The War Hits Home: The Civil War in Southeastern Virginia

A Nation Divided:
New Studies in Civil War History
James I. Robertson Jr., Editor

BRIAN STEEL WILLS

The War Hits Home

The Civil War in Southeastern Virginia

UNIVERSITY PRESS OF VIRGINIA

CHARLOTTESVILLE AND LONDON

THE UNIVERSITY PRESS OF VIRGINIA

© 2001 by the Rector and Visitors of the University of Virginia

All rights reserved

Printed in the United States of America

First published 2001

♾The paper used in this publication meets the minimum
requirements of the American National Standard for
Information Sciences—Permanence of Paper for Printed
Library Materials, ANSI Z39.48-1984.

LIBRARY OF CONGRESS CATALOGING-IN-PUBLICATION DATA

Wills, Brian Steel, 1959–
    The war hits home : the Civil War in southeastern Virginia / Brian Steel Wills.
      p. cm. — (A nation divided)
    Includes bibliographical references (p.) and index.
    ISBN 0-8139-2027-2 (cloth : alk. paper)
    1. Nansemond County (Va.)—History, Military—19th century. 2. Nansemond
County (Va.)—Social conditions—19th century. 3. Nansemond County (Va.)—Race
relations. 4. Virginia—History—Civil War, 1861–1865—Social aspects. 5. United
States—History—Civil War, 1861–1865—Social aspects. 6. Virginia—History—Civil
War, 1861–1865—African Americans. 7. United States—History—Civil War, 1861–
1865—African Americans. I. Title. II. Series.

F232.N2 W55 2001
973.7'455—dc21   2001 026035

Figs. 3-8, 10-11, 13, 15-18, and 20-22 courtesy of the U.S. Army Military History Institute, Carlisle Barracks, Pa., photographer Jim Enos. Figs. 2 (photography by Katherine Wetzel) and 9 courtesy of The Museum of the Confederacy, Richmond, Va. Figs. 12 and 14 from Jefferson Davis, *The Rise and Fall of the Confederate Government* (New York, 1881), vol. 2. Fig. 19 courtesy of the National Archives, CN-232, photograph produced by O. Kermit Hobbs Jr.

Maps 1 and 6 from U.S. Navy Department, *Official Records of the Union and Confederate Navies in the War of the Rebellion,* 30 vols. (Washington, D.C., 1894-1922), vol. 8, opp. pp. 3 and 713. Maps 2, 3, and 5 from U.S. War Department, *Atlas to Accompany the Official Records of the Union and Confederate Armies,* 2 vols. (Washington, D.C., 1891-95), vol. 1, pl. 26, vol. 2, pl. 93, vol. 1, pl. 28. Map 4 courtesy of Henry C. Murden, clerk of the Circuit Court of the City of Suffolk, and The Library of Virginia, Richmond.

⊰ CONTENTS ⊱

⊰ ILLUSTRATIONS ⊱

⊰ ACKNOWLEDGMENTS ⊱

WHEN I FIRST BECAME INTERESTED IN THIS SUBJECT, I WAS A STUDENT in high school. Through those intervening years I have had many individuals offer criticism and ideas. To each of the individuals who offered their assistance I express my sincerest gratitude.

I would like particularly to thank my colleagues at the University of Virginia's College at Wise (formerly Clinch Valley College of the University of Virginia). Chancellor L. Jay Lemons secured me a place to stay while I was conducting research at the University of Virginia Library.

I have been fortunate to work in a department with exceptional scholars, wonderful colleagues, and good friends. Thanks to Tom Costa, Mark Clark, Bill Maxwell, David Rouse, Cindy Wilkey, Elizabeth Steele, Preston Mitchell, Dana Sample, and Glenn Blackburn for setting an extraordinary example of collegiality.

I am deeply appreciative of the aid I have received, in the form of two summer grants and the first of the Faculty Leaves at UVA-Wise. This vital support allowed me to finish researching, begin writing, and finally polish the manuscript.

The Virginia Historical Society awarded me a Summer Research Internship that allowed me to have the time and access I needed to examine the important manuscript sources housed there. During this period I was able to do considerable research that would have been prohibitive to me otherwise. Thank you.

In addition, the staffs of various libraries and archives have been generous with their assistance. John Coski mailed me copies of materials from the Museum of the Confederacy as quickly as he could find them. Robin Benke and his excellent staff in the John Cook Wyllie Library at UVA-Wise helped with interlibrary loans and access to sources.

Visits to the following repositories yielded significant resources, thanks to the help of the professionals and students who worked there: University of Georgia Special Collections and Library; University of Virginia Library; National Archives; Library of Virginia; Southern Historical Collection at the University of North Carolina–Chapel Hill; Perkins Library at Duke University; U.S. Army Military History Institute at Carlisle Barracks, Pa.; North Carolina Department of History and Archives in Raleigh; Special Collections at Virginia Polytechnic Institute and State University; Woodruff Library at Emory University; U.S. Military Academy Library at West Point; and Clements Library at the University of Michigan.

A special word of thanks goes to the Suffolk-Nansemond Historical Society and to Mrs. Anna W. Rollings. Years ago Mrs. Rollings helped a young student at the University of Richmond write a paper on the Riddick family by giving him typescript copies of her family's wartime correspondence. That paper was a poor tribute to her enormous generosity, and I hope this book in some small measure will represent the heartfelt thank you that she deserves.

Other Suffolk friends also deserve recognition. Thad Williams contributed mightily by making available correspondence that enabled me to include the powerful story of Thaddeus Grashaw Williams. Giles Newsome sent me a copy of his publication of the excellent Ingalls diary. Kermit Hobbs offered his support and paved the way for any study of Suffolk in the war through his own work.

At a small college, and in a small town, friends and family abound. Although it is not possible to thank them all, I want especially to mention a few. Papa Joe and Reba Smiddy, you are blessings to everyone you touch.

Thank you for your love and support and for letting an itinerant writer "borrow" your home for a few weeks.

Ron Heise, I appreciate your friendship and your sage advice and miss the chance to benefit daily from your wit and wisdom. Enjoy your retirement, my friend. Dick Davidson, Winston Ely, and Stan Kunigelis, thanks as well for your friendship.

Of my colleagues in the profession, I especially wish to thank Emory Thomas. It does not seem so very long ago that I was in Athens writing a master's thesis on the Suffolk campaign and pestering you about a fellow named Forrest. Thanks also to my "old" colleagues Randy Patton and Glenn Eskew. To James I. "Bud" Robertson Jr. and Libba, my dear friends in Blacksburg, I cannot express enough my appreciation for all you have done for me. Your support and inspiration are as welcome as they are generous. Finally, to Ed Bearss I want to express my gratitude for working with you and having you constantly reinforce in me the need to know the battlefields themselves, as well as the human players in the drama. I cherish our association.

I also wish to express my gratitude to the staff of the University Press of Virginia, particularly Richard Holway. I appreciate the hard work and dedication he and his colleagues have exhibited in making this book not only possible but the best it could be given the limitations of its author.

My parents, Harriet and Curtis Wills, continue to offer their love and support. I am sure that I have long since worn out their patience to see this project come to fruition, but I know that I have barely tapped their love.

To my wife, Elizabeth Smiddy Wills, I owe the greatest appreciation. She carried on the multitude of household responsibilities and family chores, leaving me uncommonly free to work on this book. At the same time she patiently read the material I shoved in front of her. She was not afraid to say when something did not make sense to her. It goes without saying that this book is better for her many contributions.

I have chosen to dedicate this book to several special people. I promised my sister that I would dedicate my next book to her, which I am honored to do. This is probably the least she deserves for having me as a brother.

I also want to dedicate this book to Jennifer, William, and Courtney Sturgill. They and my daughter Lauren, to whom I dedicated my first book, have made our lives complete. I am proud of each of them in ways they will never know and love each of them deeply.

Finally, there are my fellow travelers in Civil War history. Some people will criticize us for writing only to impress each other. Happily, that is not often the case in this field. We share a collective interest with our readers concerning one of the most important and provocative periods of our nation's history. We try to tell the story the best we can. Indeed, we are readers ourselves, often profoundly shaped by what others have written.

Two writers in particular, Mary Elizabeth Massey and Stephen Ash, have seemed to echo in their work the thoughts I was mulling around in my brain about the effect of war upon the people of southeastern Virginia. Others have provided inspiration in their writings about the common soldiers and the ordinary folk, about race and war, and about the myriad personalities I have come to know, and often admire, on both sides of the conflict. To those authors and historians, many of whom will be found in the notes, I say thank you for sharing your ideas and helping to shape, confirm, and inspire my own.

The War Hits Home: The Civil War in Southeastern Virginia

"Suffolk is a small, filthy town of great antiquity,
small population, little trade, and a great deal
of Virginia dirt and Virginia pride."

Harper's Weekly, *May 2, 1863*

⊰ INTRODUCTION ⊱ *"War on Their Doorsteps"*

S UFFOLK, VIRGINIA, AND ITS ENVIRONS HAD BEEN IN THE NATIONAL
news for almost a month when *Harper's Weekly* offered its readers a
sketch of a view of the town (see fig. 1). Accompanying this sketch
on a subsequent page was a brief but telling description that declared:
"Suffolk is a small, filthy town of great antiquity, small population, little
trade, and a great deal of Virginia dirt and Virginia pride."[1]

Certainly New York City, Boston, or any other major metropolitan and
urban center in the North could hardly be described as refuse free.
Additionally, many rural communities in the part of the United States that
went to war in 1861 with its seceding section had much in common with
Southern towns like Suffolk. So, what was the writer attempting to say
and why?

By May 2, 1863, when this portrait of the town appeared, James Longstreet's Suffolk campaign was winding to a close. News stories from the

front had generated understandable curiosity among Northern readers concerning the region. As the writer explained, "The view of Suffolk, Virginia, which we publish . . . possesses some interest just now in consequence of the attack of the rebels under Longstreet."[2] Soldiers from both Boston and New York had already fought, bled, and died in southeastern Virginia. Surely the parents, friends, and other relatives deserved to know something of the area in which such sacrifices had been made. Furthermore, with a fresh campaigning season upon them, perhaps the writer hoped to spark some patriotic reaction for the fighting, bleeding, and dying to come.

For two of the soldiers who served at Suffolk, the *Harper's* depiction of the town had meaning as well. Henry E. Simmons saw it as a chance to show loved ones exactly where he had performed one of his routine duties. "There's a picture of Suffolk, Va., in Harper's Weekly May 2d," he explained, "but it only shows a front part of the town." "I picketed each side of that bridge," he noted with pride. Then he pointed out how war had altered the view shown in the picture, even in the short time he had been there. "It is blown up & all those homes near it are torn down now."[3] Another soldier thought the characterization of Suffolk was apt. Henry Marshall repeated the words from *Harper's* to the "Folks at Home" and concluded, "There is a description for you worth reading & good too."[4]

But this description of Suffolk goes beyond providing basic physical information, to injecting subjective values. Many towns on the eastern seaboard could boast "of great antiquity," because so many of them dated to the colonial period of the nation's history. Yet the writer used the words as condemnation, not celebration. Instinctively, he was suggesting the manner in which this Southern town demonstrated the backwardness of its society. Perhaps the "dirt" of this "filthy town" was directly attributable to the lack of commercial activity, to a "small population" engaged in "little trade," as the writer saw it.

Indeed, the writer saved his best insult for last. Suffolk was all of the things that a free-labor, progressive Northern urban center was not. It was stagnant, economically backward, lacking in all of the essentials for progress, but it had no shortage of "Virginia pride." To him this was the same false sense of honor that had driven the Deep South states to secede and attempt to form a new nation. It was a disease that had also come to affect George Washington's and Thomas Jefferson's Virginia. Sadly, the great commonwealth, the "Mother of Presidents," had turned its back upon its Revolutionary heritage and its nation to join these rebellious states. In doing so, it demonstrated what the writer must have considered a permeating moral weakness, as evidenced by such Virginia communities as Suffolk.[5]

Part of the great power of ideology was that the *Harper's* writer might not have realized that so many messages could be read into his few words. But just as he could not escape from the background and heritage that shaped his language, neither could Southern whites. The people in the area would have many opportunities to respond to the situations war imposed upon them. Indeed, the conflict engulfed them in waves, each of which required adjustments from them. The first wave was Confederate, with troops from outside the region filling it and impacting the lives of its citizens for the first third of the war. The second wave was Union, marked by soldiers of a different kind, who also came from outside and left their influence upon the area and its people. The policies that guided these men changed as the war continued, causing an alteration in the tone of that occupation as well.

The demands upon southeastern Virginians intensified in 1863 when a major military campaign engulfed the region. Confederate forces under Lieutenant General James Longstreet threatened the Union garrison in Suffolk while scouring southeastern Virginia and northern North Carolina of badly needed supplies, but they failed to relieve the town of its Federal presence.

The final wave came as both belligerents pulled back from the immediate area, leaving Suffolk and its surrounding counties in a no-man's-land over which both sides struggled during the last third of the war. The most common experiences of this phase were the acute shortages and constant raiding civilians had to endure.

Above all, I hope that this study demonstrates the manner in which the ordinary people of this region confronted civil war. The citizens of southeastern Virginia underwent the severest tests the American Civil War could impose upon human beings. Many of them experienced loss and heartache, struggling through hardship and suffering as they sought to defend their homes and their families in the best ways they could imagine. Some of them remained devoted to the Confederate cause throughout the war. Others found the demands of the conflict too difficult to accept and opted at various points not to do so in a variety of ways. To say that all white Southerners from the region reacted to the exigencies of war at the same level or in the same manner would be as misleading and inaccurate as to dismiss them, as the *Harper's* writer did, for pridefully defending so much topsoil.

Other people from the region entered the conflict as the enslaved property of others or as free people of color. Such individuals quickly found themselves caught up in circumstances that made extraordinary demands of them. War brought turmoil, but it also offered the unprecedented opportunity for freedom, particularly once Union soldiers established a fortified outpost in Suffolk that served as a safe haven for black refugees. By the end of the conflict, many of these southeastern Virginians would be serving in, as well as working for, the Union army or living under its protection.

Still other individuals came from outside the region. Some wore gray and came from other parts of the commonwealth or other states of the Confederacy to defend the lower tidewater. Some wore blue and came to suppress a rebellion and reunite the nation or to liberate an enslaved people. Regardless, many never left the region, dying in its camps and hospitals or on its battlefields. They became a part of this story by virtue of their service in this land so far from their own homes.

Many young men born and raised in southeastern Virginia also answered when the call to arms sounded. They joined infantry, cavalry, and artillery units that more quickly than they realized would be ordered away to distant locations. Their sacrifices on battlefields such as Malvern Hill, Manassas, Sharpsburg, Gettysburg, and Petersburg spoke eloquently of their devotion to cause and to each other. Like their Northern counterparts, many of them died in camps and hospitals far from home. Likewise, some of them deserted. Of these, many returned to honorable service, while others never chose to do so.

Under whatever circumstances this is the story of real people in the crucible of war. As Mary Elizabeth Massey wrote in her 1964 study of refugee life in the Confederacy, "Southern civilians were shocked to discover that this was a war in which they were directly and personally involved." The white civilians who lived in southeastern Virginia could not have anticipated in the slightest degree what war would mean to them and their families. "They often acted before they thought," Massey explained of such people, "for they were psychologically unprepared for a war on their doorsteps and they had little or no guidance in making decisions."[6] When the war hit home for them, it required more than any other life experience had ever demanded, forcing them to reach deeper inside themselves for the wherewithal to survive the crisis. It is a testament to their strength and character that so many of them were able to do so.

Nor did it matter what the age, gender, race, or political leaning of the individual might be. Young and old, male and female, white and black, secessionist or Unionist, Confederate or Federal, each was called upon to meet the unprecedented demands of his or her generation. This study is devoted to a better understanding of their struggles and choices and the circumstances that dictated them.

I have made every effort to keep this study from being easily labeled. It is military in the sense that the military events these people experienced are essential to their story. It is also social and political, for those elements existed as well and help to illumine our understanding. In short, this was a war that ripped at the fabric of society and profoundly affected the people who lived through it. Indeed, some may deem this work too narrative in nature or too anecdotal. Such criticism is valid but highlights nothing more than my bias toward people and away from numbers.

Nor is the study easy to characterize by its physical boundaries. It focuses on a region, not a given town, county, or state. The physical parameters of this study consist of the area surrounding the town of Suffolk, in what was known at the time of the war as Nansemond County, roughly marked by Bower's Hill and the Dismal Swamp on the east, the North Carolina border on the south, the Blackwater River and the eastern third of Southampton County on the west, and the James River on the north. The region embraces the towns of Suffolk, Franklin, and Jerusalem (modern-day Courtland) and touches Smithfield, Portsmouth, Norfolk, and nearby Gatesville, North Carolina. My intention was not to restrict the area of study to a specific county or confine it to one urban (or relatively urban) center but rather to watch the effects of the ebb and flow of war upon the people who called that region home.

Although this book focuses upon a specific area, I hope that it also provides insights that can be applied to other locations across the South. Furthermore, Northerners played a significant role as well. For however long their term of service required, they had to live, work, and fight in the region, while trying to maintain contacts with the friends and family members they had left behind. The war hit home for all.

Finally, as a note on a larger historical issue, while working on this book, I repeatedly noted the sense that the Confederacy failed because a nation and a people very much like itself defeated it. This is not to say that there were not fundamental differences between the sections but rather that once these differences brought these peoples to war, Northern whites and the African Americans who united with them exhibited the means, and the determination to implement those means, sufficient to win the war. White Southerners, for the most part, demonstrated that they had as much will to win as their opponents but, in large measure due to the efforts of those opponents, lacked the means to do so. Ultimately, most of them came to realize that peace was more important than the sacrifices that would have been necessary to wage a protracted guerrilla war. It was not the "dirt" that compelled them to defend their section but what it represented to them, and when no reasonable justification remained for continuing the defense, they did not do so. As Nathan Bedford Forrest, perhaps the Confederacy's greatest warrior, put it, "Any man who is in favor of a further prosecution of this war is a fit subject for lunatic asylum, and ought to be sent there immediately."[7] Most white Southerners accepted the verdict of Appomattox, Bennett Place, and so on not because they had failed to sacrifice or endure but because they no longer had any realistic expectation of success.

For the scholars who insist that there existed either no significant sense of nationalism or a truncated version that failed during the heat of war, the story of many of the people of southeastern Virginia throughout the conflict stands in sharp rebuttal. These people sought to secure victory until there was no victory left to win, except the conclusion of the terrible conflict that had engulfed them all.[8]

"Governor Wise lade the Dust with them."
Southampton County farmer Daniel W. Cobb on
John Brown's raiders

"Linco[l]n Causes much excite ment. War is
thretien [threatened].
Daniel W. Cobb

"They are blood Thursty for Linco[l]n and
Northern Yankies."
Daniel W. Cobb on the troops from the Deep South

⊰ 1 ⊱ *"Blood Thursty for Lincoln"*

T HE INCIDENT THAT PRESAGED CIVIL WAR OCCURRED AT THE OPPO-
site end of the Commonwealth of Virginia from the southeastern
tidewater. Even so, the events at Harpers Ferry in the autumn of
1859 resonated as few others had since Southampton Countians awoke to
similar alarm bells in 1831. The actions of John Brown immediately
brought to mind those of Nat Turner. Once again the whites of southeastern
Virginia demanded law and order, and the blacks heard a clarion call for
freedom.

A farmer in Southampton County might as well have been a world apart
from Harpers Ferry, where Brown's raid occurred, and from Charles Town,
where the sentence for attempting to incite servile insurrection would be
carried out. Still, Southampton farmer Daniel William Cobb took the time
to record his feelings regarding these astounding events amid the more banal
activities of everyday life. "A Rebelion took place . . . at Harper's ferry from

the Abalisonest," he noted. Then, with more feeling, Cobb gloated: "They
expected to do much but dun little. . . . Governor [Henry A.] Wise lade the
Dust with them."

Although a week had elapsed since the Harpers Ferry raid took place in
the beautiful little village at the confluence of the Potomac and Shenandoah
Rivers, speculation on just what had occurred there remained rife. "They
Browns Company was taken and killed," Cobb scribbled confidently,
adding, "I am toald they was 15,000 negrows" involved in the uprising. But
then, more soberly, he observed, in terms not unlike those used by the man
who had carried out the operation and soon would be facing death upon
a Virginia gallows, "I am persuaded this is the 1st of the sorte but only th[e
start of] much bloodshed."[1]

John Brown would continue to motivate people on both sides of the slavery issue, whether they saw him as an abolitionist warrior or a degenerated madman. Yet as 1860 neared, events connected with the presidential
election of that year promised to overshadow Brown's failed revolt. Indeed,
the election of 1860 mirrored the troubles facing the nation over the issue
of slavery as a new decade opened. A developing political party, the
Republican Party, had been making significant strides since its creation from
the elements of several fading parties in 1854. The party's first presidential
candidate, John Charles Frémont, had polled impressive numbers in 1856,
and a well-known, if not particularly well-liked, politician, William Seward,
seemed poised to win its nomination for 1860. If he could do so, he almost
certainly would face a formidable opponent in Democrat Stephen Douglas
of Illinois. Known as the "Little Giant," Douglas had disposed of a challenge from a lanky Springfield lawyer named Lincoln to win reelection to
his Senate seat in 1858.

Cracks and fissures in the American body politic threatened to release
powerful forces that would send events spinning out of control. At a convention in Chicago, the Republican supporters of Abraham Lincoln, "the
rail splitter," derailed Seward's bid for the nomination. It seemed that the
veteran politico had too much baggage to win, but the question remained
whether Lincoln could rebound from his loss only two years earlier to
Douglas.

This time, however, Lincoln had assistance from an unlikely source: the
Democratic Party. That party seemed poised to come apart at the seams
over the issue of slavery, a development that would certainly lead to its defeat
in the election. White Southern Democrats sought to win guarantees in
the party platform for their "peculiar institution." When such guarantees
failed to materialize, the Southern delegations, led by William Lowndes

Yancey, a "fire-eater" from Alabama, walked out of the convention. Two separate conventions later, the party had two candidates: Stephen Douglas for the Northern Democrats and John C. Breckinridge for the Southern Democrats. As if that jumble was not enough, a fourth candidate, John Bell, stood for the presidency as the candidate of an even newer party, the Constitutional Union Party.[2]

On election day Elliott L. Story, a teacher in Southampton County, recorded his vote in his diary. "Tues. 6 Taught school and went to the election and voted for Bell & [Edward] Everette." Over the next several days, Story captured the state of affairs succinctly. "Mon. 12 There is no doubt but that Mr. Lincoln is elected for our next president." This result led to a more ominous entry on November 19: "There was a great deal of talk about the secession movement of the southern states." Finally, on the twenty-second Story noted: "The papers bring news of still greater excitement in the South in regard to the presidential election. I fear the days of our happy Union are almost numbered."[3]

Nor was the Southampton teacher the only one to notice the trend of the times. "Things look very alarming from this point of view," Robert E. Lee wrote from Texas to his son Rooney on December 3.[4] So they must have appeared to a good many of the citizens of southeastern Virginia as they watched events unfold with an alarming speed in the Deep South. Yet even in the midst of such potentially divisive national events, many people tried to maintain a business as usual posture. Farmers continued to follow their time-tested routines. Clerks still waited upon their customers. The governing board of the Norfolk and Petersburg Railroad Company even managed to pull off something of a business coup with the New York and Virginia Steam Ship Company.

At their July meeting the railway company's president, William Mahone, announced a deal with the steamship firm that would ensure that "all through Freight destined for points west of Petersburg" would be handled by "our Road at Norfolk exclusively." Despite the concerns facing the country, the board seemed more wary of repercussions from other rail lines. Its members voted to seek an acceptable compromise on the language so that the partnerships with other lines might remain intact. The deal promised to be a lucrative one for the Norfolk and Petersburg's stockholders and officials and a boon to the region, unless larger events served to nullify it.[5]

Unfortunately, by mid-December such seemed to be the case. A secession convention opened in Columbia, South Carolina, on the seventeenth, with the delegates prepared to determine the fate of their state and its relationship with the nation as a whole. The momentum had been building for a defiant response of some form since Lincoln's election. A month earlier the South Carolina legislature had voted to raise a then-substantial force of 10,000 volunteers for home defense.

The president of the convention left little doubt concerning its eventual outcome. "If anything has been decided by the elections which sent us here, it is, that South Carolina must dissolve her connection with the [United States] as speedily as possible." Before the night was out, a resolution calling for a secession ordinance passed by a vote of 159–0. This preliminary action became final with the unanimous passage in Charleston of such an ordinance on December 20.[6] "The Union is dissolved," screamed the headlines.[7] And so it was.

The month of January 1861 witnessed a scramble of other Deep South states out of the Union. Mississippi voted itself out on the ninth, Florida on the tenth, Alabama on the eleventh, and after only a brief respite, Georgia left the Union on the nineteenth and Louisiana on the twenty-sixth. On February 1 Texas joined its sister Southern states, although not in time to send delegates to the initial meeting of representatives that gathered on the next day in Montgomery, Alabama. Within a matter of days, members of this convention had drafted and adopted a provisional constitution for a new nation and selected a provisional president and vice president. The Confederate States of America was born.[8]

Muted by the hue of secession was the call of former U.S. president John Tyler for a peace convention to pull the nation back from the abyss of secession and war. Suggesting that "the eyes of the whole country are turned to this assembly, in expectation and hope," the diminutive Virginian sounded more desperate than hopeful.[9] By the end of the month, the Peace Convention meeting in Washington had precious little to show for its efforts. It had squandered much of that time in argument, losing any momentum it might have had by sacrificing decision for debate. Time was running out for any solution short of war, if one actually ever existed. The task of finding peace for the nation must have seemed more Herculean than ever, and increasingly more distant.[10]

If the series of events had any impact upon the people living in southeastern Virginia, they must have come as both a terrible shock and a tremendous relief. Agitation over state's rights and slavery had been building for so long that the tension between the sections was palpable, demanding release.

On January 13 Daniel Cobb observed cryptically in his diary, "War is at hand it began in Charleston." Nothing that follows clarifies what was on his mind when he jotted these words, but the Southampton farmer must have been thinking about events in South Carolina just days previous. A

Union vessel, *The Star of the West,* had attempted to reach Fort Sumter with supplies for the beleaguered garrison there. Early on January 9 Southern shore batteries thwarted the effort, forcing the U.S. ship to return, her mission unfulfilled. Like so many others, Cobb seems to have understood that hostilities were imminent.

Still, the remainder of that day's diary entry focused not upon the "war . . . at hand" but upon a local incident that must have appeared to Cobb as a more clear and present danger than any war would likely prove to be. "A horrable death took place . . . a fiew days ago," the Southampton farmer began. Then he recounted the story of a man who had been "taken by his servants from his bead at midnight Carried out of the house and beat to death with an ax." The murder was particularly unnerving. "He beged for life," Cobb noted, "but in vain." This kind of incident shattered the myth of slave complacency that had allowed white Southerners to delude themselves into a false sense of security. Cobb owned slaves himself. Would they turn on him as they had this poor unfortunate? At the very least he would have to be more vigilant than ever in these troubling times.[11]

Throughout the months of January, February, and March, southeastern Virginia remained in a state of flux. On January 12 the Southampton teacher Elliott Story remarked that he had "found several [people] talking incessantly about secession."[12] On the nineteenth farmer Cobb observed "a grate confusion in Virginia at this time." He would use the word *confusion* repeatedly in the days to come. But for now he was concerned that "I here nothing But War no piece." Cobb reckoned that he had heard war spoken of a hundred times more than peace, a ratio that could not bode well for the chances of avoiding a conflict.[13]

The unsettled conditions continued into February, enhanced by an election at which Virginians chose delegates to a state convention, thus indicating at the polls whether or not they supported the idea of secession. The vote in Southampton County on the fourth was close between Democrat John J. Kindred, a man Cobb termed a "susceader & no Referance," and sometime Whig Charles F. Urquhart, who supported "Referance & to stay." With the votes tallied, Kindred, the secessionist, received 486 votes to his opponent's 458, but enough of those votes slid on the issue of "Referance," or referring the outcome of the convention to popular referendum, that the results for the county were inconclusive.[14] As historian Daniel Crofts has explained, "Southampton voters thereby delivered a mixed verdict, electing a secessionist while at the same time denying secessionists the free hand they wanted."[15] Daniel Cobb had voted for Kindred, while Elliott Story recorded his vote "for Charles F. Urquhart and for reference."[16]

Although he had voted for the winner, Cobb remained deeply ambivalent about affairs in his state. He poured his bewilderment onto paper on February 11, the recent election and its outcome still clearly worrying him. "Grate stir among us yet on politicks," he noted. "And where will it end I can't tell." The mixed message of the election had him perplexed: "For Its the opinion that its for the majority for disunist Canidate & [yet] in favour of Refferance. I am in the dark on the subject[.] I Can't understand. so I am within a fiew months of 50 years of age, they Can't make me Bare armes so I beleive I never will Voat a gain[.] I leave it [to the] arm-baring men[.] I Voted a Democrat ticket threwout peace and war." Exasperated, Cobb asserted, "I think I am dun with politicks, etc."[17]

The uncertainty Daniel Cobb felt was more than political. He did not want war but remained convinced that the South must have its rights defended and upheld. He captured this feeling on February 14. "The Legislater has passed some resolutions favourable of the South," he noted, "and I have learned and am inhope will settle matters without Blood shead for I am infavour of a frendly Compromise with the S. and N. on honerable turms." For him this meant "to let the S. have her fore fathers rights and let the N. have her Rights," and all would "live as here to fore."[18]

Great political questions simmered through March, adding to the unsettlement of people like Daniel Cobb. Aside from preparing for the spring planting, he kept an eye on the slave population for signs of unrest. "People has several negrows Runaway," he stated matter-of-factly, while discussing the efforts of his own workers and the current state of politics on the twelfth. Then on the sixteenth, Cobb burst out in frustration on "weather I shall leave Virginia [if] the State hangs N.," adding firmly, "I hangs S."[19]

If the focus of one man was on local events, the gaze of the nation alternated between Charleston, South Carolina, and Washington, D.C., with an occasional glance toward Pensacola, Florida. The two seaports were the most logical ones to watch for a confrontation, if either the outgoing Buchanan administration or the incoming Lincoln administration wanted one.

The likelihood of that incident occurring at Pensacola diminished as Confederates there under Mexican War veteran Braxton Bragg became less convinced of being able to storm Fort Pickens successfully. The fort was at a difficult location to assault and had already stubbornly refused to consider repeated demands for its surrender. Furthermore, the Confederates were not even in a position to halt the flow of supplies and reinforcements into the fort. They would be gambling recklessly to attempt a showdown there and wisely chose not to do so beyond words.

Increasingly it became clear that any confrontation would come at Charleston, where the Federal commander, Robert Anderson, had shifted his men in late December from vulnerable Fort Moultrie to the still-unfinished but relatively safer Fort Sumter. Even so, a ring of artillery concentrated on the position. Worse still for the garrison, there were limited supplies on hand. Perhaps they would be starved out. Perhaps the threat of overwhelming force would convince Anderson to turn the fort over without the need for hostilities or bloodshed. Mixed signals from Washington gave little sense of exactly what action the Federal government was prepared to take on behalf of the fort and its garrison. But South Carolinians and Confederates would have to take over the installation one way or another. An occupied fort in the heart of Charleston harbor was a blemish the proud people of South Carolina would not, and the Confederate government could not, let stand.

Communications passed between Confederate secretary of war Leroy Pope Walker and General Pierre Gustave Toutant Beauregard, commanding at the scene. If he believed that Fort Sumter was about to be resupplied or otherwise relieved, Beauregard must "at once demand its evacuation." Should this demand be refused, the Louisiana Creole was to "proceed, in such manner as you may determine, to reduce it."[20] Beauregard established contact with the Federals in Sumter. The Confederate States of America could "no longer delay assuming actual possession" of the fort, he stated in an ultimatum. "I am ordered by the Government of the Confederate States to demand the evacuation of Fort Sumter."[21]

Even as the hours waned on April 11, Secretary Walker hoped to take Fort Sumter without having to fire upon it. He notified General Beauregard, "[I d]o not desire needlessly to bombard Fort Sumter."[22] Inside the fort Major Anderson was prepared to offer the Confederates assurances of his compliance with their demands. He would give up the post by the fifteenth provided he had not received supplies or specific orders to the contrary. In addition he would promise not to fire unless fired upon.

Of course, Anderson could afford to wait. Perhaps he was even stalling, for relief was supposed to be imminent. The Southerners wanted the fort to submit promptly, or it might not submit at all. Thus, at 4:30 A.M. the report of a signal shot emanated from Fort Johnson. The shell burst in the air high above Fort Sumter. Quickly the air filled with explosions, as Southern artillery sent round after round toward the Union installation. Gathered on rooftops or crowding the Battery, Charlestonians watched the drama unfold with a mixture of emotions.

Inside Fort Sumter, Anderson and his garrison remained silent until about

7:00 A.M. With a limited number of men and not much powder on hand, the Federals would have to husband their resources to offer a creditable defense. Still, the outcome was virtually assured from the start. Some thirty-six hours after the attack had begun, the garrison surrendered. Interestingly, despite the volume of fire exchanged over that day and a half of bombardment, no one had yet died.

In the wake of the fort's surrender, Charlestonians reacted with cheers, speeches, and celebrations. The first victory was theirs. Unfortunately, the surreal atmosphere in Charleston received a dose of the reality to come when an accidental explosion during the surrender ceremonies cost two Federal soldiers their lives.[23]

For Daniel Cobb in distant Southampton County, Virginia, the elation at the events in Charleston was more subdued. "The Ball is open at Charleston South Carolina on last friday[.] The war has began." Still, he noted rather sadly, "Our States pain is no better at presant."[24]

Union president Abraham Lincoln responded to the attack upon Fort Sumter with a call for 75,000 volunteers to combat "combinations . . . too powerful to be suppressed by the ordinary course of judicial proceedings." The Northern chief executive asked Congress to reconvene in special session, fittingly to begin on July 4. Within days he also declared a blockade of Southern seaports.[25]

Everything seemed to be falling into place nicely for the fledgling nation. "I think the whole South will consolidate," Confederate vice president Alexander Stephens confidently predicted, "but events transpire so rapidly now that it is useless to speculate two days ahead."[26] Secretary Walker seemed to realize the unprecedented nature of the task that lay before the new nation, observing that "there is every reason to anticipate the operations of both belligerents will be conducted on a much more imposing scale than this continent has ever witnessed."[27]

Charleston remained the center of attention for the moment. Virginia newspaper editor and congressman Roger Atkinson Pryor had watched gleefully as the shells burst over Fort Sumter. He even laid a tenuous claim to having fired the first shot of the war, along with fellow Virginia "fire-eater" Edmund Ruffin. Now Pryor wanted to see the president and present him with fragments of Confederate shells he had picked up inside the fallen Union fort. Ruffin had collected some samples, too, but he sent his to friends in Virginia, a not-so-subtle jab at the state's hesitancy to take its proper place in history. Roger Pryor was in his element in Montgomery. These were heady times for him. He gave fiery speeches and enjoyed the bonfires and the boisterous cheers. All appeared to offer confirmation that he had been correct.

Unlike the prophets of the Old Testament, his message was apparently not lost upon his people.[28]

If these Alabamians seemed to be embracing the new nation with unbounded enthusiasm, the people of distant southeastern Virginia were more circumspect in their reactions. Southampton County farmer Daniel Cobb remained focused on "ploughing," "planting corn," "putting in Cotton Sead," fertilizing, and other farming activities, rather than the goings-on in Montgomery.[29] Just as news of Fort Sumter shook him into considering such matters more seriously, so did the decision of Virginia on April 17 to secede. The next day he remarked, "I under stand Virginia has seceded goin[g] S. which I hope is the Case if no other arrangemen[t] could be made in governmen[t]."[30]

By a vote of 88 to 55, the members of the Virginia State Convention had adopted an ordinance of secession. Although it called for the people to uphold this action through a referendum, the state had made its choice. It was a decision made all the clearer in its implications by the simultaneous charge of the convention upon Governor John Letcher to call for volunteers to serve the state in its defense. Suffolk representative John R. Kilby, a newspaper editor and one of the town's prominent attorneys, signed the ordinance despite an earlier reluctance to embrace secession precipitously. Once the course for separation seemed set for Virginia, encouraged by President Lincoln's call for volunteers, Kilby shook off whatever qualms remained and voted with the majority.[31]

For many of the people of southeastern Virginia, the uncertainty of fall and winter now gave way to even greater worry and confusion. "A grate Confusion among the people at presant in this County and state it goin[g] out of the Union," Daniel Cobb wrote on April 20. He had no illusions as to who was to blame for the crisis. "Lincon Causes much excite ment. War is thretien [threatened]. . . . Lincon is doing all his skill is Master off." The contemplation of a war filled Cobb with dread. It was "awfull to think of the lives that is to be lost."[32] Cobb had his opinions on such subjects fairly well set. Yet the farmer was smart enough to realize that so much of what he was hearing was based on hearsay, not fact. "The World [is] full of war news at presant," he observed on April 21, but he quickly added, "And a grate many lies a float at this time."[33] Time would soon sift the rumor from the reality, but emotion held sway for the moment.

Like his Southampton neighbor, Elliott Story watched events unfold with interest. Certainly no "fire-eater" in the mold of Roger Pryor, nor even as quick to embrace secession as Daniel Cobb, the schoolteacher came to secession hesitantly. Eventually neither he nor his state had much in the way of alternatives, as Story appears to have recognized. "It seems to me that Virginia has done all that she could do consistent with honour and justice," he explained in May, adding, "There was nothing left for her but to withdraw from the old Union and cast her fortunes with the South."[34] A month later there was not much left for him to do either. "To-day I dismissed my school for an indefinite time. The excitement of the war and circumstances connected with it has caused my school gradually to diminish till I have only about 10 or a dozen students."[35] Many individuals were leaving schools, jobs, and homes across the region to enter military service.

Throughout southeastern Virginia soldiers were beginning to assemble. Daniel Cobb noted in his diary on Saturday, April 20, "The Malitia is ordered out From the seding states & Calling for Volunteers from States." Locally this meant activity as well, with the secession of Virginia. "The Troop is ordered to Meet at Jurusalem on [next] Teusday [the] 22[d] to Make arrangements to go to Norfolk if should be wanted, or at any point of the Southern States if necesary."[36]

As if to offer confirmation, on the same day the farmer was writing these words, preparations were under way to seize Federal military installations in the Norfolk area. Governor Letcher and his advisers appreciated the importance of these facilities, even before Virginia left the Union formally. In particular, they planned to take control of the Gosport Navy Yard. With Virginia's admission into the Confederacy, the Gosport yard would become one of only two such facilities found within the borders of the new nation.

On the night of April 20, the Federals abandoned and burned the navy yard. The next day Governor Letcher claimed it for the Commonwealth of Virginia. This fortuitous circumstance gave Virginia control of a complete navy yard and an overwhelming amount of abandoned Federal property, including a huge granite dry dock, wharves, storehouses, workshops, 1,085 pieces of heavy artillery, and substantial stores of naval ordnance and provisions.[37] Cobb celebrated the victory in his diary, noting that "we have taken the navy [yard] & destroyed sevel large ships of war by fire and sinking."[38]

The capture of Federal property in the Norfolk area left the Southampton troops unsure of their next step. Before the action in Norfolk, the men had expected to go there. Since the seizure of Gosport, Cobb expressed what many must have thought: "I Cant tell where the troops will go." New orders would have to be cut for them. In the meantime, Cobb surmised, "they are to remain in Jurusalem for further orders and to get ready to March its supposed will go to Suffolk on Saturday to recive arms then where I know not."[39]

Suffolk was the largest town in the immediate region. Even so, it was a small rural community with a cluster of brick and wooden buildings fronting tree-lined streets. Troughs, hitching posts, and white picket fences marked these dirt streets. Two of the roads, the Edenton or White Marsh Road and the Somerton, ran south out of town toward North Carolina. The South Quay Road led west toward the Blackwater River, which served as a boundary between Nansemond and Southampton Counties, twenty miles from Suffolk. The Providence Church Road or Windsor Road ran northwest, connecting the town with Petersburg and Richmond. This road crossed the Nansemond River by means of a drawbridge and wound through the hamlets of Windsor and Zuni. Zuni lay on another segment of the Blackwater River at the boundary of Southampton and Isle of Wight Counties.

The Nansemond River meandered along the north side of the town, in a northeasterly direction. Marshes, deep ravines, and streams were common along the course of the river. Hampton Roads lay eighteen miles downstream. The Dismal Swamp began on Suffolk's southeast side and spread well into North Carolina. It contained dense undergrowth and swampy vegetation, as well as thick forests of fully grown trees. The Dismal Swamp was largely impassable except by small parties on foot or by the Jericho Canal, which ran along the eastern side of Suffolk.

It was the role the town played as a rail center for the region that gave it significance. Two railroads, the Norfolk and Petersburg and the Seaboard and Roanoke, connected the coastal port of Norfolk to the interior of Virginia and North Carolina via Suffolk.[40] Before the war the broad-gauged Norfolk and Petersburg offered travelers the "best travel bargain below the Potomac" at three cents for each of its eighty miles. The standard-gauged Seaboard and Roanoke charged its customers five cents for its fifty-nine miles but maintained more locomotives and cars of all kinds.[41]

In addition to railroads, Suffolk boasted a considerable share of commerce by virtue of its location at the source of the Nansemond River, a major tributary of the James River. This gave the town access to the fishing and oyster bounty of the James River and the Chesapeake Bay, as well as the Nansemond River itself. Commerce from the eastern counties of North Carolina joined goods coming into Suffolk from Norfolk, approximately twenty-four miles to the east. The surrounding counties of Nansemond, for which Suffolk was the county seat, Southampton, and Isle of Wight were composed of large, fertile agricultural regions that supplied inhabitants with such products as beef, hams, peanuts, bacon, and corn. The Confederate capital, once it moved to Virginia from Montgomery, Alabama, would be Richmond, located nearly eighty miles to the northwest.[42]

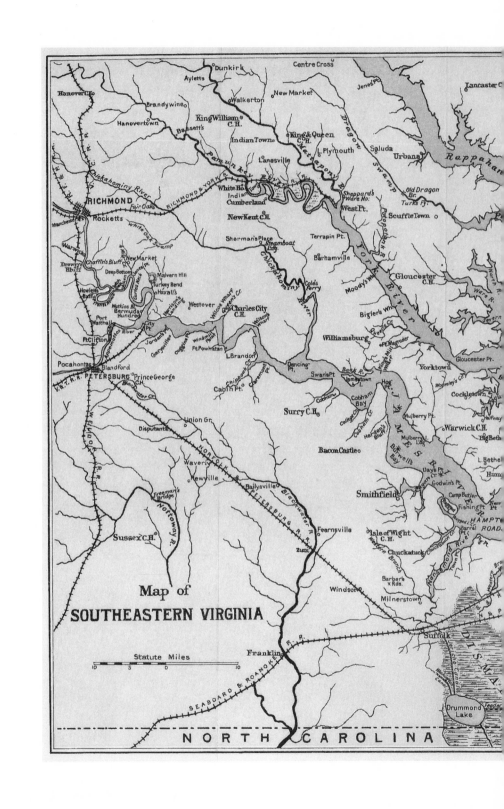

Map of
SOUTHEASTERN VIRGINIA

Statute Miles

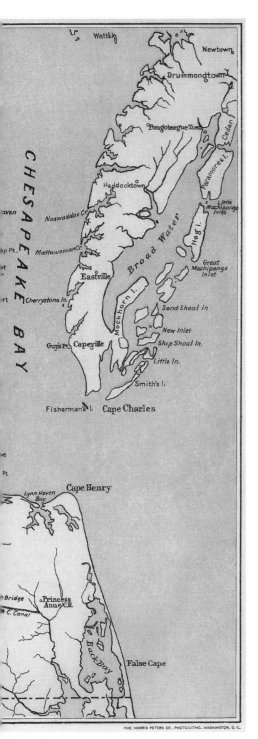

MAP 1 Southeastern Virginia. The Blackwater River is in the left center, while Gatesville, North Carolina, southwest of Suffolk, is just off the edge of the map.

Militarily, Suffolk also offered a choke point for Norfolk. Land communications between the port city and the rest of Virginia and the Confederacy ran through the town. For this reason Major General Robert E. Lee, the commander of the Virginia state forces, focused his attention upon southeastern Virginia as a potential avenue of attack against the newly acquired naval facilities. What he saw concerned him. After reading the state engineer's report concerning the area's defenses, Lee felt prompted to observe, "There is no mention of any projected work designed to prevent the ascent of the Nansemond River, by which it seems that attacking parties might approach the navy-yard from the west." Then, in the style that would come to characterize his relationships with subordinates in the Army of Northern Virginia, Lee inquired rather than ordered. "Are defenses necessary in that quarter?"[43]

Of course, General Lee raised the issue of adequate defenses on the Nansemond River in order for it to be addressed. His orders might sound rhetorical, but they were not meant to be taken as such. If the local commander saw the situation as he did, Lee would expect action to remedy the default. Left unsaid was the understanding that if they were necessary, these defenses would have to be built.

Nor were the Federals unaware of the potential weakness in the chain of river and coastal defenses the Confederates were seeking to construct or improve. On May 27 Major General Benjamin F. Butler arrived on the opposite shore of the James River at Newport News. Lee had to see such a move as a potential threat to the rail links connecting Norfolk and the interior.

As it turned out, this was precisely the idea Butler had in mind for an offensive operation. On May 29 he expressed this interest in a communication with General-in-Chief Winfield Scott. "My next point of operation I propose shall be Pig Point"; its capture would give Butler command of the approaches to the Nansemond River. "Once in command of [the defenses at Pig Point], which I believe may be easily turned," he continued, "I can then advance along the Nansemond River and easily take Suffolk, and there either hold or destroy the railroad between Richmond and Norfolk, and also between Norfolk and the South." With a naval blockade of the city, "Norfolk will be so perfectly hemmed in, that starvation will cause the surrender [of the place], without risking an attack on the strongly-fortified entrenchments around Norfolk, with great loss and perhaps defeat."[44]

It was a bold plan that could offer dramatic results. Even though it was never put into effect, fear of such a scheme sharpened the Southern focus on the vulnerability of their fixed defense system. Probably none more than

General Lee understood the threat. To counter it meant playing a chess game of sorts. He had to read his opponent's mind, as well as his movements, in order to predict with any degree of accuracy what that opponent might do. To anticipate Butler, Lee spread his intelligence net widely. He sent cavalry to the area north of Smithfield to warn of any sudden advance from that quarter. He placed an infantry company at Zuni to serve as a reserve and protect the railroad bridge there. Most importantly, he sought to awaken the Confederate commander at Norfolk, Brigadier General Benjamin Huger, to the potential danger.

"I think it not improbable that the object of the troops which are landing at Newport News may be either to ascend [the] Nansemond River to the town of Suffolk," Lee speculated to Huger, "or, if that river be too well protected for this, to cross [the] James River to Burwell's Bay, and thence, by land, to Suffolk, or some point on the railroad." Knowing the state of the defenses on the Nansemond and the disposition of Southern troops, Lee realized that either choice could prove catastrophic. "The effect of either of these movements," he warned his subordinate in Norfolk, "will be to cut off your communication with Richmond." In the meantime, Huger had better start scrounging around for reinforcements and preparing his own counteroperations.[45]

The encroachment of Union invading forces upon the region would remain the paramount concern, yet other matters troubled local military and civilian authorities, as well as citizens. Daniel Cobb remained concerned about maintaining control over the behavior of blacks and poor whites in the midst of a war. Citing the need for law and order as justification, he and other citizens from Southampton County formed defense units of their own. In late April he explained: "The siterzon[s] Meet at Jurusalem to day to [ar]rang[e] a home Guard from 16 to 60. they made the arrangement [for squads of] 5 or 10 with a offerser to a squad threwout the County and the offersers to reporte to the general Community as offen as it is necesary—there reporte is to be [on] all misconduct of negrows and lowlife white people of the County and to keep the state of affair[s] right."[46]

Whatever Cobb might hope, affairs in southeastern Virginia were certainly not "right," especially with the possibility that military action could interrupt the normal flow of activities at any moment. On May 12 Cobb lamented, "All debts and business in Cash no Credit," although he appreciated the willingness of county leaders to recognize the difficulties of the times. "We got a stay on debts preavious[ly] mad[e] untwill pease." Still, the developing situation was "better for some and worse for others."[47]

Despite such difficulties war enthusiasm permeated the region, particularly in these early days. Cobb noted that troops from Southampton
County mingled with newly arriving volunteers from "Georgia and other
States from a distant." Caught up as they were with war fever, these soldiers made an impression upon the Southampton farmer. "They are blood
Thursty for Lincon and Northern Yankies," he explained, adding, "and [God]
grant their success."[48]

The Southampton farmer demonstrated himself to be a patriotic sup-
porter of the cause in more than words. Too old to participate in the army
himself, he sent his seventeen-year-old son, Asbury, who joined what
would become Company A of the 13th Virginia Cavalry. The men chose
Joseph E. Gillette, a leading farmer and ardent secessionist, as their leader.
In an uncommon gesture of public spirit, Cobb would name his seventh
son (born at the end of 1862) Mager Gillette, in honor of his oldest son's
cavalry commander.[49]

The patriotic atmosphere offered the comforting illusion that all white
Southerners supported the Confederate cause and the war effort. "People
are all united to the South to defend there rights as Suthern men," he
exclaimed. Even so, he could not help feeling a tinge of uneasiness. "I Call
the war a horrid and abamable thing," he wrote on April 28, still months
before the bloodletting that would verify his fears.[50]

Soon the men of Asbury Cobb's cavalry unit were experiencing the first
realities of warfare: the frustrations of bureaucracy. Despite the zeal of the
days following enlistment, the men had difficulty obtaining adequate arms
in Suffolk and had to spend most of May in Jerusalem awaiting orders. When
those orders finally came, the unit moved to Smithfield and then Benn's
Church, in Isle of Wight County. The 13th Virginia then came under the
command of the politician-turned-soldier Roger A. Pryor.[51]

Although unable to join the army alongside his son, Cobb took a place
of responsibility in defending the community when he agreed to serve as
captain of one of the Home Guard units. During the latter part of May, his
squad of home guards was as active as any military command in the region.
"The Fork squad road threw the districk . . . from 10 to 4 the next morning," the captain observed. Happily he could report, "We found all servants
at home." Subsequent patrols found similar circumstances. "We Road to
night the 2nd time," he wrote on May 31, and "found all Right[.] We road
the 25th and the 30th servants all peasable."

The servants might be peaceful, but the younger members of Cobb's
squad troubled their commander. These fellows were not yet old enough
to serve in the regularly constituted military units. In the opinion of their

captain, they were not of much use to the Home Guard either. "They have put on boys 14 or 16 and what good [do] they do," Cobb asked rhetorically. "I say nun," was his instant reply.[52] Part of the reason for this poor service may have been their youth, but much of it must have been their disappointment at seeing so many others, just a few years their senior, going off to war.

Southampton County would supply seven companies of men to the service of the Confederacy: five infantry, one artillery, and one cavalry. Although coming from different parts of the county, the men in these companies were overwhelmingly farmers.[53] At the same time the Suffolk community also was raising troops for the state's, and nation's, defense. All told, the town of Suffolk and the surrounding county of Nansemond raised nine companies of infantry and cavalry, numbering some 1,500 men, to fight under the Confederate banner. Carrying such names as the Suffolk Continentals, the Marion Rangers, the Nansemond Guards, and the Nansemond Rangers, these companies were particularly reminiscent of the Revolution of 1776.[54] One company, raised in the nearby community of Windsor, took the incendiary name Isle of Wight Avengers.[55]

Soldiers from the region found themselves at various posts. Some manned the defenses that guarded Portsmouth, Norfolk, and the Virginia interior from attacks by water. One such soldier, Jonathan R. Smith, the son of an Episcopal minister and the tutor of the children of prominent Suffolk politician Nathaniel Riddick, caught the war fever as well. He enlisted on April 19 in what became Company G, 6th Virginia Infantry.[56] Stationed at Craney Island, a strongpoint located in the Hampton Roads and designed to guard the Elizabeth River approach to Norfolk, Smith addressed his correspondence to Anna Mary Riddick, Nathaniel's oldest daughter. They would share a strong bond through these letters, suggestive of a deeper affection between the two.

In his May 14 letter to "Dear Annie," Jonny provided an illustration of the soldier's life in these earliest days of the conflict. Smith shared his post with approximately 250 to 300 Southerners. They had been given an emotional send-off, leaving "the wharf amid tears and cheers of many spectators." Military duties soon garnered their full attention. "When we reached the island," Jonny explained, "we had to pitch our tents, bring up our baggage and do sundry other things not at all in accordance with my anticipations respecting soldier life." The romance of war quickly faded under a baking sun, sharp winds, and inundating rains. "I'll tell you, I never expected to become a carpenter when I enrolled myself as a soldier," the teacher observed. "But soldiers must learn to do anything and everything."

Of the soldier's life, Jonny noted facetiously: "It's no child's play to be a regularly enrolled soldier. Getting up at five o'clock—more generally at half past four—working all day, and then at night sleeping on the ground, isn't much fun, at least, not to me."

As for the Federals, they were providing little more than a momentary diversion from the daily routine. Most of the Union forces seemed content to "be idly lying about Ft. Monroe, doing nothing," although that was not the case for all of the vessels. "One of their steamers is constantly lying off the mouth of the James River, firing into every craft that comes down, from an oyster boat to a ship," Jonny explained. "The other day the Yankees fired a bomb shell into a small fleet of fishing boats, but, fortunately, they were too far off for it to take effect." Whether representing extreme nervousness on the part of the Federals or a concerted effort to disrupt local commerce, this action is an early example of the impact the war was already beginning to have on noncombatants in southeastern Virginia.

If the Northerners had chosen to attack, the Confederates defending the island would have been in difficult straits. The battery boasted eighteen mounted guns of various calibers, but Smith recognized one of the position's greatest weaknesses, aside from its isolation by water. "There are not enough men on the island to man the guns that we have here and unless more are sent, we will have to surrender to a superior force if they ever effect a landing." Perhaps sensing the concern he might have raised in his reader's mind, the soldier later boastfully averred, "If we only had men enough, we could drive off the combined fleets of England, France, and the United North."[57]

Whatever men like Jonathan Smith might write to their loved ones, the experience of war and nationhood was still very new. It was so new, in fact, that the final political act in the already accomplished secession drama did not play out until May 23, 1861. On that day the public referendum on Virginia's secession, called for by the Secession Convention, took place. In Southampton County, Daniel Cobb noted: "A pole helt for Sesesion and Union no votes for Union at Jurusalem. all voted for sesesion." Then he recorded a vote that would affect him as the owner of eleven slaves, and perhaps be the first of such measures to follow as the war continued: "A pole held for taxing infant slave children only 5 votes to the Contrary a bad taxation for slave holders."[58]

Historian Emory Thomas has suggested that the Confederacy underwent a "revolutionary experience" during the war, as the conflict tested white Southerner's prewar values and ideology.[59] This vote offers a glimpse at an opening salvo by the demands of nationalism and war upon Southern society and institutions. Here at the beginning of its struggle for independence, the new government was beginning to challenge the slaveholders' control over their property in ways that no one had anticipated. Slaveholders would continue to face assaults as the demands of the crisis increased, added to by the evolution of Union policy toward slavery and the actions of the slaves themselves.

Despite such governmental measures and his own mixed feelings about the conflict, Cobb could recognize its momentum. "Grate many volunteers going on to different points," he noted on May 27. Three days later he observed, "Jefferson Davis Came to Richmond on the 29th I am toald and says they must fite to gain the Victory or loose it."[60] Just how much he had to stand to lose was yet unclear.

By the end of spring 1861, with the events of the previous year and a half behind them, the citizens of southeastern Virginia found themselves caught up in a swirl of activity. The sleepy little town of Suffolk was awakening to the sounds of marching and drilling as it was transformed into a vast military camp almost overnight. Recruits poured into the town from the adjacent counties, eager to enlist before the war ended, as nearly everyone was convinced it would. Others, from the Deep South, rushed into the state where such action was likely to take place. Indeed, almost everyone seemed as "blood Thursty" as the farmer from Southampton County had observed, and equally determined to make a good account of themselves in the process.

"Dined to day with the most beautiful girl
in Suffolk—and it has [a] great many very
pretty ones."
Colonel William Dorsey Pender

"The Colonel is quite a lion."
Colonel Pender about himself

⫷ 2 ⫸ *A "Lion" Is in the Streets*

B
Y THE SUMMER IN THIS FIRST YEAR OF THE WAR, CONFEDERATE
soldiers seemed to fill southeastern Virginia. Some guarded the water
approaches to the region, even enjoying the occasional joust with
Union gunboats, while others performed the more mundane activities of
camp and drill field, preparing themselves for a war they had yet to com-
prehend fully. The presence of these soldiers comforted the people of the
region, allowing them a sense of security.

One of the Confederate officers marking time with his troops at Suffolk
was the colonel of the 3d North Carolina Volunteers, William Dorsey
Pender. Pender, an 1854 graduate of the U.S. Military Academy at West
Point, had left behind a pregnant wife and infant son in North Carolina.
When he arrived at Suffolk, his wife Fanny had just delivered their second
son, William Dorsey Pender Jr.[1] Pender's first written account of the area
was not calculated to endear himself to a woman who had just gone through

the rigors of childbirth. He opened his letter of May 30 well enough, expressing concerns about Fanny's health and inquiries about the newborn, but then foolishly shifted subjects: "There are lots of beautiful girls here, and [a] good many fine horses, so when I have nothing else to do, I can look at something beautiful or fine."[2]

The twenty-seven-year-old husband and father had wrestled with his conscience, at least momentarily, about leaving the side of the woman to whom he had been married for just over two years. But as summer 1861 approached, he found himself in another state training men for war. Thus, it is not surprising that Pender should write both of homesickness and a justification for being away at war early on in his posting at Suffolk: "My darling wife, it pained me to hear that you had had a relapse, and darling, how homesick it made me. . . . I sometimes feel that if it were manly and honorable I would be willing to give up all hopes of distinction and military ambition, to live quietly with my wife and children. But anyone with a military education is in honor bound to come forth these times and defend his country against the countless thousands of the unprincipled villains."[3]

"In honor bound to come forth." Embraced within that phase were the myriad reasons men went to war in 1861. Acutely aware of his responsibility as a husband and father, desirous to make his mark and establish his position, determined to serve his state and new nation, Pender was as much at war with himself as he was with the Union invaders. Before he left Suffolk, after only a few months there, he would learn a great deal more about himself.

For the time being Dorsey Pender was a brash, headstrong officer, more concerned with honor and reputation than the realities of life at war. On May 30 he exulted to his wife, "My Regiment is keeping up its reputation thus far and I only hope it will continue to do so."[4] One must wonder upon what such a reputation was based since neither he nor his men had yet seen combat. Still, he quickly added another observation: "Honey I flatter myself thus far no one need be ashamed of me. I occupy a high position for one so young and have been able to sustain myself thus far." Unabashedly he inquired, "Honey why should I not be satisfied in this world[?]"

Pender would provide an answer to his rhetorical question himself: "A fine Regt., nice gentlemen who treat me with the greatest deference—a fine horse, a good mount, the good opinion of the world, and Oh! the best wife in the world."[5] Indeed, Pender was becoming quite the social peacock and felt compelled to document the process in his letters home. On June 2 he noted, "I am treated with the greatest kindness by the people. Several invitations to dine today, as well as Sunday invitations to tea. Dined today with the most beautiful girl in Suffolk—and it has [a] great many very pretty ones."[6] Then on June 9 he gushed, "This is the most pleasant little town I ever saw. The kindest and most hospitable people I ever saw anywhere. The ladies keep my table covered with flowers and smile on me in the most bewitching manner and some of them are certainly like pinks. The colonel is quite a lion. Do not be jealous for none of them have the attractiveness of Mrs. W. D. Pender. I have not failed to let them know that I am married for *poor creatures I do not wish to destroy their rest.*"[7] The flirtatiousness continued. On June 23 he referred to "a lady" who had expressed her wish to make an article of clothing for the colonel, but who refused his suggestion that she make something for his wife. Pender speculated that she might try luring him, and then she would "see who is the loser." The lady must have been determined, for as the colonel explained, "She has intimated once or twice that she had fallen in love with me."[8] On June 26 he wrote Fanny: "I was at a gathering two nights ago, and had a very nice time dancing and flirting with a very nice girl. I am trying to get her to knit you a sac for the hair, but she said that she is not going to work for my wife, but will do anything for me."[9]

This last letter crossed in the mail one sent by Fanny and dated on the same day. She had finally had enough. The young lion was about to have his claws trimmed. First she instructed him to "Read to End." Then she struck at every point her vain husband had left exposed, demonstrating that she was no inferior at this kind of warfare.

> I have never in the whole course of my married [life] done anything deliberately that I know would pain you—your will has always been my law—and I have ever tried to obey to the very letter the commands of my lord and master.
>
> You say that the ladies seem to think I am a very superior woman—it would be a great pity to [undeceive] them, and might detract somewhat from your distinction [among them].

Quoting extensively from his recently arrived letter, Fanny rebuked her husband with his own words. Of the "flirting" incident she justifiably inquired, "Now, I ask you candidly, in your sober senses, why you wrote me such a thing as that?" Then warming to her subject, she expounded, "I feel indignant that any woman should have dared to make such loose speeches to my husband and that he should have encouraged it by his attentions, for you must have gone pretty far for a woman to attempt such a liberty."[10]

Mortified at the barrage and pained by its accuracy, the contrite husband could do no more than return the letter with a brief response. Happily, the episode seems to have struck the right chord with Dorsey Pender. Afterward, he displayed more wisdom and affection in his letters to his wife.[11]

Pender's vanity found expression in other avenues as well. Like so many other officers, he felt the responsibility for creating an effective combat-ready force but had to rely upon politicians and bureaucrats to obtain sufficient arms and equipment for the men. In this case it was not the distractions of the community and its social events that produced the frustration but the problems that emerged when the promised support failed, or was slow, to materialize. This aspect of the war could be excruciating for men who felt that the homefront seemed to be forgetting them so quickly.

Colonel Pender expressed his determination to travel to Raleigh to confront Governor Henry T. Clark over the failure of the state government to provide sufficient supplies for his command. "I started to have a row with the Governor and get what we need and have been promised or give up my command in the service." Wisely he decided instead to sound off in a letter to his wife: "I have been fooled with long enough and am determined not to stand it any longer. We are not fully equipped and have not been treated as well as others."

Pender made the sensible decision to send two junior officers on the errand to Raleigh. They would allow him to press the governor on this issue without involving himself directly in the matter. Even so, Pender remained acutely aware of the transformation he had undergone since his Old Army days. "I am not Lt. Pender any longer but Col. Pender knowing my position and worth."[12]

The two emissaries succeeded admirably, and Pender was quick to accept the credit. Six days after he had railed against the governor, he felt completely vindicated. "They were completely successful, and the Regt. is now [as] well equipped as any in the field." Then with the pretentiousness that marked his early military career, Pender concluded: "I was not light upon the Governor, for the way we had been sent off with promises, all of which had been broken. In reply he wrote the kindest letter you ever saw, saying to let him know what I wanted and he would attend to it in person." Even so, the situation left Pender ambivalent about political promises: "I find I am not capable of getting on with politicians who do not mind breaking their word. I believe them and they deceive me."[13]

However much the politicians actually supported the fighting men, at least some of the folks on the homefront felt strongly enough to argue over degrees of patriotism. In an early 1862 letter, a visitor from southeastern Virginia dashed off a quick note from "near Weldon, N.C.," illustrating this attitude. "You have to stay in Carolina to find out what a nice state it is," she explained tartly, adding, "and how many more soldiers they have sent, and how much *braver* they are than *Virginians*." Then, concluding on a particularly bitter note, she allowed that "if I had not made so many good resolutions I think I should have had many a quarrel."[14]

Of course, Virginia was putting men into the field, too. Indeed, many of those coming from southeastern Virginia engaged in the active defense of the home region, particularly in the batteries that began to arise along the rivers and estuaries at places like Pig Point and Town Point on the Nansemond River.[15] One of these men was the Riddick tutor, Jonny Smith. His plight undoubtedly mirrored the experiences of hundreds of men at posts throughout the area. "Craney Island would be a very pleasant place if there were any shade trees on it," he wrote from his encampment, "but as it is, it is a most dreary abode. The sun pours down its hot rays on us from its rise until the last golden beams cast lengthened shadows on the ground." All of the men suffered from such exposure, even with the arrival of timber for more permanent shelter than the tents could provide. Despite the hardships Smith believed himself able to adjust to army life. He was eating well enough and was relatively content with his conditions. He worried only that his unit would be transferred before they could enjoy the huts they had built. "But, as I am only a corporal, I have no say in the matter," he pronounced resignedly, "and have to go wherever those in authority say."[16]

Others found the transition from civilian to soldier life more difficult to make. In November 1861 a South Carolina soldier lamented that by the time he had joined his company, "the offices were all filled," and all that was left for him was the dubious position of *"high private."* He proceeded to single out one man who had succeeded in obtaining an "office" for himself but then had let the position of authority affect him: "They should from kindness to him if for no other reason, have left the office from him. I am afraid he will die of self conceit." The "high private" concluded that the lesson was that "brass wins the day."[17]

If adjustments to new positions of authority proved difficult for some and trying for others, there remained the important need to prepare for combat. Troops in the camps of this remote region today could be called to the battlefield tomorrow. Well-disciplined commands would have distinct advantages over those who were not. Confederate colonel W. D. Pender, who saw his regiment as a reflection of his own adequacy as an officer, drilled his men rigorously. "We are drilling four times a day having Regimental drill once each day," he explained to Fanny. "In two or three months we shall make quite a presentable appearance."[18]

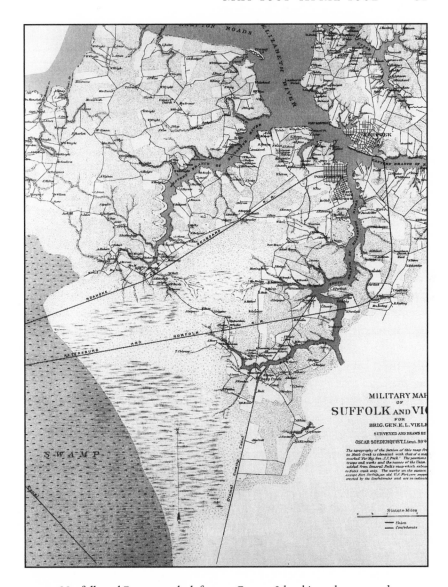

MAP 2 Norfolk and Portsmouth defenses. Craney Island is at the top, and
Gosport Navy Yard is below Portsmouth.

Earlier in the month Pender had observed, "I do not wish anything better than to be allowed to remain here long enough to get the Regt. a little
in condition."[19] His statements regarding his command remained consistent: "They begin to make quite a presentable appearance, much better than
you would suppose" (June 2); "We shall soon be worth seeing" (June 10);

and "I am proud of my Regt." (June 12).[20] These observations masked his real concern that these men, both in their appearance and demeanor, reflected upon him as their leader. In subsequent correspondence he explained straightforwardly, "I think every one has confidence in me and the men rather fear me I think."[21] The hopeful tone of Pender's statement betrays his still somewhat limited confidence in himself as an officer.

Fortunately Pender understood the need for consistency in action as well. Thus when one of his subordinate officers pressured him for a furlough in June, he refused. An angry John T. Hambrick wrote home to his wife, "I have asked Col. Pender twice for a furlow, & twice he has denied me, Saying that he could not let the captain's off, & also said that my presence was much needed." The officer complained, "I gave him all the particulars as regards my business at home, but he answered me by saying his wife was sick & also his child."

Part of Hambrick's frustration with military service in Suffolk was the almost incessant demand for drilling, particularly among officers who, like Pender, wanted the men to look good at minimum, and at maximum to be prepared for the rigors of campaigning. "I am pretty worn out with drilling," Hambrick moaned, arguing that "nine hours in the sun is no small matter." Although he adjusted the hours at drill "in the sun" to seven, with an additional hour of "examination" for the officers at night, he was clearly disgusted by the lack of martial glory he had experienced thus far.

"I hear they are going to dispence with one drill at 3 o'clock," he noted, a concession to the midday heat which, he admitted, "will make it better." Nevertheless, Hambrick was angry enough to confess, "If this thing is continued I shall have to snap. *one drill*[.] I can't nor want [to] stand it." Finally, he calmed down enough to conclude: "But, soldiers should not grumble. we are seeing a good time, when we take into consideration the soldiers of [17]76."

Having spent a significant portion of the body of his letter venting his anger at the demands of military life, Hambrick then added a postscript that sounded remarkably like his colonel: "I flatter myself that I have the best drilled company in the Regiment. . . . when my company came in from Dress Parade last evening it made me proud to look at it. . . . I believe I pass for more than my worth in the regiment. . . . I guess I think too much of my company, for I would almost wade through fire to follow it. But they had obeyed me, & acted the part of a soldier so well, I cannot praise them too much. They seem to like me, both officers and men. It would be hard to break the ties which bind us."[22]

The ambivalence Hambrick felt regarding the value of the military regimen was undoubtedly shared by the men as well. In the heat of summer, the intense drilling was not only uncomfortable, it was unhealthy. One soldier wrote in late June, "The weather is extremely hot, being exposed to the hot rays of the Sun and clouds of dust has caused Several of the men to faint while Drilling."[23] Heat and sunstroke were constant companions. Yet the need for turning volunteers into soldiers remained. In late November a soldier observed in a letter from Camp Huger in Suffolk: "Our camp is in the suburbs of the town upon an old field which affords excellent ground for drilling. And well has our Colonel taken advantage of the fact. We have been ever since our arrival here undergoing the severest drills."[24]

Nor was drilling the only constant with the soldiers stationed in southeastern Virginia; so was sickness. The rampant illness was one side effect of bringing together so many people from various parts of the state and the South, even for relatively short periods of time. People who had never been exposed to some illnesses suddenly fell deathly sick. Others suffered from changes in diet, poor sanitation, or impure drinking water. Officers took the steps they considered appropriate to safeguard the health of their commands, but diseases raged through the camps anyway.

Men from the 14th Virginia Infantry, many of whom had enlisted in Suffolk but hailed from Mecklenburg County, fell ill in droves almost immediately. At least twenty-five of them became sick within thirty days of their enlistment. Many of these, and others, had to be sent to hospitals in Petersburg, Richmond, or Williamsburg.[25] Robert Moore of the 3d North Carolina wrote home on June 15 complaining, "I have had the mumps awful bad since I wrote to you last, but I am nearly well now."[26] Nor were officers immune. J. T. Hambrick explained that he was still weak from struggling with a severe bout of diarrhea and feared. "I think all of us will have to undergo this disease," he wrote his wife. "A good many of our boys has been sick."[27]

Men from the local area fell ill as well. Robert D. Carson, a farmer from Isle of Wight County, got so sick from a bad case of diarrhea that he had to be sent to Chimborazo Hospital in Richmond. Others found the illnesses so debilitating that they had to be discharged from the service. James Council, a twenty-five-year-old farmer from Suffolk, received his medical discharge in June. Lieutenant James R. McGuire, a hotelkeeper in prewar days, remained so sick that he resigned from the army in August. William Purvis, a lawyer and farmer, continued "unfit the entire enlistment" from rheumatism and fever before finally securing his discharge.[28]

The introduction and spread of infectious diseases often proved deadly when the victims had no previous exposure or were already suffering from poor dietary and living conditions. For men like James Glasscock Sr., the barrage they underwent from sickness exacted the same price as enemy volleys. Yet because of their fatal illnesses, such men seldom if ever had the opportunity to engage the opponents they had gone into the field to fight. Within days of his enlistment in Suffolk in April 7, 1862, Glasscock fell ill. Although apparently recovering from this initial bout, by the end of June he was in Chimborazo Hospital. Forced by the influx of wounded from the Seven Days Battles out of Chimborazo into Richmond General Hospital, he received a brief furlough in July. By August, Glasscock was in Danville General Hospital. He returned to duty later that month and went back into a hospital in Winchester in September and October. Sadly, a return to convalescence at home in Mecklenburg County did not restore his health. James Glasscock Sr. died of typhoid fever on December 16, 1862.[29]

Three other privates in the 14th Virginia fared worse than the senior Glasscock, who at least recovered briefly from one illness before succumbing to another. James Riddick remained sick in a Richmond hospital through May and June before dying of pneumonia in Danville General Hospital in July. James Rideout enlisted on May 1, only to die of disease in a Petersburg hospital fifteen days later. William White joined the company on May 4 but was quickly at home, sick, before dying of disease on July 8. Two Pope boys from Southampton County, aged twenty-one and twenty-two, died of measles at a farm near Smithfield. Their neighbor, an eighteen-year-old student named Joseph T. Westbrook who had enlisted on May 11, was carried off by the same illness at the same place on July 31.[30] Whatever dreams of glory these men might have harbored for warfare, they died without ever firing a shot in anger at their opponents.

The routine for officers concerned with the health of their men was to locate good ground, good shade, and good water. But clearly such traditional precautions could not guarantee good health. By modern standards these men put themselves at risk on a daily basis, but their notions of health and sanitation conformed to the accepted norms of their day. Still, these measures could make a difference, as noted by a soldier writing home early in 1862: "The change in water made about one half the company sick for two or three days, but this morning the sanitary condition of the camp is greatly improved."[31] Yet the sad reality was that one Union soldier's prediction that "sickness will thin off our Ranks faster than the enemy can" was becoming all too true for the Confederates as well.[32]

Adding to the soldiers' afflictions were the psychological demands that military camps placed upon their occupants. Long hours of tedium matched long hours of drill. Men thrown together in common cause soon found that they did not have much in common after all. The elation and adulation that accompanied enlistment quickly dissipated under the strains of camp life. Battle would unite these men, as they faced the foe together, forced by circumstances to rely upon each other for their survival. But those days lay ahead of them.

The teacher-turned-soldier Jonny Smith observed of his camp at Craney Island, "I have found, even in my short experience, that Camp is one of the finest schools of human nature that could well be established." The comment was not meant to be complimentary, a point he rapidly made clear. "It brings to light hundreds of defects that in ordinary intercourse might have forever remained concealed." Under the glare of camp life, the true character of many surfaced, often in unflattering ways. Yet Smith, the former tutor, could appreciate the lessons offered. "I have learned more of men, their manners, their dispositions and their characters since I have been here than I ever should have learned if I remained at home, devoting myself to my occupation and my books."[33]

Soldiers could counterbalance some of the discomfort of camp life by visiting friends and loved ones at home or in camp for short periods if they obtained furloughs or lived relatively close by, but often military duties, the distance and uncertainty of transportation, or the pressure of daily routines prevented this immediate form of contact. Letters substituted, but these also proved to be tenuous connections. Although newspapers had their own drawbacks, they provided an additional source of information for soldiers and family members.

For instance, a correspondent from the Petersburg *Daily Express* kept its readers in central Virginia abreast of developments in and around Suffolk. On September 28 a feature "From Suffolk" appeared offering news of recruitment and political activity in the region. The correspondent reported "that John R. Kilby, Esq. of this town accepts the nomination for Congress in the 2d District." Kilby, the Suffolk lawyer who had signed Virginia's ordinance of secession, enjoyed enviable advantages. "His personal popularity and eminent fitness for the position," the writer started enthusiastically before catching himself, "will make his chances of success at least equal to any other."[34]

While some individuals courted office, others seem to have courted trouble. Once in the autumn of 1861 and again in early 1862, a man named Jack Fairless ran afoul of the law. Theft appears to have been his preferred vice. In the first instance he appeared before the court in Nansemond County. Although the verdict is unknown, he may have dodged punishment for that crime by enlisting in the army. If so, Fairless quickly got into trouble once more. Again accused of theft, he suffered the indignity of having his head shaved and being forced to wear a barrel. The recalcitrant soldier promptly deserted, but this would not be the last southeastern Virginia and north-eastern North Carolina would hear of Jack Fairless, who would find fresh opportunities for plunder while leading Unionist guerrillas.[35]

Of course, all was not grim death, distress, and disenchantment in southeastern Virginia. Many of the men functioned well in the camps, and others recovered from their sickness sufficiently to return to them. The men did what they could to improve their conditions, although the surest remedy for most maladies was to receive letters from friends and loved ones. In wartime situations, where conditions could deteriorate rapidly, morale played a central role. Officers hoped that by keeping morale at a high level, the men would perform better, and desertion would be less likely. Receiving mail could mean the difference between men who became skulkers and deserters and those who endured the hardships come what may. The men themselves professed to be bolstered by news from friends and family. To encourage responses, the soldiers sent out a steady stream of correspondence of their own. Camp life turned many of them not only into voracious readers but writers as well.

Often the letters became sources of propaganda. Particularly early in the war, some stationary carried patriotic messages. Such was the case with a South Carolina soldier posted at Camp Huger in Suffolk. His writing paper featured a blazing artillery piece and flag and bore the slogan "Stand firmly by your cannon, Let ball and grape-shot fly, And trust in God and Davis, But keep your powder dry," over the words "Confederate States of America." Although the South Carolinian disowned the rhyme that adorned his stationary ("I do not endorse the above blasphemous verse"),[36] many men from both North and South used such stationary to reflect and underscore their own views for the folks at home. Despite the shortages that made such printed paper increasingly rare for Southerners, the need, on both sides in the conflict, for written contact with people outside their immediate reach remained high. Letters held family and friends together whatever the circumstances at home or on the front might be.

Union soldiers had their own slogans and symbols, endorsing their commonly held views. One high-ranking Federal officer commented to his wife, "My boys look for the coming of the mail with vastly more interest than they do the advent into camp of the Secesh. If they do not get frequent letters from home and friends they feel neglected." Such was the power of the mail upon his men that he concluded in a subsequent letter: "The boys like to hear from home. . . . These letters are the links that make the chain that binds the soldier to his home and society."[37]

For this reason, letters from the front frequently followed a basic pattern. They usually included descriptions of the soldier's current location, the state of his health, questions concerning family and friends, and the conditions of the country or loved ones in other units. These letters tended to reflect the personalities of those who wrote them, but they uniformly displayed such common denominators. Thus when the South Carolinian with the militant verse on his stationary heard from a friend for the first time since enlisting, he replied with an overview of his service from the time of his enlistment in Greenville to his latest encampment at Suffolk. Of his current "home" he had a decidedly mixed assessment. "Suffolk is an old English town possessing little or no architectural beauty or beauty of location," he explained. "The low roofed houses present quite a quaint and almost comical appearance, but when one considers the age of some of them there arises a feeling of reverence almost for their dilapidated and time honored walls."[38]

Most of the soldiers who passed through the region and remained there for any length of time described it in their letters to friends and loved ones. R. Channing Price, a Confederate artillerist, conveyed the usual message to his mother on March 9, 1862. "We are at length in Suffolk after a trip much easier than expected." Then he added something more calculated to appeal to a friend than to a mother. "Yesterday was the first time since I entered [the] service that I have seen any number of ladies & you may imagine the sight was refreshing." He also wanted her to know that he was eating well enough, although he expressed surprise that the proprietor of the boardinghouse where he ate breakfast charged him and his companions nothing for their meal. The free meal left an impression on the soldier. "We have been well treated since our arrival here by every one & consequently are pleased with the place."

Price talked of attending church, which must have been more pleasing for his mother to read. But in doing so, he reported that "the town has been deserted by most of the people, consequently soldiers comprised the larger part of the congregation."[39] Despite the number of Confederate troops in the area and the backwater nature of this theater of the war thus far, many of Suffolk's residents seem to have left before the enemy seriously threatened the town. In subsequent letters he observed that all remained quiet.[40]

Civilians had some choice if they had friends or relatives they could visit in more remote locales, but the soldiers had to find ways to adapt to life as best they could from day to day. For some of them this meant foraging or hunting and fishing to supplement their army fare. Others patronized local businesses or lived off the largess of grateful residents. At this stage of the conflict, the benefits of these contacts often seem to have gone both ways. Certainly, as the units lingered in the region or established themselves in the area's defenses, local entrepreneurs grasped at opportunities for profit.

As with any large military operation, these troops demanded services for transportation and support, particularly requiring food and forage in abundance. Requisitions for charges made against the state of North Carolina or the Quartermaster Department of the Confederate States of America suggest the extent to which local residents rendered such support. When the army could not provide the necessary transportation or supplies, area citizens would step forward to do so.[41]

With the near constant shifting of men and equipment into and through the region, logistical arrangements were not always smooth. Sometimes competing needs clashed, particularly when there were multiple demands for the same transportation lines and equipment. This was true for the Suffolk quartermaster, who was responsible for responding to the demands of the batteries along the Nansemond and on part of the James, as well as meeting the needs of the military commands stationed in or around the town itself. Supplies for these batteries, including heavy artillery and ammunition, arrived as near as possible by rail and then had to be transported over the roads to the sites themselves. Snafus were virtually inevitable.

Such a snag occurred when supplies for a river battery near Smithfield arrived at the same time an infantry regiment in the area had to be moved. The Suffolk quartermaster had to inform the battery commander that he did not have enough heavy wagons on hand to haul the "two guns and ammunition from Zuni Station" for he had just "had a requisition for the moving of Col. Pender's Regiment."[42] Even a well-oiled bureaucracy could handle but so much activity, and the Confederate system, despite its demands for the proper paperwork, was hardly well oiled.[43]

As winter approached, the need for various materials to construct suitable quarters and hospitals presented new demands and offered additional opportunities. Local resident Willis Riddick seems to have recognized the need. He furnished heavy loads of hand-cut shingles for garrisons in Norfolk and at Pig Point, a battery guarding the entrance to the Nansemond River. Throughout the winter months he also furnished corn and fodder for the men and animals, as well as a number of horses and mules for ambulances and supply wagons.[44] Another Riddick supplied the 1st North Carolina with bricks to build chimneys for their hospital in Suffolk. One enterprising resident even offered his home as a temporary headquarters office for Brigadier General George W. Randolph, although Archibald

Riddick exacted $5 in rent for the privilege. This type of support contin-
ued into the spring, with various individuals selling corn, beef, fodder, and
other necessities to the troops.[45]

This assistance did not always come from white members of the community. James T. Ayer, a free black resident of Suffolk, sold the Confederates
as much in the way of chickens, eggs, bacon, and other commodities as
they sought to purchase. He was so prolific in his sales to Southern military agents in 1861–63 that Federal commissioners later disallowed his claims
to the U.S. government for compensation. The investigator observed that
"he might as well have been in the employ of the [Confederate] Commissary
Department."[46]

Local planters also made their human resources available for the war
effort. Some, like Willis Riddick, did so willingly, receiving compensation
from the government. Riddick provided four men to work as ferrymen at
the Western Branch Ferry in August, while also acting as the military inspector for the ferry. The work brought him $20.[47] Others, like Daniel Cobb of
Southampton, acquiesced reluctantly to the demands. He grumbled in his
diary in November, "Our slaves is ordered out at this time in the County
to work on embankments by the government which will throw farmers
back." Nevertheless, he intended to comply with the order, even helping
to attend to his father-in-law's quota. He spent part of Wednesday,
November 21, "delivering his negrows and getting a Receipt for them" from
impressment officers, noting, "They starte on Saturday the 24[th] to Work
on the embankments for defence of the so Confedacy." Then on the
twenty-fourth, with some of "my foalks getting up Corn," the farmer spent
his "day of[f] ten[d]ing to get Receipts for the Negrows that the Government
mad[e] recosition for."[48]

The Confederate Congress did not pass legislation allowing for the
impressment of slaves to perform such military tasks until March 1863. But
as the experiences of these and other owners demonstrate, the practice was
already under way on a local level earlier in the war. Such practices infringed
upon the owners' personal prerogatives. However, as historian Emory
Thomas has observed, "The impressment process, with its ills and inequities,
was doubtless necessary . . . and though Southern civilians complained, they
generally submitted to the infringement of property rights for the sake of
the cause."[49] This seems to have been the case in southeastern Virginia.

Whatever the fight for independence might demand, the war itself
remained, and some reminders brought it home vividly. Both sides
attempted to gain intelligence concerning their opponent's strength and
intentions. In addition to more conventional types of raiding and scouting,

this often meant employing individuals to infiltrate opposing lines. For those involved in such covert activity, this could prove to be a dangerous business to undertake. One Confederate boasted, "We took up Seven men this week on Suspicion one of them was a true Yankee and one of them was one of our men that was taken prisoner by Old Lincoln and had made his escape from the green eyed monster. The others proved to be deserters." Slipping through enemy lines occasionally provided useful information, but it meant death if the spy, or scout as they were known, happened to be caught in the act. "They were all taken down to Norfolk to have them tryed it is thought from what evidence was gotten from them here that two of them will be put to death."[50]

Colonel W. D. Pender could be equally merciless in his attitude. From Suffolk he wrote his wife, "Some of my men caught three men from Old Point [Comfort near Hampton] yesterday. They are Virginians, and to my mind are clearly traitors, and I accordingly sent them to Gen. Huger at Norfolk to be dealt with as he might think proper." In addition to these men, Pender's troops caught two deserters, for whom he had the same response.[51]

Nor were white deserters or Unionists the only ones to scout behind Confederate lines to bring information to the Federals. On November 11 Major General John E. Wool, commanding the Department of Virginia, received word at Fort Monroe that six men, "all colored, came from [the] Nansemond River last night in a small boat." One of these men arrived with a fairly detailed description of Confederate earthworks on the river and the disposition of Southern forces in the region. The informant noted the existence of two manned works guarding the mouth of the Nansemond, "about one-half mile apart—the first about four miles from the mouth—both on the left bank." Following these general descriptions were the kinds of details that probably came after the close questioning of the man. "Each mounts four guns, about 24–pounders," the report goes on. "The first is shaped thus: V V V V. The first is garrisoned by forty men of the Isle of Wight regiment, the second by eight. One gun in each fort will traverse; the chassis of the others are immovable." Additional information gave the report's writer the opportunity to editorialize: "Both open in the rear; very flimsy and trifling affairs. . . . Can land midway between them."

As for the troops stationed in the region, the informant was surprisingly specific: "The Isle of Wight regiment is at Smithfield. The Petersburg Cavalry Company is at Chuckatuck. There are thirteen regiments of South Carolina troops at the old brick church [Benn's] near Smithfield, commanded by Colonel Pender. At Suffolk there are 10,000 Georgia troops." All of these numbers made for an impressive array of defensive forces.[52]

In reality, the figures were somewhat out of date. They failed to take into account relatively recent troop movements. For instance, Colonel Pender had already left the Benn's Church area in August with his "South" Carolinians. Even so, the report indicated the variety of forces available to the Confederates, not to mention the ways in which local African Americans aided the Union cause well before emancipation. It also suggested at least one possible explanation for their willingness to do so. "This man says that the farmers are starving their Negroes to feed the soldiers."[53]

Rumors pervaded the press and the gossip mills throughout the year. In June 1861 Daniel Cobb recorded the hearsay attributed to the Federals in his diary: "I am toald they Ravished some feemales and lady. . . . I am toald they have taken 3 honerable and high minded yong Ladies and Carried them [to] frtress Monrow for what purpose you may guess etc." This kind of propaganda had the dual purpose of strengthening patriotic resolve and dehumanizing the enemy. In Cobb's case it worked perfectly. "Shuch out brakes and violence I never known of any enamay You may know they are grand low life skamps of the north."[54]

Then on June 13, as he described his own efforts to help make "Boe [Bowie] knives to Cut the Raskels of the North to Mince," Cobb vented his outrage. "Shoot Cut and Whip the Raskels of the North is my sincere praer of the harte for they are undermining Skaundels [scoundrels]." He would record other alleged Northern atrocities as he heard them, and he continued to blame them for a war the North had imposed upon the South. "No day passes but my prayer is to konker," he confessed.[55]

The ebb and flow of information and innuendo, accurate or exaggerated, filtering through southeastern Virginia generally caused the morale of the people in the region to swing dramatically. For instance, Dorsey Pender gloated about the success of Confederate arms in a small skirmish at Big Bethel, naturally attributing the success to the prowess of North Carolina soldiery as well as the hand of God. "Does it not seem that the Lord of Hosts is on our side?" he asked Fanny. "It certainly [is] a glorious thought that the troops of the old North State should win the first pitched battle, and so gloriously."[56]

Early victories such as those at Big Bethel and First Manassas helped to maintain enthusiasm for the war in many Southern circles.[57] On January 3, 1862, with the promise of a new year fresh in his mind, Thomas E. Upshaw wrote his friend Charles H. Riddick, a fellow graduate of the Virginia Military Institute, to ask for his help in raising a command of cavalry in Suffolk. Upshaw delegated to his friend the task of contacting officials in Richmond, including Charles's brother Nathaniel, a member of the Virginia

House of Delegates, to secure their aid in obtaining commissions. He gave detailed instructions as to how Riddick should proceed, specifically advising him to meet with President Davis. "Tell Jeff Davis that we are in *for the war,*" he admonished his friend, "that we are not twelve months volunteers." Upshaw assured Riddick that he would be recruiting for the command, but that it was best if "you do this part of the business because you are the *best looking* man."[58]

Upon receiving this appeal to his vanity, Charles Riddick dashed off a letter to his brother Nathaniel on the sixth. Denied the opportunity for a furlough to conduct the sales job Tom Upshaw had assigned him, Charles needed his brother's help more than ever. The secretary of war had offered limited assurances that "such a company is needed and would be received, armed and equipped when we could raise 60 men." As for the animals, "horses he refuses to furnish, but Father and some others have promised to furnish horses for all men not able to buy" their own. With such guarantees in his pocket as leverage, Nathaniel would have only "to see the President and Secretary of War" for the authority and for organizational instructions, emphasizing the desire of the two men to form "a *crack* company . . . *for the war.*" Charles concluded his letter confidently, "With your influence and that of your friends, I think the President will grant my request."[59]

Apparently the political arm-twisting worked, for on March 1, 1862, the two friends organized a cavalry company that would become Company C, 13th Virginia Cavalry. The command assembled in Suffolk with Upshaw as its captain and Riddick as its first lieutenant. The 13th Virginia would later add a second company from Nansemond County and also boasted the company from Southampton County to which Daniel Cobb's son Asbury belonged.[60]

In the spring of 1862 as people from southeastern Virginia continued to demonstrate their determination to rally to the defense of their homes, there was increasing reason to worry that such a defense might be imminent. In January, Brigadier General Ambrose Burnside led a formidable expedition into the waters of North Carolina's Outer Banks. On February 7–8 he struck the poorly prepared and woefully undermanned Confederate works at Roanoke Island. Netting some 2,500 prisoners and inflicting 100 casualties at a cost of less than 300 casualties of his own, Burnside's expedition opened the potential of a backdoor approach to southeastern Virginia, sending shock waves through the region and a new sense of the reality of war.[61]

A Virginian stationed in South Carolina spoke for many when he blasted the turn of events in a letter to his brother. "The Roanoke affair was shameful & cowardly," he proclaimed. He pointed out that the garrison had "surrendered too soon," then revised his assessment. "They ought never to have surrendered. Our motto must be victory or death."

Whatever the stain of Roanoke Island might offer as an object lesson in patriotism, Samuel McGuire, the author of the letter, was concerned about what it meant for the region. "Can the yankees take Suffolk or the Weldon Rail Road?" he wanted to know. "It seems to me that you ought to be reinforced at Suffolk, if you are to hold that place." "But," he wrote his brother, "if you ever get into a fight with the yankees, the safest way, as well as the most honorable way is to charge right boldly and straight upon them."[62]

Such bold assertions belied the despondency beneath them as the Confederates underwent a difficult spring. Roanoke Island and the fall of Forts Henry and Donelson in the western theater leveled severe blows at Southern morale.[63] The Suffolk correspondent of the Petersburg *Daily Express* shared in the gloom and general malaise. "The news from Fort Donelson has fallen upon us with terrible weight," he observed on February 19. He sought to put the best face on such developments by noting that "recruiting for old companies and joining new volunteer companies is going on rapidly."[64]

Even in his patriotic letter, Samuel McGuire could not displace his depressed feeling entirely. *"We need a great victory very much indeed,"* he wrote, emphasizing his own words dramatically. "The times are gloomy, but we must not dispond, only work the more and strike the harder. May the good God preserve us and our cause!" He concluded, "The darkest hour is just before daylight, and I sincerely hope we will have some good news soon."[65]

Instead, there were the first hints that things would get worse for the people of southeastern Virginia. In March, Channing Price wrote his mother from Camp Randolph near Suffolk, "Therre is no longer any doubt that Norfolk is to be evacuated, as the continual rumbling of heavy trains, day & night, tells, the sad tale of another city to given up to the base invader."[66]

Although Price was premature in his surmise, the Confederate grip on Norfolk would likely be tested before too long. On February 27 President Davis had already used his newly acquired authority to impose martial law and suspend the writ of habeas corpus in Portsmouth and Norfolk.[67] That action provoked a hailstorm of criticism among those who thought the Confederate government was going too far in its quest for independence. When Major General Huger attempted to carry out the directive by naming an officer to the high-sounding post of "Civil and Military Governor" with authority over Portsmouth, Norfolk, and "the surrounding country to the distance of ten miles," Virginia governor Letcher erupted. "By what authority does any man announce himself to be civil and military Governor, and organize a government at Norfolk within the limits of Virginia[?]" he scrawled angrily.

It took the good offices of General Robert E. Lee to smooth over the business, in the absence of the president. In a strong but respectful letter to Huger, Lee asked him to act "to avoid further complaint" by instructing his subordinate of "several facts with regard to which he evidently has fallen into a misapprehension." At the same time, to the secretary of the commonwealth, Lee offered the assurance that the matter would receive Davis's attention when he returned. "In the mean time, I beg you to inform the Governor that I have called the attention of Genl. Huger to the acts of the officer in Norfolk which are the subject of complaint, and directed that they shall not be repeated."[68] Lee's swift and diplomatic response seems to have settled the issue, although the prerogatives of the national government while waging a war continued to clash with those of state and local governments.

There was no doubt that military and civilian officials were concerned about affairs in southeastern Virginia. Some of the movement the artilleryman Price thought marked an imminent evacuation was undoubtedly the shifting of troops in the region. The Surry Light Artillery took up a position briefly at Hill's Point on the Nansemond River. Initially naming the post Camp Riddick, the men soon dubbed it "camp of destruction," as the weather turned harsh. The poor conditions added to the unit's health woes, leading to a number of absences from duty due to illness, as well as two deaths.[69]

Such a reassignment was also going on for some of the companies that came from southeastern Virginia. Price explained that the departure of the 16th Virginia Infantry was particularly poignant. "Many of them are from this place," he wrote from Suffolk, "& they have been so near home, that their families have not realized before that they were going to war." The traumatic scene of tearful farewells led Price to observe, "So much weeping I have not seen for many a day."[70]

Sacrifice was quickly becoming the order of the day. But just how much the people were prepared to surrender for the sake of their independence as a nation remained an open question. Public policy in the midst of war again spurred strong feelings and angry debate over a conscription bill that the Confederate Congress was considering. President Davis approved the bill on April 19, prompting instant reaction. The act called for conscripting, or drafting, "all persons residing within the Confederate States, between the ages of 18 and 35 years, and rightfully subject to military duty."[71] "Everything is in a great stir in regard to the Conscription Bill," one soldier wrote from Suffolk, "& of course it meets with much censure, but so far as I can see only from a class of men who seem determined to grumble at everything done by the Authorities for the purpose of keeping our present Army in the field." As for himself, this man felt the action necessary. "It strikes me as a very proper Bill & promises results more practical than any of the tinkering that has been done by Congress & the Legislature before."[72] Unfortunately, Congress would soon step in to provide for exemptions on the premise that the nation required some producers to remain at home to provide for those who would do the fighting. Anger over the need for conscription and the fairness of exemptions led some to dub the war "A Rich Man's War and a Poor Man's Fight."[73]

Despite the hardships, the arguments, and the often-depressing battlefield news, there were glimmers of hope. The emergence of the reborn *Merrimack,* now outfitted as an ironclad and rechristened *Virginia,* offered the illusion of security to the people of the region. This was particularly true after the vessel stunned the Union blockading fleet in Hampton Roads on March 8. Decimating the USS *Cumberland* and the USS *Congress,* the Confederate ironclad seemed destined to wreak havoc on the remainder of the Union fleet and lift the blockade. However, the next day she faced the newly arrived Union ironclad *Monitor.* The two vessels then engaged in a match that revolutionized naval warfare but ended in a technical draw.[74]

One happy resident exuded a few days later, "Were you not delighted when you heard of our grand naval battle near Norfolk?"[75] Another person believed that the *Virginia* remained a viable threat. He speculated that when she returned to fight again, the second confrontation between the vessels would be "one to which that of the 8th and 9th of March can no more compare than [a] mountain to a mole hill." There was even the rumor that a force of daring Southerners would board the *Monitor* "and take possession of her." Then, the writer envisioned, the two ironclads would turn the tables on the Federals and perhaps win the war. On the other hand, the soldier warned his correspondent, "If the Merrimac is lost, or proves a failure, your old home, Suffolk, will, in all probability, be the next battlefield."[76]

The possibility that Suffolk would become a battlefield at all, much less the next one, must have seemed remote indeed in early 1862. Yet as circumstances had already demonstrated elsewhere, the darkest hour might very well be approaching for many of the area's people. Still, if that darkness came in the form of Union uniforms, there would be other local folk for whom the darkness would bear the bright streaks of dawning freedom. At the moment there was little to dispel the sense that the war was distant and that the region might be spared its harshest elements.

MAY–SEPTEMBER 1862

"We have Suffolk, taken last evening by Major Dodge.
All quiet."
General John Wool to Secretary of War Edwin Stanton

"Suffolk is the meanest God-forsaken place
you ever saw—houses deserted, stores shut up."
Lieutenant Colonel John B. Woodward, 13th New York

⊰ 3 ⊱ *Paradise Lost*

THE PEOPLE OF SOUTHEASTERN VIRGINIA FACED ENORMOUS CHANGE in May 1862, although in the beginning few could have imagined the extent of that change. With Union general George B. McClellan breaking the impasse at Yorktown and clearing the way for his advance up the Peninsula toward Richmond, Norfolk was no longer tenable for the Confederates to hold. If Southern forces evacuated Norfolk, Suffolk would almost certainly follow. Should the Confederates retreat to the best defensive line, the Blackwater River, they would expose much of southeastern Virginia to Union occupation, or at least constant raiding, foraging, and other incursions.

Rumors of some sort of activity spread rapidly, especially among the soldiers, prompting one junior officer in Suffolk to write his brother on May 5: "All the troops here are under marching orders, destination unknown. It is rumored that we will fall back in the direction of Petersburg, or Richmond." For once the camp gossip was accurate, but then all of the signs pointed that way. "Rumors are rife that Norfolk will be evacuated in a few days," the lieutenant continued. "This is certain, that all the rolling stock on both railroads have been ordered to Norfolk," obviously for the purpose of bringing off as much war matériel as possible.[1] Another Confederate agreed, relaying a similar message to his father two days later. "It is generally believed that Norfolk will be entirely evacuated in a few days," the infantryman noted, adding, "One thing is certain they are moving large amounts of public property from there and people are leaving very fast."[2]

These Confederates were not misreading the signals. From the beginning of the month, Secretary of War George W. Randolph had warned Major General Huger to prepare himself for such drastic measures. "Send as speedily as possible the railroad iron warehoused in Norfolk and Portsmouth" to the interior for safekeeping, Randolph advised on May 1. "Lose no time," he urged, "as much more is involved than the railroad iron, and it is of great importance to have the [rail]roads clear for other purposes."[3]

Then on the third, Secretary Randolph offered specific instructions for removing excess ammunition, provisions, and supplies, as well as the heavy caliber "rifle guns of the navy pattern." With time short and available transportation limited, he knew that much would have to be left behind. This, too, must be properly disposed of before a final withdrawal took place. "Whatever public property will be of use to the enemy and cannot be carried off must be destroyed," Randolph explained, clearly preferring that Huger bring out all he could, leaving nothing for the Federals. Still, the government official cautioned the general, "You will bear in mind, however, that the preservation of your army is of the first importance and that its safety must not be too much hazarded by your efforts to save the public property."[4]

For this particular general, such leeway was enough. The secretary's suggestion that he "concentrate . . . as speedily as possible near Suffolk, leaving in position only such portion [of his command] as may be necessary to cover the evacuation," need not have been made. Huger was anxious to go. Making matters worse, the urgency spread quickly, and almost disastrously. The early withdrawal of water batteries near Smithfield, well inland of the endangered port city, threatened to expose Huger's line of retreat to assault from the flank. Robert E. Lee saw the danger and hastily notified the Confederate commander in Suffolk, William W. Loring, that such "troops must not move from position necessary to maintain communications with Norfolk before the stores, men, etc. are withdrawn from

that place; . . . the outposts must be prepared for evacuation, but not abandoned before the proper time."[5]

Civilians saw the signs as well as the soldiers. While in Petersburg, Anna
Mary Riddick received a letter that must have proved most distressing.
"Annie, what do you think of the times?" the correspondent inquired rhetorically. "I think it is dreadful. I heard yesterday that Norfolk would be evacuated very soon, also Virginia, and that she will be left out of the
confederacy altogether." Despite its exaggeration the letter, written on May
8, would prove accurate as to Norfolk's impending evacuation. All the writer
could do was to hope that Anna would be able to make her promised visit
back to Suffolk in time, telling her to "be sure to come before the Yankees
get us."[6]

Two days later General Huger confirmed the speculation by ordering
Southern forces out of Norfolk. This retreat included the evacuation of
Suffolk on the same day. Belatedly, Secretary Randolph ordered, "Major-
General Huger, or the Officer in Command at Suffolk" on May 11, to remove
prisoners and to "take up the railroad tracks on both [rail]roads east of
Suffolk as far as possible," sending the iron to safer zones. Even as the troops
withdrew, they were to "continue the same thing westward, letting the last
train take up the iron behind it."[7] At least as far as the railroads were concerned, this would be a modified scorched earth policy that would deny
the use of these lines by the enemy.

This kind of tedious activity would require a more deliberately phased
departure than Huger planned to make. General Lee also was concerned
about this aspect of the retreat, particularly reminding the commander in
Norfolk, "In retiring along the Norfolk and Petersburg Railroad it should
be so destroyed as to prevent its use by the enemy." That this had not been
done prompted Lee to complain, "So far as I can learn the road is almost
intact." He added, "The stone piers of the bridges should be destroyed as
well as the bridges themselves."[8] Unhappily for Lee, this would not be the
last time Huger's performance proved disappointing, and by the end of
1862, that officer would find himself languishing in the Trans-Mississippi
department.[9]

The pace of evacuation proved so swift that one of the retreating
Southerners lamented the necessity of leaving his regiment's baggage
behind in Suffolk to fall into the Federals' hands.[10] Another soldier also
doubted the efficacy of the hasty withdrawal from the region. From a camp
near Petersburg, Robert Mabry confided to his wife on May 12 that "the
retreat I believe was badly managed and our loss was enormous to say nothing of the loss of the Navy Yard, but still we are told it is nothing to loose

those things." Skeptical of such convenient explanations, he concluded, "I think it foretells something."[11]

Indeed, it must have seemed as if the whole world was unraveling. Channing Price moved with a portion of his battery, camped in the open at Providence Church, and pushed on the next day to the bridge crossings over the Blackwater River at Zuni, on the Norfolk and Petersburg Railroad. There they would cooperate with the 53d Virginia Infantry "for the purpose of protecting the Road." Federal shelling at Fort Boykin near Smithfield made an impression upon the retreating Confederates. Price admitted that "it was thought [that they] might land & endeavor to cut off our troops in Norfolk."

With his guns guarding the crossings, Price watched as the solemn procession strode past. "The troops from Norfolk have been passing all the time," he wrote his mother on the twelfth, "& now all have gone up, except 3 or 4,000." General Loring and his staff were among the last of the Confederates to leave the region that they had been protecting for the better part of a year. Dejectedly Price observed, "The blowing up of the Merrimac was a sad necessity was it not? as indeed was the giving up of Norfolk."[12]

Price and his fellow cannoneers shared the duty of guarding the bridges with the 53d Virginia. Benjamin Farinholt of Company B in the 53d recorded his impressions in his diary. Although not as verbose as his fellow Confederate, the infantryman had similar reactions to the events they both experienced. "Hearing heavy firing on the James River today," he scribbled on May 10. "The enemy have possession of Norfolk and have this morning marched 10,000 forces in that place. Quite lamentable." He expected to be called up to Petersburg at any time but would remain at Zuni with Price's artillery section for another ten days.[13]

Numerous soldiers from the area took the opportunity in the chaos of evacuation to desert. The 6th Virginia Infantry was especially hard hit, losing a significant proportion of its manpower. No less than ninety-two of the men in this regiment would be listed as "deserted, evac. Norfolk," "missing retreat from Craney Island to Suffolk," or some variation of this designation. Some of these men would return to honorable service. Most would not.[14]

If the soldiers felt uneasy about the sudden military developments, many area residents faced the days ahead with a tremendous sense of foreboding. Some of them left with the army, preferring to become refugees rather than face an occupying enemy force. Those area residents who remained behind felt an even greater sense of apprehension as they awaited the impending arrival of Union troops. Those who chose to stay did so for different reasons. Some had nowhere else viable to go. Others chose to remain in their homes, hoping to secure their property and weather the approaching storm. One such individual, Suffolk resident Mattie Prentiss, felt the Southern withdrawal acutely. "The day that Suffolk was evacuated, every thing looked as if everybody was dead. I felt like I had lost every friend I had in the world. It was an awful feeling."[15]

On Monday, May 12, four companies of the 1st New York Mounted Rifles rode into Suffolk, under the command of Major Charles Cleveland Dodge.[16] The officer's assignment seemed relatively simple: occupy the town and maintain order and quiet there. Dodge succeeded in his mission. On the following day the commander of the Federal Department of Virginia reported to Secretary of War Edwin M. Stanton: "We have Suffolk, taken last evening by Major Dodge. All quiet."[17]

As might be imagined, many of the town's citizens accepted this turn of events with less equanimity than the Union high command. For them, this was the worst of all possible scenarios, or so it must have seemed at the time, precipitated by the fall of Norfolk and the withdrawal of Confederate forces beyond the Blackwater River, some twenty miles away.

Suffolk residents now confronted the conditions that many Virginians had already faced or would shortly experience. As historian Stephen Ash has observed, "Virginians endured enemy occupation longer, and on a larger scale, than any of their Confederate brethren." For such people this development occurred so suddenly that adjustment to the new conditions was difficult. Thus, as Ash noted, "anxiety gave way to panic. Visions of looting and savagery, spawned by old stereotypes about the barbaric Yankees, seized the white imagination."[18]

Yet the initial presence of Federal troops hardly proved overwhelming. General Orders No. 46 called for the town's occupation force to consist of only one regiment, the 16th Massachusetts, a section of artillery, and a single squadron of cavalry. Major General John Wool, commanding the department in which this part of occupied Virginia now fell, planned to augment the garrison as quickly as possible, but the mobilization would take time and require adequate support.[19] On May 19 Wool informed Secretary of War Stanton, "I intend sending a greater force as soon as I can forward supplies." In the meantime he took steps to improve communications between Suffolk and Norfolk as an interim measure to bolster the outpost. "I will have cars running on the railroad in two or three days," he explained to Stanton, "and the telegraph line [will be] established in the course of two days to Suffolk."[20]

Suffolk's remaining citizens greeted the Federals with considerable trepidation. Stories of Yankee pillaging, stealing, and burning intimidated
many of them. One local resident recalled the prevailing mood during the
evacuation of Suffolk and its occupation by Federal forces. "The people were
greatly frightened at first by all kinds of rumors that were soon in circula-
tion. Some said that they [the Federals] were going to take all male citizens
as prisoners, others that they intended to hang certain citizens for some
alleged offense, etc." These wildly exaggerated stories caused a predictable
reaction when Dodge's troops first appeared: "The people kept close
within their houses and watched the movements of the soldiers through
the shutters."[21]

The Federals surprised some of the local inhabitants with their uniformly
good behavior and discipline. They quickly dispelled Southern fears of
wholesale arrests and other depredations. Again, this was true in other
Southern communities as well. "To the immense relief of all," according to
Ash, "the advance legions of the Yankees failed to live up to their infamy."[22]

In fact, in Suffolk at least, some of the first Union troops provided unintended comic relief. One incident illustrated the difficulty some residents
were having in making the transition from Confederate control to Union
control. It occurred when the 11th Pennsylvania Cavalry rode into town
on Sunday morning, May 18. People were on their way to church or preparing to go when the Federals appeared. As the unit passed one house, a mother
and a small boy stood on the steps and watched them go by. Thinking the
caravan of troops to be no different than any others he had seen in the past
year, the boy doffed his cap in salute and belted out enthusiastically, "Hurrah
for Jeff Davis!" The horrified parent grabbed her son as the Union commander rode over to them. "You little traitor," he said with a smile, wag-
ging his finger disapprovingly, and the column left the little rebel behind.[23]

Some Suffolk adults suffered from a similar confusion when it came to
the new arrivals. More than one local citizen offered evidence of a limita-
tion in geography, as suggested by one encounter. When a Rhode Islander
paused on the doorstep of a house as his regiment passed through the town,
an "elderly lady appeared at the door and inquired what regiment ours was."
One of the soldier's comrades proudly blurted out the name and number,
only to have the woman respond, "Is that in North Carolina?" The men
proceeded to assist her in locating Rhode Island. The writer concluded generously, "Possibly she was not up in geography." However, she must have
been up on other subjects, for he remembered, "I left the old lady solilo-
quizing upon the causes which led to the war, and its probable result to
both North and South."[24]

The majority of the Union troops might disprove the stereotypical views of them, but the actions of at least one troublemaker threatened the positive image of the whole. A Union lieutenant was concerned enough to send a report with a strong sense of urgency to the provost marshal in Norfolk. "I travelled around the county yesterday some distance," he began. "The people seem well pleased with the behavior of our troops." However, someone was "going around the county committing depredations on the people ransacking their houses killing and carrying off poultry," and so forth. "He is represented as having recently joined the [New York] mounted Rifles formerly belonging to the Rebel Army." There is no proof that this ne'er-do-well was the notorious Jack Fairless, who deserted from the Confederate army after his public shaming for theft. Indeed, there is no record that this person ever faced punishment for his behavior. But the lieutenant felt prepared to mete it out if possible. "I consider it my duty," the officer declared forthrightly, "to shoot him if caught in his acts."[25] For the moment at least, there could not have been a stronger indication of the willingness of Union officers to recognize and protect the private property of Southern civilians.

Even so, the arrival of the Union troops in the region disrupted the lives of local citizens and presented them with a stark choice. They could remain behind or seek refuge elsewhere, sharing an experience that was becoming increasingly common among Virginians. Of such communities, one historian has written that "in every invaded region many whites hurriedly gathered their belongings and took to the road, abandoning homes and farms to seek refuge behind rebel lines."[26] Of course, the fact that others faced the same dilemma was of little solace to those who chose to leave.

One person who sought sanctuary outside the occupied town for herself and her family was Missouri Ann Jones Kilby Riddick. Wife of Nathaniel Riddick, the county's delegate to the state legislature and one of Suffolk's most prominent citizens, she lived with her family in the town's most prestigious residence. Dubbed "Riddick's Folly" for its size and expense, the house was a four-story Greek Revival home that overlooked the Nansemond River. Together the Riddicks had raised five children there: three sons (Mills Edward, John Thompson, and Nathaniel Henley) and two daughters (Anna Mary and Missouri Taylor).[27]

The eldest of the children, Anna Mary (born in 1841), maintained a correspondence with her parents and siblings throughout the war. She also kept in contact with Jonathan Smith, the Riddick family's tutor before the war. By the time Dodge's troopers appeared in her hometown, Anna was already safely in the interior of the state, in the town of Petersburg. But her friend Jonny Smith sensed her dissatisfaction with her forced repatriation. In early 1862 he wryly observed, "Judging from your letter, I should suppose that you found the 'Cockade City' [Petersburg] the most *excruciatingly* agreeable place you ever visited."[28] However, Anna, the rest of her family, and many others like them were going to have to remain exiled from their homes for the indefinite future.

To make matters worse, the movement of George B. McClellan's Union army up the Peninsula toward Richmond threatened the sanctity not only of the Confederate capital but also the Riddick refuge of Petersburg. A concerned Missouri Riddick immediately determined to send her two daughters to live with her sister's family in Leasburg, in Caswell County, North Carolina. Upon hearing of Anna's departure for an even more isolated safe haven, Jonny Smith noted sarcastically, "I am glad to hear that you are so pleasantly situated, tho' really how can one expect to enjoy oneself so far from the crowded haunts of man, so far removed from all that one has been accustomed to, is more than I can conceive."[29] Despite his teasing, Jonny was happy to have her away from the fighting in Virginia.

While civilians scrambled for safe havens, the Confederates remained encamped along the banks of the Blackwater River, to which they had retreated. General Lee had feared that the Blackwater line would be too dangerous "to keep a force stationed there." He particularly worried that "it would be in constant danger of being cut off and too remote to be relieved [if attacked]."[30] Still, these units were only the precursors of men who would be stationed along the Blackwater for another year to watch the Union forces in Suffolk, some twenty miles away. The river gave the Confederates a natural defense line and base from which to wage a guerrilla-style war.

On May 19 Channing Price wrote from his new base at Ivor, farther along the Norfolk and Petersburg Railroad. His unit had continued to guard the Blackwater crossings while "a few workmen were engaged [in] taking up the Rail Road Bridge at Zuni . . . which is a splendid piece of work." Either because of the size of the work party or the commitment of the workers, Price found that the men had "made very little progress however & up to Saturday night had taken up only one of four spans." Just before they left Zuni, a party "went to work to burn the Wagon Bridge[,] which was done." When the cannoneers arrived at Ivor, they found that other units "had also burned the Bridge at Broad Water."

There was little left to do but to finish the job of destroying the "splendid" railroad bridge. Thus the artillerymen returned to Zuni, took a field-piece off the railroad cars, and "25 or 26 rounds were fired at the Bridge, tearing the Iron all to pieces, but producing no effect on the Stone Piers." As they adjusted their aim, an unusual situation suddenly developed. "Just as a beautiful shot had been made, throwing the entire span of the Iron superstructure into the River, a White Flag was seen near the Store on the opposite side of the River." The Federal officer carrying the flag bore an exchanged prisoner, Austin E. Smith, the son of former Virginia governor William Smith. With the bridge now out of commission, the men had to construct a raft for the released Confederate to cross on.[31]

The infantryman Benjamin Farinholt participated in the bridge-destroying expedition. He noted that he "went down to Zuni to bombard the RR bridge across the Black Water River which was done most effectively." The river at this juncture, best described by Farinholt as "a marshy but deep and rapid stream," was now secure.[32] Without either pontoons or bridging of some kind, it would be highly unlikely for a force of any significance to attempt to cross it. The Confederates now had a protective barrier behind which relatively small forces could prevent a passage by much larger Union forces if they appeared.

As spring wore into summer, the Federals reinforced their position at Suffolk. On May 30, 1862, the first military encounter took place between opposing forces in the area since Suffolk had been evacuated and occupied. This skirmish was typical of the military activity in the region until Longstreet's campaign in the spring of 1863. The fight occurred near Zuni, on the Blackwater River. Twenty-six troopers of the 11th Pennsylvania Cavalry rode out of Suffolk to learn if the Confederates were preparing an offensive. After determining that the rumors were untrue, the Federals turned back toward Suffolk. They never arrived. Confederates ambushed the party at Andrews Crossroads, killing one Union soldier and capturing the rest.[33]

With scouts and cavalrymen from both sides patrolling the roads between Suffolk and the Blackwater River, the going could be rough for citizens who remained in their homes and tried to continue their lives as best they could. For many, their worries included loved ones who were away from home as refugees or fighting in their nation's armed forces. Having moved herself and part of her family out of Suffolk, Missouri Riddick remained concerned for her eldest son, Mills, who had enlisted in Company I, 9th Virginia Infantry, on March 21, 1862. That regiment was now stationed in the vicinity of Richmond to defend the capital against McClellan's forces.[34]

The command did not fare particularly well in the battle of Seven Pines on June 1. During the course of the engagement, Federal forces surprised six companies of the 9th Virginia and routed them. Although the toll was not particularly heavy in lives, the blow to the unit's prestige was significant.[35] News of this disaster spread rapidly. On June 10 Missouri wrote to

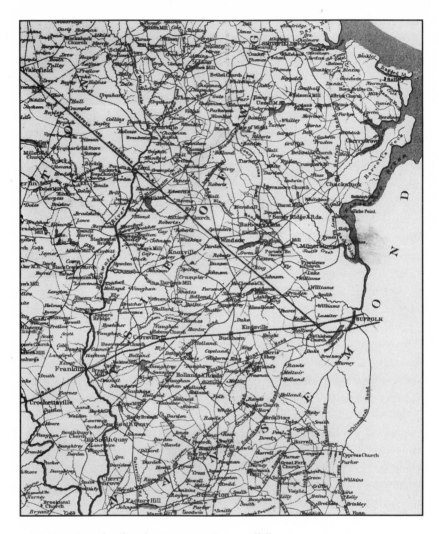

MAP 3 Roads and railroads emanating from Suffolk.

assure Anna that Mill's company was not involved in the incident. "I was rejoicing that they were not in the 9th regiment at the time[,] as they ran."[36] Jonny Smith, in a letter dated three days later, was more exacting: "The 9th Regiment was engaged, but, I am sorry to say, it has irrevocably disgraced itself."[37]

Missouri was more concerned and relieved that her child had remained safe, putting his health and well-being before any sense of honor that might attach itself to his unit. Even so, she knew life as a soldier meant hardships and dangers outside of the battlefield. "They marched in water up to their knees and slept in that condition," an incredulous Missouri complained to her daughter Anna. On top of that, her son's rations were poor, consisting of "one slice of meat and ½ lb of bread for 24 hours."[38] Mills, who wrote his sister Anna about this same time, designated his post "Camp Starvation" because of that diet.[39] This state of affairs led his mother to conclude ironically, "Who would not be a soldier[?]"[40]

Yet Missouri Riddick could not focus on her children alone. She kept in contact with whoever she believed could give her additional information about conditions in Suffolk. Sometimes these messengers were transients like her or ministers like the Reverend William B. Wellons, a Methodist pastor in Suffolk who shared news as he traveled to Richmond to see the local troops stationed in the area.[41]

Missouri was distressed that the Federals, with help from the family servants left behind to tend to the house, had discovered the "china and glass that I had secreted." Perhaps she was surprised to learn that these soldiers only cleaned the items and placed them in the house. But other Federals lived up to her expectations. Missouri explained to her daughter Anna that they broke open her bureau drawers and "took all of the bacon out of the smoke house and gave it to the servants." Still, on the whole the Federals "have behaved very well, none in town except a mounted guard that rides up and down." Most importantly, she could report, "No one stays in our house."

The news on the attitude of white residents in Suffolk was also encouraging. Although "most of the citizens have taken the parole of honour," she observed, none had taken the oath of allegiance. For Missouri this stubbornness on the part of her fellow townspeople who remained in Suffolk was an enormous source of satisfaction. "The Yanks say the people are the most obstinate they have ever seen," she noted with pride. She especially appreciated the efforts of the Reverend Mr. Wellons, who assured her that in Suffolk he "preaches every Sunday and prays for the success of the Confederate Arms, and for all in authority [in Richmond] while the house [of worship] is filled with Yankees."[42]

It was precisely this type of boldness that contributed to a change in Union policy, and most certainly in Union attitudes. Early policy had been surprisingly soft, but it began to harden against the continuous displays of Southern recalcitrance. Missouri Riddick seemed to appreciate the inevitability of this reaction. "I reckon they will begin to draw the reins a little tighter now," she concluded to her daughter on June 10.[43] Then, in her next letter on June 24 she observed that the feared crackdown had already begun to occur. The Reverend Mr. Wellons had to flee Suffolk under duress. "He says they are drawing the reins much tighter," Missouri explained. She had also heard reports "that the property of all prominent citizens that will not take the oath of allegiance will be confiscated." From this Missouri concluded despairingly, "So ours will go any how."[44]

Clearly things were getting worse. The Federals were beginning to act like invaders: "They will not allow any one to carry anything into town not even wood and the citizens are pulling down their enclosures to cook with. They have insulted two ladies. I wish I could tell all but space will not allow." In addition, the Federals were bringing in their own ministers to "preach the Gospel on its purity . . . a thing which never before has been done in Suffolk," Missouri quoted them as saying as justification.[45] This same phenomenon was occurring in Portsmouth and Norfolk as well, in an apparent effort to purge the pulpits of pro-Southern voices and influences.[46]

Whatever struggles the civilians might face, the soldiers had to endure much worse, for the war continued to rage outside Richmond. The toll of casualties from the Seven Days campaign was painfully high in companies that had enlisted in the region. In addition to the embarrassment and casualties it produced for the 9th Virginia, the fighting at Seven Pines cost companies from the region in the 41st Virginia Infantry at least half a dozen men wounded or captured.[47]

On subsequent battlefields, like those at Gaines's Mill on June 27 and Glendale on June 30, men from southeastern Virginia continued to pay a bitter price for defending their homes. Eighteen years old when he enlisted in the Southampton Greys, William F. Edwards would fall critically wounded at Gaines's Mill and die in a Richmond hospital before the summer was out. Fellow Southampton Countian William H. Felts had been detailed to Smithfield as a baker shortly after his enlistment. He was back with his unit when he died at Gaines's Mill. Richard Hill was an overseer when he enlisted in the Rough and Ready Guards. He successfully fought fever but died of the wounds he received at Gaines's Mill three days after the battle. All told, counting these men, the 3d Virginia, with men from Nansemond as well as Southampton County, lost at least ten men to death and wounds on the battlefield that bloody day in June.[48]

Waiting for some word of the fate of their loved ones in arms was particularly hard on the people at home. Individuals passed word as quickly as they could, given the limitations of the wartime postal service, but newspapers often served as the most convenient, if not always the most reliable, source for such information. On July 1 a notice appeared from "Camp Near Richmond, June 30, 1862," with the expressed desire "to relieve the anxiety of the relatives and friends of the soldiers attached to the Third Virginia Regiment." For Company F, the Nansemond Rangers, these included: "Killed: Private Alfred Lawrence. Wounded: Sergeant Sullivan, slightly with a shell; Private A. R. Cross slightly on top of the head; [and] Wm. A. Phelps, slightly in foot."[49]

The butcher's bill continued to mount at Glendale. Lieutenant William J. Haslett joined the South Quay Guards with his brother Thomas in June 1861. William was killed while leading his men on June 30, 1862. Likewise, Corporal Benjamin C. Britt, a twenty-one-year-old farmer when he enlisted, fell in the fighting that day.[50]

The combat at Seven Pines and in these early battles of the Seven Days was fierce enough to leave a distinct impression on one of the participants. In a letter to his friend Annie, Jonny Smith emphasized two messages that he hoped would reach her. The first was an insistence that she exert all her influence in preventing her younger brother John from entering the army. The second was a profession of his faith in God. "I have seriously determined to turn from my old ways and endeavor to live a new life," the soldier explained. "The sensations I experienced last Saturday and Wednesday when volley after volley of musketry was heard,—yes, and each probably ushering into Eternity many souls unprepared to meet their God,—have made me seriously reflect upon my past life and I have determined, by God's help, to so live that I may not be afraid to die, either upon the field of battle, or peacefully in bed." Jonny's closing to his dear friend Annie was particularly poignant: "I am sorry that you are so sad. Do as I am endeavoring to do. Put your faith in Him, who is the giver of all joy, and then, no matter what afflictions you may suffer, He will assist you to bear it. Sorrow may endure for the night, but joy cometh in the morning. The dawn is breaking, I think, on our country."[51]

Of all of the Seven Days, July 1 was the worst. Robert E. Lee massed his forces against a formidable line of Union men and cannon at Malvern Hill. In brave but futile charges, the Confederates attempted to crack the Union positions, only to be mowed down. Lee would lose a staggering 5,355 casualties in his quest for a decisive victory over McClellan's army. Daniel Harvey Hill, a Confederate general who watched the bloody work that day, observed, "It was not war—it was murder."[52]

Among the units who entered the maelstrom from southeastern Virginia the casualties were horrendous. Unlike many later battles, where the number of prisoners inflated the figures, those who made the casualty list at Malvern Hill were either killed or wounded. At least twenty-eight men from four regiments containing boys from Nansemond, Southampton, and Isle of Wight Counties fell dead or wounded under the intense fire at Malvern Hill. Among them were numerous friends of the Riddick family—including the tutor Jonathan Smith.[53]

The news of Jonny's death must have devastated Anna. She may have first received the news when her mother wrote of it on July 2. "Poor Johnie Smith was killed," she began. "I believe the only one of the company." Then, in that remarkably Southern manner of attempting to render death somehow more palatable, she added that "he died gloriously the ball struck his forehead and took off or mangled off [the] whole of his head." Perhaps she hoped to demonstrate that he had not suffered, but the manner of the description she gave of Jonny's death suggests that Anna's mother did not realize the depth of her daughter's affection for the fallen soldier. Yet even as she forwarded the lurid details of his demise, Missouri confirmed one of Jonny's earlier messages. "From Johnie's letters to his father and from his conduct in camp we have every reason to believe he was prepared to die. [H]e conducted a prayer meeting the night before his death."[54]

In August another relative, obviously more privy to Anna's feelings for Jonny, wrote to commiserate with her. "Our *dear* soldier boy has been taken—from much trouble to that bright world where God reigns forever."[55] Nothing else would be said on this sad matter in the correspondence that has survived. Family lore attributed Anna Mary Riddick's decision never to marry to Jonny's death.[56]

In the same letter in which she informed her daughter of Jonny Smith's death, Missouri cataloged some of the other losses among the fighting men of the community. Although, as she complained, "it is impossible to get a list of the killed and wounded," she seems to have compiled a substantial one based on information she gathered from her husband Nathaniel. "I just received a letter from your father. The 9th was engaged in the battle of the 1st the bloodiest of the war. He wrote on Yankee paper. . . . Frank Crocker is mortally wounded[,] Capt. Vermillion is killed. . . . Joe Whitehead[,] Bob Whitehead and Euclid Borland all shot in the arm and ball still in the arm of Bob, but they are doing well and are in the care of Dr. Jim Whitehead in Richmond. Col. Eley's son had both feet shot off. poor thing Nathl. will not leave until he finds out more about our folks."[57]

Of the 9th Virginia, which included the Riddicks' son Mills, the officer corps was decimated. Lieutenant James Francis Crocker, a professor and lawyer who had graduated as the valedictorian from Pennsylvania College of Gettysburg, sustained three wounds, to the throat, shoulder, and arm, although he managed to survive them. Captain Dennis Vermillion, a former ship carpenter, was less fortunate, dying as he led his men in the battle.[58]

Missouri's brother, Captain John T. Kilby, played a conspicuous role in the charge, which she proudly related. "Brother acted most gallantly," she told her daughter. "After having ascended a smaller [hill], the men flagged a little, being exposed to their fire, [but] brother seized the colors and said come on boys follow me." Another Suffolk native, Joseph Prentis, "stepped out and said Capt. I will follow wherever you lead." The Union fire was so intense that "the color staff was cut in two pieces, brother picked them up again . . . but poor Joe Prentis a few steps behind him was shot dead of the head." For the band of men with Kilby on the battlefield that day, the price was steep. "Out of 30 men he lost 4 killed and 9 wounded." Cornelius M. Dozier, "Luie" to Missouri Riddick, "was killed and the preacher Jones son Lucillius," and the list continued.[59] In a following letter she wrote simply, "Nansemond Co. suffered very severely in the last battle."[60] So it had.

A few days later Nathaniel Riddick received a grieving letter from a friend at the University of Virginia. Robert R. Prentis, the father of Joe Prentis, who had died attempting to follow Missouri's brother at Malvern Hill, hoped to retrieve his son's remains and learn something of his final days. The elder Prentis had tried to steel himself "for any event" concerning his son. Now he faced the grim reality of war's terrible cost. Even so, Robert Prentis tried a show of bravado. "I regret that not one of my six remaining sons are now able to take his place," he explained before adding dramatically, "I freely give *all to the cause*." Despite his anxiety to bring his son home, Prentis realized he might have to wait before attempting to do so. "Would it be practicable to remove his body now?" he asked his friend Nathaniel Riddick. "Or shall I postpone it 'till the fall. Please advise." Even in the midst of his grief the father attempted to anticipate all possible impediments to his sad mission. He wanted Riddick "to get all the information you can, particularly where [he was] buried, to whom it [the land] belongs and his P. office so that if necessary I can communicate with him." As he closed the difficult letter, he also made the effort to inquire after Riddick's family, expressing the hope that Nathaniel's "son and Brothers and other Relatives escaped" unscathed from the fighting. Eventually, he brought his seventeen-year-old son back to Charlottesville, interring him there.[61]

Happily, Missouri's son was safe, with confirmation provided when Nathaniel paid him a visit while collecting information on the casualties of soldiers from the area. "Thank God Mills [and] brother [John Kilby] . . . are safe," the relieved mother wrote. "Mills had his jacket sleeve and shirt sleeves cut and the ball grazed his arm."[62]

Life for the people still living in Nansemond County was as difficult as it was for the soldiers and refugees. Compounding the loss of friends and loved ones was the loss of any sense of security. Patrols from both sides roamed throughout the no-man's-land between Suffolk and the Blackwater River. Raids designed to gather intelligence or harass the enemy quickly devolved into foraging expeditions as well, leaving families little or nothing for themselves.

In the town of Suffolk itself, life for the Union troops equaled the tedium of garrison life. Of course, some of the locals who had remained behind tried their best to oppose the occupation of their town, thereby providing some excitement for the Federals. Women sang patriotic Southern songs and refused to walk beneath the U.S. flag to irritate their Union custodians. Union sentinels found the behavior only mildly irksome at first but soon came to resent this defiance. At length, the provost marshal in Suffolk threatened to jail singers of "secesh" songs and to force unwilling persons to walk beneath the Union flag whether they wanted to or not. Except for demonstrations of exhausted patience on the one hand and stubbornness on the other, the business did not amount to much.[63]

Of course, some of the Suffolk women did not see it that way: they found the provost marshal's threats intolerable. Chief among them was Mattie Prentiss. She remained firm in her Southern convictions and her utter contempt for the Union soldiers and their trappings. "The more I see the Yankees," she seethed in a letter, "the worse I *hate* them." This firebrand found life in occupied Suffolk "almost as bad as being in prison." Even when it came to commerce, she would have no truck with the invader. "The Yankees have opened three or four stores," she announced disdainfully. "I don't intend to get anything from them, unless I am obliged to do so."[64]

By the end of summer, it was clear that the Union presence, particularly their raiding and scouting expeditions, was disrupting the lives and routines of people in southeastern Virginia. Expeditions left the relative safety of the town to venture along the roads that radiated to and from the Blackwater River. These men continued to gather food, supplies, recruits, and intelligence. Whenever possible, they also tried to harry their opponents.

In August a justice of the peace of the County Circuit of Isle of Wight, W. H. Casey, wrote to Governor John Letcher to complain. "I have deemed it proper to say to you," Casey explained, "the courthouse of our county is within one hour and [a] half ride of the town of Suffolk[,] at which point the enemy have considerable forces." Such close proximity to Union forces presented myriad difficulties, not the least of which was the uncertainty that came from sporadic raids. "They have visited our courthouse on several occasions and we know not at what time they may come," the harassed public official asserted. "Consequently there are no courts held, which is a great inconvenience to the people as the municipal business of the county is entirely neglected." Although the governor had no power to halt the Union raids, he might be able to assist the local government by allowing the court to relocate to a safer point. Casey suggested a church "located in that part of the county bordering on the Confederate line, and in a neighborhood which in all probability will not be annoyed by the raids of the enemy."[65]

Nor were Northern raiding parties the only form of disruption affecting people in the region. At about the same time, planters or their representatives in nearby Gates County, North Carolina, appeared before a justice of the peace for redress of their grievances. Their problem was not so much Union raiders, or even Unionist guerrillas, but their slave property. Rather than remain enslaved, these people were fleeing across the Virginia border seeking refuge within Union lines. The proximity of Union troops at Suffolk offered a tempting incentive to those who wished to be free.

One man complained on September 29 that over the past two months four of his slaves, ranging in age from six months to thirty years, and four other slaves belonging to masters he represented had disappeared. He placed the value of this lost property at $6,000. According to the court records, these slaves had "run off from him in the County of Gates, and went to the enemy at Suffolk, Va., by whom they were received and harbored and are still harbored and detained from his service and control."[66] For such slaveowners the problem of maintaining control over their servants would only grow worse.

For the Federal troops themselves, the number of patrols required to maintain a high degree of vigilance took its toll. The work proved strenuous on both men and mounts, causing the new commander at Fort Monroe, Major General John A. Dix, to complain to Washington. "I have less than 500 mounted men at the point [Suffolk]," he explained impatiently, "and they are almost worn out by the hard service which they are performing as pickets and scouts between the Nansemond and the Blackwater."[67]

Located in a relatively exposed position, the Suffolk garrison had little choice. Letting down one's guard might lead to disaster, doing little for one's military career. Indeed, local Union commanders complained bitterly of the lack of opportunity for glory, commendation, and promotion in this relative backwater of the war. Brigadier General Joseph K. F. Mansfield, commanding in Suffolk since June 13, eventually complained his way out of southeastern Virginia. He found the action he craved and a Rebel bullet at Sharpsburg.[68] Yet other military considerations, more than officer complaints, led Federal troops to move in and out of Suffolk throughout the summer and early fall of 1862, much the same way the Confederates had the previous year. Unseasoned units came into the area as the more veteran regiments transferred to more active posts.

Even with the failure of McClellan's Peninsula campaign to take Richmond, there was plenty of activity. Some of these transferred Union troops participated in the fighting in late summer, as did the Confederates from the region who served under General Lee. Indeed, it was Lee who sought the fight, hoping to hit John Pope's Army of Virginia in the northern part of the state before McClellan could extricate his army and join him. Pope had 63,000 men in the field, McClellan 100,000. Together they would badly outnumber the Army of Northern Virginia.

The result was a dramatic stroke at Pope's communications at Manassas Junction by Thomas J. "Stonewall" Jackson. When the Union general turned to punish Jackson, Lee brought up James Longstreet. Following a bloody confrontation near the Brawner house on August 28, Pope sent his men against Jackson's the next day, hoping to crush them. Near the climax of that fight, with some of Jackson's men reduced to throwing rocks because they had run out of ammunition, Lee unleashed Longstreet. The gray tide smashed into the Union forces, sending them reeling. For a second time on the field of Manassas, a Union army fell back in hasty retreat.[69]

Among those who faced Pope's army at Second Manassas were men in five regiments who hailed from the lower tidewater. As at Malvern Hill, virtually none of them were captured, but this time there were more dead than there had been in the earlier battle. Ten of these men were killed or mortally wounded in the fighting. John T. Luke and Charles Nelms both enlisted in the Nansemond Guards on the same day in August 1861; both lingered with wounds into September 1862 before they died. Corporal William H. Babb had been married to Lizzie since 1855. He was killed in action at Second Manassas. Less than a year before the couple would have celebrated ten years of marriage, Nathaniel Riddick made a claim on her behalf for $77.[70]

Missouri Riddick spent the late summer months keeping up with her scattered family, scratching for news about Suffolk and cataloging the progress of the wounded and the bereaved. Jonny Smith's family continued to take his death hard. His mother had confined herself to her room in grief, while his father could do nothing but talk about him. "He wishes to collect everything that Jonnie wrote," she told Anna, "and every paper that had his name on it; he has brought more than fifty copies of the Express that had his death [notice] in them and sent them away to his acquaintances." Then, in wording that suggests she still did not realize the depths of her daughter's affections for Jonny Smith, Missouri remarked offhandedly to Anna, "I suppose you got one."[71]

Communication with Suffolk was getting more and more difficult. The Federals seemed to be trying to suppress what some white Southerners referred to as their "Underground Railroad," connecting those behind Union lines with those beyond them through messengers and smuggled goods.[72] On August 1 Missouri noted that "Mr. Cowling has been arrested," which complicated matters as "he came up every week and was a medium of communication."[73] In another letter she observed that "all the boats on the river have been destroyed by Yanks except a few for the use of their detectives or spies, they also have a guard stationed every half mile on the south shore of the Nansemond[;] the tents can be seen."[74] Despite persistent rumors to the contrary, she finally admitted to her younger daughter, Zouzie, "Now as to Suffolk, I don't think the scamps meant to give it up."[75]

Northern impressions of this occupied territory remained mixed at best but were always tinged with an understandable disdain by the common soldiers. William Henry Snow of the 6th Massachusetts reported to his wife in distant Lowell on September 17, "I went over to the town of Suffolk a town of 1500 inhabitants before the war but now consisting only of Negroes children cripples and women." He was particularly struck by the "Large No of Negroes of both sexes here," whom he deemed "useless and idle," as well as "a large no of secessia women." "The men," he explained, "are all of[f] shooting yankeys as the Little boys say." Such sentiments were increasingly generating antagonistic feelings toward the local folk among the men in the lower ranks. "We are encamped in a Large orchard belonging to a capt in the rebell army there was a good many apples when we come here but [in] two days [we] Picked the apples cut down many of the trees and dug ten wells and burned up a mile of good rail fence." The soldier concluded with an object lesson some of his superiors had yet to grasp: "We are an expensive set to keep out the rebells will find out soon."[76] An officer complained that such activities affected his dietary choices as well. "An army like ours cuts up everything in the surrounding country so soon that we are limited very much in our supply of such common luxuries" as fruit, he fretted after wishing for "some of those apples" from home "once in a while."[77]

Theodore Skinner of the 112th New York was less caustic when he wrote his parents, "This place is a bout six miles from north Carolina the country a round hear is very pleasant." His regiment was enjoying Southern hospitality as well: "We encamp on a rebels farm he went away with the reble army." Hoping to ease his parents' concerns for his health and well-being,

Skinner continued, "We have plenty to eat and drink," then thinking quickly, added, "I mean water for you know that I don't drink nothing but water."[78]

John B. Woodward of the 13th New York noted succinctly of his surroundings, "Suffolk is the meanest God-forsaken place you ever saw—houses deserted, stores shut up."[79] At least for a time under Union occupation, the town remained tightly controlled. According to one historian of the community, "No article of merchandise, however insignificant, was procurable at the stores without an order from the Provost Marshal."[80]

Despite such control General Dix was upset enough at the transfer of veteran troops from his district that he threatened to forsake his Suffolk outpost altogether if Washington remained uncooperative.[81] Union general-in-chief Henry W. Halleck immediately sought to give his disgruntled subordinate every assurance. He ordered Dix to "retain troops sufficient to hold them [Suffolk and Yorktown] till others arrive."[82] The assurances must have been enough, for Dix reacted with even greater determination to hold Suffolk, promising Halleck in reply, "No effort will be spared to maintain our position there."[83]

On September 21 Dix transferred a new commander to Suffolk. Once Major General John James Peck arrived, the situation in the garrison town changed significantly. The people of the region, from the harried local officials to the worried local farmers, would discover that the Union presence in the region was about to increase rather than decrease. Peck would make sure that reminders of that presence also grew, giving people like Missouri Riddick the feeling that conditions in Suffolk would continue to get "worse and worse."[84]

"The country will soon be robbed of everything."
Suffolk resident

"Do you know where Pryor is?"
Union general Dix to General Peck

"I expected every moment some of us would be
hit and did not have to wait long to have my
expectations realized."
Private Solomon Lenfest, 6th Massachusetts

⊰ 4 ⊱ *A Deserted House*

THE MAN WHO HASTENED TO SUFFOLK AT THE END OF SEPTEMBER 1862 was amply qualified for the duty he would have to perform. A native of Manlius, New York, John Peck was a graduate of West Point (Class of 1843) and had served with distinction in the Mexican War. Twice brevetted for "gallant and meritorious conduct" in Mexico, Peck served in the West until 1853, when he resigned his commission. As a civilian, John Peck embarked upon an active business career in Syracuse, his wife's home. He also found time to dabble in politics. Twice nominated for Congress (1856 and 1858), Peck served as a delegate to the Democratic National Conventions of 1856 and 1860. Then, with the outbreak of war in 1861, he returned to the military, accepting an appointment from President Lincoln as a brigadier general of volunteers.

Beginning in the defenses of Washington, General Peck saw his first active service in George B. McClellan's Peninsula campaign in 1862. He fought well in the preliminary engagements, losing a horse at Fair Oaks (or Seven Pines).[1] Confederate general D. H. Hill recalled years later, "All day Sunday and Sunday night General J. J. Peck, of the Federal army, had strong working parties strengthening the intrenched camp and making it more secure for the eleven thousand five hundred men who sought refuge there."[2] This tendency to improve his position by entrenching was one of Peck's virtues and would serve him well in the months to come at Suffolk.

Peck's performance in the Peninsula campaign earned him a promotion to major general on July 4, 1862. When that campaign came to a halt, he remained at Yorktown, now the outpost for the Federals on the Virginia peninsula. By mid-September he had accomplished his task of improving the defenses there so thoroughly that Major General John A. Dix, the Department of Virginia's commander, sent him to do the same thing at Suffolk.[3] Indeed, Dix declared, "I have no one who can do it so well."[4]

The Suffolk commander's first task was to familiarize himself with his new command and assess Confederate strength and intentions in the region. To that end he personally surveyed the labyrinthine road network leading into Suffolk. At the same time he dispatched Colonel Samuel P. Spear and the 11th Pennsylvania Cavalry on a reconnaissance in the direction of Carrsville and Franklin.[5] Sam Spear and Charles Dodge became so ubiquitous in southeastern Virginia that they inspired one Union soldier to create a toast in their honor: "Here's to our cavalry commanders, may the enemy never dodge our Spears or spear our Dodges."[6]

Once he had gotten an initial impression of the area, Peck turned his active attentions toward the post's greatest deficiency: its lack of fortifications. In a report on conditions as he found them, he remarked, "No artificial defenses were found nor had any plan been prepared . . . [therefore] I prepared a system, and . . . commenced Fort Dix." Naming the first earthwork for his immediate superior was shrewd, for Peck planned far more extensive defenses for his charge. "From that time until the present [May 1863] I spared no pains for placing the line of the [Nansemond] river and [the Dismal] swamp in a state of defense."[7]

Peck's men went to considerable pains to carry out their commander's elaborate plans. No longer were the garrison's duties confined to drilling and scouting. Details of men took up shovels, axes, and picks to construct lines of entrenchments, supported by artillery strongpoints. One of the laborers confided in his diary, "I have been at work on Ft. McClellan shoveling all day and feel somewhat tired to-night."[8] Many more days of similar duty lay ahead of him and his comrades. To his credit John Peck remained a hands-on leader when it came to developing this defense system. One Union soldier noted in his diary in December, "Gen. Peck was round looking at the forts."[9]

Upon completion, Peck's system stretched approximately ten miles. The intent of these defenses was to cover the roads and railroads leading into Suffolk. Peck began by erecting a series of redoubts along the southern flank of his position. Fort Dix commanded the White Marsh or Edenton Road.[10] Fort Union's guns would command the vast open field west of that road, while Fort McClellan guarded the Somerton Road. Fort Nansemond anchored the southwest corner of the system, flanking the Somerton Road and covering the area to the west of that artery. All of these were square earthen fortifications, open only at a narrow entrance in the rear of each.

North of Fort Nansemond stood the South Quay Batteries, which covered the approaches from South Quay and Franklin. The batteries also fronted the railroads and fields between the town and a branch of the Nansemond that dumped into Savage's Mill and Kilby's Mill ponds. Fort Rosecrans occupied the northwest corner of the system. This position and its neighbors, like the other artillery strongpoints, were interconnected by a series of rifle pits and trenches.

Along the north flank lay Fort Corcoran, a large lunette which commanded the approaches to the town from the northwest quarter. To its right stood Fort Peck, a small redan which guarded the drawbridge over the Nansemond River over which ran the Providence Church Road that led to Windsor and branched off toward Chuckatuck. Batteries of artillery supplemented these less formidable works, as did the natural defensive line of the river.

Forts Jericho and Halleck supported Suffolk's eastern front. Both were significant redoubts. They guarded the approaches from Portsmouth and Norfolk, as well as both railroads in that section. Thus even should the Confederates penetrate the Union lines between Suffolk and Portsmouth and Norfolk, there would be no vulnerable point to attack. Furthermore, Jericho Run and the Jericho Canal supplemented the defensive value of this sector of the lines. A line of breastworks also ran southward, completing the connection to Fort Dix.[11]

Union general George Gordon assessed the defensive works thoughtfully when he arrived in Suffolk in the spring of 1863. "The entire fronts are swept by artillery and musketry," he began.

These surprisingly strong works were begun in September, 1862, under General Peck's supervision. Up to that time Suffolk had been under the command of General Mansfield, and had been guarded in

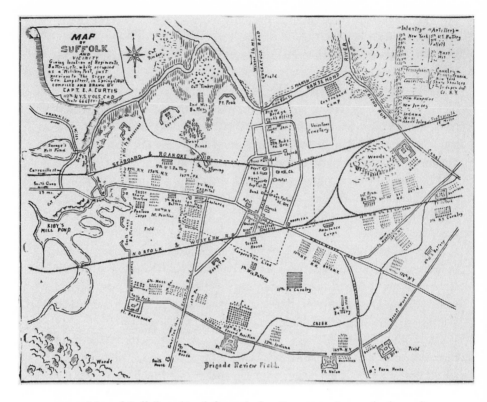

MAP 4 Map of Suffolk and its defenses before Longstreet's assault, drawn by Capt. E. A. Curtis of the 112th New York.

the usual manner, by pickets thrown out to the front and on the main roads, by patrols of troops, and by gunboats on the waters of the Nansemond River. The dense pine forests which then surrounded the place came almost up to the town on the south, affording shelter for an attacking force. Now, however, the timber had been removed, and no cover was to be found nearer than half a mile, while in some places the ground was uncovered and clear for more than a mile. . . . By a vigorous use of the spade in the hands of soldiers and "contrabands," Suffolk had been made impregnable.[12]

Yet no matter how formidable the defensive system might be, the Union commander never achieved a level of comfort with his work. One officer assessed Peck's character rather harshly: "Gen. Peck was a nervous, dispeptic gentleman who would fret himself to exhaustion for fear that he might be caught napping. Many a night have I when General officer of the day, laid out with the pickets, to guard against imaginary surprises." The same officer concluded more generously, "Well, I do not really find fault with his vigilance, but I do with the misfortune [to the men] that attended his [unsettled] digestive apparatus."[13]

Wisely, Peck chose not to remain passively behind his elaborate defenses. He wanted to maintain the initiative over his opponents and keep them off-balance and on the defensive. For that reason the Union general kept "about one-third of his force constantly in motion . . . to harass the enemy on the Blackwater by all practical means." With evident pleasure Dix later observed of Peck's methods, "Frequent expeditions were made; the enemy was repeatedly attacked."[14] The Suffolk commander's strategy had the benefit of giving his men practical combat experience in addition to increasing their engineering prowess.

Throughout October clashes with the Confederates on the Blackwater occurred with renewed vigor. The most significant of these was a Federal combined arms operation that entered the region early in the month. Three Union gunboats pushed along the Blackwater River from North Carolina toward the town of Franklin. Lieutenant Commander Charles W. Flusser led the task force, consisting of the *Commodore Perry,* the *Hunchback,* and the *Whitehead.* For the army's part in the combined operation, General Peck agreed to send Colonel Spear over the surface roads to Franklin.

Major General Dix outlined the reason for the operation in a letter to his naval counterpart, Rear Admiral Samuel P. Lee, on September 24, 1862. "I had last evening an earnest request from Major-General Peck, commanding in Suffolk, that two or three gunboats should be sent up the Chowan and Blackwater rivers as far as Franklin, where the enemy have a force of from 10,000 to 12,000 men. If this can be done I think we shall be able to disperse this force and destroy the bridge at this place."[15]

Lee immediately contacted Flusser: "You are hereby directed to give all the assistance in your power for the accomplishment of this object, with such of the gunboats as can be used for this purpose."[16] Flusser, considering the army's information inaccurate and overblown, assured Lee that he would eliminate the sole Confederate battery he expected to encounter "if the army clears away the sharpshooters from the banks."[17]

Dix considered Flusser's timetable to move against Franklin on October 3 to be "too early." He sent a messenger requesting a delay, but the rider could not reach Flusser in time. Despite the short time allowed, Peck managed to dispatch Spear and some 2,000 men on the second to serve as the army's contribution to the operation.[18] In view of the numbers that he attributed to the Confederates at Franklin, Peck was clearly relying on the Federal gunboats to provide the bulk of the firepower.

In the beginning the operation seemed to be coordinated well enough. While Spear and his men moved toward the Blackwater, Flusser's squadron lay only about three miles from Franklin. They left their moorings for the final assault just ahead of the time that the naval commander and a representative of the army had agreed: 6 A.M. on October 3.

The gunboats began "shelling the banks [of the river] as we went," according to Flusser. Then, as they rounded one of the many bends in the river, less than a mile from their destination, "the enemy opened fire on us from a place of concealment on the bluff overhead." The narrow channel prevented the Federals from using their guns right away. Flusser "ordered his men to shelter themselves as they best could," while trying "to steam past, but the river here is very narrow and we ran into the bank."

One Confederate thought he saw the perfect opportunity to capture a prize. Exhorting his comrades to follow, he raced forward. Flusser reported that the display of courage cost the soldier his life, although two Confederates, describing the actions of one of their friends years after the war, recalled that he returned from the misadventure unscathed.[19]

At last freeing the gunboat from its exposed position, Flusser succeeded in bringing it to a point where "our guns would bear." Under blasts of canister and shell, the *Commodore Perry* laid a covering fire for the *Hunchback* "as she rounded the bend and she in turn covered the *Whitehead*." The three vessels steamed past this difficulty only to encounter another. The Confederates had blocked the river ahead of them. "This barricade could have been removed," Flusser later reported, "but not under the terrible fire to which we were exposed."

By mid-morning the Union naval task force had made no further headway. Forced to content themselves with lobbing shells at the pesky Confederates, they waited for an indication of the arrival of the cooperating land force. Finally, at about 10:15, the frustrated Union naval commander ordered the operation broken off. "The enemy continued to fire at us from every available point until 2:30 P.M.," he reported. "They also attempted to block the river in our rear, by felling trees, through which obstructions we pushed with a heavy head of steam" and the help of a favorable current.

Flusser particularly singled out Lieutenant William B. Cushing for his "great gallantry" in the action. He had manned a fieldpiece "amid a storm of bullets." Master's Mate John Lynch fell beside him, shot through the heart, one of two fatalities on Flusser's vessel.[20] The brave lieutenant very nearly lost his life as well, while serving the howitzer. With every volunteer dead or wounded, Cushing faced a force of Southerners as they rushed toward the grounded boat. His howitzer's fire staggered them, but their leader, "a splendid looking fellow with long curly hair," kept coming. Cushing had no weapon to defend himself as the sword-wielding antagonist approached, but a sudden shot brought the Confederate down. Looking for the source of his salvation, the naval officer noticed a wounded man propped up with a smoking weapon in his hand. "Close one, sir," the fellow called out to his grateful commander.[21]

On the *Hunchback* the fire was just as severe and deadly. Boatswain's Mate James Ritchie took a fatal round while sighting his gun. The Confederate shell that hit him also killed a "contraband" named Frank Davis, the "grapeshot passing through both, killing them almost instantly." Davis probably served on board the vessel as a laborer, because he died near the gun, and not as a pilot with the commander, Edmund R. Colhoun, who shouted his orders "through the speaking tube in the pilot house how to fire" the howitzers.[22]

The crew of the *Whitehead* suffered the least of the three Union gunboats, although it had to take the lead as the vessels pulled back from Franklin. Commanding officer Charles French explained, "I am only surprised that the casualties [four men wounded] were not greater, considering our exposed situation and the upper works being so cut up with musketry." The losses might have been greater, for like Flusser's *Commodore Perry*, the *Whitehead* ran aground briefly. Seaman Edwin Smith plunged into the murky waters and swam ashore with a rope to pull the vessel off the sandbar on which it was caught. Somehow he accomplished his mission and managed to avoid being struck by the Confederate fire.[23]

The Southerners harassing the gunboats on their return journey included several foolhardy souls as well. Two of these men recalled years later that they had found a bluff of their own, dug a hasty rifle pit, and settled to await the Union vessels as they dropped back down the Blackwater. Although armed primarily with double-barreled shotguns, these fellows "endulged in the faint hope of capturing" the gunboats by felling trees in the river as obstructions.

The participants recalled catching the Federals on the decks unprepared to receive their fire but quickly conceded that the Union artillery got the best of their encounter. "The firing was so rapid and accurate from the gunboats above and below our rifle pit," one of them admitted, "that we could no longer expose ourselves, and we practically ceased firing." One shell caused the soft sand of the rifle pit's wall to collapse, and two of the men had to be pulled out by their feet and legs. Above the din of battle, they then heard shouted instructions indicating that a force was about to be sent against them. "We then had a very short conference and concluded that 'discretion was the better part of valor,' and decided to leave the pit at once, which we did in a hurry."[24]

Flusser later reported that the hostile forces opposing him during this fight included civilians and African Americans. "I neglected to state in my report," he added on the thirteenth, "that the people who fired on us near Franklin were not only soldiers, but there were men without uniforms, and also some negroes."[25]

The cooperating land force fared no better in their drive toward Franklin. "The enemy was there in greatly superior numbers," Dix explained to Admiral Lee, "but our men kept him at bay during the entire day, waiting for the gunboats." They left Franklin "having lost 1 man killed and 6 wounded and missing." Dix added that Spear's force might have "remained another day, but two scoundrels from New York, belonging to a regiment of mounted riflemen deserted in the night and passed over to the enemy." The deserters threatened the land-based force by providing the Confederates with "the amount of our force." Under the circumstances "we thought it best, especially as we had given up [on] the gunboats, to withdraw."[26] Thus the combined arms operation sputtered to an inglorious end, thwarted by the Southern forces that Peck, Dix, and Lee had hoped to disperse.

Despite the failure of this joint expedition, the Federals remained active in southeastern Virginia. By the end of the year, skirmishes had taken place all along the Blackwater from Franklin to Zuni, in addition to others on the roads near Carrsville, Windsor, and Providence Church. Hardly a crossing point or a crossroads in the region missed a visit from probing Union cavalry patrols.[27] Frequently the soldiers marched out and marched back without seeing any Confederates. Occasionally, they took the opportunity to forage independently. Food was the common target, especially meats, vegetables, and fruits to supplement normal soldier fare. The foragers were so effective that one Suffolk lady lamented in late October, "The country will soon be robbed of everything."[28] A Union officer writing to his wife in December agreed with this assessment. "The country is so cleaned out that one can forage to no purpose now," Alvin Coe Voris explained. "The chickens have left the country in disgust—I should say, of disgust of the Union Army."[29]

General Peck seems not to have appreciated the liberality with which the men under his command indulged themselves at the local citizens' expense. While some officers were vigilant in attempting to hold the men in their commands in check, Colonel Samuel Spear found the need for restraint less compelling. He dutifully had an order from Peck "strickly forbidding foraging of any description" read before his command and then remarked: "Boys, I know you won't steal. That order does not apply to my regiment. Keep on doing as you have been doing and you will be all right." He thus nullified Peck's order among the men of the unit who most needed to hear it.[30]

The targets of the foraging tried many ways to protect their property. One choice was to hide produce and livestock. But with roving cavalry units appearing without warning, this required a lot of luck. Some tried subterfuge, such as a Quaker family whose beliefs prevented them from lying, yet who wished not to be stripped of everything they had produced. Their solution was to leave a token ham strung from the rafters, while hiding the bulk of their hams beneath the floorboards. Thus when foragers appeared, the farmer could honestly say that all the ham he had was in the smokehouse.[31]

Another farmer tried declaring himself to be a "good Union man" before asking for protection of his property. Again, Spear and his men proved ready for the ploy. As the men scrounged the farm and "proceeded to help themselves" to what they found, the farmer hurried to Spear to make his case. When the colonel demanded that the man prove his loyalty by taking the oath of allegiance, the farmer hesitated but finally agreed. Expecting Spear to intervene after the makeshift ceremony, the farmer was shocked to see him do nothing to stop the plundering. A new protest prompted Spear to ask if he was not a "good Union man" as he had claimed. When the farmer replied that he was, the officer pointed out, "If you are a good Union man you will not object to my boys having a few chickens."[32]

Some Union soldiers expressed resentment toward local black families, particularly in the wake of President Lincoln's proclamation of emancipation for slaves in rebellious regions. Cavalryman George Starbird apparently harbored no desire to secure the rights of these people. He not only condemned them as unfit persons who "will starve without lifting a hand to save themselves," he was not above helping himself to such food as these families had. To one local black family, he explained that he expected to be fed whenever he wished and that his benefactors could let the Emancipation Proclamation "pay for it."[33]

In addition to foraging and hoarding, there were also the effects of speculation. Shortages drove prices higher, making goods more difficult to purchase when they could be obtained at all. "I am a Little Superised," one soldier remarked, "to see that flour and grain is so high as it is in the market." He added, "I think it is the result of Large Speculation," although he predicted, perhaps more hopefully than realistically, "that spring will reduce the price materialy."[34]

People living in the no-man's-land were not safe from Confederate troops either. Equally eager Southerners made the same requests for support, requisitioning the food and forage not already taken by the Federals or safeguarded by the farmers themselves. For the families thus victimized, the color of the uniform was beginning to make no difference to their empty larders and dinner tables.

Wartime disruptions could take a variety of forms, from military raids and foraging expeditions to attempts by slaves to reach the safety of Union lines in Suffolk. On the night of November 30, 1862, a band of slaves led by a free black man named Merrit Spratley made a dash for Suffolk. The thirty-five individuals included Spratley's wife and two infant children. Complicating matters was the fact that while Spratley was a free man, his wife and children were not.

Unfortunately, their race for freedom fell short when a patrol apprehended the fugitives and arrested them. Merrit Spratley appeared before the Southampton County Court the following February to face the charge that he "did aid and advise" his wife and children, "slaves the property of Nicholas Williams to abscond and escape from their said master." Despite his plea of not guilty, the court ruled against him. The presiding justice sentenced Spratley to "be sold into absolute slavery," in lieu of sending him to prison.[35] Thus for his "crime" of seeking liberty for his loved ones, this free man lost his freedom, as the system designed to perpetuate slavery demonstrated its continued power and commitment to the "peculiar institution," even in the midst of war.

While local whites sought to find ways to retain their way of life, their family members in the military continued their service as best they could. The Army of Northern Virginia made its way onto Maryland's soil in General Robert E. Lee's first invasion of the North, with the boys from lower tidewater trudging along with their units. Some of the Confederates moved against the Union garrison at Harpers Ferry, while others moved farther north. Then, in one of the greatest intelligence coups of the war, Union general George McClellan became apprised of the Confederate army's dispositions when Lee's "lost order" (Special Order No. 191) fell into his hands. The information showed that Lee's army was divided and vulnerable to attack in detail. A now confident McClellan ordered an advance toward South Mountain.

One of the points McClellan planned to hit was Crampton's Gap, only six miles northeast Harpers Ferry. Swift movement not only would discomfort the Confederates but would relieve the Union garrison there. He gave the assignment to Major General William B. Franklin. With 12,000 men, Franklin faced a force of only about 500. Yet the Southerners held a strong defensive position that proved impervious to Union assaults for most of the day. Finally, near the end of September 14, the line broke.[36] Two companies from Suffolk and one from Isle of Wight, all part of the 16th Virginia Infantry, were taken prisoner in droves. Among them was Major Francis Davis Holladay, who earlier had suffered a wound at Malvern Hill. Lemuel J. Stephens, a farmer when he enlisted in the Isle of Wight Rifle Greys, died in the fighting. At least twenty-one members of the Marion Rangers, the Suffolk Continentals, and the Greys fell into Union hands, with many of them going on to incarceration at Fort Delaware.[37]

The push against Crampton's Gap nearly saved the Union garrison at Harpers Ferry and may have changed the course of the battle that followed near Sharpsburg, Maryland, along the banks of Antietam Creek. As it was, the fighting on September 17 turned that day into the bloodiest single day of the war. Again, southeastern Virginia offered up its sons. This time it was the 3d Virginia, with two companies from Southampton County and one from Nansemond. Of the former, Major Charles Fox Urquhart, a graduate of the Virginia Military Institute (Class of 1860), who had only recently received his promotion, died at the head of his troops.[38] Ironically, Urquhart had run as the Unionist candidate for the state convention in 1861, when the farmer Daniel William Cobb helped narrowly to defeat him. Now, the man who had, in Cobb's words, desired "to stay" in the Union was killed fighting in the cause of the Confederacy.[39]

Writing in October from near Winchester to Anna Riddick, a friend from prewar days, Lieutenant Thomas Washington Smith expressed the sense of loss that the year's campaigning had meant to him personally. "But suffice it to say I have seen some hard times and trials," he wrote, "but above all I lost my dear young friend at Manassas, Poor Johnie Darden. You know how much I was attached to him. I had him with me ever since I first went in service. . . . I miss him so much." He was but one of the list of those who had died. "We have lost a great many men from our Regt. and several from our Company," the lieutenant explained. "We had one of the hardest fights at Crampton Gap you have ever heard of." After moving on to other subjects, he returned to "the Crampton Gap affair." "You know we had to fall back there for want of reinforcements. Our 600 men held 12 or 16,000 Yankees in check for two hours or more," Smith noted proudly. "We fell back and took a new position and the scoundrels were afraid to attack us any more."[40]

In the same month Anna received two more letters from the Winchester area. One was from another friend, Euclid Borland, who had healed from his Malvern Hill wound. He had welcome news of her brother. "I saw Mills day before yesterday and gave him the letter I had for him," Borland noted. He added a word about the conditions that plagued everyone in camp. "But like all the rest of the soldiers and officers too, [he] had to stop and *scratch* every now and then."[41]

Then she heard from Mills himself. He had made the rounds, too, but was expecting to march at any time. "We keep three days rations in our haversacks all the time," he explained. "We only get beef and bread now. I have been living on that ever since I left Richmond." Of course, the army had made the time to hold a formal review for some distinguished guests. "Gen. Longstreet review[ed] his Corps last Monday and two or three English Lords were on the field." But more than anything else, he was getting tired of soldiering. "Ask Father to try to get me a soft position somewheres," Mills told his sister.[42]

While these men from southeastern Virginia coped with conditions in the Shenandoah Valley, others watched the line along the Blackwater. Duty had more than its share of hardship for the men posted there. "On Picket 7 miles above Franklin, Va. on the Banks of the Blackwater," a North Carolina soldier wrote his wife complaining strongly about his lack of footwear. "If I do hapen with the luck to get home," A. C. Myers observed, "I should want the Boots to ware myself Especially if I should hapen to go home as near Barefooted as I am now."[43]

By the end of the month, he could report some relief for the worst off, but there was still plenty of room for criticism of the Confederate Commissary Department. The biggest problem was that Myers could not get a furlough so that he could get himself properly outfitted. "The different companys has petitioned to send one man home from Each company to get Blankets shoes clothing etc.," he explained. But even this suggestion "was disapproved & no man [has been] allowed to go home." All of this might have been tolerable if the government was doing its job of provisioning the troops. Instead, Myers had found that "the government cannot furnish Blankets, overcoats and has not yet furnished but one hundred & Eighty pairs of shoes for the Regt. & that only furnished those who was barefooted."[44] It was enough to strain even the strongest patriot.

The Confederates on the Blackwater might not be getting shoes and blankets, but at the beginning of November 1862, they received a new commander—Brigadier General Roger Atkinson Pryor. A native of Petersburg, Pryor was the former newspaper editor, U.S. congressman from

Virginia, and ardent secessionist who had witnessed the opening drama at Fort Sumter. His arrival in the region prompted one Confederate soldier to exude, "A more energetic, vigilant and judiciously brave officer I have never seen."[45]

Pryor began his tenure on the Blackwater in the same fashion Peck had started his in Suffolk, with his attention focused on security. The Confederate general explained, "On assuming the command . . . I immediately set myself to the work of fortifying the line, and so disposing the troops as to guard it with the greatest possible security." The Virginian kept his men busy "obstructing fords, digging rifle pits, [and] throwing up epaulements." He also had bridges constructed over the river to facilitate his own offensive operations.[46]

These intrusions into the no-man's-land between Suffolk and the Blackwater enabled Pryor to boast of supplying his forces with provisions taken from within the enemy's lines, although requisition receipts suggest that he actually purchased substantial quantities, particularly of beef, from friendly local suppliers.[47] In any case, his operations proved so successful that he claimed to be able to send a surplus back to Petersburg.[48] Pryor enjoyed the advantage of knowing something of the region, as well as having a base of people sympathetic to the cause for which he was fighting. He established an effective intelligence system by which he obtained "the earliest & most accurate information of the enemy's movements, both in Norfolk & Suffolk."[49]

In the meantime, the Union commander's desire to fortify Suffolk may have reached the point of becoming counterproductive. The morale of Peck's men suffered under the fatiguing work details. Men who had expected to fight found digging trenches increasingly intolerable. William Hyde of the 112th New York believed that although the work was necessary, "The effect of the constant digging was to abate soldierly pride and ambition in the Regiment."[50] Likewise, Edward Boots of the 101st Pennsylvania complained to his mother: "The work of fortifying this place still goes on briskly. . . . They are working away to-day, though it is the Sabbath day. I do not know the reason for it, but suppose that Gen[.] Peck wishes to get done fortifying before winter sets in & I hope he will, for we are tired of it."[51]

Fortunately for Peck, the troops often made light of the tedious work, even in his presence. On one occasion the commanding general found that a guard, an Irishman, had failed to take proper care of his rifle. The officer reprimanded the guard for having "a rusty gun." The soldier responded, "Sure, Gineral, indade, it's a bit rusty for want of use, but bedad it's mesilf as has a spade down at me tint, bright as new shillin', that yez can see yer face in liek a lookin' glass."[52]

Others confined their humor to the trenches, but it was no less biting concerning General Peck. One of the laborers, weary of his long hours of toil, remarked to a comrade, "I say, Bill! I hope Old Peck will die two weeks before I do."

"Why, so?" asked Bill.

"Because he will have hell so strongly fortified, in that time, that I can't get in."[53]

The men battled their circumstances with a variety of weapons. In addition to humor came an almost incessant indulgence in complaining. "All grumble in the army," one officer explained to his wife, "from the poorest soldier in the rear rank to the Major General. It is the soldier's privilege." This pattern went down the chain of command and back up again, with everyone targeting someone else for their problems. "So you see," the officer continued, "there is a complete circuit of complaining." Then he concluded of this particular glue that bound the men together, "Who has the best right to exercise this privilege is not determined and probably never will be."[54]

Undoubtedly all could agree with the colonel of the 112th New York when he wrote that the men in his regiment "have done but little since coming here but dig, making forts and rifle pits." So many of the men were occupied by the fatigue duty that it was virtually impossible to conduct regimental drills. Drilling by squads usually had to suffice until the work was completed.[55] Posted in Suffolk with the 6th Massachusetts, Henry Ingalls spent the bulk of his time on fatigue duty at various points in the defense line. The working parties usually operated on a rotating basis. "We work 1 hour and [have] 1 hour off," he recorded in his diary.[56] Such duty was not without risk. As part of a team of about forty men assigned to clear trees "in front of fort Nansemond," he watched as one of the trees killed a member of the working party from a different company. "It struck him across the neck and he was killed instantly," Ingalls wrote. He may not have known that Dennis McCarthy, the accident victim, was just twenty-two when he died.[57]

Accidents and unusual deaths were not uncommon for soldiers on either side of the conflict. Whether such cases stemmed from the movement of troops, particularly when the men rode atop boxcars on trains, or from simple carelessness, the exact toll will never be known. These deaths staggered friends and comrades just as severely as the more common and expected combat fatalities. Joseph Wallpole, for instance, a farmer who had enlisted in the Southampton Greys at Jerusalem on May 3, 1861, went into the hospital in Richmond on November 8, 1862, suffering from "moris serpentis," or the "bite of a serpent." He lost his leg to amputation before finally losing his life on November 15.[58]

Even with an elaborate defense system being constructed, Union generals Peck and Dix continued to worry that a sudden Confederate thrust was imminent. Dix's announcement to Major General Henry Halleck in early October that "Suffolk had been put in good condition, and we have no concern of attack," rings hollow. His new troops were "very raw," and the rebels always seemed poised to strike if the messages from African-American refugees, or "contrabands," were to be believed. This is why Peck had to remain active, Dix reasoned, constantly sending probes toward the Blackwater to ascertain Southern aims.[59]

The reality of these expeditions frequently differed from what appeared in the reports that the officers submitted. For instance, Peck termed the probe to Franklin in early October "a nice fight," with the object of the expedition being "fully attained." He set the Union loss at 2 killed, 5 wounded, and 1 missing and estimated the Confederate casualties at between 75 and 100.[60] Yet Nate Lampheur, a member of the 130th New York, related a different tale. Although he did not participate himself, he eagerly soaked up the news from those who did. "The detachment from our regiment came in tired worn and footsore without seeing an armed rebel and without having fired a gun except at hogs, fowls and beeves among which they made great havoc."[61]

Solomon Lenfest of the 6th Massachusetts participated, coming away from the expedition with a similar description of it. Writing in his diary, Lenfest noted, "We left here at 4 PM Friday (Oct. 3) with a brigade of 3,000 men marching 11 miles without stopping, arriving at 9 PM and camping in a cornfield." The next day they joined the rest of the regiment "and camped for the day on the grounds of a Seccesh who is in the rebel army. We helped ourselves to sweet potatoes, apples, grapes, and everything else we came across that was eatable." The only "rebel" he mentioned seeing was "quite a pretty girl."[62]

A colleague in the 6th returned with a less pleasant recollection. He had met two ambulances as they were bringing back the dead and wounded. "In one was stretched the stiffening body of a man just slain." It was, he recalled, a scene that spoke "more eloquently than words." Even so, he found time to lounge in the field, smelling the sweet potatoes and ham as they cooked, before assembling with his unit for the return trip to Suffolk.[63]

That trip, like the others before and after it, was made through desolate country. The soil was already badly depleted and the farms in relatively poor condition. Wartime demands did not help. One Northerner noted, "This section of the country is all after one pattern: wide tracts of forest; at long intervals 'plantations,' on which scattering stalks of corn, long and lean, stand on a thin and famished soil; roads of the wretchedest kind; houses, with rare exceptions, perfect tumble-down concerns, inhabited by old men, women, and children; and a general poverty strickenness everywhere."[64] This area stood in sharp contract to the well-kept houses and gardens the Confederates saw near the Blackwater or in the towns of Suffolk and Smithfield.[65] This soldier was convinced, "Really, of itself alone, [this section is] not worth conquering; and were it not for the principle involved in this struggle, we often said that we should be better off without than with such a tract as South-eastern Virginia."[66] A Union officer expressed the same feeling to his wife in a letter, adding the matter of race to the equation. "This is a miserable country," Alvin Voris observed exasperatingly, "nothing but Virginia and niggers. The whole eastern Va. is not worth fighting for, niggers thrown in."[67]

The expedition undoubtedly was more exciting for the cavalry and artillery, which reached the river first. They experienced the "furious cannonade" and took and inflicted the casualties.[68] By the time the slower-moving infantry columns had marched out, there was no skirmish to fight and nothing to do but march back. Lampheur was surely correct when he told his sister and brother, "The Expedition advanced to Franklin on the Blackwater the advance skirmished a little and the whole force returned without having accomplished anything of importance as I can see."[69]

The ship's log of the USS *Stepping Stones* indicates that the navy was taking a more active role in helping to guard the Nansemond River as well. In October, after a period of waiting for orders and initiating repairs, the vessel took one of many runs to Suffolk, developing a pattern of patrolling that ranged from the town to the Western Branch of the Nansemond and back. It was tedious work, with little to do but record the few vessels that passed, indulge in some oystering, and punish the occasional sailor for falling asleep at his post. Yet these patrols became an increasingly important part of Peck's vigilant defense of Suffolk in the months to come.[70]

Peck also maintained an elaborate system of pickets posted on the major thoroughfares into Suffolk. The Union commander seems to have left as little open to his opponents on the Blackwater as was humanly possible. For travelers there was a pass system to which they had to adhere. This was true of even the most innocent-looking citizen wandering into town. Pulling duty "at the lower end of the town," Massachusetts soldier Henry Ingalls wrote in October: "Have just been to the Provost Marshall's with an old woman. She came over the draw bridge." A month later, while stationed near the outer perimeter, he examined "the passes of all who passed us on the road." Again, there seemed to be no immediate threat, but there was a great deal of activity. The day being a Saturday and a market day, he observed, "There has been a good deal of passing to day: country folks going to the market."[71]

November brought no respite for the weary Federals, particularly as the weather became less hospitable. Expeditions, particularly for those on foot, became exercises in masochism. In one case Nate Lampheur watched as his men struggled along the roads back to Suffolk from another trip to Franklin. "The men were terribly fatigued," he wrote, "and it was with great difficulty that we could get them [to move] along. . . . Their feet were blistered and sore and it was almost impossible to get them to move." When stragglers fell out, Lampheur left them in squads so that they would be able to help each other in case of trouble. He got most of them back into camp but assessed the business bitterly. "I am satisfied we have accomplished nothing. Anything at least but the loss of a few of our men. I pray that this may be the last of these foolish recconnoisances."[72]

The people of the region, however, held on to their hopes that a day of liberation would come, ending the occupation of their homes. Many residents remained outwardly hostile toward the Union soldiers who walked their streets. One such soldier, Zephaniah Gooding, wrote of an encounter he had with the locals. "They is not but a few citizens hear perhaps 200 in number they is four Churches in the place and they hold meetings I have been every Sabbath since we have been hear." Despite Gooding's piety, the people were not particularly hospitable toward him or his comrades in blue. "They congregate in the corners of the streets and talk to gather and when we pass them they will look as cross as the ———." Finally, he had enough. This time when he walked by "one of the women on the sidewalk she made up a face at us and I asked her what she smelt oh how made she wus." Delighted at her response to his jest but exasperated by her attitude, Gooding told his brother, "I do not have eney simpathy for eny such people."[73]

At about the same time, Jennie Boykin wrote her friend Annie Riddick to say that such matters were not so amusing. "I had so sincerely hoped that I could spend the winter at my dear home," she explained, "but we find now, it is impossible for us to think of it, with such a large force as the Yankeys have now in Suffolk they will be making continual raids along and in the lines." Then listing the crimes for which she held "the Yankeys" responsible, she added, "I make occasional and brief visits Home . . . and when I leave every time I hate the Yankeys more." There was not much else for her to do but endure; still, "One week at *Home* is worth a whole year of Refugeeing."[74] It was an assessment with which Anna Riddick undoubtedly concurred.

Just as the people of the region were watching him with a jaundiced eye, so Nate Lampheur was keeping a close watch on the people back home. Writing from Suffolk on November 2, the New Yorker observed, "I look with great anxiety for the result of the election in our state." To his family he stated unequivocally: "You are fighting the most important battle of the war. You must not fail." For this soldier the election was a referendum on the war and his small part in it. He saw the election of Horatio Seymour, the Democratic candidate for governor, as tantamount to a rejection of all he had gone to war to defend.[75]

The result went against Lampheur's wishes, and he demonstrated his disappointment in his next letter. "The most disastrous and humiliating defeat the Union cause has suffered since the opening of the war is the loss of the election in New York State." In his mind the vote was a repudiation of the "loyal men of the North [who] have gone into the field by the tens of thousands." With these good men gone, "the cowardly, the indifferent, the doubtful, the lukewarm loyal and the openly disloyal [were able] to combine under the leadership of base advocates of treason who have worked upon their weak and cowardly natures against not only the [Lincoln] administration but their friends and neighbors whom they cheered off to the war and who are liable any day to become the victims of this unparalleled duplicity and treachery." Lest his friends assume this indictment lay at their feet, Lampheur added, "You have done all that you could do for us and must continue to do so for as sure as the policy of Seymour and his supporters prevails it will become a disgrace to be a soldier in the Union army and an honor and glory to have served in the Confederate ranks."[76]

Several inches of snow fell in early November, creating very muddy conditions and adding to the misery of refugees and soldiers alike. Peck still found time to stage grand reviews for important visitors he hoped to impress. General Dix's appearance in mid-November prompted a caustic response from one of the participants. "I thrashed about on my sorrel horse at a great rate," one officer noted in a letter, "and marched my men *up* and *down* as gay as a holiday." This soldier concluded sarcastically, "Well these grand reviews will soon crush out the wicked rebellion."[77] Several days later he was still fuming. "All the armies and navies of this post were out in thier glory," he exaggerated. "This is the third review we have had since I came here," he added before repeating his declaration that these reviews were sure to crush the rebellion.[78]

Whatever they thought of these reviews, the troops in Suffolk enjoyed Thanksgiving. One private even stopped long enough to jot in his diary a reminder of why he was there. "I did not think one year ago that to-day would find me amid such scenes as these," Solomon Lenfest wrote, "but here I am fighting for the cause of liberty." Peck did not let the day pass entirely without duty. Fatigue details worked on the fortifications for some hours before the men could drop their spades and enjoy the holiday. There were games aplenty and food shipped specially from loved ones back home. Lenfest "received a box" that made for as sumptuous a meal as if there had been no war going on at all. "Thanksgiving of 1862 will always seem much pleasanter from this item," he concluded gratefully.[79]

Combat soon replaced the festive mood of the holidays. Both Spear's 11th Pennsylvania Cavalry and Dodge's 1st New York Mounted Rifles continued to ride out on patrol. On one of these occasions, the Union cavalry enjoyed a spectacular success. Peck had sent out the force in response to reports from "contrabands" that the Southerners had crossed the river "tearing up the rails" on the Seaboard and Roanoke Railroad and "throwing up [defensive] works near the railway." When Confederate cavalry approached while the Federals were eating breakfast, Colonel Spear reacted swiftly and drove them off, killing between ten and twelve of their men and capturing twenty. The spoils included horses and equipment, and the "famous Petersburg Rocket Battery" of seventy tubes.[80] The prisoners Spear's men brought back presented many of the Federals with their first close-hand view of their enemy. Private Lenfest of the 6th Massachusetts was impressed sufficiently to record, "The prisoners were the roughest specimens of humanity I ever saw and their bloody faces and heads, where they had been slashed by the cavalry, were horrid to behold."[81]

Apparently, Pryor enjoyed successes of his own. On December 22 Confederates left the Blackwater near Zuni to interrupt Federal attempts to obtain votes for the area's seat in the U.S. House of Representatives. Approximately 200 men from Colonel Dodge's cavalry command were escorting the ballot box as it moved through the no-man's-land between Suffolk and the Blackwater. The after-action report noted that Lieutenant Colonel Onderdonk, commanding the escort, "succeeded in extricating himself," which lent credence to Confederate newspaper reports that their "dash on the Yankees" had been successful. Those reports noted that the "protectors fled in great confusion and were chased ten miles at full speed." The Union report claimed the capture of "2 of the enemy" and "the loss of 4 horses, but no men," while the Confederates boasted only a "trifling" loss.[82]

Either way, the Southerners seem to have largely accomplished their goal of disrupting the election. Although one Northern account suggested that "the election went off quietly in Suffolk," with forty-nine votes cast, a correspondent from the *New York Daily Tribune* offered further corroboration of the Confederates' claim. "A few votes were cast in Suffolk," he noted, but "no returns will be received from Isle of Wight, Windsor or Smithfield—the rebels from the other side of the Blackwater came over to put a quietus upon Union men who might try to vote." The correspondent explained that a detachment of the New York Mounted Rifles was escorting the ballot box "out to the rebellious sections named . . . when [it] was set upon by an overwhelming rebel force and had a hard race for Suffolk."[83]

Christmas brought some welcome relief to the Union garrison in Suffolk. The day was unusually warm, with the men spending part of it marching in a dress parade and performing drills. As at Thanksgiving, the men had part of the day to themselves to spend as they saw fit. Some chose to reflect upon home and family, while others engaged in various sporting activities.[84] Lieutenant Colonel Alvin Voris described the way the men in camp celebrated the holiday. "A shout would commence down a mile or more to our right," he explained, "till some 20 regiments had exhausted their throats in giving volume to the round. A thousand men cheering at once is a 'big thing.'" Christmas Eve also brought out the mischief in some of the men. "The boys could not go to sleep," he noted; "they wanted to burn gunpowder, wanted to have fun miscellaneously, and they did have it in spite of orders or officers of the day."[85] Although the officers made their own social rounds the next morning, a few days afterward Voris lamented, "Santa Claus did not come by Suffolk, so I had nothing in my stockings."[86]

The New Year brought no real changes in the intentions of the Union and Confederate commanders in the area. Both sides wished to seize the offensive, and with it the initiative. In mid-January, Pryor characteristically boasted that he would "be in Suffolk by the middle of the week."[87]

General Peck must have either gotten word of Pryor's boast or sensed it, for activity on the defenses suddenly increased dramatically. On January 14 Henry Ingalls noted the correlation between the general's concern and the soldiers' workload. "Gen. Peck expects an attack and there is a large fatigue party [out] today. There is more to work on fatigue to day than ever before since we have been in Suffolk."[88] Two days later the men were still busily engaged in perfecting the defenses, despite rainy weather. "Went down between Fts. McClellan and Union and worked on the breastworks," the Massachusetts soldier wrote. "We expect an attack. Work on the Fts. Is to be rushed."[89] Finally, on the twentieth, the frenetic pace abated somewhat. Ingalls was still "on fatigue," this time "at the new works below Ft. Nansemond," but there was a sense of relief as well. "Peck has got over his fright and is peaceful again."[90]

The pressure may have appeared to ease in the eyes of the soldiers, but increased Confederate activity created enormous problems for Dix and Peck. Often intelligence reports were contradictory and unsatisfactory. Pryor might try to attack Norfolk or Portsmouth. He might move into North Carolina. No one was sure. Dix plaintively questioned Peck, "Do you know where Pryor is? Have you any reliable intelligence from the enemy, as to his force or his movements?"[91] The Suffolk commander could do little to comfort his superior. He continued to send out scouts, sometimes using the *Stepping Stones* to ferry small parties of men to drop-off points along the Nansemond River.[92] The Federals were off-balance and unsure. Peck continued to strengthen his entrenchments and maintain a high level of alertness, but the walls of his fortifications were beginning to take on the grim aspect of prison walls.

Now Pryor finally had the opportunity to seize the initiative. He could strike while his opponent was unsure. On the evening of January 25, he crossed the Blackwater River with a force of some 1,800 infantry, cavalry, and artillery. He had several objectives. He expected to "shut the enemy up in Suffolk," interrupt communications, and gather food and forage from Union-controlled areas.[93] By January 29 Pryor rested his force at Kelly's Store, about eight or nine miles northwest of Suffolk, twelve miles from the Southern lines at Franklin, and less than two miles north of Buckhorn Station on the Seaboard and Roanoke Railroad.[94]

On the same day word reached Suffolk that Pryor had left his Blackwater lines and ventured within striking distance. Peck saw his opportunity and grasped it. He mobilized a special task force of some 4,800 infantry, cavalry, and artillery. Once scouts had returned confirming the information, Peck instructed the expedition's commander, Michael Corcoran, to "proceed cautiously . . . [locate Pryor,] and force him from his position, inflicting all the loss possible."[95]

The assignment suited the Irish-born general. The most colorful of the figures who joined Peck at Suffolk, the feisty soldier differed considerably from his chief. He remained embroiled in controversy throughout his military career. Born the son of a British army officer on September 21, 1827, Corcoran emigrated to New York in 1849. Entering the 29th New York Militia as a private, he rose to the rank of colonel. In that position he achieved singular fame among Irish Americans and incurred the ire of native Americans with a public snub of the visiting Prince of Wales in 1860.[96]

Corcoran very nearly paid a heavy price for his refusal to parade his command in honor of the English dignitary. Roundly criticized for insubordination, Corcoran was relieved of his command and ordered to go before a court-martial. Fortunately for the proud soldier, war intervened to prevent his disgrace; the army dropped all charges. Corcoran resumed his post and prepared to lead the 69th New York to war.

Although many Irish Americans stood divided in their loyalties, Corcoran had reasons for supporting the United States in the conflict. As he explained to a Fenian official, "It is not only our duty to America . . . but also to Ireland. We could not hope to succeed in our effort to make Ireland a Republic without the moral and material aid of the liberty-loving citizens of these United States."[97] Furthermore, Corcoran saw the war as an opportunity to obtain "a little practice" which could serve the Irish cause in the future.[98]

Having committed himself to the Union cause, Corcoran led the 69th New York into the battle of First Bull Run. In the ensuing defeat the Confederates captured the Irish general. Incarcerated in Richmond, Corcoran soon became involved in a contest of wills between the United States and the Confederate States. Chosen by lot to share the fate of captured Southern privateers, considered pirates by the Federal government, Corcoran lived under the constant threat of execution. Finally, after languishing in various Southern prisons, the Irishman was exchanged in August 1862. Corcoran returned to the North as a hero. Immediately he sought to organize a new Irish brigade, vowing to return to Ireland if necessary for recruits. He did not have to bother. Irish Americans responded to the call with enthusiasm, and within a month the newly promoted brigadier general commanded a "Legion" which bore his name. By the end of 1862, the fiery Irishman and his men were in Suffolk.[99]

So it was Corcoran who led the task force out of Suffolk at 1 A.M. on Friday, January 30, in hopes of catching and defeating Pryor's Confederates. Each man had three days' rations and sixty rounds of ammunition. The column of march included nine regiments of infantry, one regiment of cavalry, and two batteries of artillery. The expedition also included a wagon train for supplies and an ambulance corps.[100]

Pryor's force remained encamped near Kelly's Store. According to his report the Southerners deployed every conceivable security measure, anticipating a Union advance against them. Pryor sent out cavalry patrols to warn of approaching Federals, directed a company of infantry to be placed in advance of the main camp on either side of the road, and posted 100 sharpshooters well along the main road toward Suffolk to ambush the Union cavalry as they came up.

Swamps and thick stands of pine dotted the land on which Pryor disposed his troops. The Southern general used the terrain features to his advantage. He deployed his infantry on both sides of the main road leading to Suffolk, approximately half a mile west of Kelly's Store (the Deserted House), which lent the battle its name. This road divided at the house, one fork leading through the swamp directly toward Suffolk. The other fork ran perpendicular to the main road, leading north and east past the Ely house toward Providence Church. A huge open field surrounded the house. The swamp bordered this field and lay about a quarter of a mile to the east of the Deserted House. Thick forests ran from the swamp to the north and south of the house. The Seaboard and Roanoke Railroad ran south of the house, approximately a mile and a half on the Confederate right.

With the Confederates settled comfortably in their bivouac and the pickets set, Pryor was prepared for whatever might transpire. "As was expected, about 3 o'clock, the enemy's cavalry approached our men in ambush."[101] But Confederate junior officer James Clark, writing to his wife just over a week later, suggested that the pickets relaxed their vigilance as the night progressed with no hint of danger. He explained that the Southern camp "was surprised by them. The first thing we knew a bombshell came through the pines about 3 1/2 o'clock in the morning of the 30th."[102]

Another Southerner, this one in the 63d Virginia, implied years after the war that the Confederates were surprised when he noted, "While [we were] in camp during the night, the enemy captured our pickets and sent a shell whizzing across our camp."[103] On the other hand, a Union account seems to confirm Pryor's contention that the Federals had not surprised his command. "At this time the moon had gone down, and it was impossible to distinguish the exact position of the foe. The pickets fled at the approach of our cavalry." Yet when the Federals sent forward a small detachment to "feel" for the Confederates, it ran into "a party of men" who fired a volley at them, at which point the Union artillery came up.[104] Although it is reasonable to assume that any volley would have been heard in the main camp, thereby alerting it, this would not be the first time that atmospheric conditions muted noise from troops relatively close to a firefight.[105]

Whatever the case, at approximately 3:20 A.M. Union cavalry hit the Southern pickets. An explosion of small-arms fire greeted the Federal cavalrymen as they came up the road. The volley threw the blue horsemen into momentary confusion and emptied several saddles.[106] But the cavalrymen quickly rallied. The Confederate pickets then retreated, with

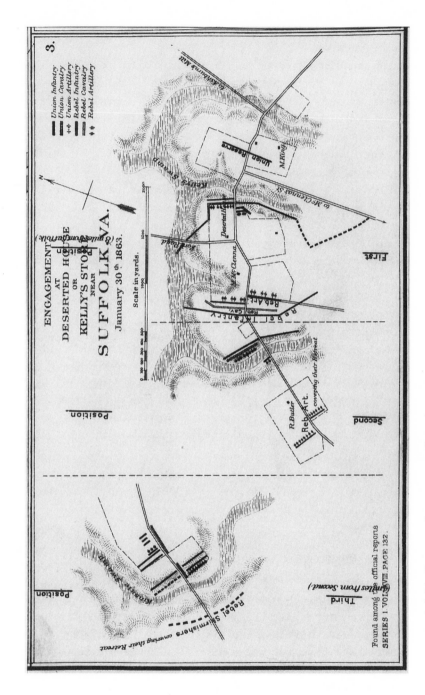

3.

Union Infantry
Union Cavalry
Union Artillery
Rebel Infantry
Rebel Cavalry
Rebel Artillery

ENGAGEMENT
AT
DESERTED HOUSE
OR
KELLY'S STORE
NEAR
SUFFOLK, VA.
January 30ᵗʰ 1863.

(8 miles from Suffolk.)

Position

N

Scale in yards.

First.

Position

Second

Third

(9 miles from Second.)

Found among the official reports
SERIES 1. VOL. XVIII. PAGE 132.

MAP 5 Battlefield of Deserted House or Kelly's Store, on January 30, 1863.

some of them undoubtedly killed or captured as they slogged through the swamps and woods.[107]

By all accounts both sides hustled their artillery crews into action. The unlimbered pieces quickly began to blaze away at each other, with the Union artillery occupying the ground near the Deserted House for most of the duel to follow. The firing continued as the rest of the Union column raced toward the fight. Spurred by the "thrill of animation," the blue infantry-men deployed in line of battle and rushed forward at the double-quick. They waded a creek, pushed through the swamp, struggled amid the pines, or pressed their way up the road to get in front.[108]

Approximately ten minutes after the fighting had begun, the full fury of artillery fire added to the sights and sounds of the ever-widening battle. James Bowen of the 130th New York watched the spectacle. He never forgot what he saw:

> Through the darkness we saw the flash of the cannon, and instantly their missiles of death came blazing and screaming through the air, tearing through the tree-tops or bursting in our midst, until it seemed as if pandemonium was let loose upon us. This fearful crash of cannon and deluge of shells came so suddenly and unexpectedly that the men were for a moment dazed, but quickly regained composure. . . . The pyrotechnical display, in the pitchy darkness of the night, possessed all the elements of sublimity and terror. The flash of the guns and the long, bright lines made by the burning fuse of shells as they flew, either way, in curves through the air, made a grand and beautiful picture, which, but for the destruction wrought, would have been most enjoyable.[109]

The pre-aimed Southern artillery was particularly effective. Pryor's can-noneers executed a steady and destructive fire, especially on the Union infantrymen moving along the road from Suffolk. These Federals hustled into position. Once there, they lay on the ground to avoid the murderous fire. Private Lenfest remembered:

> Shells were flying all around us and bursting over our heads. I expected every moment some of us would be hit and did not have to wait long to have my expectations realized. We had not been lying down more than 15 minutes when I saw a shell coming and ducked my head. Then came a crash and a thud and I was bespattered with brains and blood and a wail of distress arose just beside me that showed where the shell had struck. A young fellow at my side raised

himself partly up exclaiming "Oh God, I'm killed, I'm shot" and fell back right onto me. It proved however that only his leg was shot off. Just beyond him Lieut. Sawtelle of Company B was groaning and Lieut. Blood exclaimed "here is a man with the top of his head shot off." I began to feel a little sick but there was no escape and 15 pieces of artillery were playing on us all the time.

For nearly two hours Lenfest and his Massachusetts comrades lay on the ground, exposed to the brutal Confederate fire. Lieutenant Edward D. Sawtell, who had joined the Union army as a twenty-eight-year-old farmer, was shot "through the breast" and lived only long enough to be taken to the rear. Lenfest observed that "another man had the top of his head taken completely off and a third had the side of his head crushed in. Another had his leg cut off at the knee and still another had his right arm shot off." In all, the young soldier counted three men killed and two others wounded within six feet of him. He felt fortunate to leave the battlefield unscathed.[110]

The Confederates had also suffered severely, particularly the officers. Early in the artillery duel, a shell fragment struck Thomas Pogue, colonel of the 50th Virginia. Tearing through his thigh, the fragment ripped a main artery. Within minutes the Confederate colonel bled to death. Others suffered grievous wounds as well. Two men of the 50th, William Patterson Barnard, nineteen, and Orvil M. Perkins, twenty-two, both farmers when they enlisted in 1861, received severe wounds from the shelling. The two men survived the battle only to have their wounded limbs amputated. Neither lived long after the surgery. Altogether the regiment lost no less than twelve men killed, wounded, missing, or captured, many of them from the artillery exchange.[111]

In the 54th Virginia officers again paid a steep price. Captain Thomas P. Dobyns and Lieutenant John S. Lacy died in the fighting, while seven others from the 54th were wounded, and four were captured. William King wrote to his wife Mary on February 1: "We lost several men of the 54th. Capt. Dobins was killed Lieutenant Lacy killed i and my brothers escaped un hurt . . . i am very thankful that i was Spared."[112]

Despite the physical damage inflicted upon them, the Confederates, like their Union counterparts, remembered the awesome beauty of the artillery exchange at Kelly's farm. Private John W. Wade of the 50th Virginia noted, "The Canon Shot flew thick among us." Burning fuses in the darkened sky particularly drew their attention: "I cold see the canon balls flying with a streak of fier to them for it was before day." The geography impressed this farmer from Floyd County, too. "This is level country," he explained, "and no hills to Shelter a man from a canon ball."[113]

The hot artillery duel, in which both sides suffered so greatly, continued until 6 A.M. At 5:15, Union general Corcoran decided to turn to his infantry to carry the day. He ordered the 167th Pennsylvania to advance on the enemy. The order repeatedly went unheeded. Corcoran then learned that the regiment had lost all of its field officers. The men were a "confused mass, mixed up with other regiments, and [they] filled the entire road, leaving it impassable and creating a temporary confusion among some other regiments in the rear." Corcoran truly had a problem, for panic in this regiment might easily spread into other units. But the Union commander managed to withdraw the leaderless unit before any further damage was done.[114]

One Union account bitterly assailed the Pennsylvanians. Even though the approach was difficult and intimidating—"The only way to advance was through a sort of gorge, with heavy timber and swamp-land on each side of the road"—the writer was merciless toward them. "Like the veriest cravens that ever cursed a noble cause," he sneered, "nearly every man of this regiment skulked, and all were as deaf to the calls of their commanding general as they were insensible to the demands of patriotism and the ordinary dictates of manhood."[115]

Corcoran called upon the soldiers of the 69th and 155th New York Regiments to prevent further chaos, together with the 13th Indiana and the 130th New York, brought up to replace the demoralized Pennsylvanians. At 6 A.M. the Federals made the dash toward the Confederate lines. When they pressed across the field, the Southerners began to pull out of their positions. As a result the attack met with little resistance, and the Federals easily occupied the Confederate main line.[116] But according to one writer, the victory might have been much greater. "The delay occasioned by the supineness of the Pennsylvania regiment lost us the golden opportunity to capture a large portion of the enemy's cannon and many prisoners."[117]

Pryor later explained that he had retreated upon receiving word that Union reinforcements were arriving in railroad cars on his right flank. Already outnumbered rather severely, the Southern general contended that he had withdrawn to avoid capture or destruction.[118] At least one private disagreed with his general's analysis. "I am bound to say they whip[ped] us this time," explained Joel Mankins of the 50th Virginia, "for our men left the field in time of the fite."[119]

Both sides claimed victory. Each commander generated a circular of congratulations to the participating units, commending their valor and sacrifice. Each claimed to have been thwarted in achieving greater results only by the other's failure to remain on the field.[120] Actually, neither side was ready to renew the action in earnest. In the battle of Kelly's Store or Deserted House, neither side won a clear-cut victory. The Confederates succeeded in inflicting greater losses upon their opponents but withdrew from the battlefield, leaving it to the enemy. The Federals could claim the field but little else, as Pryor slipped back to the safety of the Blackwater.

In the battle the Federals lost 23 killed, 108 wounded, and 12 missing or captured. The Confederates reported 8 killed and 31 wounded. They listed no one as captured, but Corcoran believed the number of Southern prisoners taken to be about 30. Peck placed the number at 13. Total Union and Confederate casualties were roughly 143 and 52, respectively.[121]

As the opposing forces positioned themselves immediately after the fighting, an anxious Abraham Lincoln wired the Federal commander for news. Undoubtedly, the answer the president received to his query, "How has Corcoran's and Pryor's battle terminated?" was unsatisfactory at best.[122] Neither side emerged from the fighting with a strategic or tactical advantage. However, the battle of Kelly's Store or Deserted House at the end of January 1863 gave both sides a foretaste of the events that would occur later that spring.

For now, the status quo held. Suffolk remained squarely in Union hands, and the region between the town and the Blackwater continued to be a no-man's-land. Given the proximity of large bodies of Federals in Suffolk, the colonel of the 54th Virginia was probably closer to the truth when he concluded, "Whenever we cross the Blackwater River we are considered within enemy lines" or, as Pryor would have to attest, within the enemy's reach.[123] It remained to be seen if the balance of power in southeastern Virginia could be shifted back in favor of the Confederates, or whether the region was destined to remain in Union hands and under their control.

"Perhaps, sweetheart, perhaps I say, you will
see your soldier sooner than you think."

George Pickett to LaSalle Corbell

⚔ 5 ⚔ *A Winter of Discontent*

THE CONFRONTATION AT KELLY'S STORE ON JANUARY 30, 1863,
left a bitter taste in John Peck's mouth. He had hoped that Corcoran
would bag General Pryor and eliminate the Confederate threat on
the Blackwater River. His failure to do so left Peck with the frustrating reality of Pryor's presence. Although Peck called the engagement a "handsome
affair" and offered Corcoran and his men "my warmest approbation for
the[ir] brilliant achievement," he clearly was disappointed at Pryor's "narrow escape from capture."[1] Nevertheless, Peck enjoyed the satisfaction of
attracting the notice of the Confederate high command in Richmond.
Increased activity on the Blackwater and Suffolk line did little to allay
Southern fears, while the battle of Kelly's Store drew additional attention
to the area and magnified those fears. In his May 5, 1863, report, the Suffolk
commander pleasantly noted, "My labors alarmed the authorities at

Richmond, who believed I was preparing a base for a grand movement upon the rebel capital."[2]

One of the more macabre sidelights of the battle Corcoran and Pryor had just fought was the interest the battlefield generated among the local residents. While the conflict at Kelly's Store was a small engagement compared to Sharpsburg and Gettysburg, it was the most significant set-piece battle that had occurred in the region. Consequently the battlefield turned into something a tourist attraction. Because both sides had removed their dead and wounded, what these curiosity seekers found was the detritus of war: broken equipment, abandoned accoutrements, shattered trees, a war-torn landscape, and dead horses. Compared to the running fights that so typified campaigning in southeastern Virginia, the encounter had left a great deal to see. For those who visited the site, the battlefield, as well as the casualties it produced, caused this war to hit home to them in a profound way.[3]

Not everyone found the battle worthy of such attention. The Southampton County farmer Daniel William Cobb wrote in his diary on February 1, "I understand Prier is in a fight on Black water for the last 2 or 3 days I [have] not hurd the result."[4] Also conspicuously absent from Cobb's notations was any opinion regarding the implementation of the Emancipation Proclamation. Announced as a preliminary measure on September 22, following the battle of Antietam, or Sharpsburg, the proclamation went into effect on January 1, 1863. It specified that all persons "held as slaves" within the states or parts of states then in rebellion "henceforth shall be free." The document put the Lincoln administration on record for black freedom, but it would only take effect in areas that remained in rebellion. Specifically excluded were some areas, including Norfolk, already under Union control. "Ironically, the only Afro-Virginian slaves who could openly celebrate the proclamation were in areas exempted from its provisions," one historian has noted. Still, Norfolk set the scene for "one of the largest black public commemorations in the state," with a parade, a band, and other forms of open celebration.[5] At the beginning of the new year, this proclamation would be effective in Nansemond, Isle of Wight, and Southampton Counties. Perhaps just as significant, the final proclamation called for ex-slaves to be taken into the Union army.[6]

Many slaves had not waited for President Lincoln to act or for the arrival of Union soldiers to enforce his will upon people who did not necessarily recognize his authority over them. Those who managed to escape to Union-held territory found safe haven, as historian Ervin Jordan put it, "Lincoln's exemptions notwithstanding." Likewise, historian Philip J. Schwarz has found that when the slaves "took advantage" of the wartime disruptions and the changes in Union policies regarding emancipation, "they created a fugitive slave situation never before encountered by Virginian slaveowners." Indeed, he noted that the state Auditor's Office itself affirmed that "at least five thousand Virginian bondspeople had fled to the enemy" between the advent of the war in 1861 and the early months of 1863.[7]

In early 1863 planters in Gates County, North Carolina, continued to press their claims for runaway slaves who had sought refuge in Union lines at Suffolk. Members of the Riddick family in Gates County sought representation for themselves or represented others who wished to register such losses. Three appearances before a county justice of the peace offer a glimpse at what must have been a much more widespread phenomenon. The numbers associated with these claims must have been astounding.

The claims made from January 18 to February 21 asserted the loss of seventeen slaves, ranging in age from children of three and four to a fifty-two-year-old adult. The claimants placed the value of these runaway slaves at $13,000 and noted that they had gone to the enemy at Suffolk during the preceding five months.[8] How many of these people sought freedom because of the Emancipation Proclamation is not known. It is certainly possible that these seventeen slaves anticipated Lincoln's actions and left for Union lines on their own account. Yet the fact remains that they risked everything in their quest to be free and sought that freedom within the Union lines at Suffolk.

By contrast, local Unionist reaction was anything but stellar. At the end of 1862, the assistant adjutant general of Brigadier General George W. Getty's staff, Hazard Stevens, left that post to enlist men for the 1st Regiment Loyal East Virginians. Destined to win the Medal of Honor for his exceptional valor, Stevens failed to convince Unionists from the lower tidewater to rally to the Federal banner, even with the offer of a $100 bounty ($25 down and the rest at the "expiration of the term of service"). He set up one of the recruiting stations for the unit at Bernard's Mills, a few miles east of Suffolk. After a brief stint on Getty's staff during the battle of Fredericksburg, Stevens returned in January to find that not much in the way of enlistments had taken place in his absence. "I have used every effort to obtain recruits during your absence without any success whatever," his lieutenant, Joseph Throckmorton, explained. "I have kept the three recruits I have with me constantly employed . . . the Sergeant and myself have also exerted ourselves to the utmost but to no avail." As historian Richard Current has noted, "All together the efforts of Stevens and his subordinates netted only enough men to fill one company of the First Loyal East Virginia Infantry." For a man as devoted to the cause of Union as Stevens, the failure to recruit more men must have been supremely disappointing. As it was, the eighty-four men raised found use on the Eastern Shore of Virginia for the rest of the war.[9]

The war also was having an effect on the rail system in the region. By the end of 1862, the Norfolk and Petersburg line was reduced by half to forty operative miles for the Confederates. The Seaboard and Roanoke was down from fifty-nine miles to twenty-three usable by the Southerners. Since their arrival, the Federals had worked to convert the Norfolk and Petersburg to a standard gauge (4 ft. 8½ in.). They constructed a Y connection that linked it to the Seaboard and Roanoke (already a standard-gauge line), which would facilitate the movement of men and supplies along both lines. This effort gave the Federals use of almost half of the Norfolk line and thirty-six miles of the Seaboard road.[10]

The Confederates tried to interdict these lines, but with the conventional troops distant on the Blackwater and the Suffolk garrison between them and the converted or repaired sections of these railroads, they had to rely upon guerrillas. Even so, the unconventional could prove useful, for harassment purposes if nothing else. On January 16, 1863, a message went by signal from the military governor of Norfolk, Brigadier General Egbert L. Viele, to Colonel David W. Wardrop: "Some rebels appear to have got through between you and Suffolk. Gen. Peck's Pickets are skirmishing on the track between here and there." Shortly, Wardrop, who commanded the Reserve Brigade, wanted to know if Viele had any further intelligence from Suffolk. Viele responded anxiously: "The Pickets at Suffolk were attacked at two points by Guerillas who were repulsed. Watch for them."[11] This activity seems to have produced more fear than any real harm, but such fear often brought on exaggerated reactions. An officer of the 13th New York recalled that among the false alarms was an instance of the tending of a small sick child. The father, walking up and down the stairs with a lantern at night, caused an officer of the picket guard to suspect that he was signaling to guerrillas.[12]

Of course, the alarms were not always false. The same writer noted in the latter part of 1862 that "guerrillas are seen almost daily and every now and then one is caught and brought in. They constitute a sort of independent picket and convey from house to house tidings of any unusual movement here." But the gathering and dissemination of news were only part of the activity going on in the no-man's-land. "They also stop rebel deserters and contrabands from coming in." Considering the guerrillas on a par with criminals, this soldier proclaimed, "Their actions are a disgrace to humanity." One Federal happily conveyed the capture of "six men & one

Officer," having "bin looking for them some time[.] they are the ones that have bin shooting our pickets all the time."[13]

The *Stepping Stones* continued to play its role in disrupting Southern communications and guerrilla activity. The ship's log lists on February 26 an expedition to Bennett's Creek "to destroy all Boats that was in use and Bring out all of eny Value." The boat's crew "distroyed 7 cannoes 6 Punts Brought out 7 Boats."[14] A seaman who joined the gunboat about this time later recalled:

> Our work was principally at night, made necessarily so by the rebels, or those who were in league with them in carrying on trade across the river. Their plans were to watch the movements of the vessels, and, by a well understood code of signaling arranged by passing a window with a lamp, they would cross the river, where they would meet friends and where wares could be exchanged for money, and mails taken into the rebel lines. It always seemed strange to me that this border between the conflicting territories should be so imperfectly guarded. It would not have been difficult for a cunning man to pass between Washington and Richmond continuously by this route. Our duties were to break up these operations, and to arrest those engaged therein. . . . But it was only owing to some clumsy action of their own, like using lighted signals, that we ever caught them. Could it be expected of a single vessel to guard a narrow river a distance of eighteen miles against these communications? The most effectual way of preventing them was to destroy all the boats to be found, and we were so diligent in this work that the conspirators carried their boats on wagons to a safe distance within their lines.[15]

Union forces were effective enough in disrupting or interdicting transportation networks in the region that the Confederates apparently gave up all hope of reclaiming the rail lines and began to dismantle the Seaboard and Roanoke east of the town of Franklin.[16]

For these men stationed along the Blackwater line, the winter of 1862–63 struck particularly hard. From his "camp near Blackwater Bridge," Sergeant Samuel H. Pulliam wrote a long letter to a relative, much of it illustrative of the discontent that marked the lives of the men serving there. He was grateful to receive news from the homefront. "I wish I could get them more frequently," he observed of her letters. "They are among my greatest pleasures in camp life."

Not much else was so pleasant. "We have not been paid for more than six months," the Southern artillerist moaned, "& have received not one arti-

cle of clothing from the government since the first of last May." Only
through the "contributions of benevolent citizens from different parts of
the state" had the troops obtained "a very limited supply of shoes blankets
shirts & socks." The shortages had left the bulk of the command in poor
condition. "Many of our company are *very ragged & barefooted, & all* are pen-
niless." The majority of the men endured the conditions as best they could.
Still, Pulliam observed with more than a hint of disdain, "There have been
eight or ten desertions from the company in the past four weeks from the
meaner portion of our men." Although many "are quite discontented," he
predicted that "pay & a sufficiency of clothing will do much to alleviate
this state of affairs."

The Confederate sergeant found it particularly frustrating that he could
not keep the men occupied with drill. Speaking of the book of tactics, he
complained, "I can rarely put [it] in practice as the ground does not admit
of battery drills." In this isolated region, camp life must have seemed particularly displeasing. "At times my duties keep me very busy, & again I almost
die of ennui," Pulliam explained. To make matters worse, the appearance
of smallpox in the region threatened the men. "Gen. Pryor has ordered that
all the troops be vaccinated at once," he remarked. "We had many of our
members vaccinated today—Myself among them though probably uselessly."

Nor were the Southerners the only disgruntled ones in the region.
Sergeant Pulliam noted that "several deserters from the enemy have
recently crossed over near here & represent the whole northern army as
discontented." They turned out to be angry over some of the same issues
as their Confederate counterparts. "They have not been paid for some time
& are getting as tired of the war as ourselves."[17]

One unit in particular, the New York Mounted Rifles, was susceptible
to this malady, but more by design than reaction. Some of the men who
wanted an immediate furlough, or at least to be shed of the grueling life
of a soldier for a time, went into the Confederate lines where they turned
themselves and all of their equipment over in exchange for a parole. Not
only did the Confederates gain valuable equipment, but granting the
parole took another Union soldier off the line, because such men were not
eligible to return to duty until properly exchanged. Northern commanders
soon caught on to the ploy and took steps to halt it. Their method was to
declare the individual a deserter rather than recognizing his status as a
paroled prisoner of war. Under these terms the "deserter" faced summary
punishment rather than a furlough, prompting soldiers thinking about such
a recourse to seek more legitimate means of obtaining furloughs.[18]

Perhaps pushed by their shortages, the Federals continued to exact a toll from nearby civilians and their property. As Pulliam told his aunt, "We are very near a wealthy portion of North Carolina, now in the Yankee's hands, which has been woefully ravaged. Nearly all the negroes have left & all the crops have been taken from the owners." The sergeant also found signs of destruction on expeditions into the no-man's-land east of the Blackwater. Expressing the hope that his kinfolk might "be spared the horrors of a desolated mansion & ravaged lands," he concluded, "Such has been the fate of many, whose houses I have visited on our marches."[19]

The hardships, the desolation of the countryside, and the raids by the Union forces in Suffolk were not all the concerns Southerners confronted in the region. On February 8 they received an additional scare when the first brigade of the Union 9th Corps arrived at Newport News. The Hampton Roads area had long been used as a staging base for amphibious assaults on the Confederate coastline. Troops stationed there en masse posed a serious threat not only to southeastern Virginia but also to the entire Confederate Atlantic seaboard. Southerners could not take such a threat lightly.[20]

Despite numerous appeals for assistance, the Davis administration seemed primarily concerned with the protection of the capital. The Army of Northern Virginia was positioned to offer Richmond protection from a Federal attack in any of three directions. However, Petersburg, the key to Richmond's supply lines and the capital's southern front, lay relatively exposed. Only the dispatch of troops from Lee's army could make the Confederates in this vulnerable flank feel safe.

General Lee telegraphed Secretary of War James A. Seddon (in office since November 1862) that he would send Major General George E. Pickett and his division to Richmond on February 15. He planned to hold Major General John B. Hood's division "in readiness" to accompany Pickett's command, should the need arise. Lee was unsure as to the 9th Corps's intentions. He speculated that it might be sent as near as Suffolk or as far as South Carolina. Lee assured Secretary Seddon that if the former was the true destination, "General Pickett's division will be ample to resist it."[21]

The flustered secretary of war hastily wired General Lee on February 15 that President Davis wanted an "adequate force" to be sent toward Richmond.[22] Seddon observed that Pickett's force would probably "suffice."[23] All of this was contingent upon Lee's judgment concerning Joseph Hooker's intentions on the Rappahannock line. Although the roads in the vicinity of the Rappahannock were in dreadful condition because of the weather, Hooker's huge army remained the principal threat.

Lee already had assured Seddon that "Pickett's division can meet and beat it [the 9th Corps] wherever it goes."[24] However, Seddon's dispatches led Lee to reevaluate the situation. In response to the secretary's urgings and the potential threat to Richmond, the Southern commander directed Hood's division to move toward the Confederate capital on February 16.[25] The next day the greatly relieved war secretary expressed his gratitude to Lee for his "characteristic vigilance" in hastening Pickett and Hood toward Richmond. With Lee's acquiescence Seddon posted the soldiers on the south side of the James River. From that point they could render service to Pryor on the Blackwater or defend Petersburg and protect the capital.[26]

On February 18 Lee instructed Lieutenant General James Longstreet to assume command of his two divisions. "The transfer of a portion of the Federal Army of the Potomac to Hampton Roads," Lee observed, "has rendered it necessary to move two divisions of your corps toward [the] James River. I desire you to join them, and place them in position . . . whence they can be readily moved to resist an advance upon Richmond by the enemy from his new base." Lee also informed his lieutenant, "Should the movement of the enemy from the Potomac render it expedient, your other divisions will be ordered to join you."[27]

Longstreet was to have control of a major portion of his army corps, led by men who shared with him almost identical backgrounds, training, and experience. Longstreet, Pickett, and Hood boasted sterling martial records. Each was a West Pointer, a Mexican or Indian Wars veteran, and a tested Confederate field officer. In the spring of 1863, their troops were veterans of the hardest fighting and the bloodiest battlefields in the eastern theater. They had an outstanding reputation as Lee's finest shock troops.

Their leader, James Longstreet, was a South Carolinian, born on January 8, 1821. He entered West Point at the age of sixteen and as a cadet had a history of academic difficulty.[28] Although voted the "handsomest cadet at West Point" by his comrades, he only passed mechanics after two attempts.[29] When Longstreet graduated in 1842, he ranked fifty-fourth in a class of fifty-six. Upon his graduation from the military academy, Longstreet moved to posts in Missouri, Louisiana, Florida, and Texas. His first combat experience came in the Mexican War, where he served with distinction in numerous battles. Severely wounded during the storming of Chapultepec, Longstreet earned two promotions for his "gallant and meritorious conduct" in Mexico.[30]

The Mexican War veteran married and returned to duty in the West. There he settled into the position of army paymaster. Despite such a passive military assignment, Longstreet maintained his "buoyant" spirits, his enjoyment of life, and "an enviable capacity for food and drink."[31] The outbreak of hostilities in 1861 interrupted this pleasant existence. Longstreet tendered his resignation and traveled eastward, hoping to obtain a comparable position in the Confederate armed forces. Instead, as a West Pointer with a long and varied service record, Longstreet won a field commission as a brigadier general in June 1861.

The newly appointed general seemed amply suited for his new role. Forty years old in 1861, he was imposing at six feet two and over 200 pounds. Longstreet's chief of staff, G. Moxley Sorrel, considered him "a most striking figure . . . a soldier every inch, and very handsome, tall and well proportioned, strong and active, a superb horseman and with a unsurpassed soldierly bearing." Sorrel added that his commander was usually pleasant in his "disposition with his chums, fond of a glass, and very skilful at poker."[32]

Sadly, fortune intervened to alter Longstreet's attitude. Scarlet fever took the lives of three of his children in January 1862. The tragic deaths left Longstreet a changed man. The former gaiety yielded initially to grief, which gave way to a calm, unobtrusive self-possession. The James Longstreet who led his men toward Suffolk was a quiet, reserved man, absorbed in thought and less communicative than before. Tragedy had made him a soldier and little else.[33] In the words of one newspaper editor, Longstreet had become "an officer who devoted his whole mind to the war."[34]

As a fighter, Longstreet was both tenacious and dependable. His men called him a "Bulldog." Yet "Old Peter," as his friends knew him, had a strong temper that could be harsh and combative. At First Manassas, Sorrel saw him in a "fine rage," in which he flung his hat to the ground and uttered "bitter words" at not being allowed to pursue the routed Federals.[35] However, in the manner of his day, Longstreet usually exercised strict control over his temper and generally exhibited a calm and resolute demeanor. His physical capacity continued to be significant. Arthur Fremantle recorded, "The iron endurance of General Longstreet is most extraordinary: he seems to require neither food nor sleep."[36]

After the first Confederate victory at Manassas, Longstreet received a promotion to major general. He then saw service on the Peninsula and in the Seven Days Battles, where he turned in a solid performance. Longstreet's efforts assured him of General Lee's support and confidence, which he confirmed at Second Manassas with a timely counterattack that destroyed the Union left flank. In Lee's first invasion of the North, Longstreet earned both his commander's enduring admiration and a new nickname—"Lee's War Horse"—with tenacious fighting in the fields adjoining Antietam Creek. Following the Maryland campaign, Longstreet participated in the battle of Fredericksburg where his men easily smashed repeated frontal assaults against their position behind the stone wall of Marye's Heights. By this time James Longstreet was a lieutenant general, having been, only two years earlier, an army paymaster. Now, in the spring of 1863, an opportunity for independent command awaited him. Longstreet seemed prepared to make the most of it.[37]

Longstreet enjoyed other advantages in the upcoming campaign as well. He would be working with officers with whom he was already quite familiar. One of these men was a thirty-eight-year-old Virginian named George Edward Pickett. Tall and thin, Pickett wore his auburn hair in ringlets and sported a goatee. For all his panache, it was his hair that caught the attention of others. Sorrel noted, "Long ringlets flowed loosely over his shoulders, trimmed and highly perfumed."[38] Years later Longstreet recalled Pickett's "glossy hair worn almost to his shoulders in curly waves of wondrous pulchritude."[39] There was no doubt that he was picturesque. In contrast to his reserved chief, Pickett was also impulsive and romantic. He was a widower who had been revitalized by the love of a young woman not half his age.[40]

Despite their temperamental differences, Pickett shared many attributes with Longstreet. Born in Richmond on January 28, 1825, he also attended West Point. Pickett's conduct while there was an exaggeration of Longstreet's. Before his graduation the young cadet garnered an impressive four full pages of demerits. When he graduated in 1846, Pickett was dead last in his class.[41] Again like Longstreet, Pickett served in the Mexican War. He, too, participated in the storming of Chapultepec, where he took the regimental colors from the badly wounded Longstreet to become the first soldier to scale the parapet and hoist the flag over the fortress. He received one of his two Mexican War–related brevets in response to this action.[42]

Once the fighting ended, Pickett served on the Texas frontier. He married in 1851 but lost his wife later in the same year.[43] Five years later Pickett transferred to the Washington Territory. With a small force of U.S. Army regulars, he received additional praise for his part in preventing a British landing on disputed San Juan Island in 1859. The approach of hostilities in 1861 presented the Virginian with a dilemma not unlike that of Paymaster Longstreet. However, Pickett had little difficulty in making a decision. He tendered his resignation from the Old Army and offered his services to his native state and new country. Obtaining a colonelcy in July 1861, Pickett was a brigadier general by early 1862.

As one of General Longstreet's brigade commanders, Pickett fought with distinction during the Seven Days Battles. The colorful officer fell at Gaines's Mill with a severe wound but recovered to rejoin his command after Lee's first invasion of the North. Promoted to major general in October 1862, Pickett participated two months later in the repulse of Burnside's men before the stone wall of Fredericksburg.[44]

While recovering in Richmond from his Gaines's Mill wound, Pickett received at least two visitors of some import. One was President Jefferson Davis, who wished him a speedy recovery; the other was LaSalle Corbell.[45] Sallie was the dashing Virginian's dearest love. A native of Chuckatuck, a small village in Nansemond County not far from Suffolk, she was pretty and vivacious. Before 1863 was gone, the fifteen-year-old would become General George Pickett's "child bride of the Confederacy."[46] In the meantime Pickett wrote to her as often as time and circumstances would permit. In one of these letters, written in February 1863, he hinted at the upcoming Suffolk campaign. "Perhaps, sweetheart, perhaps I say," Pickett intoned romantically, "you will see your soldier sooner than you think."[47] The two shared a deep-seated love, which would greatly affect the general's performance before Suffolk.

James Longstreet's other principal lieutenant was John Bell Hood. A Kentuckian by birth and a Texan by choice, Hood was his superior's physical equal. Six foot two with a long, grave face and sad blue eyes, Hood's most telling feature was his voice. Edward Pollard observed, with journalistic flair, "He was remarkable for a powerful melodious voice, that rang out words of command as with the blast of a trumpet, and never failed to be heard in the storm of battle."[48]

Like Pickett, Hood stood in contrast temperamentally to Longstreet. Hood biographer Richard O'Conner noted this difference.Whereas Longstreet was "inclined to deliberation," "Hood was all for flying into action." Longstreet was too realistic (even pessimistic), too cautious, and too ponderous for Hood. Hood was brave, ambitious, and rash to the point of recklessness. Though relations were not always harmonious between the two men and on occasion sparks did fly, nevertheless there was an element of mutual respect between them.[49]

Despite their differences in temperament, the backgrounds of the two officers were generally similar. Born on June 28, 1831, Hood entered West Point in 1849. Like his superior, Hood found academic life at the military academy difficult at best. He struggled in both his studies and his conduct. In his senior year the cadet came dangerously close to being expelled as a result of the demerits he had gathered. When Hood graduated in 1853, he ranked forty-fourth out of fifty-two.[50]

Hood's military career began in California. He then transferred to one of the two newly created cavalry regiments in 1855 and duty on the Texas frontier. Hood found the service pleasant, despite being wounded in an Indian engagement. The young officer found himself drawn toward a strong association with Texas and the South. Moreover, Hood was able to renew his acquaintance with Robert E. Lee, who had been superintendent of West Point while Hood was there. This association, particularly for Hood, would play a fundamental role in shaping his mental attitude during the Suffolk campaign.

In 1861 Hood resigned his commission and received an appointment as a lieutenant on April 17. Promotions followed in rapid succession: captain, major, lieutenant colonel, colonel, and then, on March 2, 1862, brigadier general. Hood's rise was nothing short of phenomenal for its swiftness; just over thirty years old, he had advanced from first lieutenant to brigadier general in slightly less than a year.

Hood's initial combat record confirmed the wisdom of these early promotions. His troops were hard fighters who earned a reputation for being in the thickest action. Furthermore, Hood had the luck of performing well before important audiences. As Richard McMurry has suggested, "It had been his good fortune to fight his battles under the eyes of the three ranking commanders of the army—Lee at Gaines's Mill, Longstreet at Second Manassas, and Jackson at Antietam."[51]

Yet, like Pickett, Hood had romantic and social distractions. Whenever in close proximity to the capital, he attended social functions in the city. The gallant Texan appeared at the most socially important parties: those of President and Mrs. Davis and of General Joseph E. Johnston's wife. He knew that laurels could be won in the ballroom as well as the battlefield.[52]

Moreover, during the spring of 1863, Hood first met and "surrendered" to Sally "Buck" Preston. His combat prowess was no match for this "sophisticated, cosmopolitan young belle."[53] The would-be suitor was so awestruck by her presence that he could not resist a last look and a comment to a friend, Dr. John Darby. As he rode off, she hurried over and eagerly inquired what the departing soldier had said. Darby replied, "Only a horse compliment— he is a Kentuckian, you know. He says, 'You stand on your feet like a thoroughbred.'"[54] There is no record of her reaction, but clearly Hood was in the height of infatuation. Later, when his troops sat entrenched on the outskirts of Suffolk, he pined for Buck Preston and the exciting life of Richmond.

These were the men who would comprise the Confederate leadership core when their troops crossed the Blackwater. Despite their common military backgrounds, Longstreet, Pickett, and Hood shared few temperamental characteristics and differed significantly in most. But as Longstreet approached southeastern Virginia, he had more to worry him than just his immediate subordinates or the details of a military operation. Longstreet suddenly found himself thrust into the command of an entire department, much of which effectively lay outside his reach. The department, of which he assumed command on February 26, consisted of eastern Virginia from Richmond to the coast, as well as the entire state of North Carolina. Though nominally one department, Longstreet's new command was too large for one man to control effectively and was practically three separate subdepartments. Each of these subdepartments had an individual commander, who was responsible to the department commander.[55]

Major General Arnold Elzey commanded the Department of Richmond, which incorporated all of the city's defenses north of the James River. Major General Samuel G. French commanded the Department of Southern Virginia. This department consisted of the area east of Powhatan County and south of the James, including the Blackwater-Suffolk line. Major General Daniel H. Hill had the unenviable authority over the largest of the subdepartments—the Department of North Carolina. He was responsible for that entire state, already threatened by Federal invasions via the coast and the irascible will of Governor Zebulon Vance. Although mostly outside of Longstreet's future zone of operations, Hill's command would never leave the "War Horse" free to wage war at Suffolk.[56]

Civilians throughout much of Virginia were facing their own challenges, particularly from food shortages and a crippling inflation rate.[57] In the spring of 1863, bread riots erupted across the South. President Davis had to quell one such riot in Richmond personally.[58] Tension filled the Confederate capital, causing an officer in Lee's army to tell his wife on April 5, 1863, "Bread, alias plundering, riots are becoming common, some of the rioters in Richmond will probably get sick of it before they get through with it."[59]

These conditions affected soldiers as well. In January 1863 Lee explained to Secretary Seddon: "As far as I can learn, we have now about one week's supply [of provisions]. . . . After that is exhausted, I know not whence further supplies can be drawn. The question of provisioning the army is becoming one of greater difficulty every day."[60] Nor was the situation likely to improve in the foreseeable future, with a planting season, not a harvest, pending.

Other necessities were lacking as well. Quartermaster items such as shoes and blankets for the soldiers were in critically short supply, with even the reserves being depleted.[61] Thousands of soldiers were without boots, shoes, or blankets. The shortage of shoes was so critical that Longstreet had to detail eighty men from his command to the quartermaster general in Richmond as shoemakers.[62] Lee also had to divert men from military operations to facilitate the gathering of provisions and supplement the government agents in collecting cattle.[63]

A shortage of draft animals and particularly artillery and cavalry horses threatened the effectiveness of the army as a fighting unit. The lack of forage menaced those animals spared from the fighting with starvation. By February 1863 the situation had reached "crisis proportions," and Lee was forced "to scatter his cavalry so widely to subsist the animals as to render it almost useless."[64] Lee also realized that working the horses on insufficient nourishment would cause them to be "incapacitated for duty in the spring, when their services will be more required." He understood the implications for the rest of the army should this happen. "Without forage for the horses, provisions for the infantry cannot be transported, nor can efficient means be adopted to expel the enemy at this inclement period."[65]

Most of Virginia was showing the effects of almost two years of war. The state had supported major armies from both sides, complete with their full complements of men, horses, mules, and other animals, as well as its own civilian population, which swelled with non-Virginians who flocked to the state when Richmond became the capital of the Confederate States. These facts, coupled with the difficult weather conditions and questionable rail transportation, made much of the state a difficult supply base from which to operate.

It was into this troublesome atmosphere that James Longstreet traveled to Richmond on February 18, 1863, to assume command of the two divisions sent there by Lee. Unfortunately for him, things were about to get worse. In assuming his position Longstreet came under the orders of four different individuals: President Davis, General Lee, Secretary of War Seddon, and Adjutant General Samuel Cooper. This complicated the chain of command under which Longstreet would have to function, particularly if the missions each man assigned him were to prove incompatible. Furthermore, he would be expected to accomplish all four of these separate and distinct missions simultaneously, and in the midst of a military offensive against a stubborn and aggressive foe.[66]

The first of these missions was the protection of Richmond from the southern and southeastern approaches. President Davis initiated this mission himself, in response to the arrival of the Federal 9th Corps on the Virginia peninsula. This was the reason for the transfer of Longstreet and two of his divisions from the Army of Northern Virginia to the Richmond vicinity. The arrival of these men in the area fulfilled this mission and safeguarded the capital. It was with surety that Seddon could write to Lee,

"General Longstreet is here, and under his able guidance of such troops no one entertains a doubt as to the entire safety of the capital."[67]

Lee was responsible for Longstreet's second mission. He asked his subordinate commander to be prepared to rejoin the Army of Northern Virginia, if necessary. Although Lee expected Joseph Hooker and his army to remain in winter quarters in the near future, he was wary of any surprise offensive the Union commander might undertake. In early February he wrote his daughter Agnes and mentioned Hooker's recent activities. "He is playing the Chinese game. Trying what frightening will do. He runs out his guns, starts his wagons & troops up & down the river, & creates an excitement generally. Our men look on in wonder, give a cheer, & all again subsides 'in statu quo ante bellum.'"[68] General Lee may not have been frightened by his adversary's antics, but he was watching them very closely. Should they turn out to be more than just frolics, Lee wanted Longstreet and his veterans back with him.

At one time or another, Secretary Seddon, General Lee, and General Cooper defined Longstreet's third mission. They wanted him to drive the Federal forces out of their garrisons in southeastern Virginia and northern North Carolina, or at the very least to hold them there while his men gathered and secured all food stocks, forage, and other quartermaster supplies that could be found. To the Southerners these regions represented largely untapped areas under enemy occupation. Obtaining supplies from them would not only benefit the empty coffers of the Army of Northern Virginia but also deprive the Union forces of these same products.

On April 16, 1863, Lee expressed an additional motive in a wire to President Davis: his desire to "assume the aggressive by the 1st of May." The Confederate commander cherished an elaborate vision. Before Hooker could assume the offensive, Lee wanted to clear the Shenandoah Valley and invade Northern territory again. In this way he not only expected to draw the Army of the Potomac out of Virginia but also anticipated aiding other Confederate commands. He explained to the president, "I believe greater relief would in this way be afforded to the armies in Middle Tennessee and on the Carolina coast than by any other method."

However, General Lee needed to accumulate adequate stores of supplies in order to undertake this second grand invasion of the North. It was with this scheme in mind that he supported Longstreet's mission of gathering food and supplies. Lee told the president: "I had hoped by General Longstreet's operations . . . to obtain sufficient subsistence to commence the movement. . . . It must, therefore depend upon the success of these operations unless other means can be devised for procuring subsistence."[69]

Clearly, Lee was contemplating an invasion of the North at the beginning of May. He expected that such a move would forestall Hooker and preserve the initiative for himself. Had his plan materialized in this way, Lee would have invaded the Union a month earlier than he actually did, while Stonewall Jackson still lived and Joseph Hooker remained in command of the opposing army. A battle of Gettysburg might never have transpired or at least would have featured a different lineup of leadership and abilities. In this light Longstreet's operations in southeastern Virginia take on a new meaning, not only for what they accomplished or failed to accomplish but for what they almost accomplished.

Finally, Secretary Seddon explicitly and General Lee implicitly dictated Longstreet's fourth mission: if possible, he was to capture the Federal outpost at Suffolk. By doing so, Longstreet could clear a relatively untapped area of badly needed foodstuffs and supplies, as well as capture a sizable Union post. Suffolk's capture would be a handsome prelude to Lee's plans to invade the Union, for it would enhance Confederate morale and divert Hooker's attention.

Thus it was that Longstreet and his command prepared to cross the Blackwater River. He would have to juggle these diverse and distinct missions, while holding the enemy at bay. At the same time "Old Peter" had to confront the reasons for these missions: the perceived threat of the Union 9th Corps in Newport News, the Confederates' need for food and supplies, President Davis's determination to protect Richmond, Lee's desire for the return of his command in the event of a Union offensive, and the commanding general's plan to invade the North a second time.

FIG. 1 Wartime Suffolk as it appeared in *Harper's Weekly*, May 2, 1863. In the foreground is the Providence Church or Windsor Road over the Nansemond River.

FIG. 2 The "Ladies of Suffolk" presented this battle flag to the Marion Rangers, Company A of the 16th Virginia Infantry. It features the commonwealth of Virginia's motto, "Sic Semper Tyrannis."

FIG. 3 William Dorsey Pender, a North Carolinian, was stationed in Suffolk early in the conflict.

FIG. 4 Union cavalry commander Charles C. Dodge rode into Suffolk at the head of the New York Mounted Rifles in May 1862, claiming the town for the Union.

FIG. 5 Samuel Spear led his 11th Pennsylvania Cavalry on frequent expeditions to the Blackwater River and helped to keep General Peck advised of Southern activities in the region.

FIG. 6 Union major general John James Peck built a formidable line of defenses and stubbornly resisted Longstreet's assaults in the spring of 1863.

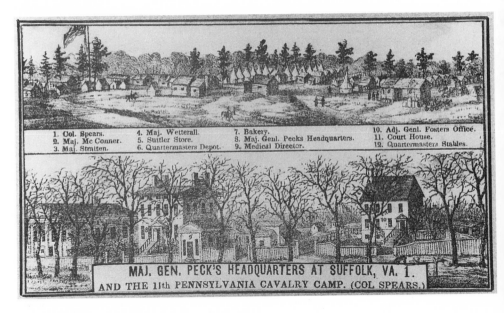

1. Col. Spears.   4. Maj. Wetterall.   7. Bakery.   10. Adj. Genl. Fosters Office.
2. Maj. Mc Conner. 5. Suttler Store.   8. Maj. Genl. Pecks Headquarters.   11. Court House.
3. Maj. Stratten. 6. Quartermasters Depot.   9. Medical Director.   12. Quartermasters Stables.

MAJ. GEN. PECK'S HEADQUARTERS AT SUFFOLK, VA. 1.
AND THE 11th PENNSYLVANIA CAVALRY CAMP. (COL SPEARS.)

FIG. 7 Peck's headquarters at Suffolk, part 1.

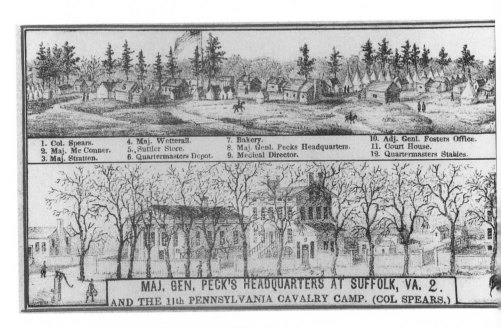

1. Col. Spears.   4. Maj. Wetterall.   7. Bakery.   10. Adj. Genl. Fosters Office.
2. Maj. Mc Conner. 5. Suttler Store.   8. Maj. Genl. Pecks Headquarters.   11. Court House.
3. Maj. Stratten. 6. Quartermasters Depot.   9. Medical Director.   12. Quartermasters Stables.

MAJ. GEN. PECK'S HEADQUARTERS AT SUFFOLK, VA. 2.
AND THE 11th PENNSYLVANIA CAVALRY CAMP. (COL SPEARS.)

FIG. 8 Peck's headquarters at Suffolk, part 2.

FIG. 9 Fiery Virginia newspaperman and congressman Roger
Atkinson Pryor hastened back
from collecting souvenirs from
Fort Sumter, to accept a field
command that included men
from southeastern Virginia. On
the Blackwater River line by 1862,
he tangled with Union forces
under Michael Corcoran at
Deserted House in January 1863.

FIG. 10 After his en-
counter with Pryor
at Deserted House,
Michael Corcoran,
a volatile Irishman,
served at Suffolk dur-
ing Longstreet's 1863
campaign.

FIG. 11 Lt. Samuel Blood of the 6th Massachusetts wounded himself in the foot as he cleaned his gun at Suffolk. Then he let the Confederates do it for him at Deserted House.

FIG. 12 James Longstreet, Lee's "War Horse," came to Suffolk in 1863 to fulfill a number of missions, especially to gather badly needed supplies for the Army of Northern Virginia. Later criticism suggested that he was using his independent command at Suffolk for his own purposes.

FIG. 13 *left* George Edward Pickett was deeply in love and badly distracted at Suffolk. FIG. 14 *right* John Bell Hood also was distracted by love during the 1863 Suffolk campaign.

FIG. 15 Col. Edgar Kimball of the 9th New York met his end at Suffolk when he confronted General Corcoran at a picket post.

FIG. 16 George Washington Getty was clearly the best general on either side in the Suffolk campaign.

FIG. 17 Samuel Phillips Lee, a relative of Confederate general Robert E. Lee, served with distinction in the U.S. Navy. Cooperating with the army, he and his subordinates captured Fort Huger and its battery on April 19, 1863.

FIG. 18 Roswell Hawkes Lamson (*standing*) and William Barker Cushing (*seated*), S. P. Lee's subordinates, complemented each other very well.

FIG. 19 While facing General Longstreet at Suffolk, General Peck sent out probes to test Confederate strength, including this one on May 1, 1863, when the 99th New York crossed the South Quay Bridge.

FIG. 20 On May 3, 1863,
Col. Benjamin Ringold
of the 103d New York fell
at the head of his troops
assaulting the Confederate
works. He lingered into
the night before dying
of his wounds.

FIG. 21. *left* In his letters to his sweetheart, Capt. David F. Dobie, 118th New
York, explained his role in a lightning raid on Suffolk designed to capture Con-
federates visiting their homes on furlough.   FIG. 22 *right* Wiry and combative,
William Mahone served as president of the Norfolk and Petersburg Railroad
Company before the war. His actions at the Crater helped the Confederates
retain Petersburg until April 1865.

"A sudden, vigorous attack on Suffolk
would doubtless give you that place."

Lee to Longstreet, March 27, 1863

⊰ 6 ⊱ *The "War Horse" Jockeys for Provisions*

THE COMPLEXION OF THE SITUATION, FOR JAMES LONGSTREET AT least, changed temporarily in mid-March. Perhaps sensing the long-anticipated Federal offensive, Lee advised him to begin preparations for returning to the Rappahannock.[1] Longstreet responded that Hood's men were being maintained along the railroad for that purpose. He also proposed to return to Lee personally, "unless there is a fine opportunity to strike a decided blow here, in which case I think I had better act promptly and trust to your being able to hold the force in your front in check until I can join you."[2]

Federal cavalry crossed the Rappahannock on March 17. Longstreet continued to quibble over which troops he could send back to Lee. He also stubbornly insisted that Lee should be content to hold the line against Hooker while the Confederates drove "the enemy out of North Carolina." Longstreet stressed the necessity of obtaining badly needed supplies, a fact of which Lee was certainly aware, and observed that any troops sent back to Lee would further tax the supply system and thus do more harm than good.[3] However, Longstreet's arguments demonstrated the strategic limitations of his thinking in this instance. Clearly, Joseph Hooker's Army of the Potomac presented a greater threat to Richmond and the Confederacy than the scattered Union commands of southeastern Virginia and North Carolina.

Lee responded by requesting that all three generals and both divisions return to the Army of Northern Virginia. The "War Horse" reluctantly but obediently moved Hood's division back toward the Rappahannock. Hood's Texans received their orders early on March 18. They marched through Richmond to the small village of Ashland and halted for the night. On March 19 Lee canceled the alarm. The crisis had passed with the repulse of the Union cavalry at Kelly's Ford. Both Lee and Longstreet could now breathe a little easier. Hood's Texans could not. After having made the exhausting twenty-five-mile march to Ashland, they were blanketed by snow at their night encampment on the nineteenth. The next day, the Confederates retraced their steps back to Richmond.[4]

The communications that ensued from this time between Lee and Longstreet throughout the rest of the Suffolk campaign have raised questions about the relationship enjoyed by the two generals. Did Lee give Longstreet too much leeway in his orders? Did Longstreet argue with his chief out of self-promoting ambition? Did Lee and Longstreet work well together?[5]

To be sure, the two generals had a unique relationship. There is no doubt that they enjoyed a mutual trust and respect. In his memoirs Longstreet took pains to explain that he and Lee maintained "relations of confidence and esteem, official and personal." He further noted that Lee invited his views on strategy and general policy, often using him as a devil's advocate.[6] It could well have been due to such invitations that Longstreet was not averse to stating his opinions plainly or offering alternative views to his chief. It may also have been that by promoting the case of his closeness to Lee, Longstreet hoped to mute the growing criticism he felt from those who disapproved of his postwar politics or his relatively mild critique of Lee's generalship.[7]

Despite his unique role in Lee's top command structure, or perhaps because of it, Longstreet had a special affection for Lee. Edward Pollard, editor of the Richmond *Examiner,* observed that Longstreet's relations with Lee "were not only pleasant and cordial, but affectionate to an almost brotherly degree."[8] Colonel Fremantle recorded a similar impression: "The relations between him [Lee] and Longstreet are quite touching—they are almost always together. . . . [I]t is impossible to please Longstreet more than by praising Lee."[9] Whenever circumstances permitted, he camped near Lee.[10] It was Lee who greeted Longstreet affectionately at Sharpsburg and bestowed upon him the sobriquet "War Horse." Still, Longstreet did not have the degree of affection for Lee that others, such as John Bell Hood, maintained, and it was this difference in degrees that would be magnified during Longstreet's campaign into southeastern Virginia.

Whatever later critics might conclude, Longstreet obeyed the recall order, but he felt no compunction in offering his commander an alternative point of view. His suggestion that Lee hold the line of the Rappahannock with the troops he had on hand may have been unrealistic strategically, but it was hardly irresponsible. A recent study of the operations along the Rappahannock line in late 1862 and early 1863 has suggested that this "Dare Mark" line had significant psychological power for the troops and commanders on both sides.[11]

Nevertheless, Longstreet has taken criticism for seemingly challenging Lee's authority for his own benefit. Biographers H. J. Eckenrode and Bryan Conrad have used Longstreet's statements to demonstrate what they believe was the general's unbridled ambition. These biographers particularly cite Longstreet's calls for more men prior to the Suffolk campaign as evidence that he actually intended to make himself the premier Confederate commander in Virginia. They argue that Longstreet sought to elevate his status by diminishing the size of Lee's army, while correspondingly increasing his own.[12]

However, it should be remembered that this was James Longstreet's first command independent of Robert E. Lee. He would be making the decisions in it, even if he sought advice from his mentor, as he did. He would be responsible for the operation as it unfolded and accountable to his commander, the war department, and President Davis for its outcome. It was only natural that under these circumstances he would be even more cautious than normal. In addition, the intelligence system upon which he depended in planning the campaign was largely unsatisfactory and was prone to distort numbers by inflating them, thus feeding his caution and his desire for more men. Sufficient evidence to support the Eckenrode and Conrad thesis convincingly continues to elude other Longstreet biographers and students of this campaign.

Lee biographer Douglas Southall Freeman thought that he was culpable for giving Longstreet too much discretion and for permitting his lieutenant to "browbeat" him.[13] Freeman noted that during the time he corresponded with Longstreet, General Lee was quite ill. "He had not been sleeping well, and in some way he contracted a serious throat infection which settled into what seems to have been a pericarditis. His arms, his chest, and his back were attacked with sharp paroxysms of pain."[14] Lee was irritated at this untimely deterioration in his health. "I fear I may be unable in the approaching campaign to go through the work before me," he complained to his wife. A bit later, with an uncharacteristic self-indulgence, he wrote, "Old age & sorrow is wearing me away, & constant anxiety & labour, day & night, leaves me but little repose."[15]

The symptoms got worse before they improved. The doctors, "tapping me all over like an old steam boiler," confined the general to strict bedrest for a time, to which the patient reluctantly acquiesced. General Lee regained his health in time to lead the Army of Northern Virginia onto the battlefield of Chancellorsville. Nevertheless, as Lee biographer Emory Thomas explained, Lee "never completely recovered from the illness of March and April 1863."[16]

Longstreet may have unwittingly taken advantage of a sick man. Yet Lee held his ground in calling Longstreet's men back during the Kelly's Ford scare. Lee was unlikely to allow any subordinate to sway him from a course to which his own mind was already set. Furthermore, it was in the interest of Lee's grand strategy of carrying the war once again to Northern soil for Longstreet to remain in southeastern Virginia and gather supplies. Thus, if Longstreet felt that his operations required more men, Lee had to consider that notion at the very least.

"Old Peter" was not an insensitive subordinate. On March 19 he candidly observed to Lee, "I know that it is the habit with individuals in all armies to represent their own position as the most important ones, and it may be that this feeling is operating with me." This explanation recalled his usual role as Lee's devil's advocate. "I am not prompted by any desire to do so, or to attempt to do, great things. I only wish to do what I regard as my duty—give you the full benefit of my views."[17] It was left to Lee to accept or reject those views.

Instead, Lee kept his "War Horse" in limbo. On one hand, he continually directed Longstreet to turn all of his "energies to obtaining supplies, subsistence, and forage for the army." On the other hand, Lee expected his subordinate to keep Hood's men where they could easily be moved to support the Army of Northern Virginia.[18] This left an already indecisive Longstreet even less sure of his position. He now considered the possibility of a campaign against Suffolk to be "advantageous." However, to undertake such an operation, he suggested that "at least one division in addition to what we have would be necessary."[19]

Lee balked at the request, unconvinced that his lieutenant really needed all the men he desired. He certainly did not expect that Longstreet would need two divisions to gather supplies. Yet, though Lee preferred for Longstreet to hold both Pickett and Hood in reserve, he tacitly approved an aggressive course for his subordinate: "If, however, you see an opportunity of dealing a damaging blow, or of driving him [the enemy] from any important positions, do not be idle, but act promptly. If circumstances render it impossible or disadvantageous for you to rejoin this army when attacked we must withdraw toward you, if we cannot resist alone." Lee was expressing the fullest measure of confidence in his "War Horse." He asked Longstreet to keep him advised but left operations in the area under the authority and judgment of that officer. The only advice Lee offered "Old Peter" was to keep the "general plan of operations" in mind as he conducted his own campaigns. The commanding general was prepared to support his lieutenant provided such assistance did not jeopardize the conduct of the war as a whole.[20]

While this frenetic exchange of communications occurred between Longstreet and the Confederate high command in Richmond and on the Rappahannock involving his preparations for a movement across the Blackwater line, the people of the region, Southern civilians and Northern soldiers alike, went on with their lives and their routines. According to Solomon Lenfest, stationed in Suffolk with the 6th Massachusetts, "February has passed quickly and quietly away without any event of importance to disturb the monotony of soldier life."[21] As March wore on, he had little to note in his diary besides the usual picket and guard duty, drill and review, prayer meetings and chapel. The exception was an incident he recorded on March 6.

It was unusual to have a general appear on the picket line, but that is what Lenfest thought he witnessed about midday on March 6. "General Foster and Col. Folansbee came out" to where he was standing watch, and a lieutenant instructed him, along with another soldier, to accompany the officers. The pickets "escorted" the entourage "through the woods about 2 miles to a house where it was suspected the rebs got information." While Lenfest stood guard, the three officers went in and "pumped the 2 women who were the only persons at home, but without any particular gain of information."[22]

General Peck was maintaining his usual high level of alertness, but it is unlikely that Lenfest saw "General Foster" at Suffolk. Major General John G. Foster, commanding the Department of North Carolina, was headquartered in New Bern. More likely the officer was Colonel Robert S. Foster, commanding the brigade in which the 6th served, accompanied by Colonel Albert S. Follansbee of the 6th. At any rate, a Suffolk resident recalled that "the Yankees would from time to time search the citizen's house to see if any stray Confederate had come to spy on them."[23]

Sometimes Peck's vigilance paid off. On March 6 he reported to Major General Dix that three Union noncommissioned officers had successfully "passed themselves for Confederates and had the freedom of the house of a leading rebel near Windsor, from whom they picked up many items." The intelligence suggested that 20,000 to 25,000 Southerners now stood poised on the Blackwater line under the command of "a new general" awaiting the signal to cross the river. Even more disturbing, Peck learned how thoroughly his opponents were gathering information on his command. "Their spies knew all about Suffolk," he explained, forwarding their numbers to Dix as confirmation.[24]

Prisoners and deserters brought in by scouting expeditions confirmed that Confederate forces were assembling on the Blackwater. Reports from Southern newspapers indicated that James Longstreet was at Petersburg in command of a new military department. It was becoming apparent that John Peck's tendency to worry was not without cause. Peck and Dix cautiously developed a special code for use in some of their communications, hoping to secure them from any prying Southern eyes. Private Lenfest would have been proud to know that they gave Suffolk the name "Boston."[25]

Peck kept his patrols active as well. On St. Patrick's Day he forwarded the news that a ten-man patrol of the troubled New York Mounted Rifles had "captured the noted forager, Brown, and 6 men between Windsor and the Blackwater." Peck viewed the capture of Brown as a coup, because he had "managed many of the supply trains of General Pryor."[26] It was also an important act of redemption for the Mounted Rifles. Having lost at least twenty deserters, "many to the enemy," and with a commander in whom Dix no longer had confidence, the unit must have earned some measure of relief and pride from the operation.[27]

The day brought considerably less fortune for a second Union expedition near Franklin. Colonel Samuel Spear led the ever-active 11th Pennsylvania Cavalry on an ill-fated expedition to the Blackwater. Attempting to gain information on Confederate strength in the area, he approached the river near Franklin. Capturing a lieutenant commanding the Southern pickets, the Northern cavalrymen chased the others into their lines. Then, impetuously and foolishly, Spear dispatched a force to charge the main Confederate works. The Southerners repulsed two attacks with some loss to the Federals.

Spear then brought up a battery and blazed away at the Confederate position before withdrawing.[28]

Confederate James R. Boulware noted in his diary that the victory might have been greater than it was, a common lament of the fighting men on both sides. However, this time it was not the commanders but the cavalry who were to blame. "Our cowardly cavalry refused to charge them after they (the Yankees) had been thrown into confusion the second time or we might have taken the whole of them," the South Carolinian wrote with contempt.[29] In a letter to his brother, Boulware continued his tirade against the North Carolina cavalry. "The cowardly cavalry came along and were showing our boys some pieces of shell they had picked up,—saying it was Yankee shell.—Our boys laughed at them terribly and told them we had bumped against too many [pieces of shell] to notice them."[30]

Another Confederate, John M. White, concurred. Writing his sister on the twenty-second, he took his own swipe at the North Carolina cavalry. "Last week a Regiment of Yankee Cavalry with four pieces of Artillery made a bold charge on our cavalry pickets early in the morning driving them in at a run (which is not unusual) [and] following so close upon their heels as to prevent the Infantry pickets from firing" at the Federals for fear of hitting their own men. White was particularly unkind to the junior officer who had managed to get himself captured. "The Lieutenant in charge of our Cavalry outpost fell from his horse and was taken prisoner," the South Carolinian remarked, adding caustically that he was "the only man we lost."[31]

Northern accounts of the expedition varied in their assessments, although tellingly very little appeared on paper about it. The writer of a regimental history of the 11th Pennsylvania later concluded, "The colonel may not have been in proper mental condition when he ordered these charges which caused the loss of twenty-eight men killed and wounded, proving that the enemy were determined to resist the passage of the Blackwater at this point."[32] Yet Spear may have been the unwitting victim of new Confederate weaponry at the scene. Accustomed to striking at soldiers who could not do him much harm without deploying artillery, he found himself in a fight with men with improved arms. As one of the Confederates observed, "The prisoners we took expressed much surprise at our Enfield rifles and stated that they fully expected to take the post."[33] Spear, hardly shy in testing Rebel strength anyway, probably did not realize what his men would face until it was too late.

Bold but reckless, the skirmishing provided little to compensate for the unnecessary casualties it caused. One officer, Lieutenant Samuel Monday, received a mortal wound in the attack, while another, Lieutenant G. B. Knight, was unhorsed and fell into Confederate hands. The losses would have been greater had the Southern artillery pieces not misfired during the second charge.[34] General Dix tried to varnish the action by insisting to General-in-Chief Henry Halleck on the eighteenth, "Our loss is trifling."[35] They buried Lieutenant Monday a few days later.[36]

These raids left scars on the local communities that the participants increasingly considered badges of distinction. One Union soldier wrote poetically, "We took our departure and Windsor was itself again (with variations). To the people of Windsor, we are 'thought lost to sight, [but] to memory *dear!*'" This warrior proudly cataloged the effect of the Union expedition: "We've burned their fences, destroyed their railroad and thus lessened the value of their property." The Federals left behind only camp refuse that included "enough old papers to provide the south with literary matter for five years to come."[37]

March 17 also brought a flurry of activity in the Union camps at Suffolk, particularly among the Irish troops. Brigadier General Michael Corcoran and his men demonstrated a particular zest in celebration. "Gathering all the horses he can, he mounts them with his best riders; mounts all the buglers he can obtain," one witness recalled. "Then joined by his whole staff . . . [Corcoran] brings the whole cavalcade in full uniform, bugles sounding furiously and the mounted bands playing 'St. Patrick's Day in the Morning.'" The man considered the drama a "stirring show" and noted that the infantry regiments soon turned out in a "grand procession" of their own "through camp."

It was all good fun, although in their exuberance some of the Union soldiers demonstrated that racism knew no bounds. Seizing one of the 13th New Hampshire's black cooks, some of Corcoran's celebrants sought to humiliate the man for their own enjoyment. They stripped him of most of his clothes and began "painting him in patches, bars and stripes, yellow, green, red, blue—every color they can muster, and then turn him loose." The terrified victim of this treatment ran back to his camp, "as if for dear life, scared half out of his wits, and looking worse than the evil one."[38] As far as the record suggests, such harassment went uncorrected, because few Union commanders felt any compunction to appease black victims, especially against white perpetrators.

White Southerners in the region generally could count on better treatment, although they continued to display their anger when pressed. As one Suffolk resident had to admit, the Federals "did not interfere seriously with its people," who remained "quiet" for the most part. Nevertheless, the Union

presence was a constant reminder of military occupation and, as such, provoked its share of angry outbursts.[39]

People in the surrounding area, particularly those living between Suffolk
and the Blackwater, were subject to tangible examples of Union might as
well. One woman wrote her sister from Chuckatuck on March 9 of the
appearance of Union cavalry. "They did not steal as much as we had
expected they would," she had to confess, "although they went into the hen-
houses at Mr. T's and stole fowls and [eggs]." Still, she could not bring herself to express less than total hostility toward them. "I never had such
indignant feelings toward them as I had yesterday when they came in flaunt-
ing *their flags* and looking as if the very earth belonged to them," she noted.
"The flag too that we once loved and reverenced to be so poluted and
despised by the foul use to which it has been applied by the vile invaders
of our lov'd, our native land."[40]

The Federals could be provoked, too, particularly by fire from Southern
guerrillas. The worst of this kind of activity seemed to occur in North
Carolina. In mid-March, Peck passed along word of guerrilla activity
"below Gatesville."[41] But such activity was not confined to the nearest
county in the neighboring state. One New Hampshire soldier in Suffolk
observed on March 24, "Our pickets go out every morning for 24 hours. . . .
The worst danger is from 'Bush-whackers,' men who pretend to be farmers in the daytime, and who shoot our pickets at night."[42] These Southern
"combatants" were just as contemptuous as the Northern "stay-at-homes"
who would not risk themselves on the battlefield, and the soldiers tried hard
to punish them for their effrontery.

Another source of irritation was the increasing efforts by the regular
Confederate forces to set ambushes for the Union reconnaissance patrols.
Confederate brigadier general Micah Jenkins, who superseded Roger Pryor
as commander on the Blackwater in early March, advised Longstreet on
the twenty-fourth that he had a plan for sending out forces for this purpose on the main roads leading to the river.[43] Apparently he succeeded in
obtaining permission, for at the end of the month Peck reported to Dix:
"Yesterday the enemy came over to the vicinity of Carrsville with one or
two regiments of infantry for the purpose of ambushcading our patrolling
parties. They were secreted in woods on both roads, about 2 miles from
this side the place." This squad managed to avoid the trap, losing only
one man in the process, but the scheme tested nerve and patience alike.[44]

Of course, all was not seething anger in southeastern Virginia. Young
people from both sides found opportunities for romance and diversion. One
Suffolk resident recalled that the town's young ladies "often repulsed" the

romantic inclinations of the Union men, but that the soldiers' "many acts of kindness," and, no doubt, their availability, "soon won some over."[45] Yet when the Union officers decided to hold a ball, it allegedly took threats against the fathers and their property to convince these ladies to attend. According to Emma Ferguson, even then many of the women got the last word by attending but refusing to dance.[46]

However, at least one of these romances threatened danger for the Federals in Suffolk. A member of the New York Mounted Rifles recorded that he and a lieutenant in the command called upon "a couple of fair young ladies whose acquaintance he had made, at an old Virginia farmhouse situated in a lovely spot on a bank of the Nansemond." The writer became disturbed when his companion began "denouncing the Yankees and extolling the Confederates." Thinking the move a tactic designed to woo the Southern women, he inquired and was "considerably shocked to hear" that the sentiments were genuine. Even so, the man dismissed his friend's "treasonous" notions as part of the latter's "disputatious" nature and refused to participate in subsequent arguments with him on the subject.

Shortly thereafter Peck assigned the two men to engineering duty on the fortifications. The lieutenant proved adept at the task, but remained as contrary as ever, and was openly dismissive of his superior officers and the Union cause. His remarks prompted the provost marshal of Suffolk to give him close attention. While under surveillance, the officer aroused further suspicion when his orderly sergeant abruptly defected to the Confederates.[47]

This desertion gave Peck reason to worry. On March 30 he nervously reported: "A sergeant of the engineers deserted Saturday night to the enemy. He has been on the [earth]works all the time and can give much valuable information."[48] According to the lieutenant's former friend, the sergeant even rode the officer's horse into Confederate lines. Apparently the officer decided not to attempt to hide his complicity by claiming that the horse had been stolen. Making matters worse, the next day the provost marshal "intercepted a letter" from the sergeant to his sister in New York which contained a note from the lieutenant "saying, that her brother had safely joined the Confederates, by whom he would be much better treated than he had been by the 'Yankees.'"

Armed with what he considered conclusive evidence against the lieutenant, the provost marshal arrested him. Trial and conviction by court-martial followed, with the officer sentenced to be "shot to death." In the end, the unwise, if not disloyal, Union officer received clemency, which allowed him to obtain a dishonorable discharge from the service. Ironically, his compatriot, the sergeant, tried to return to Union lines a year after his desertion. Apprehended by men of his own company, he stood trial and went to prison before he also was allowed to leave the army.[49]

Whatever assistance Longstreet might have gained from such knowledgeable deserters, he faced a daunting task as he poised his command to move across the Blackwater River. He alternated between the expectation of simply holding the Federals in their works and the hope of actually attacking and driving them out of Suffolk. Yet "Old Peter" had to keep at least a portion of his command ready to return to Lee if needed. Above all, he knew the Confederates desperately needed the supplies he would extract from the area, and those convoys would require protection.

Longstreet also knew the potential of the regions from which his commissary agents would draw supplies. His corps commissary, Major Raphael J. Moses, reported that supplies were abundant, but they were in areas dominated by Federal forces.[50] To gain control of them, the "War Horse" would have to attack fortified Union posts at Suffolk and at Washington and New Bern, North Carolina. Under such circumstances he understandably wanted as many men and as much assistance as he could get.

Longstreet was a talented and capable field general. Still, this was to be his operation alone; there would be no place to hide mistakes, no convenient shadow to provide obscurity. The glory or the blame would fall upon him. Perhaps for this reason "Old Peter" betrayed a lack of self-confidence in his correspondence with General Lee. He turned to the Confederate commander for firm guidance. Yet Lee was unwilling to issue direct orders himself, preferring to defer to his lieutenant because he felt that Longstreet was in the best position to judge local matters. Nevertheless Longstreet wanted a redefinition of his primary mission, more troops, and a direct order to attack Suffolk.[51]

Lee indirectly obliged his subordinate. He reiterated Longstreet's primary mission: "I consider it of the first importance to draw from the invaded districts every pound of provisions and forage we can." The commander was reluctant, however, to send any more troops from the main army. "If this army is further weakened we must retire to the line of the Annas and trust to a battle nearer Richmond for defense of the capital," he postulated. The problem was that this would expose "a broad margin of our frontier" and "renders our railroad communications more hazardous and more difficult to secure." Lee felt that by all reports the Federal forces before Longstreet were at best only equal in numbers to that officer's own forces. He was certain that the tasks set for his lieutenant could be accomplished without additional men. Furthermore, Lee advised Longstreet, "A sudden, vigorous attack on Suffolk would doubtless give you that place." But the commander left the "propriety of this step" to Longstreet.[52]

The mixed signals did little to clarify the situation. Longstreet should hold back troops. He should attack Suffolk if possible. The men should gather supplies. They must be made ready for a rapid return to the Rappahannock. With the guidance Longstreet was receiving from his trusted chief, no wonder he chose caution above all other possibilities. Longstreet had kept Hood's troops north of Petersburg, ready to march in either direction. But to have any hope of success in obtaining the needed supplies in the face of an aggressive enemy, much less of attacking a strongly defended town like Suffolk, he had to have those men with him. Thus "the War Horse" rather tentatively informed Lee that he was moving them closer to Suffolk. He acknowledged to his superior that the new position would "throw me far away from you" but considered the move "indispensable" if his supply-gathering operations were to prove successful.[53]

Pickett's and French's men already had moved south through Petersburg in early March. Some of these men continued to move on to Franklin and the Blackwater line. Others followed later in the month. Thus, by piecemeal and leisurely deployment, Longstreet's Confederates moved ever closer to Suffolk. It was the kind of careful movement of troops that illustrated that general's uncertainty, not his unbridled ambition.[54]

Inclement weather complicated these preparations. On March 20 nearly six inches of snow fell on the Suffolk area, and a much heavier snowfall blanketed the Richmond area. Cold and blustery weather pervaded southeastern Virginia throughout the first week in April. Roads remained treacherous as they first froze and then thawed.[55]

Longstreet was fortunate to have a capable commander in Micah Jenkins on the Blackwater line. Throughout the latter stage of preparations, the twenty-seven-year-old South Carolinian proved to be an effective officer. He was also well liked by the men. One of them compared him favorably to the man he had replaced, Roger Pryor. "The Genl is the complete opposite of the late commander of the 'Forces of the Blackwater'—being sociable & pleasing in his manner & address—pious & a good officer.[56] Another Confederate, bemoaning the manner in which some obtained promotion, noted that "Jenkins fought for his and deserves it."[57] Yet Jenkins's transfer to the Blackwater, and the transfer of other troops from that area, had left Pryor without a command. The fiery Virginian considered the entire affair an insult to his honor and left the region in a huff.[58]

Jenkins remained active, pushing his pickets out toward Suffolk and sending scouts to the town to obtain accurate reports of Federal strength. He continued to concoct schemes to ambush the Union cavalry patrols of Samuel Spear. He also busied himself with the security of the Blackwater line. On March 24 he wrote Longstreet, "I am working hard to make the line here impregnable."[59] Four days later, after extending his patrols, shifting units, and establishing new picket posts, Jenkins proudly observed, "This arrangement, in my judgment, renders the line of the Blackwater perfectly secure."[60]

In the meantime reports reached Lee that Burnside's 9th Corps was leaving Newport News. Federal intentions remained unclear, but because Longstreet would almost certainly face fewer Union soldiers in his push toward Suffolk, he could no longer justify his requests for more men from Lee.[61] Lee wrote, "You are . . . relieved of half the force that has been opposed to you. You will therefore be strong enough [now] to make any movement that you consider advisable." However, the Confederate commander added a word of warning. "So long as the enemy choose to remain on the defensive and covered by their intrenchments and floating batteries I fear you can accomplish but little, except to draw provisions from the invaded districts."[62] Lee proved remarkably prescient.

Longstreet added a new dimension to his campaign planning at the end of March when he asked Lee's aid in obtaining support from the Confederate navy. Longstreet believed that this assistance would be essential if he was to succeed in capturing Suffolk. "I believe with you," he wrote Lee in early April, "that a sudden vigorous attack upon Suffolk would give me that place, but I see no chance of getting the garrison unless I can get assistance from the Navy."[63] There was actually little Lee could do to facilitate matters that concerned the Confederate bureaucracy. Earlier he had warned Longstreet that any move against Suffolk would have to be accomplished by control of the Nansemond River. However, rather than involving the navy, Lee suggested that batteries of field artillery placed along the course of the river would achieve the same effect.[64]

Whatever help the navy might or might not offer him, Longstreet determined to proceed with his plans. In two distinct communications with Lee on April 4, Longstreet presented his timetable. "I hope to be able to cross the Blackwater on Wednesday [April 8] or Thursday [April 9] next and to get what supplies there are east of that stream and, if I find it possible, to make an effort to get that garrison [Peck's]." He projected that the entire operation would require two weeks. Longstreet then inquired, "Can we afford to consume this time and reach you before the enemy can move?"[65] Lee could only answer that he did not know when Hooker would advance, although indications showed that he was prepared to do so once the roads dried sufficiently.[66]

The movement into the region promised to be difficult. Longstreet summarized some of the obstacles for Lee in early April. "I do not deem it practicable to make movements concealed in any portion of this country," he explained. "In the first place I do not suppose the enemy so very careless as to admit of it," which Peck had demonstrated time and again. "Second, there are many people in the eastern counties who sympathize with the opposite cause," he noted, particularly of the counties of North Carolina east of the Chowan River from which he planned to obtain supplies. Finally, there was the question of "our transportation," which Longstreet considered "most indifferent." This latter problem would be the most difficult to overcome, "rendering slow movements almost impracticable; rapid movements out of the question."[67]

"Old Peter" was sending his chief a gentle warning. Once the commissary and quartermaster trains fanned out, it would take time to recover them. Still, he pledged to Lee, "I shall move, as I have said, across the Blackwater as soon as I can get substantial crossings, and at least make a forced reconnaissance while I endeavor to draw off subsistence and quartermasters' stores. If more can be done without great sacrifice I shall do it."[68]

Jenkins sent Longstreet all the information available on the Union garrison. He included a map of the region's confusing network of roads. On April 6 Jenkins set the size of the Suffolk garrison at 12,000 to 15,000 troops and enthusiastically exhorted Longstreet, "If you succeed in capturing them it will be the most brilliant affair of the war and would be attended by glorious results to the cause."[69] Longstreet replied simply, "I desire that you have your command in readiness to cross the Blackwater on Friday [April 10]."[70]

As the start of the campaign neared, the Confederates continued to seek accurate intelligence on Union dispositions in Suffolk. In addition to what Jenkins could provide, George Pickett notified Longstreet that according to his intelligence, the Union garrison was facing a critical point when the nine-month enlistments "of a good many [units] would soon expire." Pickett offered to send a trusted scout named Schriver to Suffolk by the circuitous route of Newport News and Norfolk. "He says he will have no difficulty reaching Suffolk by the route," the general assured his commander, "but much by any other." The main impediment to the mission seems to have been money. "I have none except Confederate money, which will not pass," Pickett astutely recognized. He suggested using state funds, then added, "I think it worth trying."[71]

Yet all was not going according to plan. Four days before Longstreet proposed to move against Suffolk, he received bad news from the navy.
Secretary of War Seddon informed him that the navy could not clear the
obstructions in the James below Richmond in time to offset the Union gunboats in the Nansemond. Seddon advised him to proceed with the operation without the navy.[72] By this point Longstreet felt himself already
committed to an assault timetable and could not justify, in his own mind
at least, terminating the operation.

Longstreet wrote Lee stating that he had decided to do nothing more
than gather and draw out supplies from the region and would refrain
from an all-out assault on the town unless the opportunity offered. His
expectations seem to have changed with the bad news from the Navy
Department. His caution began to dull his enthusiasm. Now Longstreet
was thinking in terms of a grand foraging expedition alone, rather than
the capture of Suffolk and its sizable Union garrison. Furthermore, he
delayed the start of the campaign to "Saturday [April 11], possibly not before
Sunday [April 12]."[73]

General Lee made a token effort to pry loose naval support for his subordinate. On the ninth he sent a confidential message to Seddon: "General
Longstreet proposes to cross the Blackwater with a view to obtaining supplies from the counties of Nansemond, Isle of Wight, etc. He is apprehensive
that the enemy may move up the James River and get in his rear, and asks
whether he cannot obtain some cooperation from the Navy." Lee seems to
have realized that there was little anyone could do for Longstreet on this
subject. "I am not aware that the Navy can operate below the obstructions
at Drewry's Bluff," he admitted.[74] Even had he been successful, the inertia
of the Confederate bureaucracy would have prevented the assistance from
being given in a timely fashion. In the campaign to come, Longstreet would
have to operate without the help of the Confederate navy.

Meanwhile, the Union forces under General Peck were slowly becoming aware of the possibility of a major Confederate movement against
Suffolk. As early as February 20, reports of Southern reinforcements from
Richmond had reached him.[75] At the beginning of March, deserters established that Pickett and Hood commanded the Confederates.[76] Subsequent
reports placed Longstreet and Stonewall Jackson at Franklin, just a few miles
distant.[77] Still others put Longstreet in the West and claimed that the entire
Army of Northern Virginia was on the move toward "North Carolina and
the Blackwater."[78]

On March 5 a reconnaissance by Spear's industrious cavalry sorted out
some of the confusion. He set the Confederate forces on the Blackwater

at 20,000 men, with Longstreet in Petersburg with his two divisions. A report of Jackson's presence found no corroboration to sustain it.[79] Armed with these updated reports and articles from the Charleston *Mercury,* Peck felt more accurately informed. He was certainly aware of the considerable Confederate force within striking distance of his command at Suffolk.[80]

Reports of an imminent attack upon the town reached General Peck in mid-March. Dix hastened George Getty's division from Newport News to Suffolk in response. Although the alarm proved premature, the Federal commander remained in a high state of alertness throughout March and into April. He now expected a Confederate advance upon his post with every new day.[81]

The preparations the Union commander continued to undertake reflected his desire to leave nothing undone before any potential Confederate threat materialized. Having done so much to improve the defenses surrounding the town, he now sought to upgrade the defenses along the Nansemond River. This line remained vulnerable, except for whatever defense the navy could muster. One soldier complained to his wife on April 3, "I was very much disappointed on arriveing here, for I expected to see some kind of a *Fort,* but there was not so much as a shovel full of dirt thrown up."[82] Peck would expect these men to throw more than a little dirt in order to secure his river flank.

Peck was fortunate to have subordinates who would remain as prepared as he to respond to any moves the Confederates might decide to make. In addition to Michael Corcoran, the feisty Irishman who had tangled with Pryor in January, the Union commander's other division commander during the Suffolk campaign was George Washington Getty. Although not as colorful as Corcoran, Getty was amply qualified for his part in Peck's command. Born in Georgetown, D.C., on October 2, 1819, Getty was a West Pointer who graduated in 1840 ranked fifteenth in a class of forty-two. The young officer participated in the Mexican War, where he earned a brevet promotion to captain for gallant conduct. In 1848 Getty married a Virginian, Elizabeth Graham Stevenson, and he subsequently fought against the Seminole Indians in Florida in 1849–50 and 1856–57.

Getty was serving in the West when the Civil War broke out; despite his wife's Southern birth, he remained in the U.S. Army. He began the war as a captain but quickly secured an appointment as a lieutenant colonel in September 1861. Getty took part in McClellan's Peninsula campaign in 1862, serving at Yorktown, Gaines's Mill, and Malvern Hill. Following McClellan's withdrawal, the new colonel fought in the Antietam campaign.

For this service Getty became a brigadier general in September 1862, and he subsequently commanded the 3d Division of the 9th Corps at Fredericksburg. His command remained in reserve for much of the battle on December 9, but at about 5 P.M. the troops left their positions and entered into the cauldron of Southern fire. By dusk the survivors of Getty's badly mauled command limped back to the relative safety of the town. The slaughter his men experienced at Fredericksburg taught the general a bitter lesson about attacking a well-entrenched enemy. Later at Suffolk, Getty would have the opportunity to apply his knowledge on both the offensive and the defensive.[83]

Peck remained uncertain as to the exact nature of Longstreet's threat until April 10, the day before the Confederate advance was set to commence. Near the end of the day, he received the contents of a captured Southern mailbag, which plainly indicated "that General Longstreet would attack me at once with from 40,000 to 60,000; that he had maps, plans, and a statement of my force, and that General [D. H.] Hill would cooperate."[84] Although greatly exaggerating the numbers, such a report could not help but stir the already-skittish Union commander into action. Immediately he quickened the pace of preparing his men for the Confederate advance that he now knew was coming.[85]

The captured report was correct about one thing. Daniel Harvey Hill was supposed to cooperate with Longstreet's imminent campaign. In fact, Longstreet and Hill had agreed that the latter would proceed first, by launching an assault against New Bern, North Carolina. When that fizzled, Hill attacked the Union garrison at Washington, thirty miles north of New Bern. The Confederate commanders intended that neither the Federals in Virginia nor those in North Carolina would be allowed to render assistance to the other. Harvey Hill, a former mathematics professor, miscalculated his chances of liberating these North Carolina coastal towns but succeeded in turning the operations into foraging opportunities. It was the kind of lesson Longstreet might soon have to repeat in southeastern Virginia.[86]

Longstreet ordered Jenkins to cross the river on April 10 and "take up some strong position between the Blackwater and Suffolk," to serve as a screen for the main body as it crossed. This would enable the Confederates to pass over the difficult barrier unopposed. Longstreet advised the young officer to maintain pickets on the opposite bank in order to prevent a surprise sortie by the Federals until he took up his screening position. He also suggested that cavalry cross the river at Blackwater Bridge, near Zuni, and "move on the flank via Windsor," thus providing further protection for an advance. So that Jenkins's men would be prepared, he ordered them to cook four days' rations and pack their entrenching tools. Pickett and Hood were to cross the river on April 11.[87]

On the night of Wednesday, April 8, James Longstreet left his headquarters at Petersburg and proceeded to Franklin to start his long-planned campaign.[88] His swift departure meant that the "War Horse" would have to spend time soothing the bruised ego of Major General Samuel Gibbs French, the commander of the Department of Southern Virginia. A native of New Jersey fighting with the South, French, born November 22, 1818, was three years Longstreet's senior. Like his three future colleagues in the campaign, Sam French had attended West Point, but he fared considerably better, graduating in 1843 ranked fourteenth in his class. He served in Mexico, was severely wounded at Buena Vista, and received two brevets. French resigned from the U.S. Army in 1856 to manage a plantation he had acquired through marriage.

At the outbreak of war, French offered his services to his adopted state, Mississippi, and subsequently entered Confederate service. Despite his earlier military experience, his service for the South was largely lackluster. Nevertheless, he was appointed brigadier general in October 1861 and promoted to major general in August 1862.[89] French was an Old Army man who knew his rights and obligations well. He paid close attention to how he was treated and was particularly cognizant of military usages. He appreciated deference to his military experience and rank. In short, he was almost certain to cause great difficulty at the slightest provocation and would have to be handled carefully.

Longstreet seems to have failed at this from the outset. He did little more than inform French generally of his plans, despite the latter's important role as commander of the Department of Southern Virginia. Then on April 9 French realized that Longstreet had started toward Suffolk with troops from his command. Angrily he accused his commander of taking "from me a division and a number of batteries . . . without informing me." French reasoned that Longstreet had given his troops to Micah Jenkins, a personal favorite of the latter. Although he did not personally begrudge the young South Carolinian for taking his troops, French wanted his men back. He followed Longstreet to Suffolk, incensed at his superior's insensitivity. This anger promised to shape his reactions to Longstreet's leadership in the weeks to come.[90]

The signs of impending military action were there for almost anyone to see. In addition to the rumors and speculation, there were the people who seemed to be fleeing to safety before the whirlwind struck. "Because of the little excitement along the front, the colored people are hurrying within our lines in large numbers," wrote a member of the 13th New Hampshire. "They come in poor, destitute, starved and ragged. Rations are delivered them by the government."[91] These men, women, and children became the latest inhabitants in a "contraband camp" near Suffolk on the banks of the Nansemond River. Peck used some of them to provide him with information on Southern activities. There seemed to be a lot for them to pass on to him lately.[92]

As James Longstreet hastened toward his first independent campaign, his mind must have raced with activity. Perhaps the rush of events had caused the unintended snub of French, but a month of planning had preceded his departure. He had wrangled with General Lee for more men and the Naval Department for gunboats, receiving neither. Still, he took steps to assure good communications between himself, the War Department, and the Army of Northern Virginia by ordering the extension of a telegraph line into the part of southeastern Virginia he would shortly be entering. Whatever his critics might contend, these were the actions of a conscientious subordinate, not a power-driven military megalomaniac.

There was much to do and much to oversee, but at least "Old Peter" could take comfort that the men he was leading were his own battle-hardened veterans. He still expected that he could complete the operation in only two weeks, and nothing about the advance seemed to indicate any reason to be concerned about such an ambitious timetable.[93] It must have been an enormous relief simply to have the operation finally begun.

Longstreet's Confederates took their first steps onto the contested soil of southeastern Virginia at first light on a lovely spring Saturday, April 11, 1863.[94] Officers of the formations barked their orders, and the columns shook into motion. The grizzled veterans were in a jaunty mood as they crossed the Blackwater River on planks laid over pontoons. During the march one Southerner observed that his comrades were "as careless as if nothing of importance was on hand."[95]

Although the day grew increasingly warm as the columns wound their way over the crooked country roads, few of the Confederates straggled. Except for ambulances and ordnance wagons with additional ammunition, the heavy wagons remained on the far side of the river for the time being. This lessened the congestion and the dust the men would have to endure. The wagons would be sent along once the attackers had advanced, because Longstreet expected to fill them with the region's produce for Lee's hungry army. For now, he wanted nothing to impede the progress of the troops, and they were the beneficiaries.[96] Besides, he still held out the hope that he could surprise Peck, and perhaps even capture Suffolk and its garrison if he struck quickly enough.

By 4:00 in the afternoon, these hearty Confederate veterans were poised to drive the Union pickets in and deploy before the town. For some of them, including Mills Riddick in the 9th Virginia, this advance meant a home-coming.[97] It remained to be seen whether it would be happy one.

"The noise became deafening, all the batteries
around Suffolk were engaged in shelling the
woods in every direction."

Suffolk resident Emma Ferguson on Longstreet's appearance
before the town, April 11, 1863

"I thought for awhile the vessels would be
knocked into pieces."

Union sailor battling Confederates on the Nansemond
River, April 1863

⫷ 7 ⫸ *The War Hits Home*

U NION LIEUTENANT AMOS THAYER PEERED ACROSS THE LANDSCAPE
for a sign of enemy activity. His mind's eye conjured the sight of
advancing ranks of screaming Southerners. The night before, the
camps had been full of rumors. He watched the roads carefully for even
the slightest indication that this time the rumors were true. Surely so large
a force as that purported to be moving against Suffolk could not remain
long hidden from his well-trained eye.

Thayer had a special task. It was his duty to prevent the Confederates
from surprising the Union garrison in Suffolk. The vast network of fortifications surrounding the town would be of no value if the Southerners swept
into them before the Federals could react. Thayer's post was a treetop signal station which occupied a key position at the juncture of the South Quay
and Carrsville roads leading into Suffolk. These routes were the most likely
ones for an advancing force of Confederates to use.

Cavalry pickets occupied posts 1,200 yards farther along the roads, and together with intermediary infantry pickets, they provided cover for the signal station itself. In the event of trouble, Thayer instructed these pickets to report to him. Customarily, the pickets' horses remained saddled and bridled for instant action. Should the horsemen need immediate assistance, the infantry could offer that help temporarily until the signals had been given and they received reinforcement or retreated into the works. Usually the hours passed slowly, and the signalmen made nothing more than routine transmissions. But that was not to be the case on Saturday, April 11, 1863.

At about 3:30 that afternoon, a lone figure approached the Union signal post. He was a former slave from the area, and he hastened to the station to explain that he had just seen large numbers of Rebels coming toward the town. Thayer instantly understood that this meant the rumors were true. The Confederates were coming. The Union lieutenant signaled the news to Suffolk. "A few minutes" later, he watched as the startled cavalry pickets dashed past his post "at a furious rate." Some of the pickets rode barebacked, their horses already soaked with lather from the race for safety. Clearly not all of the pickets had received the information Thayer had obtained. Unperturbed by what he was witnessing, the signal officer calmly reported: "Pickets driven in. Reinforcements needed."

The Confederate infantry that would drive the Union cavalry outposts so unceremoniously past Thayer arrived with surprising swiftness. Between 3:30 and 4:00 P.M. they set upon the cavalry outposts, capturing a lieutenant and fifteen cavalrymen. Several of the startled horsemen managed to escape. Thayer bravely attempted to rally the scattered infantry pickets, while awaiting aid from the main garrison. He needed to buy time. However, in short order the Confederates reached the signal post, and sharpshooters rendered further signaling impossible. Happily for the beleaguered Union force, cavalry reinforcements arrived, allowing Thayer and his men to evacuate their post.[1]

Longstreet's sudden appearance before Suffolk seems to have stunned General Peck. Despite his extensive preparations and the efforts he had taken to divine Confederate intentions, it was almost as if the Southern legions had risen mysteriously out of the ground in front of him. He ordered the destruction of the drawbridge across the Nansemond leading from the north directly into the town. But in his haste Peck failed to notify the Union cavalry picket at Providence Church. Consequently, as the horsemen fled back toward the town, they were shocked to find the bridge gone. With the Confederates coming uncomfortably closer by the minute, there was nothing to do but swim or surrender. So the men plunged their mounts into the cool water, emerging safely within their own lines.[2]

One Union witness captured the drama of the moment. "We saw them beyond the bridge," he wrote of the cavalry vedettes, "riding fast toward our lines, and as they passed the fort they called out, 'The rebs are coming! the rebs are coming!'" The soldiers in Suffolk fell into line, urged by the commands of officers and the staccato of drums. "The excitement was intense," the man remembered. As the infantrymen nervously tested their weapons, the cavalrymen raced past, "their horses' hooves sending up little clouds of dust, the artillerymen in commotion, their officers shouting orders for them to train their guns on the road beyond the bridge."[3]

In the rush of excitement, the surprised Union commander not only stranded his cavalry pickets, he very nearly forfeited his critical riverfront flank as well. In his haste to reinforce the lines surrounding the town, Peck recalled most of the forces he had deployed along the Nansemond. Only a relatively small force of three companies from the 13th New Hampshire remained to guard the river. This force was to hold its position at Fort Connecticut, two miles out of Suffolk, and "observe the river, resist any attempt of the enemy to cross until the last moment, and then fall back to Suffolk over the corduroy bridge across Broer's Creek, taking up the bridge" as they went.[4] This would leave the east bank of the Nansemond River across from Norfleet's Point untended and undefended. In addition, General Getty was instructed to blow the Seaboard and Roanoke Bridge over the Jericho Canal.[5] In effect, should pressure from the Southerners prove too great, Peck was prepared to bottle himself up in Suffolk and hold on there until help could arrive.

Hazard Stevens, the man who had attempted unsuccessfully to enlist Unionists from the region, assessed Peck's strategic choice harshly. "It is clear that General Peck expected to be invested on both front and rear," he wrote after the war, "but the haste and panic in which he abandoned the most and indeed only endangered part of his defences was inexcusable, and came near costing him dear."[6] Steven Cormier, a student of the Suffolk campaign, has observed, "By issuing these orders, Peck did not exactly abandon the river flank, though his decision to withdraw Dutton's regiments virtually surrendered its security to the gunboats."[7] One of the Union gunboat commanders who served in the campaign wrote on April 12, "The Gen said he depended on the gunboats to defend this side and keep the river open—which is more than ought to be assigned to us, but he seems to think 'gun boats' can do any thing even in a narrow stream where it is more difficult to maneuver than to fight them."[8] By anyone's estimation, Peck's actions in this regard represented a gamble, particularly should the Confederates recognize the weakness and aggressively seek to exploit it.

Peck considered such a course unlikely. He was convinced that the naval vessels in the Nansemond were sufficient to repel a Confederate crossing and safeguard his vulnerable flank. The army had two converted tugboats in the river. The *Smith Briggs* and *West End* each carried fieldpieces manned by detachments of the 99th New York Infantry.[9] Both vessels huddled close to the main works, near the drawbridge that Peck had ordered destroyed. They could be used to supplement the fire from the fortifications on the northern front of the town. But neither was likely to resist long against sustained fire from Confederate fieldpieces.

The navy had employed the converted sidewheel ferryboat *Stepping Stones* in the river to curtail local smuggling. With the appearance of Longstreet's Confederates, the vessel could be used as a true gunboat by taking advantage of its armament and shallow draft to patrol the river. The *Stepping Stones* carried eight 12- and 24-pounder smoothbore guns and two 12-pounder brass rifled howitzers mounted on each end of the boat. Unusually large quantities of small arms were available to provide additional protection for the crew on the narrow waterway. The small dispatch boat *Alert* offered further support, although it carried only two guns.[10]

Despite these vessels and his confidence in recalling most of the infantry forces from the riverfront, Peck remained concerned. Dispatches raced from both Suffolk and Fort Monroe urging Admiral Samuel Phillips Lee to assist the army against Longstreet. The Union army commanders knew the importance of a swift response from their naval counterparts. The security of Suffolk, and perhaps Norfolk as well, depended upon the successful resistance against a Confederate crossing of the Nansemond.[11]

Admiral Lee responded with guarded pessimism:

> If the enemy have the means of crossing the Nansemond, and wish to do so in force under cover of their artillery, the two small navy and the small army vessels called gunboats (which are frail little river or harbor steamers, mounting in all but a few pieces of fixed artillery) should not be considered enough to prevent it. The Nansemond is a mere creek above the Western Branch, and musketry alone can command the decks and drive from their guns the crews of these little crafts, which are liable to be disabled in their exposed boilers, etc., by a few discharges from small and scattered fieldpieces.[12]

This prognosis was hardly cheering. Yet Peck seemed perfectly content to rely on Admiral Lee's "little crafts" to defend his most vulnerable flank.

Compounding the emotional strain of defending his post against an attack by a host of Confederates, John Peck suffered physical injury on his first day of the Suffolk campaign. Naval officer R. H. Lamson wrote to his future wife from aboard the *Mount Washington* in the Nansemond River "off Suffolk" on April 12, "Gen. Peck was injured yesterday by his horse falling and was in a carriage driving from point to point, with aids and guard galloping after."[13] The Union general remained hobbled by the mishap for the duration of the Suffolk campaign and required a period of recuperation afterwards before returning to active duty.[14]

The advance of the Southern troops on Suffolk affected more than General Peck. It caused great consternation among the Federal troops of all ranks. One Union soldier wrote the next morning, "Yesterday just before sundown we were ordered 2 beat the long roll every man jumped for his musket for we knew they were here and moveing toward us for our picket was drove in some without a cap on or a horse."[15] A member of the 112th New York noted, "The wildest excitement prevailed in town, and every camp was in commotion."[16]

One Suffolk resident, Emma L. M. Ferguson, described the scene in vivid detail:

> Their appearance created the greatest commotion among the Federals, the whole army commenced to pour into our town from the surrounding country. . . . The Confederates began to move toward the town and force the Yankees to draw in their pickets, as they were forced near town they fired every house as they passed along. . . . In Suffolk the greatest excitement prevailed. Couriers were straining their horses up and down the streets. The noise became deafening, all the batteries around Suffolk were engaged in shelling the woods in every direction, the booming of cannon, the noise of bursting shells and the sound of musketry combined made one continuous roar; the smoke from cannon and burning houses hung like thick clouds over our town which seemed doomed to destruction. . . . Amid all this excitement and commotion couriers riding along the streets rattled at the windows of the houses and told the frightened inmates to hold themselves in readiness, for if the "rebels" came any nearer town they intended to burn it and evacuate.[17]

Although the Federals had no actual intention of burning the town, General Peck faced one of the fundamental dilemmas of war: he had to wage war in a town containing civilians. On the one hand, he had a military duty to hold Suffolk at all costs. On the other hand, he had a human-

itarian duty to try to prevent civilian casualties. Peck could serve both interests by evacuating the noncombatants from Suffolk, and he gave orders
almost immediately to do so.[18]

From this earliest moment, as the smoke curled up from houses already
ablaze, it was clear that the fighting at Suffolk would cost local citizens dearly.
Many of the houses and farms not damaged or destroyed by artillery and
small-arms fire or cleared to provide open fields of fire for the batteries
would be converted into makeshift hospitals and headquarters for the troops
of both sides.[19]

The Confederates who stormed east down the South Quay Road were
John Hood's men. They enjoyed early success in driving the pickets into
the Union lines, but the alertness of the Federal garrison and the lateness
of the hour held that success to a minimum. The Federals easily checked
the Southerners with a blanket of artillery fire from their chain of fortifications. The Confederates wisely halted their advance and awaited the arrival
of their comrades. Pickett's men bivouacked for the night within reach of
the town.[20]

Throughout this first night of what would become known, erroneously,
as the "Siege of Suffolk," soldiers on both sides toiled on their lines, digging rifle pits and extending their earthworks and defenses. As a Union naval
participant explained, "Fortifications seemed to have risen on the banks of
the river as if by magic."[21] Pickets lay in advance of both main lines to provide an early warning against attack and occasionally took potshots at their
opponents across the way.

The initial excitement within the Union lines subsided during the night.
The Confederate appearance seemed to vindicate the months of agoniz-
ing, backbreaking labor. Men who had become known as "The Basket-
Makers of the Nansemond" were the heroes of the hour.[22] They no longer
criticized Peck. As one of the laborers observed, "All who had heretofore
complained because of the severe fatigue duty demanded by General Peck
in constructing fortifications, now commended his wisdom and vigilance,
realizing that their hard labor was not in vain and the old general's head
was level."[23]

In the meantime, the Union navy responded swiftly to the army's
call for help. On the morning of April 12, Admiral Lee dispatched the
Mount Washington, under Lieutenant Roswell H. Lamson, to the lower
Nansemond. He sent the *Commodore Barney,* under Lieutenant William B.
Cushing, into the upper Nansemond.[24] The *Stepping Stones,* the *Cohasset,*
and the *Alert* rounded out the tiny flotilla. The *Mount Washington* and the
Commodore Barney were converted sidewheel river steamers; the *Cohasset*

was a converted tug. Each of the vessels carried a variety of armaments. These additional gunboats instilled further confidence that a Confederate crossing could be prevented.[25]

In any case, Admiral Lee would be working closely with the army to safeguard the Suffolk garrison. Lee was himself a Virginian (and a third cousin of Robert E. Lee). Born in Fairfax County on February 13, 1812, he became a midshipman on November 22, 1825, and served aboard vessels in the West Indies, the Mediterranean, and the Pacific. He participated in the Mexican War, assisting in the capture of the coastal town of Tabasco. Through the mid-1850s Lee conducted coastal and oceanographic survey studies.

When the war broke out, Lee was off the Cape of Good Hope, bound for the East Indies. Already boasting thirty-six years of naval service, the officer immediately returned to the United States. After a tour of duty off Charleston, Lee assumed command of the sloop-of-war *Oneida,* which participated with distinction in battles on the Mississippi River from New Orleans to Farragut's twin passages of the Confederate stronghold of Vicksburg. Shortly after making captain, Lee went in September 1862 to the eastern theater of the war as acting rear admiral of the North Atlantic Blockading Squadron. A professional, no-nonsense naval commander, Lee rendered effective service in his new post. He was a careful and conscientious officer, unwilling to take risks but thoroughly devoted to duty.[26]

The key to army-navy cooperation in Suffolk lay primarily with naval lieutenants William Barker Cushing and Roswell Hawkes Lamson. These two men would have to secure the army's relatively vulnerable Nansemond River flank. Thus, Peck relied upon them as much as he did on his army commanders, and his relations with Cushing and Lamson had a profound effect upon his defense of Suffolk.

William Cushing was perhaps as colorful a figure in the navy as Michael Corcoran was in the army. Born on November 4, 1842, in Delafield, Wisconsin, Cushing was the youngest of four boys. His father, Dr. Milton Cushing, died when William was four years old, and the family moved to Fredonia, New York, where the widowed mother supported her children by teaching. Young Cushing was "very pugnacious, good-natured generally, but very quick to resist an insult, and he would fight any boy or man without the slightest hesitation." These boyhood traits remained with Cushing throughout his wartime career.[27]

In 1856 young Cushing obtained an appointment as a page for the House of Representatives. The next year he won appointment to the U.S. Naval Academy at Annapolis, Maryland. There he failed to apply himself to his studies, choosing rather to cultivate his talents as a practical joker. One of these pranks resulted in a recommendation for Cushing's dismissal from the academy. Cushing's senior-year report in February 1861 editorialized, "'General conduct bad; aptitude for the naval service not good; not recommended for continuance at the Academy.'" Fortunately the navy allowed Cushing to resign instead of dismissing him.[28]

Despite Cushing's poor record, the timely intervention of friends enabled him to secure an assignment aboard the USS *Minnesota* in early 1861. Cushing demonstrated his worth and again became a midshipman in October 1861. On July 16, 1862, at the age of nineteen, he was a lieutenant, and by the time the war brought William Cushing to Suffolk waters, he was just over twenty years old.[29]

Cushing's compatriot on the Nansemond was R. H. Lamson. Born in Burlington, Iowa, Lamson was several years Cushing's senior. He went to war at an early age, enlisting in the Washington State Volunteers to fight against Indians in 1855–56. Appointed to the naval academy in 1858, Lamson was the first cadet appointed from Oregon. He graduated second of the eighty-four members of the Class of 1862. "A tall handsome man with a neat beard and serious eyes,"[30] the young officer saw wartime service at Port Royal and Hatteras Inlet in 1861 and the following year was promoted to lieutenant.[31]

Cushing and Lamson became "fast friends" as a result of their service in the Suffolk area.[32] Admiral David Porter characterized them as "both brave, energetic men—Lamson with the capacity of one older and more experienced, and Cushing with dash and vigor never exceeded."[33] Both men were anxious to prove themselves as naval commanders, and they chafed under the confining subordination of the navy to the army at Suffolk.

Admiral Lee was convinced that the vessels were vulnerable to battery fire from the banks of the river. He correctly criticized the "impolicy" of "relying upon what are called ferryboats in New York and gunboats here" to defend the Nansemond River flank. He feared that the Confederate artillery "properly placed" would prove "more than a match" for the "little improvised gunboats" with which he sought to defend the river. Lee believed the frail craft would offer "insufficient defense" for Peck's lines.[34] Hoping to avoid a calamity, Lee gave his two young naval officers specific instructions, ordering Lamson and Cushing to "occupy the safest and most commanding positions." They were to fire judiciously and keep their vessels in motion. Under the worst circumstances the two naval commanders were to destroy rather than surrender their vessels.[35]

Neither Lamson nor Cushing ever considered the latter course. Instead, each commander sought to improve his vessel's defenses. Lamson employed a shipment of boiler iron as rifle screens. Both officers lined the interior of their pilothouses with iron plates. The pilothouses made highly visible and vulnerable targets, but the pilots' safety was paramount if the boats were to remain in the narrow channel of the river.[36]

Sunday, April 12, broke bright and beautiful.[37] With all of his forces now on the field and rested, Longstreet decided to press the temporary advantage his vanguard had gained on the previous afternoon. At 4:00 A.M. George Pickett's men prepared for the advance, but they did not attack until nearly midday. Longstreet apparently saw little reason for haste. Although he wanted to test the formidable Union earthworks, the "War Horse" was content to probe for weak spots in his own good time. Tentative fighting marked the rest of the day.[38]

Late in the afternoon rain began to fall over the combatants. The weather provided an appropriate setting for a bizarre incident which threatened to incite a mutiny within the Federal ranks and demonstrated that not all fighting would occur on the front lines or between opposing sides. This strange event involved two flamboyant characters, fiery Michael Corcoran and Lieutenant Colonel Edgar A. Kimball of the newly arrived 9th New York. Kimball, a veteran of the Mexican War, was just shy of his forty-first birthday. He had served at Roanoke Island and Sharpsburg, where he established a reputation as a courageous fighter. The popular commander and his unit had reached Suffolk after a fatiguing thirty-mile march from Portsmouth. The business of settling his men into camp, acquainting himself with the area, and renewing old friendships kept Kimball awake through much of the night.[39]

As he was strolling with a friend in the early morning hours of April 13, Kimball became embroiled in an argument at a nearby road. A number of riders were moving toward the front lines. The hour was late. The group seemed suspicious to the new arrival. He stepped in front of the riders and challenged them. Unbeknownst to the colonel, he was face to face with General Corcoran. Likewise, Corcoran did not know the identity of the officer who had challenged him. The Irishman later explained:

> I asked if it was Dr. Heath, (one of the surgeons of the Irish Legion,) and was answered by another order to halt, with the additional remark, "It is none of your —— business. I want the countersign." Perceiving it was not the Doctor, I requested to know the object of his halting me, and his name, rank, and other authority, but could not obtain any

other reply than that it was none of my —— business. I repeated the questions several times and received similar answers, with the exception that the countersign was not demanded more than once; and he said, "You can not pass here."

Corcoran stated that he had never met Kimball before that fateful evening. He believed that Kimball had "no authority to demand the countersign" and that under the circumstances "I would have been derelict in my duty had I yielded to his demand." Neither man was prepared to take the chance that the other was not an enemy intruder. Given the close proximity of the enemy, Corcoran and company might actually have been Confederates scouting the Union perimeter. On the other hand, Corcoran was correct in withholding the password from an individual who was both strange to him and maintaining a threatening manner, but the confrontation threatened disaster.

Corcoran continued to confront his unknown challenger:

> I expostulated with him on such conduct, and told him to remember that he was not on duty, and had no right to be there and stop me from proceeding, and that he must let me pass. I asked him if he knew who he was talking to, and then gave him my name and rank, telling [him] my business there, but it was of no avail. He answered: "I do not care —— who you are." I again told him that I should pass, and warned him several times to get out of my way, and attempted to proceed. He thereupon put himself in a determined attitude to prevent my progress, and brandishing his sword in one hand, and having his other on a pistol, as I then supposed, made a movement toward me with the evident design of using them, making an impolite statement that I should not pass. It was at this point that I used my weapon.

The hot-tempered Irishman's shot struck Kimball in the neck, severing an artery. As Kimball fell, he gasped, "Damn you, fire again!" Although the confrontation occurred near a hospital, the wound proved mortal.[40]

With emotions still raw, Edward K. Wightman wrote to his brother on the thirteenth. "The troops were at the time under arms and expecting an attack at any moment. Camp rules were therefore strictly enforced." The ingredients were ripe for what followed. "Gen. Cocoran and staff attempted to pass a sentinel without the countersign, and Kimball, who happened to be near, backed the soldier. Cocoran drew his pistol and fired. . . . But the lion-hearted old man was up again in a moment, and with his sword drawn, contemptuously calling upon Cocoran to 'fire again.'" Wightman declared that Corcoran's actions were inexcusable. "He knew [it was] Kimball when he fired."

But Wightman also unwittingly offered another explanation for the violent confrontation. He remarked that while the command camped at Norfolk, "we slept under cover, and I felt no other inconvenience than that resulting from Col. Kimball, who was a little tight, stepping on me as he passed back and forth during the night."[41] Years later a remorseful George W. Griggs sought to repudiate his past as a provider of distilled spirits to the troops. In an 1895 article for the local newspaper, he admitted, "Most of the survivors of the glorious 89th, especially those in Windsor [New York], will remember the eating and drinking house of Griggs & Nolen at Suffolk, Va. when that regiment was stationed there." He had no difficulty drumming up business. "The firm mentioned had the only permit to sell liquors of anyone in the department, and our receipts for eating and drinking ran from $300 to $1,000 a day." According to Griggs, Kimball was "tight" again on the night he confronted Corcoran: "While in a state of intoxication [Kimball] ran from his tent, seized Gen. (Michael) Cocoran's horse by the bridle, drew and flourished his sword, and demanded of the general the countersign." Griggs made no effort to pass the blame to something or someone else. "Griggs & Nolen sold Kimball the whiskey that caused his death."[42]

Whatever the cause of the incident, word spread of Kimball's death. The reaction was immediate and emotional. One soldier remembered, "There was such confusion and the scene for a time savored somewhat of insubordination, not to say mutiny."[43] Another recalled, "The boys raved rather than talked, and many would have gone through the whole legion for the blood of the assassin."[44] However, General Getty quickly intervened. He calmed the heated tempers by promising a complete investigation of the shooting. At the same time Getty ordered the regiment to a new sector of the line, in close proximity to the Confederates. One member noted that for the rest of the campaign the 9th was "so fully occupied with the enemy in front that if his satanic majesty had wished to brew mischief he could have found no heart or hands in the regiment to do it for him."[45]

Internal problems of a different sort worried Longstreet in this early phase of the Suffolk campaign. By the time the distraught and bitter Samuel French arrived in the Suffolk area to reclaim command of his men, Longstreet had become aware of just how desperately he needed to unify the command of his artillery. Knowing French's reputation as an artillerist and not willing to place that officer with infantry, Longstreet offered the new arrival command of his artillery. French refused, explaining, "I told him I did not intend to give up the command of my division to any one, but that I was willing to give all the assistance I could."[46] Longstreet subsequently ordered the artillery to report to French, ignoring the latter's hostility toward the assignment. French promptly reassigned the batteries to the chiefs of artillery of Pickett's and Hood's divisions and despite the gesture remained angry.[47]

Through the thirteenth, Hood's men consolidated their positions along the Nansemond River and harassed Union gunboats. All day they peppered the vessels with small arms, but to little avail. The Confederates needed heavier firepower. Teams of Southerners worked throughout the night in shifts, throwing up earthworks and rifle pits. As the laborers carved gun emplacements in the bank of the river, Confederate artillery crews dragged their guns into place.[48]

Also on the thirteenth occurred one of the inevitable tragedies associated with war. During an advance along the Somerton Road, a family became trapped between the lines. As shot and shell tore through the frame of their home, the father, mother, and seven children huddled in terror in the cellar. When that sanctuary proved inadequate, they raced for the relative safety of some nearby trees. The mother, Judith Kilby Smith, never made it. As she hurried along, encumbered by a six-month-old baby in her arms, a projectile smashed into her, killing her instantly.[49]

Versions vary as to the origin of the shot. At least one Northern account attributed it to a Confederate soldier who shot her when she failed to heed his calls for her to stop. Another Northern version, purported to be by a witness, explained that Union fire had brought her down. "I saw yesterday lots of rebs & their officers riding white horses," a member of the 15th Connecticut wrote. "I could . . . see our pickets and see them wound & kill each other & see them brought in & see a woman brought in that was shot in the head they said she was secesh of the worst stamp and insulted our pickett in the worst [way] till they shot her."[50]

The letter suggests that the soldier saw a woman's body "brought in" but did not see her death. His account is so out of line with other versions as to be based upon rumor, not fact. A more convincing explanation for the woman's death comes from accounts that indicate she fell while fleeing her home, the accidental victim of indiscriminate picket firing. According to the history of the 11th Pennsylvania, based upon the memories of witnesses from the unit, "A family whose house was burned just outside our works, attempted to seek safety by fleeing to our lines, and while doing so the wife was killed."[51]

Her husband, George R. Smith, stayed with her after shuttling the children to safety with a friend. He carried her body into Suffolk to the home of her brother, John R. Kilby, the attorney who had reluctantly cast Suffolk's vote for secession in 1861. A Union cavalryman recalled the scene vividly. "It was particularly sad to see the little boy running on before, waving a flag of truce, while his father followed, driving a team in which lay the body of his wife."[52] Her brother was one of five men about to leave under guard for Fort Monroe, as his sister's body passed.[53] Her mother, forced into town when her own home burned, went to the residence where Mrs. Smith's body lay. Seeing her lying there, the mother asked if she were faint or sick. No one could answer. Suspecting something was amiss, she girded her strength, walked over to find her daughter lifeless, and fell into grief.[54]

Another local family was much more fortunate in their encounter with skirmishing near their home. Major Samuel Wetherill of the 11th Pennsylvania recorded in his diary on the twenty-fifth, "We drove in the pickets from Everett's Lane to the edge of the woods, where their rifle pits were ranged." As other troops moved up, he "moved to the right to Elisha Everett's house and kept our howitzer going." Suddenly he became aware that civilians were in the residence, trapped by the combat. "I was surprised to find Mrs. Everett, the children, and an old slave, Zack, in the house." The Union officer jumped into action to prevent tragedy from occurring here. "I ordered the family to the cellar" and told the servant to create a shelter of fence rails and bedticks. "This saved them, as several shells exploded in the house," he attested modestly. But he thought his greatest service to them came when, under orders to pull back and burn the structure, Wetherill pleaded that because the Federals had arrested her husband "as a precaution," the family was dependent upon the Union troops for their protection. "This saved the house," he noted with satisfaction.[55]

As families caught in the grip of war endured personal drama, Union general Peck had to concentrate on the defense of his line. By itself the Nansemond River was an uncertain impediment to Longstreet's advance. If the Navy would remain resolute in patrolling and defending it, the river could be barricade enough to ensure the Suffolk garrison's safety. For their part Lamson and Cushing were determined not to let Peck down. At daylight on the fourteenth, Lamson's flotilla steamed upriver. The *Mount Washington* led the column of gunboats, followed by the *West End* and the *Stepping Stones*.

Approximately two miles from Suffolk, Lamson came upon a fresh earthwork at Norfleet's Point. He confidently steamed past, expecting only Hood's sharpshooters. But this time the Southerners rolled seven artillery

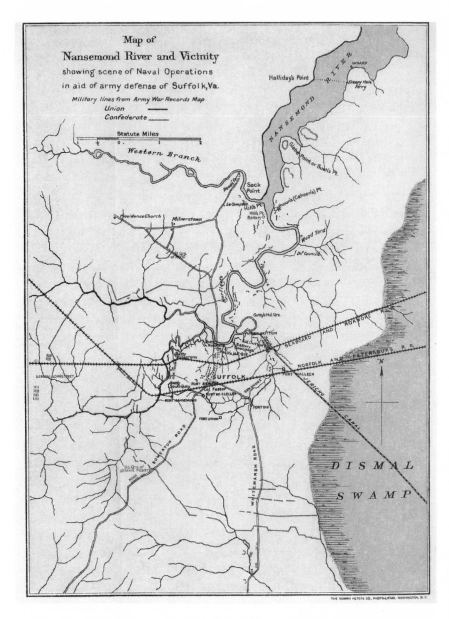

MAP 6 Nansemond River and vicinity. The Hill's Point Battery, or Fort Huger, is located strategically where the river narrows on its course to Suffolk.

pieces from under cover and into the earthwork. The Confederate artillerists opened a brisk fire and quickly disabled the *Mount Washington* with a shot through the boilers. The engines lost steam, causing the vessel to drift against the riverbank. Scalding water and escaping steam drove the crew from the disabled craft. However, once the spewing water and steam had subsided, they courageously returned and manned the guns.

The other ships of the flotilla were in only slightly better condition. The *West End* was also stuck fast. The *Stepping Stones* had prudently withdrawn a short distance in order to protect the hull of the boat with an intervening point of land. Nevertheless, the Confederates battered the vessel unmercifully. A member of the crew later described the experience:

> I thought for awhile the vessels would be knocked into pieces before we could change our position, as every shot seemed to hit one or the other of the vessels. . . . I never was exposed to such an artillery fire before or since. It seemed as if the whole atmosphere was filled with deadly sounds. The sharp shriek of solid shot, the shrill [sound] of Whitworth rifled shot, the noise of elongated shell that seemed to flutter above our heads then explode with a loud report and scatter its deadly fragments of cragged pieces of iron with a quick hum and buzz among us, produced a medly of sounds too thrilling and terrible to be described, and which I have not yet forgotten.[56]

Lamson now had no choice but to signal the *Stepping Stones* to come up and tow his vessel out of range of the Southern guns. Under heavy fire the *Stepping Stones* moved up to the *Mount Washington,* attached two lines to the stricken vessel, and pulled her to safety. Then the *Stepping Stones* returned to assist the *West End.* Confederate sharpshooters peppered the gunboats as they retired toward the bar at Hill's Point and wider water in which they would be able to maneuver with greater ease.

The battered flotilla was not yet out of danger. The Confederate fire had badly damaged the *Mount Washington*'s helm, and as she was being towed near Hill's Point, the helm broke. The vessel became completely unmanageable and once again drifted aground. Two tugboats came to tow her free, but to no avail. Quickly the Confederates brought up fieldpieces to batter the disabled gunboat. Sharpshooters deployed to hamper efforts to tow the boat.

Observing the developments from comparative safety, Lieutenant Cushing decided to bring up the *Commodore Barney* to cover the disabled craft and silence the Southern batteries. Cushing had little difficulty achieving his task; however, the Confederate artillery soon deployed into new positions. The *Commodore Barney* responded to the new threat with determination, but at fearful cost. Cushing later dramatically related the experience to his mother:

> Well, it was a hard fight, and at close quarters most of the time; so close that their infantry riddled the two vessels with bullets. Crash! go the bulkheads—a rifle shell was exploded on our deck, tearing flesh and woodwork. A crash like thunder is our reply—and our heavy shell makes music in the air, and explodes among our traitor neighbors with a dull sullen roar of defiance. . . . Crash! Crash! Splinters were flying in the air; great pools of blood are on the deck, and the first sharp cry of wounded men in agony rises upon the soft spring air. The dead cannot speak—but there they lie motionless, lifeless, and mangled, who a moment ago smiled on the old flag that floated over them, and fought for its glory and honor. Sprinkle ashes over the slippery deck—the work must still go on. The rifled gun— my best, is disabled, for three shots have struck it—the muzzle is gone, the elevator is carried away, and the carriage is broken. Steady men, steady! Fill up the places of the killed and wounded—don't throw a shot away. The wheel of the howitzer is torn off by the shell, and the gun rendered useless—never mind! Work the remaining guns with a will—for we can and must be victorious.[57]

The sparring continued throughout the day. Finally, at high tide the *Stepping Stones* attempted to pass a towline to the *Mount Washington*. Confederate sharpshooters riddled one sailor with bullets as he tried to work the line across the gap between the vessels. Others took his place, and the Federals soon towed the crippled boat across the bar and out of range. For the first time since Longstreet had arrived before Suffolk, the Nansemond River, and thus the door to Norfolk, lay open.

The tiny Union naval force had suffered severely during the day's engagements. Casualties were five killed, fourteen wounded—several severely—and one missing, believed to have been killed and lost overboard. The Confederates heavily damaged the Union vessels, with Lamson's *Mount Washington* in the worst condition.[58] Lamson explained in a letter on the fourteenth: "I am well and safe, have been fighting rebel batteries from 6½ this morning till 6 this evening. The rebels fired into my engines and exploded one of my boilers." He concluded: "The Mt. Washington is a wreck of splinters. I shall have her towed down with the wounded, and I shall remain on board the 'Stepping Stones.'"[59] Even though the Southerners had driven off the ships, they had failed to sink any of them.

Because of the events of April 14, 1863, the initiative lay squarely with Longstreet. The severe chastisement of the Union gunboats left the river flank more vulnerable than ever. The opportunity existed for a Confederate crossing operation which might easily net Peck's entire force, and perhaps Norfolk as well. Quick action could redeem a region lost since May 1862 and give Longstreet a handsome victory, too.

But it would not be as easy as that. Perhaps the most complicating factor was that Longstreet had objectives other than combat in this early phase of the Suffolk campaign. From the series of tents that constituted his headquarters in the field, located approximately a mile and a half from the point at which the railroads crossed outside of the town, the Confederate commander directed a rapidly expanding operation.[60] To fulfill the mission of obtaining supplies for Lee's army, he ordered Henry L. Benning's brigade to escort and assist the commissary agents as they gathered supplies in the northern counties of North Carolina. "Old Peter" gave Benning meticulous directions for guarding the valuable train of wagons. He maintained a continuing interest in these operations and kept in constant touch with Benning's detached force. Longstreet could not afford to abandon the important task of securing commissary and quartermaster supplies.[61]

By any reckoning the Confederate commander had much to consider, and because this was an independent operation, there would be no one else to blame if things turned sour. To take advantage of the opportunities presented to him, Longstreet had to grasp them, and early indications were that he would not do so. The limited success of the initial Confederate attacks may have lulled Longstreet into being content to hold the Union garrison in the town while his commissary and quartermaster agents scoured the region. Or perhaps he did not realize the opportunity opened to him. Whatever the case, the "War Horse" was not yet prepared to press home his advantage. There was also a very real danger that delay would allow the initiative to pass over to his opponent.

APRIL 15–19, 1863

"Here when all was quiet along the lines my
Soldier would ride in from his headquarters
almost every night between the hours of
sunset and sunrise to see me."

LaSalle Corbell on George Pickett at Suffolk

"I don't think his division benefited by such
carpet-knight doings in the field."

Moxley Sorrel on Pickett at Suffolk

⊰ 8 ⊱ A *"Knight" in Suffolk*

AT SOME POINT IN MID-APRIL, MISSOURI RIDDICK RECEIVED THE
news that every parent dreads to get in wartime: something had
happened to her son Mills. He had fought in Lewis Armistead's
brigade in the skirmish on the Somerton Road with the 9th Virginia. They
pushed the pickets back but then encountered a converging fire from several Union forts that stopped them in their tracks. Armistead's decision to
pull back out of range prevented the casualties that would have come with
an assault against the main Union works. A second attempt, this time with
the support of a battery, proved only marginally more successful in forcing the Federals back into their entrenchments. Mills Riddick, the young
man who had lived in the home that General Peck now occupied as his headquarters, was wounded in the fighting.[1]

A friend of the family subsequently wrote the soldier's mother. "I have
just heard that you received a dispatch stating that your son Mills was

wounded," the friend reported. "I do sincerely hope that it is not so please let me know if it is so when and where he was wounded and have you heard if our army is it in or near Suffolk yet." Groping for news of any sort, the friend at last pleaded, "Please let me hear from Mills."[2] Struck within sight of his hometown, Mills Riddick was fortunate to be able to recover from his wounds. Others would be less fortunate, including a comrade of Riddick's in Company I. Alfred Van's service record listed him as having "died later [in the] hospital.[3]

Against the backdrop of the fighting now engulfing his home district, the requisition of his house, and the wounding of his son, political life for Nathaniel Riddick continued. Riddick had held his post in the Virginia House of Delegates since before the war. An open letter from "SOLDIERS AND REFUGEES" to "THE VOTERS OF NANSEMOND COUNTY" announced his candidacy for reelection. Appearing in newspapers in Petersburg and Richmond, the letter reminded those voters of the Suffolk resident's qualifications for the office. "His experience in that body, his fidelity to our interest and cause, and his sacrifices for them, in peace and in war, are known to us all." With early word of Longstreet's operations in the area beginning to filter through, the notice exhorted voters to give Riddick what his service ought to "entitle him to receive," their "unanimous support."[4]

Military operations proceeded at Suffolk despite the rain that fell during the night of the fourteenth and into the next morning. Between 2:30 and 3:30 A.M., the Federals conducted a heavy reconnaissance down the White Marsh (or Edenton) Road. The object was to ascertain the disposition of the Confederates along George Pickett's portion of the lines. The Union force, under Colonel J. P. McMahon of the 164th New York, consisted of three companies of infantry, two of cavalry, and a mountain howitzer. Major Alexander Patton of the 1st New York Mounted Rifles commanded the cavalry and the howitzer.

This force left Fort Dix and proceeded cautiously down the White Marsh Road. The men felt their way along in the predawn darkness. When they struck, the Federals charged so rapidly past eight barricades on the road that they captured several Confederate pickets, including a sentry at the edge of the Southern camp. Suddenly the Union force encountered the entire 17th Virginia, drawn up in line of battle. Unshaken by this development, Patton drew back his own advance to allow McMahon's infantry and the howitzer time to catch up.

Upon their arrival McMahon's foot soldiers deployed in an open field opposite the Southerners and to the right of the road. They quickly formed into line of battle. Deploying skirmishers to cover their flanks, the Federals launched a brief, unsuccessful cavalry charge. The infantry then rushed forward on the Confederate left and, joined by the fire of the howitzer, drove the Southerners back through their camp. After a second successful charge, the Federals withdrew to their main lines.

This reconnaissance resulted in light casualties for both sides. The attacking party lost two cavalrymen wounded and captured, three infantrymen killed and nine wounded, and one howitzer crewman wounded. The 17th Virginia suffered three men wounded and four captured. The Union reconnaissance demonstrated that the Confederates remained "in considerable force in short distance from his outposts."[5]

About the same time Colonel Samuel Spear of the 11th Pennsylvania Cavalry led another force down the Somerton Road. This force consisted of four companies of infantry, four companies of cavalry, and two pieces of the 7th Massachusetts Battery. Its object was to determine the strength of the Confederate troops facing Colonel Robert S. Foster's front.

The Federals also sought to disperse the Confederate sharpshooters who were using outlying buildings for shelter as they harassed the Federals behind their earthworks. From these relatively safe havens, they played havoc with Union infantrymen and gun crews. They found the large Brothers house particularly useful for this purpose and dug rifle pits to complement the building's strength. Corcoran ordered Spear to drive the Confederates from the house and burn it. However, the order proved extremely difficult to carry out. Spear tried to urge the infantry companies to charge, but the soldiers resisted his most vehement orders. Despite several gallant rushes by Spear's horsemen, the effort failed.[6]

While so much took place on his segment of the line, George Pickett had something or, more accurately, someone else on his mind. He was in love. Longstreet's movement against Suffolk placed Pickett considerably closer to his sweetheart, Sallie Corbell. Like so many other local residents, Sallie had sought refuge behind the Confederate lines when Longstreet first appeared. She went to live with an aunt at Barber's Crossroads, approximately ten miles from Suffolk. Sallie had already received at least one visit from Pickett when his division first camped near the Blackwater River. Longstreet now inconveniently posted the Virginian on the extreme opposite end of the Southern lines from Sallie's refuge.

At first the love-struck suitor tried to persuade Sallie herself to make the journey that would unite them. From "Camp" he wrote on April 15: "As you know, it is imperative that I should remain at my post and [it is] absolutely impossible for me to come to you. So you will have to come to me. Will you dear? Will you come?"[7] For the moment at least, George Pickett seemed willing to put duty above affairs of the heart. But the heart quickly intruded.

When his pleadings failed to produce the desired result, Pickett acted himself by calling upon her as often as time and circumstance permitted. The thirty-mile ride did not deter him from making frequent visits. Sallie recalled, "Here when all was quiet along the lines my Soldier would ride in from his headquarters almost every night between the hours of sunset and sunrise to see me."[8] A colonel in the 56th Virginia confirmed that Pickett was "continually riding off to pay court to his young love" and complained that in doing so he left "the division details to his staff."[9]

At first Pickett sought and obtained Longstreet's permission for these visits. Soon he was going so frequently that he decided to ask Moxley Sorrel, Longstreet's chief of staff, instead, for the necessary clearance. Sorrel later remembered:

> Perhaps he had wearied Longstreet by frequent applications to be absent, but once he came to me for the authority. My answer was, "No, you must go to the Lieutenant General."
>
> "But he is tired of it, and will refuse; and I must go, I must see her. I swear, Sorrel, I'll be back before anything can happen in the morning."
>
> I could not permit myself to be moved. If anything did happen, such as a movement of his division or any demonstration against it, my responsibilities for the absence of the Major General could not be explained. But Pickett went all the same, nothing could hold him back from the pursuit.

Sorrel was quite correct when he concluded, "I don't think his division benefited by such carpet-knight doings in the field."[10]

Pickett was negligent in leaving his command on such a frequent basis in the face of the enemy. The fact that he did so on his own is perhaps not surprising, but that he rode off with Longstreet's permission on some of these nocturnal visits is, on the face of it, nothing short of astonishing. Yet there was one possible explanation for Longstreet's approval of Pickett's indulgence. Longstreet took particular interest in Pickett. The two men shared a great deal of past experience, in particular their Old Army association. Sorrel observed that Longstreet was "exceedingly fond" of Pickett and explained that "Old Pete" "looked after Pickett" and often required one of his staff officers to stay with the Virginian "to make sure he did not get astray."[11] But during this courtship Longstreet encouraged Pickett's lax behavior, rather than restraining it.

When the Federals struck the 17th Virginia on the morning of April 15, they initially caught the Confederates sleeping in their tents. No mention is made in Southern accounts of this action of Pickett's presence at the scene. He may have been returning from a nocturnal visit to Sallie Corbell or sleeping off the effects of long hours in the saddle. At least, despite their embarrassment, the Confederates did not have to pay for George Pickett's behavior on this occasion as they would later at Five Forks.

Regardless of Longstreet's affection for him, the flashy Virginian suffered criticism from some of his colleagues. Colonel William Dabney Stuart of Richard Garnett's division complained about Pickett's behavior when writing to his wife, and Colonel Eppa Hunton, also of Garnett's division, was particularly harsh. He recalled rather caustically seeing the general leaning over his horse's neck in order to protect himself from enemy fire as the two men rode along an exposed portion of the line. Because officers were supposed to set the standard for unflinching courage and disdain toward the opponents shooting at them, Hunton considered Pickett's actions most unmanly. He berated his superior's moral failing and tried to counteract it by riding "bolt upright in my saddle."[12] Pickett undoubtedly was attempting to spare himself for more courtship, although given his penchant for nocturnal wanderings, it is a wonder that he was not dozing as he lay on his horse's neck. At one point in the campaign, Colonel T. G. Barham of the 24th Virginia Cavalry did find Pickett asleep in an unusual place. The colonel sought to rest against a fence, when the rail upon which he was leaning gave way. It fell on top of a man sleeping below, awakening the fellow abruptly. The man, George Pickett, stood up bellowing curses at the disturbance.[13]

While Pickett was trying to catch a nap whenever possible, the commanders of the Union gunboats in the Nansemond River had to maintain their vigilance. The riverfront remained vulnerable and open to Confederate exploitation. George Getty spent much of the fourteenth personally reconnoitering the area opposite the strong Confederate battery at Norfleet's farm. This was the battery that had pummeled the Union fleet, disabling the *Mount Washington*. The strength of the Confederate position alarmed Getty. Summoning artillery crews, supporting troops, and laborers from the "Contraband Camp" in town, the industrious Union officer set about counteracting the Southern activity across the river. Getty's reactions would do as much as anything to ensure that the Confederates would not cross the Nansemond without a fight, if they tried to cross at all.

As night fell the Union general placed sharpshooters on the point across from the Southern position to dispute any Confederate crossing and harass their gun crews. Behind this defensive screen he deployed the 10th New Hampshire and a section of artillery. Throughout the night of the fourteenth, these troops dug rifle pits.

Getty also carefully selected two sites for Union batteries, based upon his observations during the day and his past experience as an artillery officer. The two sites, Battery Kimball and Battery Morris, were 1,200 and 900 yards, respectively, away from the Norfleet Battery across the Nansemond. The blacks and Union artillery crewmen worked with a vengeance through the night. By midnight they had completed Battery Kimball. Getty put two 20–pounder Parrott guns and one 3–inch gun into this position. By two A.M. the diligent laborers had finished Battery Morris as well and had three 10–pounder Parrotts in position there. Finally, the Federals constructed screens from tree limbs and underbrush to mask the two batteries they had so painstakingly built.

At daylight on the fifteenth, the Federals cut away the screens that masked the guns of Battery Morris and opened a brisk fire on the Confederates across the river. The aroused Southerners quickly responded in kind. Soon they were blazing away energetically at Battery Morris. Unwittingly the Confederates had fallen victim to Getty's simple but effective plan. The Southern fire exposed the position of each gun, allowing the Union gunners in Battery Kimball, still undetected, to sight their own pieces with accuracy. While the Confederates focused their attention on Morris, the artillerists in Kimball threw aside their screens and commenced firing.

The battery commander in Kimball initially directed the fire of the three Union guns at only one of the Confederate pieces. The gunners then fired successively at the other two Southern artillery pieces. The strategy worked to perfection. In short order, all three Confederate guns fell silent. All the while, the guns of Battery Morris continued to fire as well. This, when coupled with the other battery and the fire of the sharpshooters on the point, who sprayed the embrasures of the Confederate battery, proved most effective. Southern attempts to run off the sharpshooters with blasts of canister failed, and the combination of rifle and cannon fire proved too much for the Norfleet Battery. After two hours the Confederate fire slackened. At the end of three, it ceased altogether.[14]

Despite this local Union success, Peck still feared a Confederate river crossing most of all.[15] If the Confederates succeeded in driving the gunboats off and interposing a force between Suffolk and Norfolk, it would place Peck's garrison in a most precarious position. He need not have worried. The safety of the river flank rested upon the indefatigable Getty and the talents of naval commanders Lamson and Cushing, not upon the distraught

Peck. Getty personally surveyed his lines and supervised the placement of reinforcements. He ordered the construction of roads and bridges to mitigate the river's twisted course and the confusing network of country roads behind it. The marshy terrain meant that many of these military roads had to be corduroyed on long stretches.

Such work required many hours of fatiguing toil. Details of infantrymen detached from their regular units served as "Pioneers" to complete the tasks. Often short of adequate tools, these teams of men worked in all types of weather and conditions. Their strenuous exertions resulted in a considerably less contorted line of march for units and supplies along the Nansemond River.[16] Peck augmented the effort to strengthen the river line by directing his signalmen to open a line of communication with Getty's front.[17]

Yet even with Getty's efforts on land, Admiral Lee was not optimistic. He complained loudly to Secretary of the Navy Gideon Welles, condemning the gunboats as "weak river craft" and the Nansemond as "a mere creek." But he saved his final swipe for Peck and Dix. "The army authorities make frequent, urgent and embarrassing calls on me for gunboats to assist them in holding weak detached posts and long, weak lines, which they can not hold, and which the gunboats could not make secure even if I had the number and kind which these extraordinary calls require."[18]

Although he did not share his commander's pessimism, Lamson was not satisfied with his army counterparts either. He remained skeptical of any assurances. "They say that the rebel batteries are all silenced," he explained, "which I suppose means that they [the Confederates] have rolled the guns a little back into the woods." The naval officer was also critical of army operations. "They keep a very poor lookout along the river," he remarked caustically. "I have shelled [the] rebels twice from where I am lying, and the army wished to know what I was firing at." Nevertheless, Lamson and Getty cooperated in most areas. The general offered the lieutenant supplies, while the latter promised that he would assist the infantry "in any way possible."[19]

The naval commanders had reason to be wary. The Nansemond River continued to be dangerous for Peck's forces in Suffolk. On the same morning the Federals blasted the Norfleet Battery into submission, Confederate general French rode toward the river to fulfill his role as commander and adviser of the Southern artillery on the Nansemond. His objective was "to endeavor to destroy the gunboats of the enemy in the Nansemond River," which meant finding even better locations for batteries. To that end he ordered the batteries of R. M. Stribling, W. D. Bradford, and J. C. Coit to take up positions along the river, hoping to lure the Federal gunboats into another duel.[20]

By the evening of the seventeenth, General French had more than just a professional grudge against the Union gunboats, he had a personal one as well. During the day Cushing put pickets on the left bank of the river to prevent a surprise attack from an unseen battery. About noon French's chief engineer, Henry J. Rogers, went down to the river to site positions for the Confederate guns. Accompanied only by an armed civilian as a guide, the engineer approached to within 300 yards of the vessels in the river. He did not expect Cushing's countermeasures on land, and the pickets captured him.[21] That night Longstreet dashed off a note to French: "I regret to learn that Lieutenant Rogers is probably captured. I hope that we are more troublesome to the gunboats than they are to us."[22]

To settle the score French contrived another unpleasant surprise for the pesky gunboats. This time, however, he would strike them where they least expected it and would therefore be most vulnerable: at anchor. He detailed "sixty good riflemen" from the 6th South Carolina for the special duty. Their captain found three Union vessels anchored "close up to the shore, not suspecting any disturbance." Silently they "crawled up so near as to hear the conversation of the watch on board one of the boats."

At dawn the Southerners struck. One of the adventurers remembered: "The nearest boat had a sentinel on shore, who fired at us and made for his boat. Then we opened on every man in sight, brought down one out of the rigging, and kept the port holes of the vessel so hot they could not get to fire their guns. Steam was up, however, and this boat rapidly backed away down the stream, and so did two others which were in easy range of us." As the boats steamed away, they shelled their audacious assailants with canister. However, the Confederates suffered no casualties in the affair.[23] As Colonel John Bratton wrote his wife two days later, "God favors the brave."[24]

April 18 was as warm and fair as the previous day. The lines remained generally quiet, with only intermittent firing. Even the river flank stayed unusually inactive. Captain Robert M. Stribling, commanding the battery in the formidable Confederate work at Hill's Point, reported, "Saturday was a day of comparative quiet, no shots of any consequence being fired at the fort and we not firing at all."[25]

Turner Vaughan of the 4th Alabama was on picket in Fort Huger, the work Stribling's battery occupied. He noted the presence of three Union gunboats in the lower Nansemond but was little disturbed by them. By mid-afternoon he was forced to take cover, but not because of enemy shelling.

He noted in his diary: "2 o'clock in the fort. I am lying in a bomb-proof—a pit dug in the ground and covered with a plank and dirt for the men to get into to escape fragments from bursting shell. It is cool & pleasant in here and I have entered it to avoid the hot sunshine without. The gunboats have thrown 12 shells at us, some of them bursting on the edge of the fort[.] our batteries have not replied. No firing going on at present except by sharp shooters."[26]

An air of complacency gripped the Confederates. All seemed well. They had penned Peck up in Suffolk, with no apparent recourse beyond staying put or falling back to Norfolk. Their batteries had punished the Union gunboats and restricted their movements. The audacity of the raid on the gunboats confirmed this feeling. Colonel Bratton mirrored this attitude in a letter to his wife on the evening of April 19: "A party was sent off to fight the gunboats and they are now engaged and have been for some time. We will not hear the result until tonight. It is safe on our side. We may capture or sink them, or should we fail, they can only stay in the river and we withdraw. They cannot capture or rout us. We feel no uneasiness about the result therefore. It will be either that they have been captured or have escaped. We fear nothing for our party."[27] The Confederate batteries and Union gunboats renewed their duel on the morning of April 19. The noise of the fighting prompted Longstreet to inquire of French, "Please let me know the result of the furious cannonade now going on as soon as you learn."[28] In turn, French asked for the same information from the chief of artillery, Major L. M. Shumaker.[29] Neither Confederate officer went to the river to investigate personally. French felt ill, and apparently Longstreet was too busy with the affairs of running a campaign.[30] However, both men were concerned about the infantry support for the river batteries. Longstreet wanted to know if the batteries were properly supported.[31] Perhaps encouraged by his superior, French instructed Shumaker: "Show this to Colonel Connally and have him post his regiment to repel any landing of infantry against the batteries. They had better move down near the battery of Stribling's."[32]

Two companies of the 44th Alabama, under Captain D. L. Bozeman, provided close support for Stribling's battery at Hill's Point. The 55th North Carolina, under Colonel John Kerr Connally, offered general support for all the batteries posted along the Nansemond. Stationed at various points on the Reed's Ferry Road, Connally's regiment had been in reserve near the river for only two days when French ordered it to move toward the river. The order came late in the afternoon of the nineteenth.[33] Connally did not know precisely where the batteries were or how he should support them.

Rather than march the entire regiment to the river, he sent two officers to investigate. As darkness began to fall, they had not returned to report. Connally continued to wait, well to the rear of Hill's Point and out of supporting distance.[34]

In the meantime, the Federals were preparing to make an attack that had already failed twice. Lamson had vowed to Admiral Lee on the eighteenth, after the first failure, "I shall not be satisfied unless I take the battery that knocked the *Mount Washington* to pieces."[35] Despite the setbacks, the naval officer remained determined. Getty supported the idea and agreed to supply the infantry for an assault.[36]

At 5:30 P.M. on April 19, 130 men from the 8th Connecticut and 140 men of the 89th New York waited at Council's Landing. These men embarked upon the *Stepping Stones* and settled behind canvas screens set to mask their presence aboard the vessel.[37] Getty paused only long enough to suggest that Peck prepare to exploit a successful assault by using the point as a base for a general attack on the Southern left flank.[38]

As the gunboat moved down the river, the Confederate cannoneers watched. The Southern guns stood ready with double canister to rake the vessel as it attempted to pass. But this time things would be different. Getty later reported, "At 300 yards above the battery Lieutenant Lamson headed his boat inshore, but striking on a spile she glanced off, and, borne on the ebb-tide, was on the eve of shooting in front of the battery." If this happened, canvas would be of little protection against canister; the result would be a bloody disaster. However, Lamson saved the situation when he immediately "reversed the paddlewheels and backed her aground."[39]

Lamson's quick reaction saved the vessel from drifting in front of the Confederate guns but brought the boat aground thirty feet from the bank. Again, the moment for success hung in the balance. Seeing this, the equally quick-minded and courageous Hazard Stevens rushed to the fore and jumped into the river. Standing in the waist-deep water, he called for the others to follow. The soldiers plunged into the muddy water after him. Holding their weapons above their heads, the Union infantrymen scrambled ashore. The men fixed bayonets and raced toward the fort. They shouted as they dashed across a field and into a ravine in the rear of the Confederate work.[40]

The sudden dash caught the Southerners completely by surprise. The gunners had time to pull only one gun from its position and turn it to fire into the attacking Federals. The Alabamians opened a fierce musket fire, but the attackers' momentum proved too much. Following behind Getty's soldiers, Lamson led four 12–pounder boat howitzers into position. He discharged two rounds of canister, and the battle was over essentially before it had begun. The Federals swarmed over the rear parapet of Fort Huger, sealing Stribling's fate.

In a matter of minutes, Hill's Point was firmly in Union hands. The victory gave the Federals five fieldpieces and fifteen chests of artillery ammunition. The 54th Alabama lost five officers and sixty-six men captured. Stribling's battery lost four officers and fifty-five men captured. However, Stribling's caissons, limbers, horses, and gear were a half mile from the fort and thus escaped capture.[41] The Confederates suffered no killed or wounded, obviously surrendering as soon as it became clear the position was lost.[42] However, the Federal losses of four killed and ten wounded was testimony that the Confederates had offered at least some defense of the position.[43]

The victors hustled their prisoners across the river and immediately "turned to fortifying the position and preparing for [a counter]attack." The men hastily dug rifle pits. Getty set out pickets, manned the captured artillery pieces, and positioned the gunboats to "sweep the plain in front over which the attacking party must pass." By morning, he had secured his new line.[44]

Connally heard the Union cheers and rushed toward the fort to launch a counterattack. On the way he met two companies of the 48th Alabama under Captain Leigh R. Terrell, sent to relieve the two companies that had just been captured. Connally knew nothing of the terrain around Hill's Point, and Terrell's description persuaded him that an attack "would be worse than folly to . . . attempt." Even so, Connally deployed his men near the fort, rearranging his lines when they came under heavy Union fire. About 1 A.M. General Evander M. Law arrived on the scene and ordered the North Carolinians to pull back. Connally obeyed. No counterattack would occur on this night.[45]

The Federals took their prisoners into Suffolk and placed them in the city jail for safekeeping overnight. As the dejected defenders filed into town, they found an unusual greeting awaiting them. Ladies from Suffolk gathered on the streets and sidewalks to cheer the men, which undoubtedly lifted their spirits. Indeed, the captured artillerists and infantrymen became so buoyed by the reception that they responded in kind, cheering the onlookers themselves.[46] The next day the Federals paroled their prisoners and moved them out of Suffolk. Within a matter of days, the enlisted men would be exchanged. "Send the exchanged men to Franklin, to rejoin their companies," Sorrel wired to the station at Ivor.[47] For the officers the wait was only slightly longer. They went to Fort Delaware where they were quickly paroled and exchanged as well.[48]

Longstreet awaited word of the affair at his headquarters. He ordered troops to the vicinity of Hill's Point to prevent a general collapse and instructed French to "hurry down" to the river. Once there, he should "ascertain the facts in the case and apply the remedy." In ignorance of the situation, and perhaps out of frustration, the "War Horse" added, "If it is true that the enemy is on this side he should be driven into the river." Longstreet also worried that other batteries might be in danger as well.[49]

The business at Fort Huger, or Hill's Point, was a major setback for the Confederates. Until the nineteenth, they had done remarkably well and exhibited the confidence to show it. Now with this lightning strike came a blow to the psyche as well as the loss of a fortification that had demonstrated its worth against Union gunboats in the early days of the campaign. In one assault the Federals had managed to reverse the fortunes of war on the Nansemond and place Longstreet, not Peck, on the defensive.

"He is a Jersey man, low bred and vulgar. His heart cannot be in his business."
Southern diarist on Confederate general Samuel French

"I am exceedingly anxious to hear from Suffolk and vicinity and cannot hear."
Thaddeus Williams, 6th Virginia, April 1863

⊰ 9 ⊱ *"Waiting for the Wagons"*

SAM FRENCH WAS IN A POOR SPOT. ALREADY DISGRUNTLED WITH Longstreet anyway, the Confederate general suddenly found himself the target of newspaper editors and diarists alike. Fairly or unfairly, popular feeling ran against French, in large part due to his Northern birth and the coincidence of Fort Huger's loss. Because French felt that he bore no direct responsibility for the disaster, he considered such personal criticism unwarranted. Still, he was sensitive enough in the years following the war to write rather extensively in his memoirs about it.[1]

An editorial in the Richmond *Daily Examiner* on May 2 blasted him unmercifully: "A great responsibility attaches to some one for this stupid and shameful piece of business. The accounts that have been published and universally accepted—at least no contradiction of them has appeared—concur in giving the glory of the performance to Gen. French, another, we believe, of our Southern Generals of Northern birth, a class to whom we owe so much, from the fall of New Orleans down to the free gift of one of our best batteries to the Yankees at Suffolk."[2]

Privately, diarists also excoriated French for the embarrassment. John B. Jones, a Confederate war clerk, observed in his diary on April 22, "The loss of the two guns and forty men the other day, on the Nansemond, is laid at the door of Major-Gen. French, a Northern man!"[3] One lady lashed out at the general with great fury in her diary. "We lost a Battery last week by General French's mismanagement. He exposed and failed to support it." Then she concluded rather viciously, "He is a Jersey man, low bred and vulgar. His heart cannot be in his business."[4]

The field commanders also hurled charges and countercharges. Provocative confrontations led to questions of honor as the Alabamians impugned the reputation of the North Carolinians. Colonel Connally of the 55th North Carolina took offense. One Confederate noted that "it was the talk all over the army that Colonel Connally's regiment had behaved badly the night before." With such talk ringing in his ears, Connally rode over to General Law's headquarters to determine the veracity of the rumors he had heard. If they were true, there would have to be a challenge to meet on the dueling plain or a retraction to all that had been said to impugn his command. Connally was so angry that he did not even bother to dismount when he confronted Law. The general replied that he had gotten a report to that effect, and Connally then sought out the officers who had made it. Neither Captain Terrell nor Captain John Cussons expressed any willingness to amend what they had said. Indeed, Cussons, an Englishman who had come to America and was known throughout the command as "Law's wild man," deliberately goaded the North Carolinian. "No, Colonel, I did not," he offered when Connally asked him if he had accused the North Carolinians of cowardice, "but I tell you what I now say: That if you gave your men orders to retire when the enemy appeared in their front, they obeyed orders d——d promptly last night." "I hold you responsible sir, for that remark," came the instant reply, to which Cussons calmly observed, "All right, Colonel, I will be most happy to accommodate you."[5]

There was nothing left but the field of honor. Satisfaction must be gotten for such an outrage. Connally issued a challenge to duel, joined by Major Alfred H. Belo. Captains Terrell and Cussons accepted the challenge. The Alabamians had the right, as the challenged party, to choose the weapons they wished for the affair. Apparently with the intent of hitting someone, Terrell chose double-barreled shotguns. Cussons decided upon the Mississippi rifle. Both agreed to engage their opponents at forty paces.

All designated seconds to negotiate, as prescribed by the code duello, and to carry on if the need arose.[6]

On the appointed day, April 28, the combatants assumed their places. The two pairs of antagonists stood in adjacent fields, but neither pair could see the other. Cussons stood opposite Belo, his long black hair falling against his gray suit. Belo wore his dress uniform. Both held their rifles at the ready as the elaborate process played out. Finally the countdown came and shots followed, but neither man hit the other. One of the seconds inquired if the duelists were satisfied. Belo replied that he was not, and the men fired again, this time with a round passing through the North Carolinian's coat, grazing his neck near the shoulder. Although seen to wince, Belo never admitted that he had been struck, but he was angry enough to demand a third round of shots. "Major, this is d——d poor shooting we are doing today," Cussons called out. "If we don't do better than this we will never kill any Yankees."[7]

Suddenly a doctor from the other field rushed up. "Don't fight so d——d fast," he called out, waving his hat to catch their attention in time. "We are about to settle this matter over yonder." Connally and Terrell had reached a satisfactory agreement before exchanging any shots with the shotguns. As far as they were concerned, the matter was concluded. Despite later disagreement over exactly what had been said, the men met at an ambulance to share drinks of whiskey and salute each other's courage. Almost certainly Cussons and Belo repeated their agreement that they would all have to exhibit better marksmanship "when we meet the enemy again."[8]

There is no evidence that either Longstreet or Hood was aware of the duel, officially or privately. However, knowledge of the duel was widespread. The *Rome (Ga.) Tri-Weekly Courier* mentioned the affair on two occasions.[9] Hood biographer Richard McMurry has concluded: "If he did not know, he was ignorant of what was transpiring in his division; if he knew and did nothing to stop the duel, he was guilty of irresponsibility. In either case, the Texan . . . did not exercise effective command."[10]

If nothing else, in the wake of the shocking setback at Fort Huger, the air of complacency permeating the Confederate ranks disappeared. Recriminations replaced smugness as Southern leaders sought to shift responsibility and place blame. Southern newspapers generated or fed rumors and speculation. How could the enemy have surprised an entire battery and its infantry support? Who was responsible for the loss that led to the parade of "rebel" prisoners through the streets of Suffolk? The only thing that was certain was that most of the Confederates positioned near or alongside the river would exercise more vigilance from this point onward.

One exception may well have been John Bell Hood. Perhaps he, like Pickett, had his mind on something else. The Texan sorely missed his Richmond associates, especially Buck Preston. Recalling a parlor game he played with Buck, Hood confided to his friend Dr. Darby, "I say, doctor, this is not as pleasant as [being at] the corner of Clay Street *and* [playing] *casino.*"[11] Boredom, coupled with the embarrassing loss of the battery at Fort Huger on his sector of the line, contributed to Hood's misery. The "lights and laughter" of the Confederate capital seemed far removed from the quiet banks of the Nansemond.

Hood also missed his association with Robert E. Lee. Lee had been superintendent of West Point when Hood was there and has been described as the "greatest influence of West Point on Hood."[12] Lee and Hood renewed their association in Texas; once again, they were on good terms. Lee even offered the younger man "fatherly advice" on the benefits of marrying well. These personal experiences with Lee profoundly influenced Hood, who wrote of his "affection and veneration" for Lee.[13]

The desire Hood had to return to the Richmond limelight, or at least to serve again on a more promising front under Lee, was apparently more than he could handle. He felt prompted to write Lee: "Here we are in front of the enemy again. . . . I presume we will leave here so soon as we gather all the bacon in the country. When we leave here, it is my desire to return to you. If any troops come to the Rappahannock please don't forget me."[14] Even after the war he would recall his mind-set in those days. "I was most anxious to rejoin my old chief, General Lee. Never did I so long to be with him as in this instance, and I even proceeded so far as to apply for permission to move with my division to his support."[15]

Hood was an unhappy general at Suffolk, and his attitude was reflected in his performance. When it is recalled that Fort Huger was located in General Hood's sector of the line and under General French's command, the surprise victory of the Federals on April 19 is much less enigmatic. The Confederate high command had paved the way through negligence and indifference. Hazard Stevens, the Union officer who received the Medal of Honor for "gallantly leading a party that assaulted and captured the fort," thought the assault fortunate to succeed.[16] "If a regiment had been posted near the fort in support," he observed, "the attack would probably have failed, and in that event few of the assailants could have escaped."[17] This affair would become another of the "what-ifs" of Suffolk that the Confederates would later be asking themselves.

After their triumph at Hill's Point, the Federal services enjoyed complete harmony for only a brief time. On the night of the victory, Admiral Lee wrote Cushing: "Congratulate the general [Getty] for me. I willingly assist him and let the gunboats remain. He is of the right sort."[18] But doubts remained. The admiral feared that new Confederate batteries might be unmasked to menace his gunboats. Despite rumors that the Southerners were retreating, he wanted the gunboats out of the upper Nansemond. Lee planned to leave only the *Stepping Stones* to aid the army.[19]

In the meantime, Getty was reconsidering his own situation. His men held a strong position on Hill's Point. The gunboats and artillery easily dispersed one tentative Confederate sortie on the morning of April 20. Nevertheless, Getty had his doubts. He was expecting a Confederate attack against his force at any moment. And if such an attack proved successful, he would lose considerably more men and equipment than Stribling and Bozeman. After consulting with Peck and in ignorance of Lee's orders for the gunboats, Getty decided to evacuate Hill's Point.[20]

Getty arranged with Lamson to have the troops and equipment transported from Hill's Point. Lamson was understandably disturbed by the decision, but he carried out his task with characteristic professionalism. He explained to Lee: "General Getty will evacuate the captured battery to-night. I shall run down with the last load of troops, land them at Sleepy Hollow [Hole], and join Lieutenant Cushing."[21] The ferrying operation began at dark and proceeded uneventfully. By midnight the evacuation was complete. Getty's entire force was safely within Union lines.[22] Hill's Point and Fort Huger once again belonged to the Confederates. The feud between the navy and army continued unabated, and the Union flotilla now lay in the lower Nansemond.

Even with the Federal evacuation of Hill's Point, the Confederates were in no condition psychologically to exploit it. They had lost their fighting spirit. From top to bottom Longstreet's corps no longer seemed to have confidence. The capture of Fort Huger made the Southerners on the river fearful of a repetition. One Georgia sergeant confided in his diary: "A little after dark I reached my post, put out two sentinels to watch out and keep the yanks from landing a force on this side. I expected the boat [to] land some men on this side that night, as they had landed some a few nights before, and captured five of our guns and 150 men, but they did not attempt to land, everything was quiet. I was up the most of the night watching the gunboats."[23]

Longstreet himself no longer seemed to care about seizing the initiative. He appeared increasingly content simply to avoid further losses. Moxley Sorrel, his assistant adjutant general, kept up a steady stream of messages that reflected the defensive tone of the Confederate high command at Suffolk. On April 21 he wrote General French to ask "what arrangement or disposition you have made for watching the gunboats or other movements of the enemy on the river."[24] French replied, "Inasmuch as the troops of General Hood extended to Hill's Point I did not think the watching of the movements of the enemy [there] devolved on me." Then in a backhanded manner he observed, "I will thank the general to state what should be the number and character of the forces he wishes me to send there, and if he wishes it to be done to-night."[25] To his credit Sorrel responded succinctly and dispassionately. Longstreet wanted French to "keep at least a lookout on the river to discover what may be going on," and other arrangements would follow.[26] Of course, this was to be done not for the purpose of ambushing the gunboats, as the Confederates had done earlier, but to keep the Federals from jolting them again with another sudden assault.

On the twenty-second Longstreet had the unsavory task of making a report of the Hill's Point debacle to Secretary Seddon. "We were so unfortunate as to meet with a serious disaster on the 18th in losing Captain Stribling's battery, 55 of his men, and 70 [men] of General Law's brigade," he explained. After providing an overview of this untoward development, Longstreet attempted to justify his delay in forwarding this information to Richmond. "I have not made any report of the facts because I had hoped to have General French's report of the facts officially." The dilatory response of this subordinate forced the "War Horse" to wait no longer. "As well as I can judge at present," he assessed strongly, "the misfortune is due to the entire want of vigilance on the part of the troops in the front." Left barely concealed was the implication that because General French had immediate authority over the dispositions and actions of these men, he must bear the requisite responsibility for their successes and failures.[27]

Still stinging from the necessity of having to forward such a negative report, Longstreet directed Sorrel to communicate once more with General French. The message contained strained references of respect, but Sorrel's tone was quite different than it had been on the previous day. "The enemy retired from this side of the river yesterday, and the lieutenant-general commanding expects that you will resume the responsibilities of the river batteries and their protection, if it is agreeable to you," he observed at Longstreet's behest. He ended on a blistering note chiding French for not making the proper disposition of supporting troops for the batteries on the river. Things would have to be different from this point. "The commanding general expects you to make such arrangements as you deem necessary to secure the river from another surprise," Sorrel pointed out. Longstreet had had enough. There was to be no repetition of Fort Huger. "He will be glad to offer suggestions upon any particular point on which you may have doubts," Sorrel concluded.[28]

Also on the twenty-second, Sorrel wrote General Hood regarding abatis, a defensive measure.[29] It was a message he would repeat to French five days later.[30] At the same time Longstreet's adjutant warned Pickett: "I am directed to caution you against any of the enemy's efforts to surprise [you]. Extreme vigilance and energy are required, and it is expected that you will give the subject every attention."[31] Perhaps Longstreet felt the need to exercise greater control over his subordinate commanders, while emphasizing the defensive more than ever.

News of Longstreet's campaign was slowly filtering out to those from the area who were far away. For young John T. Riddick, word had finally arrived of his brother's wounding. He wrote his sister Annie from the Virginia Military Institute in Lexington, where he was learning to be an officer and a gentleman, on April 19. "I received your letter yesterday and was extremely sorry to hear that Mills was wounded and I wish you would answer this letter as soon as you receive it and let me know how he is and where he was wounded at." Then he added quickly, "But I hope he was not mortally wounded." The events in John's old hometown had taken his mind off his studies. "Tell Pa I would like very much to come home and see Mills and also to go to Suffolk and every since I heard of the news about Mills and Suffolk I have not opened a book."[32]

The emergency of Mills's wounding had passed when John sat down to write his next letter to his sister on the twenty-eighth. The letter was filled with the innocent reflections of a boy who had not yet seen combat for himself. "Tell Mills that I will write him next week if I can possibly get time," the younger brother promised. In any case Annie should "tell him to come up here. I have the best drill corps he ever saw to show him but I cannot say anything about our uniform."[33]

Another native of the region, Thaddeus G. Williams, serving with the Army of Northern Virginia near the Rappahannock, also expressed the terrible pain of not knowing exactly what was happening near his hometown. "I am exceedingly anxious to hear from Suffolk and cannot hear," he complained to a friend participating in Longstreet's campaign on April 22, 1863.

"Will you please be kind enough to write me all the news of any importance from Suffolk, and Genl. Longstreets Army[?]" Williams had hoped
to be part of the operation himself, but orders to that effect had been coun-
termanded, and he was forced to remain in central Virginia while other
comrades moved off to the southeast toward Nansemond County and
home.

Briefly digressing in his letter to note that "we are not expecting any fight
at this time up here," Williams returned to the subject uppermost in his
mind. "I do sincerely hope that we may soon get news of the surrender of
Suffolk and the whole Yankee Army to General Longstreet's forces. Please
write me all the news from the entire Community of Nansemond." Then
the captain unloosed a torrent of pent-up anger: "I am very glad to know
that you and your family succeeded in getting out of the lines of the hated
Vandals, for you never would have seen any pleasure as long as you
remained subject to their insults, and under their Iron rule for it seems to
me, that they are the most detestable set of beings that God in his wisdom
has ever [allowed] to inhabit this Earth; and I am in hopes that the time will
soon come when we shall get rid of them entirely from our once peaceful
and happy Homes."[34]

While soldiers from the area serving elsewhere hoped to hear of a decisive victory, the Federals began to suspect in late April that "the attack on
Suffolk is only a grand foraging expedition." This view gained credence from
the corroborative stories of deserters, one of whom acknowledged "that
wagons were running night and day carrying provisions of all kinds across
their pontoon bridge on the Blackwater."[35]

Whatever else he might hope to accomplish, Longstreet reiterated the
primacy of the food-gathering mission to Secretary Seddon on April 17.
"The principal object of the expedition was to drew out supplies for our
army. I shall confine myself to this unless I find a fair opportunity for something more." But, if "something more" did not present itself, Lee's "War
Horse" was unlikely to seek it out actively, given his penchant for caution.
He had every reason to be content with the present state of affairs. "The
reports of bacon and corn are very favorable thus far," he assured the war
secretary.[36]

Indeed, Longstreet's Confederates were gathering a great abundance of
bacon, corn, and fodder and hauling it to Franklin for shipment to General
Lee. With transportation for these supplies often short, the Southerners
impressed horses and wagons or improvised with oxen, mules, and carts.[37]
Supplies poured in as Longstreet's net swept wide over southeastern

Virginia and northeastern North Carolina. The account for John Riddick during this period read:

April 17th	500 Pound Fodder	$2.00	10.00
" 18th	15 Bushels Corn	$1.90	28.50
" "	640 Pounds Fodder	$2.25	14.40
" 19th	360 "	$2.25	8.10
" "	20 Bushels Corn	$1.50	38.00
" "	450 Pounds Fodder	$2.25	10.00
			109.00

Received at South Quay the 19th day of April 1863 [38]

Jethro Riddick delivered 100 bushels of corn and 2,484 pounds of fodder on April 13 to Cyprus Chapel, earning $169.68. On the nineteenth he took twenty barrels of corn, worth $200; 1,885 pounds of fodder, worth $42.41; and an additional 1,200 pounds of fodder, worth $27.00, to South Quay. He returned on April 21 with 45 bushels of corn ($90.00) and 1,100 pounds of fodder ($26.25) for a total in receipts of $116.25.[39] Edward C. Riddick took home $40.00 for the "Forty Gallons Vinegar @.50" and the "Ten Bushels Peas @ 2.00," "Received near Suffolk, Virginia on the 29th of April 1863."[40]

Of course, not everyone was prepared to yield so readily to the hungry Confederates. Some undoubtedly tried to deny the prying Southerners from access to their animals and goods in their barns and larders on the grounds of their own or their family's self-preservation. Others harbored latent Unionist views, if not outright loyalty to the U.S. government and its forces. Naval lieutenant R. H. Lamson recommended one such man to General Peck a few days after Longstreet's appearance in the region. "A Mr. Singleton who lives near Western Branch came up and says he has a number of horses and mules, and a quantity of corn which he fears will fall into the enemy's hands. I directed him to you."[41]

Despite the existence of even larger pockets of Unionism in eastern North Carolina, the sweep of the neighboring counties there also yielded impressive results for the Confederates. A list of producers in Gates County hinted at the wealth of supplies available there, although some of the men on the list were either Unionists or unwilling to accept Confederate scrip from commissary and quartermaster agents.

1. Frank Winslow . . . 2 miles from Bridge   60,000 lbs bacon (5 miles from Sandy Cross on the Edinton Road)
2. Wiley Riddick (on Middle Swamp in 1 mile of Wiggins Cross Roads)   corn fodder & bacon 50 lbs.

3. Benj. Saunders (Middle Swamp / 2 miles from Riddicks)   300 Bbls. corn   25,000 lbs. fodder   20,000 lbs. bacon
4. Wm. Jesse Savage (Wiggins Cross Roads)   30 bbls. corn   5,000 lbs. fodder   5,000 lbs. bacon
5. Jno. Hill (Middle Swamp)   150 Bbls corn   5,000 lbs. fodder   10,000 lbs. bacon
6. Saml Herrell (Middle Swamp)   200 bbls. corn   20,000 lbs. fodder   10,000 lbs. bacon
7. Joshua Whidbee (Middle Swamp)   150 bbls. corn   15,000 lbs. fodder   10,000 lbs. bacon
8. Wm. Harrell (near Sunbury)   150 bbls. corn   10,000 lbs. fodder   5,000 lbs. Bacon
9. Geo. Costen, Davis Parker, Tom Walton, Dick Oden, Wm. Beaman, Bob Ballard & numerous others[42]

These astounding figures of abundance represented the untapped wealth of a region that had lain beyond Confederate grasp since 1862. One historian noted that this operation secured "enough meat to feed Longstreet's army of 20,000 men for nearly a month at the current bacon ration of a quarter pound per day!"[43] A Virginian wrote his wife in late April, "We got a fair chance of bacon & corn from around there." Even so, he could not resist taking a shot at his fellow Southerners. "You would be amused to see the merriment the boys have at the ignorance of some of the N.C. people of the low country," he explained. "Some of them seem to be ignorant of the war going on & said when asked some thing about it that they beleived it was away out in Virginny or somewhere out that way."[44]

"We have already gotten out 1,000,000 lbs.," a Southerner gloated excessively about bacon, adding, "and still a great quantity is yet in these counties around here and in the edge of N.C."[45] Another, probably remembering the lean winter months, could scarcely contain himself. "O, my ain't we in it?" the Texan exuded. "We just swim in bacon." They were enjoying "big rations," he reported, "and all the time we have an immense wagon train hauling out bacon, corn, wheat, flour and great droves of beeves. It's a big haul we are making."[46] There was reason to celebrate, even for Longstreet.

In addition to the foraging operation, Benning's soldiers and John A. Baker's North Carolina cavalry drove Union sympathizers, or "buffaloes," from the region.[47] The worst of the bunch, a band organized by Confederate deserter Jack Fairless, had enjoyed a period of almost unrestricted freedom to plunder. By supplying the Federals with information and assistance when they wanted it, he received the trappings of military authority. But by the time Benning and Baker went into the region for Longstreet, Fairless had already died at the hands of his own men. Attacks from Southern militia and regulars subsequently dispersed the band of renegades.[48] This left these Confederates free to sweep the area of the remnants of guerrillas, while gathering food and forage from local farmers. Benning and Baker were even successful in ferreting out supplies being hidden from them, including 100,000 pounds of bacon hidden "in a corn crib covered with corn."[49]

On the lines at Suffolk, the lethargy of siege warfare began to affect both attacker and defender. In reality the little town was not besieged. The Federals maintained their communication with Norfolk via the railroad, relatively undisturbed. Union gunboats continued to ply the waters of the Nansemond, albeit with considerably greater caution. Blue-clad reinforcements poured into Suffolk in increasing numbers, making it less likely that Longstreet could change matters even if he wanted to do so. But the Federals were not yet confident enough to challenge the Confederates with more than reconnaissances in force.

On the days when the skirmishing on land subsided and the soldiers remained within the relative safety of their earthworks, life could still prove dangerous on the front lines. Long stretches of time often passed with little or no action, but because both sides employed sharpshooters with deadly effectiveness, the exposure of any target would prompt a quick reply. One soldier wrote his brother on April 24, "The rebs still beset us." This activity was becoming more than annoying. "The firing of Secesh sharpshooters is now so close that sentries can no longer mount the parapet. It is no unusual thing for the rifle balls to pass through our tents."[50] In the exposed camp of the 99th New York, a bullet struck a soldier in the leg as he lay on his bunk reading a book. Another suffered a wound to the forearm when he extended a tin cup to a colleague for a refill of coffee.[51]

The *New York Herald* praised the exceptional qualities of the 99th New York: "The manner in which these brave boys have borne the constant annoyance of the rebel sharpshooters has never been excelled by any troops in the world." The newspaper writer noted that Confederate fire riddled the soldiers' tents and threatened the company streets along which the men had to walk, before concluding proudly, "This [exposure] would demoralize any troops in the world unless of the highest morale."[52] The Federals tried to lessen this harassment by directing artillery fire against the Southern rifle pits, but this only served to expose the gunners themselves and seems not to have had any considerable impact on their targets.[53]

There were also moments of humor, intentional and otherwise. Comrades later remembered close calls and entertaining incidents. Longstreet himself chose to relate one in which the Confederates enjoyed a practical joke at their enemy's expense. His story featured a captured Federal signal post and a stuffed figure the Southerners dubbed "Julius Caesar." A Confederate, whom Union fire toppled from the perch unceremoniously the previous day, apparently dreamed up the "scheme by which he hoped to get even with the Yankees."

Under the protective cloak of nightfall, the soldier climbed to the platform, fixed "Julius Caesar" tightly to it with a rope, and scrambled back. He now had only to wait for daylight. "A little after sunrise 'Julius Caesar' was discovered by some of the Federal battery officers," Longstreet explained, "who prepared for the target—so inviting to skillful practice." However, this time the man did not tumble from his seat to the derisive cheers of the Federals. "The new soldier sat under the hot fire with irritating indifference," until the Confederates began to cheer "Julius Caesar." "The other side quickly recognized the situation," Longstreet recalled, "and good-naturedly added to ours their cheers for the old hero."[54]

James Longstreet was remembering this incident many years after the fact. It may actually have occurred as he recalled it, or it may have been a memory based upon an event witnessed and recorded by a member of the 11th Rhode Island. In a letter dated April 20, Henry Simmons recounted an incident at a captured signal station "out a mile or so from our works." A few Confederates had taken the opportunity to climb the abandoned tower, approximately "50 feet or so high and commenced doing every thing they could to insult our folks. At least two or three went up & began slapping the *seat of their pantaloons* at our folks." The Federals could not ignore such taunting indefinitely. Soon "some artillerists in one of the forts brot a 6 pound Parrott gun to bear on them and [at] the very first shot down came the scamps heels over head." Apparently the Confederates learned their lesson, for as Simmons proudly added, "The cannon ball took them out of it & they have not been up since to go through their performance."[55]

The men even used the sharpshooting threat as a diversion from the boredom of trench warfare. A New Yorker explained to his brother: "Our men amuse themselves, when at leisure, by throwing nails over the heads of the Mass. and New Hampshire men encamped near us and seeing them dodge and duck. The nail makes a noise very much like a bullet."[56] One group of Union soldiers made braving the gauntlet of Southern fire a part of their daily ritual for gathering water at a nearby spring. Running relays, the men relished taunting each other until a "volunteer leader" agreed to make the first dash and risk the enemy fire. Then each in his turn would brave the gauntlet until all were safely at the spring out of sight of their Confederate tormentors. "The return was equally exciting," remembered one of the men, concluding that "no doubt it afforded amusement to the Confederate sharpshooters half a mile away." Fortune smiled on the participants in these deadly games, for the writer recalled that "none of the boys was hit."[57]

In addition to other dangers, the Confederates found the heavy guns of the Union riverine units particularly worrisome. Unless they took a direct hit from one of these large projectiles, the annoyance was tolerable, but if a shot fell accurately, there was no protection. A Union soldier later found gruesome evidence of one shell's effectiveness. "We see where a shell from one of our gunboats had lodged in a large hut, had burst and torn some men into hundreds of pieces, shreds, and scattered them all about," he explained. The only word he could find for the scene he had just described was "horrible."[58]

Although subject to fire from Union gunboats, Longstreet's Confederates had the freer hand at Suffolk. They scoured the countryside for food and forage at will. They pelted enemy gunboats. Small parties of Southerners melted into the Dismal Swamp, reemerging in the Union rear to harass isolated pickets and sabotage the rail lines. Sometimes individuals crossed the lines as well to garner information on Union dispositions for Longstreet.[59]

The Great Dismal Swamp, extending from North Carolina into the region of Virginia between Suffolk and Norfolk, was an impressive natural phenomenon. Union general Peck worried that it might offer the Confederates an avenue for attack over some unknown road or cart path, but it acted as an effective barrier to troop movements, especially once the rains set in late in April. Both sides dispatched patrols into its murky depths, but conditions mitigated against anything on a more grand scale. On at least one occasion, competing patrols had to agree to suspend hostilities long enough to help each other get out of the swamp. Lieutenant Colonel Martin Buffum of the 4th Rhode Island was undoubtedly correct when he observed, "In my opinion not the least apprehension is to be felt of any attempt to construct roads at any point between Lake Drummond [in the heart of the Swamp] and the R. Road [to Norfolk] for the passage of any force whatever."[60]

Whatever diversions the men might find, they continued to engage in the same activities that had been marking their time at Suffolk. The correspondent of the *Rome Tri-Weekly Courier*, attached to a Georgia regiment, explained to his readers: "Throwing up breastworks, planting batteries, changing positions, scouting and doing picket duty is still the order of exercises."[61] One Federal soldier wrote his wife concerning the fighting, "We are shelling tham by spells day and night; we have got so used to it that we cannot go to sleep unless there is a few shotts fiered every few minutes."[62]

There were no sweeping motions of grand armies here. Brief skirmishes and desultory picket and artillery firing were the standard. Men fought or dug. They stood watch or slept. They marched or tried to entertain themselves in their makeshift camps. And through all of the monotony of this style of warfare, men bled and died. They fell victim to a shell's jagged shrapnel or a sharpshooter's bullet. Some died less glamorously from disease or infection. The wounded sent back to hospitals at Fort Monroe or Petersburg told a grim tale of the toll both sides were paying in a type of warfare that would become commonplace in 1864–65.

For the remainder of the campaign, which lasted until May 3, the number of significant skirmishes dropped dramatically until near the end. On April 23 Cushing launched a raid on Chuckatuck in retaliation for an incident in which Confederate scouts killed a seaman, wounded another, and captured three others after luring them ashore with a white flag.[63] On the following day Corcoran launched a reconnaissance in force on the southern flank. He suffered thirty-five casualties before returning to the main Union line.[64]

However, the Confederates were not destined to remain at Suffolk much longer. As late as April 27, Lee suggested that Longstreet strike a blow at Suffolk if it would be damaging.[65] But on April 29 Adjutant General Cooper warned him to "be prepared to move your command . . . with the least practicable delay."[66] The next day he instructed the "War Horse": "Move without delay with your command to this place [Richmond] to effect a junction with General Lee."[67] Hooker and the Union Army of the Potomac were finally on the move. Lee could no longer leave Longstreet at Suffolk. He needed him on the Rappahannock.

Confederate general French, undoubtedly still smarting from receiving the blame for the loss of Stribling's battery at Hill's Point, jotted in his diary on April 30, "'Waiting for the wagons' is still the song." The weather was not making the waiting any easier. "Terrible thunderstorm," he added on the thirtieth, remarking, "Lightning injured a number of men."[68] A variety of factors were complicating the movement of the wagonloads of supplies that hindered Longstreet's return to Lee.

In Richmond, General Cooper remained anxious, but he was unwilling for Longstreet to sacrifice the success he had achieved thus far in gathering food and forage. He clarified his peremptory April 30 order the next day. "Old Peter" was to move with "all possible dispatch [but] without incurring loss of train or unnecessary hazard of troops."[69] The "War Horse" responded with vigor. Sorrel instructed the chief quartermaster to "push the trains across the Blackwater as rapidly as you can make them go, night and day, until they are all across." The staff officer added a sense of urgency: "This is a matter of the greatest importance, and you are expected to display unusual energy in the accomplishment of the orders of the commanding general."[70] He ordered Benning to return to the Suffolk area with dispatch, leaving Baker's cavalry to guard the wagon trains.[71]

On May 2 Longstreet notified Cooper, "I cannot move unless the entire force is moved." But he added, "I will endeavor to move as soon as possible."[72] Sorrel continued to apply pressure for speed on behalf of his superior. He instructed Baker to help get the wagons across the Blackwater.[73] Although, as an anxious John Bell Hood observed, Longstreet made "every effort . . . to get to Lee at the earliest moment," the job proved daunting.[74] Longstreet's wagons were scattered throughout the countryside of southeastern Virginia and northeastern North Carolina. Thus, "the march was consequently delayed."[75]

The restlessness of the Federal forces bottled up in Suffolk made the task of regrouping and marching to Lee's aid especially monumental. Any Confederate disengagement would be harried to the fullest; Peck was not about to let his counterpart off the hook easily. The first few days of May promised to test the resolve of Longstreet's Confederates, the civilians they were leaving behind in southeastern Virginia, and the Confederacy as a whole.

"I have not lost many men. But I have lost some
of my best soldiers."
John B. Hood, at Suffolk, to R. E. Lee

"I want to see old Suffolk once more."
A young refugee to his sister

⊰ 10 ⊱ *No-Man's-Land*

JOHN J. PECK KNEW THAT JOSEPH HOOKER WAS ABOUT TO STRIKE
at Robert E. Lee on the Rappahannock. He logically deduced that
Longstreet would soon hasten to rejoin his superior. For two of the first
three days of May, Peck pressed the Confederates along a wide front.
Just as Longstreet had probed for weaknesses in the Union defenses several weeks earlier, so the Union commander looked for signs that the
Southerners were trying to disengage.

Late in the day on May 1, the 99th New York pushed out on the South
Quay Road, under a protective screen of artillery fire from the forts facing
the road. The Confederates remained strangely quiet until the Federals
began to form, and then they tried to disrupt the process. When it was clear
that their musket fire from long range was just attracting enemy artillery,
they ceased firing. The Southerners then allowed the lead elements of the

Union line to advance well out into an open field before unleashing a deadly storm of musketry upon them.

The Confederates in the rifle pits particularly targeted the color bearers. No sooner would one fall when another person would step up and reach for the banner, only to be hit himself.[1] "As they neared the enemy's works, the fire grew hot and furious and the men dropped by tens," a witness explained. "Three times I saw the stars and stripes fall, but they were caught up again in an instant and floated out as bravely as ever."[2] Finally the order came to pull back to the Union lines. Sergeant William Stetson, one of the participants, remembered that the men were reluctant to obey. "Four times the bugle from the South Quay battery sounded the recall before it was heeded, and then, what were left together, began the retreat, the enemy keeping up a constant fire, and singly and in squads, as best they might to protect themselves, the boys who were able, made their way back to camp."

The sergeant failed to hear the call to retreat and quickly found himself separated from his fellows. When he realized his position, he worked his way back toward his lines. "The first comrade I found was Jim Calloway, of Company D, lying in one of the ravines, shot through the cheek and bleeding profusely," he recalled. Going to the river, Stetson managed to attract the attention of some Union sharpshooters, who sent a small boat over to him. He returned to the wounded man, dragged him to the river and into the boat, and rowed to safety. James Calloway would survive but left the service shortly afterward due to disability from the wound he had suffered at Suffolk.[3]

The Confederates defending these works included men from the maligned 55th North Carolina, led by Major Alfred H. Belo, one of the duelists after the fall of Fort Huger. Belo and his men intended to erase whatever doubt remained about their fighting integrity. It was he who ordered the men to wait until the Federals moved close, so that they could use their shorter-range smoothbores to advantage. "They came in easy range," Belo explained, "and I gave the command to fire and broke them up in great disorder." When the Union troops rallied and tried to push forward again, Belo was ready for them. "This time I let them come a little closer and ordered my men to take good aim and shoot low." The result was predictable. "At the command a deadly volley was poured into them and continued so that they were routed back inside their breastworks." Whether the Federals were recalled or driven back, the effect was the same. When another officer offered to bring up reinforcements, Belo quietly replied, "No, I think the battle is over and won."[4] The Union commander, Colonel David W. Wardrop, noted only in his report, "The enemy was found

in strong force and the regiment was obliged to retire." He set his losses at
"13 killed (or died of wounds) and 31 wounded."[5]

During a lull the Federals sent out parties to bring in the dead and
wounded, "the enemy giving us aid to that end." Stetson spent the evening
"in the hospital at Suffolk," sitting up with a number of badly wounded
friends, two of whom died early the next day. "The casualties in the charge
eventually proved to be eleven killed or mortally wounded, and thirty-two
more wounded, some slightly, but many seriously," he noted. "We took out
two hundred and ten men, and so, twenty per cent of them were killed or
wounded."[6] Not much had been accomplished except to demonstrate that
the Confederates were still outside Suffolk in force, and this had been done
at a terrible cost.

Two days later another sizable Union contingent surged across a temporary bridge over the Nansemond and raced up the Providence Church
Road. These men, from several different regiments, were part of a three-
pronged operation to test Confederate strength along a wide arc. Theirs
was to be the main thrust. One of the men in the 13th New Hampshire
recalled that his regiment was up early on the third. They marched into
town, arriving about 8 A.M. and assembling near the courthouse with the
other regiments that would make the attack. Time seemed to drag as the
men anxiously awaited the signal. Finally, after a respite of "an hour or two,"
word came, and the regiments moved out.

The 103d New York led the way across a makeshift bridge of "canal boats"
with planking laid over them. Following came the 25th New Jersey, then
the 89th New York, and finally the boys from New Hampshire. Three
Connecticut regiments provided support for the others through the day.
Confederate artillery targeted them as they crossed and scrambled past "the
ruins of Capt. Nathaniel Pruden's house." To one Union witness the
Southerners appeared to be trying to hit the Union troops and the bridge
without "throwing shells into the city."[7]

Hazard Stevens, the man who had plunged into the water in the assault
of Fort Huger at Hill's Point on the nineteenth, watched as the 103d New
York and 25th New Jersey fanned out on the right side of the Providence
Church Road, while the 89th New York and 13th New Hampshire deployed
on the left. He described the action more mundanely than he had the assault
on Hill's Point, failing to note his own significant role in the drama.[8]
According to a member of the New Hampshire regiment, it was Stevens
who boldly broke the impasse that occurred after the Federals had crossed
the bridge. Climbing onto a fence, Stevens, according to this man, "waves
his hat and shouts: 'Forward!' 'Forward!'"

In a moment more almost every man in the Thirteenth is in a wild rush for the woods and the rebel rifle-pits and trenches within them, over fence, ditch, brush and what not, some with bayonets fixed, some fixing bayonets as they run, and all yelling like madmen. The enemy fires into us two quite regular volleys, and follows with a brisk firing at will before the charge is over, and a number of men in the Thirteenth are seen to fall; but the distance, 300 or 400 yards, mainly over the descending and clear ground of a cornfield, is made as quickly as men can run, and just as we enter the woods the enemy takes to his heels, leaving his dead and a few wounded in our hands . . . At 1:15 P.M. the enemy is in full retreat, the rifle-pits [are] in our hands.

During the rush the men of the two regiments on the right side of the road mixed together, making command and control difficult. Holding their captured ground, the men began to reestablish their formations and take stock. A battery under the command of the son of the abolitionist Henry Ward Beecher went into action nearby. "Lieutenant Beecher's battery exchanges rapid shots with the rebel battery in the dense timber and supported by a strong body of infantry, all of which our charge has unmasked," the writer recalled. "The firing continues until dark, many of the shells from both friend and enemy, going over our heads, cutting up the trees, treating us to the falling branches, and occasionally bursting near and giving us little rattling showers of the pieces and small shot."[9]

Some of the very bravest of the Federals died trying to encourage their comrades or exposing themselves to enemy fire for their friends' sake. Captain Lewis Buzzell, of the 13th New Hampshire, recognized the danger the Confederate sharpshooters represented to his men. Moving up behind a tree in hopes of spotting the sharpshooters who were harrying his men, Buzzell unwittingly offered himself as a target. A sharp-eyed Southerner drew a bead on the Union officer and squeezed the trigger carefully. "Oh—I'm killed!" the officer cried out, staggering "a step or two, and instantly falls forward upon his face, dead." Buzzell's death in this manner hit "the Regiment like a cold-blooded murder committed in their midst," the writer observed, "and not as a stroke of war."[10]

Another Union officer who fell on this day was Colonel Benjamin Ringold of the 103d New York. He had ridden back and forth on a white charger throughout the day conferring with General Getty and seeking to implement his instructions. Near the end of the day, musket fire ripped through Ringold, toppling him from his horse. Soldiers managed to bring him to a hospital, but the colonel would not live through the night.[11]

The sacrifice did not afterwards seem to validate the orders to advance that sent these men across the plain at Suffolk. General Peck viewed this action strictly as a reconnaissance in force. The units did not have the strength to hold more than the initial line of rifle pits the men captured, and Peck had no intention of keeping even these indefinitely. That evening, after achieving their limited success, the attackers withdrew, having suffered some sixty or seventy men killed and wounded.[12] One of the men who died from his wounds was a Presbyterian chaplain in the 25th New Jersey, Francis Butler, who had paused in the open to tend to the wounded men.[13]

For the many wounded Union soldiers, the nightmare had only begun. The regimental surgeons established a field hospital, where the stewards brought in the wounded on parts of a fence. One of these hospital attendants later recalled: "A Lieutenant from the 103d N.Y. was the first one brought in, shot straight through his head. Next a man of the 89th N.Y., then another of the 103d, then one of our own 13th boys shot through the body—and so they came all day long. Men were cut, torn and mutilated in every conceivable manner. The day was very hot and we had all we could do until after dark."[14] On the other side of the lines, his counterparts in gray were equally busy attempting to save their own casualties.

In conjunction with the attack along the Providence Church Road out of Suffolk came two smaller sorties along the Nansemond River. One was a party that crossed very early in the morning near Fort Huger. Poor visibility from darkness and fog, as well as ignorance of the area, led the contingent from the 4th Rhode Island to miss its crossing near Hill's Point by about a half mile. "I had urged upon him the importance of taking a guide," Colonel Arthur Dutton explained concerning the lieutenant colonel who led the force, but "he declined to do [so], pleading a perfect understanding of the position."

The resultant delay worried the colonel, who was supposed to have his men rendezvous with a second force near Reed's Ferry. He was even more concerned that a strong Confederate force would occupy Fort Huger, which would be in his rear as his men moved away from the river. Fortunately only Southern pickets occupied the work, whom the Rhode Islanders easily dispersed. But this was about all that Dutton's column was able to accomplish. When it tried to push inland from the river, the advance ran into stout resistance and fell back.[15]

The other force proceeded to Chuckatuck, where it confronted Confederate cavalrymen who seemed none too eager to fight. Cautiously pursuing them in the direction of Reed's Ferry, the hookup point with the Hill's

Point force, the Federals encountered a fork in the road that required them to divide into several smaller detachments. The commander of this Union expedition, Major Hiram Crosby of the 21st Connecticut, left an artillery piece and "a sufficient support" with orders "to command" both roads as they branched out from the fork. The rest of the men proceeded a short way on the Reed's Ferry Road until Crosby felt comfortable enough with the security of his position there to detach men to reconnoiter the Everett's Bridge Road, under the cover of the artillery piece.

Despite his painstaking efforts to avoid any Confederate trap that might ensnare his men, Crosby's decision to send the small patrol out on the Everett's Bridge Road encouraged the Southerners to strike. What followed was a short but sharp fight. "One of our cavalrymen was shot in the arm near the elbow," according to a participant. "Another cavalryman was hit six times and instantly killed. One bullet went into his left eye coming out of the back of the head; another went into his mouth, coming out near his right ear." These shots alone would have been enough to kill him, but "another went through his right side; another through the calf of his leg; another hit him on the hip; and another went through his neck." The Union trooper never knew what hit him.[16]

Reuniting after their brush with the enemy cavalry, the Federals next ran into Confederate infantry pickets at the Western Branch. Here the Southerners were in an awkward position, with their backs to the river. A spirited thrust netted the Union cavalrymen sixteen prisoners: a lieutenant and fifteen enlisted men. Yet this small force could do no more. Unable to effect a rendezvous with the Hill's Point force at Reed's Ferry, the men gathered their prisoners and returned to their lines.[17]

R. H. Lamson, the courageous Union naval commander, wrote to his future wife about the Confederates taken in the action on the third. "I have seen a number of Rebel prisoners to-day, rough looking fellows, but good fighters," he noted, then adding with a sense of mutual respect, "They were in the battery that fought the Mt. Washington and say they thought they would capture her without failing when she got aground."[18] More than exchanging war stories, these prisoners and the almost inevitable deserters that came into the lines would have interesting things to say about Confederate activities.

Rumors suggested that Longstreet was about to pull back from Suffolk. Such reports put Peck in a quandary. With Hooker finally moving into the wilderness near the Chancellor residence against Lee, the pressure would be on "Old Peter" to return. But the resistance to the operations sent against him demonstrated clearly enough that Longstreet and his men were firmly entrenched at Suffolk. Peck did not want to overplay his hand, but he wanted to convince his adversary that it was indeed time to go.

In retrospect, John Peck need not have worried. The evidence of resistance was deceiving. The "War Horse" had already issued elaborate orders for a phased withdrawal. During the night of May 3, while the exhausted soldiers who had fought on the Providence Church Road slogged their way back across the Nansemond into Suffolk, the Confederates began to pull out of their trenches and head for the Blackwater River. Longstreet set a strong picket to try to prevent stragglers and deserters from getting through to the Federals. This, and the orderly withdrawal, bought the Southerners a respite of a few hours.[19]

Even so, deserters managed to slip through the cordon. Colonel Dodge reported immediately following the campaign, "About 11 o'clock on the evening of the 3d instant the officer of the day reported with two deserters, who informed us that the enemy were rapidly withdrawing their forces and *en route* for the Blackwater." Dodge put his cavalrymen in the saddle and started his preparations to harry the Southerners. "Investigation and additional deserters soon confirmed the first report," he noted, and the pursuit was under way in earnest. In view of the difficulty in making any headway against the Confederate positions the day before, what Dodge saw next must have been astonishing. "Advancing rapidly but cautiously we soon arrived at the enemy's earthworks, which were found quite deserted." From that point it was a matter of capturing stragglers and deserters and making contact with the Confederate rear guard.

Near Holland's Crossroads, a small Nansemond County community southwest of Suffolk, the Union infantry halted its march. The Confederates had gotten too far ahead for the foot soldiers to catch them. However, the cavalry continued along the familiar road toward the Blackwater River. They picked up more prisoners, by one account "some 40 or 50," before they, too, called off the pursuit.[20] Nothing was going to stop Longstreet from reaching the safety of the river except infantry, and the Union infantry was too weary or too out of position at the beginning of the retreat to accomplish that task.

As the Confederates pulled back, the retreat was filled with suspense and tension, especially for the men of the rear guard. They were the ones who could expect to be hit by the enemy at any moment. One Southerner later recalled:

This falling back from Suffolk was done in regular military order, as if expecting the enemy to make hot pursuit. The trees along the roadside were chopped nearly down by the corps of sappers and miners—"sappling miners," as some of the boys called them—ready to be felled across the road by a few licks of the axe when the rear guard had passed. At the bridge across [the] Blackwater, troops were deployed in line of battle on either side of the road; the artillery was also in position, in battery, unlimbered and ready for action; General Longstreet was at the bridge seeing to it that every detail was carried out.[21]

Despite the well-ordered retreat, not everyone was so anxious to leave the region. A number of Southerners took advantage of the night and confusion to slip away. Among them were several members of the 9th Virginia. At least a dozen men, most of them farmers in the prewar period, had had enough of the bloody harvests of civil war. They only wanted to go home and resume their lives. On the other hand, the small number of men who had joined the 9th as recruits during the campaign, with minor exceptions, marched off with their new comrades when they recrossed the Blackwater River.[22]

In the early morning hours of May 4, the Federal pursuit finally tangled with the Confederate rear guard. However, the Union force was too small to hinder the Southerners as they crossed the Blackwater to safety. Other than gathering up handfuls of Confederate stragglers and deserters, the Federals could do little but return to Suffolk.[23] "Old Peter" was gone. His Suffolk campaign was over.

Yet as the men serving with Lee could have told him, by the time Longstreet disengaged at Suffolk, he was too late to have any effect whatsoever on what had been transpiring along the Rappahannock. It was on that front that Lee tested his opponent's resolve, launching the most famous flanking assault in the war with his trusted lieutenant, Thomas Jonathan "Stonewall" Jackson. That attack, coming late on May 2, smashed into the Union 11th Corps as it sat to supper. By the time the attack sputtered out, the Federals were on the defensive. However, when Jackson rode forward in the gathering darkness to reconnoiter for the next day's fighting, his men mistakenly fired into his party, severely wounding him.[24]

Although Jackson's command would fall to the cavalryman Jeb Stuart, who led it with dash and daring, the Confederacy was destined to lose its finest general.[25] Still, Lee and his army fought on steadfastly. Men from the southeastern part of Virginia bore their share of the combat at Chancellorsville, as their casualties attested. James F. Bradshaw, a twenty-year-old farmer, had enlisted at Windsor, in Isle of Wight County, two short

years earlier. He would die at Chancellorsville. Corporal Commodore
Saunders, in the 41st Virginia, had already sustained a wound at Malvern
Hill the previous summer; now, in the spring of 1863, he would fall again,
but this time mortally wounded. Others, like Richard Henry Byrd, Neverson
Howell, and Thomas W. Savage, would be captured and sent to Union prison
camps until exchanged.[26]

Lee's victory relieved the pressure in central Virginia for a time, enabling
the general to plan and set into motion a second invasion of the North.
But Longstreet's withdrawal did not relieve the Federals in southeastern
Virginia of all their concerns and responsibilities. As the weary combatants
settled back into their previous positions, the need remained first to count
the costs of the recent military operations. In human terms the price was
relatively low compared to the bloody toll exacted at Chancellorsville. Peck
stated his own losses as 44 killed, 202 wounded, and 14 missing, a total of
260 men.[27] The Union naval flotilla suffered 11 killed, 16 wounded, and 4
captured.[28]

Confederate losses were more difficult to establish. With the command
in motion and the distractions of Chancellorsville and the subsequent death
there of Stonewall Jackson, Longstreet had much more than assessing casualties on his mind. Peck offered the estimate of 500–600 killed and wounded,
500 deserters, and 400 prisoners, although his numbers were surely on the
high side.[29] The Confederates had lost five artillery pieces of the famous
Fauquier Artillery, "fresh from the foundary,"[30] in the debacle at Fort Huger,
and the valuable artillerists who had served them, in addition to losses associated with various skirmishes throughout the campaign. John Bell Hood
lamented to Lee on April 29, "I have not lost many men. But I have lost
some of my best soldiers."[31]

Just as the Federals had suffered at the hands of sharpshooters, the
Confederates lost some exceptional soldiers to the same kind of skill. A
Texan, I. N. M. "Ike" Turner, had shown great promise as a warrior before
he stood on the earthworks at Fort Huger to get a better vantage point for
observing the fighting with the Union gunboats. Across the way a Union
soldier spotted him and sent him tumbling with a mortal wound.[32] Fellow
Texan John Bell Hood decried the loss to Lee, saying that a "more noble
and brave soldier has not fallen during this war."[33] Likewise, a Virginia
colonel noted painfully, "We lose a good many men by skirmishing and
among them a great many officers picked off by sharpshooters."[34] Such
losses would prove cumulative, as the pool of talented junior officers who
were available for promotion to higher rank or responsibility diminished.

Nor were the soldiers the only ones who suffered. In addition to the destruction visited upon the area by the arrival of the Confederates and the fighting, their departure left local residents vulnerable to reprisals and retribution. For those Federals who lost friends and comrades to snipers' bullets, the temptation to seek vengeance was sometimes too great to overcome. Historian Steven Cormier has written that "some of the most concentrated destruction of civilian property occurred in the final hours of the campaign."[35]

One Union witness recalled the pursuit of the Confederates. "The early part of our route was all along lighted by houses set on fire by our Cavalry advance, in revenge for injuries received from riflemen lodged there during the siege."[36] A soldier in the 117th New York attested to the thoroughness of the destruction. "I was on picket the night of the retreat," he explained to his father. "Our men burned every house as they advanced. We could see over twenty from our post."[37] Solomon Lenfest of the 6th Massachusetts observed that during the "GRAND SKEDDADLE OF THE REBELS FROM SUFFOLK," his command moved out in pursuit. "After marching about 15 miles [on the Somerton Road] it was found that the rebs had crossed the river so we countermarched returning to camp and burning all the houses along the road."[38] Another member of the regiment explained to his parents that during the pursuit "on the somerton road about 15 miles . . . we took about 80 prisoners & don what had ought to have bin done long ago & that is we burnt about all of the buildings on the road."[39]

Others were anxious to sightsee following the Southern withdrawal. One soldier noted in his diary on May 12 that he had been assigned to picket duty on the Providence Church Road. "Since the enemy left Suffolk I've been very anxious to see the works of the enemy, and also our own defenses." As he set out across the bridge over the Nansemond, "repaired by supporting the framework in the centre upon an old canal boat," he noted the widespread destruction. Then, as he approached them, the Union soldier began to realize the extent of the main Confederate works. "Line after line of breastworks we pass and still we found them. Shot and shell lie around in every direction, and the useless *debris* of an army lies about in all directions—old coats, canteens, plates, cups, haversacks, etc."

It was not until John Habberton reached the little country church that gave the road one of its local names that he saw the unvarnished residue of war. "I went up to the church to see what was to be seen," he observed. It is unlikely that he ever forgot the scene that unfolded before him. "The floor of the church was covered with pools of blood. It had evidently been used as a hospital." The soldier found the walls marred by graffiti and "about a dozen graves" in the front churchyard marked only by "a shingle bearing the name, regt. and state of the deceased."[40]

In the aftermath of Longstreet's retreat, a considerable correspondence passed between Union commanders in the region over the viability of maintaining the Suffolk line. Dix informed General-in-Chief Halleck on May 10 that he was ready to give the place up. "Suffolk is no longer of any use to us as a position for making friends of the secessionists," he argued. "The population there and in the surrounding country are bitter and implacable." Besides, he could defend Norfolk more effectively by pulling back to a defensive position closer to the port city.[41]

Halleck responded affirmatively to Dix's proposal, even going so far as to venture, "Suffolk is a most ill-chosen position for defense. . . . Why it was ever occupied I do not know."[42] But both men knew that much needed to be done before the Federals could evacuate the Suffolk line. S. P. Lee hoped to use the infantry to level the abandoned Confederate defenses on the river, but Dix had already informed Halleck and now explained to Lee that "all the troops at Suffolk have been constantly occupied since the retreat of the enemy in leveling his intrenchments, which are very extended and solid."[43] Dix knew, as the admiral did not, that the pending withdrawal would require the demolition of the Union works as well. Halleck had been clear on this point: "When abandoned, the works of Suffolk should be destroyed."[44]

The Federals spent the next few months removing rails and leveling Confederate fortifications. Private Lenfest noted in his diary on May 6, "I was on fatigue [duty] to-day tearing down the rebel breastworks that are very strong and protected by good abatis."[45] The 6th Massachusetts set out once again from Suffolk on May 13, on what a participant noted was the "EIGHTH BLACKWATER MARCH." Arriving at Carrsville, the men were told that the expedition was undertaken to protect workers assigned to "take up the tracks of the Seaboard and Roanoke Railroad."[46]

Almost from the beginning, the expedition ran into trouble from the Confederates. The working parties consisted of a "large force of colored laborers [who] were set to work tearing up the [rail]road, at a point about five miles from the Blackwater river." As the men strained to lift the rails and clear the tracks, the Confederates fired blindly at them from across the river. Although well out of range of this immediate threat, the workers "dropped their tools and scattered in every direction, and could not be brought up to work again that day."

It was just as well, for the Confederates then sent a force across the river "to interfere with our operations." Two drafted Pennsylvania regiments panicked. "On this occasion," a New York account noted caustically, the

Pennsylvanians "got into confusion, fired wildly and wounded some of their own men, soon broke and ran, some of them keeping the railroad track until they reached Suffolk." The 13th Indiana blunted the attack and drove off the Confederates. As darkness settled on the fourteenth, some of the Federals went out to retrieve the abandoned tools.

At dawn on May 15, the Union infantry consisting of the 6th Massachusetts and the 112th New York held positions on either side of the road, about a mile from Carrsville.[47] "Our forces were hardly in position," a participant recalled, "when our skirmishers (Cos. A, B, and F) were driven in and the rebs advanced to the edge of the woods opening a heavy fire of musketry." The Federals hunkered down behind a rail fence as the Confederate fire passed overhead. In reply, a battery opened on them, and when the Union infantry "rose up and gave them a volley or two," the Southerners dropped back.

It was now time for the Federals to take the offensive. Once again deploying skirmishers, the blue line surged forward. The attack immediately proved irresistible. "We advanced some distance into the woods, the rebs falling back just out of range." Then, as the Union units shifted replacements to the front, the Confederates struck once more. The artillery was less effective in the heavy growth, but again the Union infantry fire convinced the Southerners to retreat. Private Lenfest called the fight "the Battle of Hebron Church," noting that the 6th Massachusetts lost twenty-one men killed and wounded.[48] The 112th lost one man killed and two wounded.[49]

At some point on this day, Private S. G. Sweatt of Company C, 6th Massachusetts, performed so heroically that he later received the Medal of Honor for his actions. Private Lenfest recalled that as two companies, C and I, moved up to relieve two others (his Company G and H), the "rebs advanced in large numbers." Catching the two units "near the edge of the woods," the Confederates hammered them, "driving them back with considerable loss to Company C, 2 killed and 6 wounded."[50]

Sweatt was pulling back toward cover with his unit when he realized that several of his comrades had been hit. According to the Medal of Honor citation, "When ordered to retreat this soldier turned and rushed back to the front, in the face of heavy fire of the enemy, in an endeavor to rescue his wounded comrades, remaining by them until overpowered and taken prisoner."[51] Three of his fellow infantrymen also fell into Southern hands, all three subsequently dying of the wounds they had received.[52]

The next day, Saturday, May 16, the Confederates "made another attempt to break our lines." This time the fighting involved a battery and the 165th

Pennsylvania. Casualties were relatively light, with "five or six" wounded, including one mortally. On the return march a bad case of straggling and a stray shot from a "bushwacker" caused one of Michael Corcoran's units, the 170th New York, to panic. "It was quite dark and misty," one man recalled, "and the Regiment began to fire wildly into each other." The result was greater loss than the Confederates had inflicted, with four killed and ten wounded. "So much for ill discipline and whiskey," the writer noted bitterly. "It was currently reported that their Colonel was drunk."[53]

The Confederate view of the several days of skirmishing near Carrsville is reflected in a letter by a member of Jenkins's brigade. From "Camp near Franklin, Va.," John M. White described the recent skirmishing to his sister. "We have just returned from another four days skirmish with the enemy," he began. "Although the balls and shells and grape shot flew pretty thick around us yet [we] were not allowed to engage them. We sustained a loss of 12 or 15 men during our trip." Despite their efforts the Confederates were unable to impede the Union objective. "The enemy have succeeded in tearing up the RR from Carsville to Suffolk, they have taken the iron away." In addition, "they burned several houses and wantonly destroyed much property."[54] Indeed the frustration was so great for one Southerner that he resorted to a unique form of communication with his enemies. "Found a letter in road addressed to the first Yankee officer that passes," a Union soldier recorded in his diary. The author of the letter blamed the Federals for "his being obliged to take up arms to avenge the wrongs done to the ladies of Nansemond and adjacent counties. Seemed to think that plundering was done by order." After struggling with the contents, the bluecoat concluded that the "sentiments . . . were essentially southern and the orthography was miserable."[55]

In the aftermath of the engagement, the 6th Massachusetts continued to protect the working parties. Lenfest noted that for three days the work went smoothly, without interruption by the Confederates. "These days were spent quietly," he noted, "as the enemy had fallen back to his fortifications [on the Blackwater] while the work of taking up the track went forward." Finally the men from Massachusetts started back toward Suffolk, stopping to encamp on the old battlefield of the Deserted House. Within a matter of days, these men were on their way home. On May 26 Solomon Augustus Lenfest would write his final entry, telling of his journey back to Massachusetts, to the arms of his beloved Jennie, whom he later married. "So closes my career as a soldier," he noted, ending service that had been almost exclusively spent in Suffolk.[56]

If Lenfest and his Massachusetts comrades were going home, others remained in southeastern Virginia. Small-scale raids and guerrilla activity continued to plague the Federals and were beginning to take a toll on the men in the field. Increasingly, a hard-war policy was beginning to have resonance for more than just the Northern hardliners. Not surprisingly, this meant that the men in the field were more willing to adopt it as a means of combating the Confederate resistance they faced.

It was with this end in mind that Major Franklin Stratton, commanding the 11th Pennsylvania Cavalry, submitted a short report on June 11. He had sent out a detachment under a junior-grade officer "against the small detachments of infantry which the enemy has been sending out lately for the purpose of attacking our pickets and small parties." Stratton either did not realize or chose to ignore the fact that with their limited numbers the Confederates would only be able to send out small forces, for which pitched battles would have meant suicide. His strike force "intercepted" approximately fifteen Southerners, killing and wounding several, despite the accidental and premature discharge of a weapon that warned them in time to allow most of them to escape. Had it not been for the accidental warning, Stratton assured his superiors, the Confederates would have suffered "the complete destruction of their party, as I had given directions to give no quarter in [the] action."[57]

The next day a much larger force, consisting in part of the 155th New York Infantry, set out for the Blackwater. Over the next several days, it ranged along the South Quay Road to Franklin and over to the Blackwater Bridge and back, passing through the area of Carrsville several times. With the Federals set to pull back from Suffolk soon, these expeditions were supposed to keep the Confederates off-balance. As it turned out, they did little more than wear out men and horses.[58]

Although the Union commanders could not know it precisely, the Confederates were in no shape to exploit a Union withdrawal. They, too, were shifting troops from the region. Lewis Henry Webb, a member of a North Carolina battery, wrote on June 12 that he was preparing to leave, "& now adieu: to South Quay, where I have spent six months most pleasantly, fallen in love, & become engaged to be married." He spent a few minutes of free time visiting his fiancée before hastening back to the battery. "The troops are all leaving the line of the Blackwater except a few pickets," he observed. Webb reluctantly accepted the orders to leave with his battery but felt a sense of helplessness in doing so. "The Blackwater is to be evacuated," he explained, "and now while waiting here & viewing the removal of everything of a public kind, my heart is saddened, when I think that the good people whom I have here learned to love, & her who has promised to be my wife, are to be left defenceless."[59] With many of the men who had guarded them being reassigned, the people in the area must have shared this soldier's concern for their safety.

Still, the movement of men from the Blackwater did not leave that line entirely uncovered. Union general Corcoran informed his superior, General Dix, on the eighteenth, "Colonel Spear found the fords all blockaded and guarded, with their opposite banks generally so steep that crossing, unless by bridges was considered impracticable." There might be relatively few Confederates holding the line, but resistance remained. "The casualties of yesterday," Corcoran added, "were 2 killed and 11 wounded."[60]

The Union soldiers in Suffolk had repulsed Longstreet's advance and endured over a year of sparring with Confederates on the Blackwater, but their determination to stay the course remained strong, if a letter written on June 10 is any indication. Expressing anger at the surrender of Harpers Ferry, Joseph Brooks surmised, "It was either caused by gross imcompetency, or treason." Having survived his own "siege" successfully, he felt justified in questioning the actions of others. Of a comrade who had gone home at the end of his enlistment and announced that he "has done fighting the rebels," Brooks pronounced, "I am sorry, as he might do his country some good in the field, but he is of no value at home." As for himself, the soldier explained to his friend, "My principles remain unchanged, and however I may differ from others in the manner of prosecuting this war, yet I can see no excuse for a man who withholds his support from the government in its honest endeavors to put down this Hell borne Rebellion." The war was bound to end someday, and when it did, "we will have a heavy reckoning to settle with those who assisted to bring on these troubles, but till then I am at the service of my country. Through thick and through thin, through good report and through evil report I am bound to stand by her." Brooks closed his argument with a strong rhetorical flourish: "The war may last for years, I presume it will, but we are bound to triumph sooner or later. The people of the loyal states will never submit to a division of these United States." Then he added with finality, "We have men enough and means enough, and we will use them."[61]

The Southern fighting men were maintaining their morale as best they could, too. South Carolinian John White, fearful "that we are left here in these piny woods to be devoured with ticks," nevertheless felt strongly enough about his "cause" to assert, "Although we have fought well yet [even] if we are conquored we need not look to Europe for help or sympathy, we do not desire the sympathy's of the world." Resentment against Union depredations helped to build morale. When he left the Blackwater line with

Jenkins's brigade in mid-June, White paused at Weldon, North Carolina, to dash off a quick note to his sister. "We arrived at this place yesterday afternoon," he noted on the sixteenth, having "left 1400 Yankees on the oppo[site] side of Blackwater burning houses and pillaging generally." He concluded that the marauding came from being unable to defeat the Confederates on the battlefield in the region; "they seem determined to be avenged on Rebeldom by acting the part of incendiaries and demons." He had to admit, though, that the Federals had been successful. "They have burned nearly all the dwellings between Blackwater and Suffolk." Yet White thought that the reason the Federals gave publicly for the destruction—"Our Scouts have been bushwhacking them and they plead this as an excuse for their acts"—was inadequate.[62] Either way it seemed that once more the civilians in the region were suffering as much, if not more, than the people who were supposed to defend them.

Of course, their defenders were suffering, too. Disease among the fighting men remained a scourge. This proved a demoralizing loss to those who had survived the battlefield with friends and relatives only to watch them ravaged by sickness. Such was the case for John Newton Smith and Charles Croft. Smith had enlisted at Suffolk in June 1861 in what became Company I of the 13th Virginia Cavalry. In February 1863 he had written his sister to express his sorrow "to hear the Yankees bother you all so much." He hoped to have a chance to help his kinsmen by making the Federals "leave you all in peace" but did not expect to "have a chance at them in Nansemond, for I think we will be kept here sometime yet."[63] To his father a few days later, Smith was more adamant. "I expect as you say there will be some heavy fighting in old Nansemond yet."[64]

By June 1863 Newton lay desperately ill at Hanover Academy Hospital. His kinsman, Charles Croft, stood vigil with him, becoming so fearful for his life that he dashed an anxious letter to the stricken man's father. "Newton is very sick he was takened about two weeks ago with the intermitant fever."[65] He followed this with an even more urgent letter on the eighth. "He was taken worse last night," the distraught cousin explained. "If there is not some change in him I do not think he can stand it much longer if you ever want to see him alive again you must come amediately"[66] Before this letter had a chance to reach its destination in distant Somerton, in lower Nansemond County, the ravaged soldier, who had been steadily "getting mighty weak," gave up the struggle. Almost two years after he had entered the service, John Newton Smith "departed this life." Charles Croft sent the final message the next morning, June 9, 1863. "His last request to me was if he died he wanted to be burried at home." Croft tried to offer some solace to the now-grieving father. "He died in his right sinces. . . . I sit by his side until I saw he was dying I could not bear to see him die."[67]

The surgeon in charge of the hospital informed the company commander in September of the soldier's passing with the clinical coldness of a man inured to death. Smith had died "leaving effects and money to the amount of $47.70," which had been turned over to the proper authority according to the regulations. It did not need to be said that typhoid fever had claimed another victim. "You are requested to transmit this notification to his legal representative," the doctor explained, "who will be paid this amount on application to the Second Auditor of the Treasury, C. States of America at Richmond, Va."[68] The following March, Captain Alexander Savage, who had enlisted with Smith on the same day in Suffolk, finally settled accounts with the boy's father. He enclosed a certificate for the army clothing allowance "not drawn." The valuation, $136.13, was to have covered the soldier's clothing demands for a year. Then, having attended to this duty, Savage wrote that he would "be pleased to hear from you & [get] the news generally in old Nansemond."[69]

Rumors of an impending Union evacuation of the region were reaching Southern ears. Even so, Daniel Harvey Hill informed Secretary of War Seddon on June 21 that "Suffolk has not been evacuated," giving a survey of current Union troop dispositions. Still, their level of activity was suspicious. "This looks very much like evacuation," he remarked, "as they usually cover their retreats by feigned attacks."[70] Information slipped out of the "commissary at Newport News, who supplies Peck with all his fresh beef. The same authority reports that Suffolk will be entirely evacuated." There were other signs: "Negroes are being enrolled as fast as caught. A number have been carried from Suffolk to Newport News."[71]

Indeed, the Federals were feverishly laying the groundwork for an evacuation of Suffolk. After telling his sister that his regiment and several others had been busily engaged in "building two forts" and felling trees as obstructions at Bower's Hill, Aaron Blake of the 13th New Hampshire happily welcomed assistance in the work. "They have been picking up all of [the] Contrabands they could find & setting them to work on a Fort," he observed of his Union superiors to his mother a few days later. He wearily concluded, "I am glad of it."[72]

In the ensuing weeks the Union soldiers and work crews who remained in the area finished dismantling the railroads. "We have destroyed the Seabord & Roanoak R.R. and the Petersburg and Norfolk R.R. for twenty miles out of Suffolk," one soldier boasted, "so that the rebels when they pay us another visit will not find such convenient transportation. We have run the rails into Norfolk." This last measure would be particular effective. "It will trouble them to rebuild the roads as they are very short of rails." Demonstrating that Union soldiers used Confederate newspapers for intelligence gathering, he noted, "Their roads are so badly worn that an order has been issued prohibiting them from running on any R.R. in the Confederacy at a faster rate than ten miles an hour."[73]

At the end of May, a member of the New York Mounted Rifles recounted the frenzy of activity. "We have all been out of camp for the past 3 weeks doing picket duty," he told his sweetheart, "while the contrabands were tearing up the track, but it is all torn up now nearly to Suffolk." With this work nearing completion, "there is a great deal of talk of evacuating Suffolk entirely and I think the whole place will be burned to the ground if we should leave it." The news apparently had not yet reached the residents. "The Secesh around here appear to be quite contented since the Rebels left for their own soldiers robbed them five times as much as our men do." There was little left behind. "The whole country is nearly spoiled," he stated dispassionately, "and thousands of acres of timberland have been burned over."[74]

Union general Dix was sending instructions to his subordinate in Suffolk, Michael Corcoran, that mirrored the orders General Lee had sent to Benjamin Huger a little over a year earlier. On June 20, 1863, he explained, "Do not commence destroying [the defensive] works till all the ammunition and ordnance stores are removed."[75] On the twenty-eighth he was more precise:

> Destroy the entrenchments at Suffolk as speedily and thoroughly as you can, but do not sacrifice thoroughness to haste. The forts should be completely demolished. If necessary, impress negroes into your service for the purpose, directing the quartermaster to keep an account of their work, so that they may be fully paid.
>
> When the works have been destroyed, fall back to the new line near Portsmouth and Norfolk. When you leave Suffolk, you will take care that there is no destruction of private property by your men.

General Dix was particularly adamant about the latter part of his orders. Had Suffolk residents been aware of his protective cloak they might have been less uneasy about the Union withdrawal. "I shall hold you responsible for any violation of this order," Dix stated unequivocally, "which is not intended merely for your brigade but for all the troops under your command."[76] This last point may have been a veiled reference to the cavalry's tendency to consider that such orders did not apply to them.

With the destruction of the rail lines and earthworks in the area complete, the last of the Union soldiers prepared to pull back to defensive positions at Bower's Hill and Deep Creek, nearer to Portsmouth.[77] Rumors had circulated that the Federals would burn the town of Suffolk in retribution for the toil and blood spent in defending it, although under the guise of striking a blow at the enemy.[78] A lieutenant in the Confederate signal corps relayed the desperate news. "Women and children are ordered to leave Suffolk. The enemy say they intend to burn it."[79]

Then, on July 3, 1863, as the war took a decisive turn on the gentle rolling slopes of Cemetery Ridge near Gettysburg, Pennsylvania, the Federal forces evacuated Suffolk and established their new picket lines. As the United States celebrated its independence from Great Britain, Corcoran forwarded a report that many Suffolk residents would find cause for celebration as well. "The evacuation of Suffolk was completed at noon yesterday," the Irish general noted. "The works are destroyed and every article of public property removed." He added clearly, "No private property was injured in the least, and your directions were in every respect complied with."[80] Henry Smith wrote his sweetheart to tell her that "Suffolk is now entirely evacuated, the earthworks thrown down, quarters burned, everything of value removed and it now looks as lonely as any of the rest of Virginia."[81]

The Confederate officer who reconnoitered the abandoned town reported directly to Secretary Seddon a few days later: "Our troops in Suffolk. Enemy fallen back to and fortifying Bower's Hill." The "enemy left nothing," but, he noted incredulously, "Suffolk [was] not destroyed." As an explanation, the Confederate officer added, "Special instructions from Corcoran prohibiting it."[82]

Whatever the feeling in the Union ranks regarding their withdrawal from Suffolk, the soldiers' morale seems to have remained high, while that of much of the local citizenry seems to have dropped. One Federal wrote home on July 24 to tell of his transfer to a new post at "Camp Bower's Hill," which was "about eight miles from Portsmouth." He noted the simultaneous exodus to Portsmouth of "most of the citizens that used to be at Suffolk," although he gave no explanation for their actions. These individuals may have been Unionists going with the army as it pulled back from the region, or they may simply have sought safety outside of the no-man's-land between the contending forces. Either way, Henry Lyle liked what he saw. "I don't think the Rebellion will last much longer," he observed, confidently predicting that "the Bogus Confederacy will cave in."[83]

Bower's Hill would remain the main line of Union defense for Norfolk for the rest of the war, although picket posts spread as far toward Suffolk as Bernard's Mills, a few miles from the town. Of course, both Federals and Confederates would continue to send troops into and through the area, assuring the residents that they had not seen the last of soldiers in their midst. The good news for many was that they would now stand a better chance of seeing friends and loved ones who had fled or were serving in units in other parts of the state. In any case, people in the region were entering into a new phase of the conflict, one in which they would be caught between the opposing forces. These circumstances promised that they would face new challenges in the months ahead.

"We gained nothing but glory, and lost our bravest men."
Virginia captain in the aftermath of Pickett's charge at Gettysburg

"I want to see old Suffolk once more."
A young refugee to his sister

"Can we do nothing for the people of Suffolk?"
Confederate brigadier general Matthew Ransom

⊰ 11 ⊱ *"Nothing but Glory"*

S UFFOLK WAS CLEAR OF UNION OCCUPATION FORCES, BUT IT WOULD remain in a no-man's-land between the opposing lines for the remainder of the conflict. Federal patrols and military expeditions would continue to traverse the region, but the searing daily presence of blue-coated soldiers pacing the streets or standing guard was gone. Now that they were out from under a provost marshal's regulations, the residents could breathe a little easier. But there might be reason to regret the loss of discipline and order a regular army could represent.

What the withdrawal of Union forces revealed was a community destitute of many of the basic necessities that people had taken for granted before the war. In the initial days following the evacuation, residents scoured the empty campsites for discarded goods. Some of them found a bonanza in tossed aside or misplaced items. Decorum was the last thing on these scavengers' minds, for people who had been forced to do without for a year or more found the castoffs quite acceptable.[1]

For the Confederate soldiers from southeastern Virginia serving with General Lee at Gettysburg, July 3 proved to be one of the most devastating days of the war. As friends at home were celebrating the end of Union occupation, many of these men were preparing to participate in one of the most famous charges in American military history.[2] It was approximately 3:30 P.M. when the men in Lewis Armistead's and James Kemper's brigades stepped out of the shadows of the trees in which they had been assembled. The shells of battery and counterbattery fire sliced through the air as the men dressed their lines. Armistead's men would advance in support of Richard Garnett's brigade and Kemper's. After the exhortations that came from commanders trying to motivate the men to carry out the terrible work that lay ahead, the soldiers in gray and butternut moved out across the long space between them and a tiny copse of trees near a low stone wall nearly a mile away.

When the smoke cleared from "Pickett's Charge," the survivors staggered back across the field or marched solemnly at bayonet point as prisoners. Far too many lay dead or dying on the field. Armistead himself lay mortally wounded, having taken a mere handful of his boys across that stone wall in a fleeting moment of glory and victory that quickly faded as Union reinforcements moved up. Kemper, too, was down. As was Garnett. Men from Suffolk, Nansemond, Southampton, and Isle of Wight had followed their commanders into the inferno and paid a grievous price. Corporal John T. Beach of the 9th Virginia was hit in the arm and leg and taken prisoner by the Federals. Lieutenant Walter Butts also fell into enemy hands. He was twenty years old when he enlisted at Chuckatuck in Nansemond County; he would be buried in a cornfield at Gettysburg after dying there on July 11. The list of casualties was so great that a recent historian of the regiment succinctly observed, "The charge at Gettysburg destroyed the 9th Virginia."[3]

The men from southeastern Virginia in James Kemper's brigade suffered even worse than their comrades in the 9th. No less than thirty-six men died, suffered wounds, many mortal, or were captured on that fateful day. Officers and common soldiers alike went down in the hail of Union musketry and canister that snuffed out Pickett's charge. Brothers John C. Arthur and Patrick H. Arthur, both farmers in their early twenties when they enlisted and both lieutenants by the time they reached Gettysburg, went down during the preliminary bombardment. John Calvin did not survive his wounds. Many others fell on or across the way. Altogether, the

Southampton Greys (Company D) lost seven killed and one wounded; the Nansemond Rangers (Company F), four killed and six wounded; and the Rough and Ready Guards (Company G, also of Southampton County), two killed and two wounded, with many more from all three companies taken captive.[4]

Other units with companies from southeastern Virginia had casualties as well. Lieutenant Richard Franklin Chapman of the 16th Virginia under William Mahone would have his wounded leg amputated by a Union surgeon. He would not survive. Others, like Julius Ward of the Bilisoly Blues (Company G) of the 41st Virginia, which had enlisted near Bower's Hill, died in the battle.[5] As one Confederate officer lamented, "We gained nothing but glory, and lost our bravest men."[6]

The news from north of Mason and Dixon's line and along the Mississippi, where the fortress city of Vicksburg fell to Ulysses S. Grant on July 4, was particularly grim this summer of 1863. Yet if the fortunes of their nation looked dismal, Confederate soldiers from the region could at least take advantage of the Union withdrawal from Suffolk to visit the homefolk, provided they could obtain furloughs. They still had to take care to dodge Union cavalry patrols and raiding parties, but it must have been a welcome compensation to see familiar faces on familiar ground once more.

Some refugees also chose to return. One of those who returned wrote her friend Anna Mary Riddick with a sense of relief, "We have reached home and have not been disturbed."[7] At about this same time, August 1863, orders went out for a tighter rein on the flow of people and goods across Union lines. Elaborate orders put into place strict regulations. Union brigadier general Henry M. Naglee particularly focused his efforts on shutting down the flow of illegal or contraband goods that had become a staple of Southern life and communication to and from southeastern Virginia. "Any person attempting to pass letters, information, or merchandise across [the lines] . . . will be imprisoned and severely punished," his order read, "and the goods [will be] seized, as well as all other personal property within this department belonging to all implicated, will be confiscated." In addition, he established rules for registering boats and obtaining licenses. Consumers could only buy limited amounts of goods, "to prevent an accumulation of goods for contraband purposes," he explained. "Weapons of all kinds, powder, and all items of a contraband character are prohibited, and will be seized whenever found," with violators subject to arrest and loss of property.[8]

The order was more than posturing. Naglee's adjutant issued instructions that an army captain designated for the duty should seize or destroy vessels in the Nansemond River, particularly those not properly registered after the deadline of August 15.[9] In addition, Naglee himself advised a subordinate that he should detain any "refugees or deserters or contrabands that may come to you." Refugees in particular were to be advised that "under no circumstances will they be permitted to recross the line."[10] Within a few weeks, when Naglee assumed control of the newly established Department of Virginia, he would have the opportunity to implement such measures on an even grander scale.[11] He would shortly order harsh measures to bring an end to guerrilla activity, including the destruction of homes used as refuges for such people. "Report all persons that give aid and comfort to guerrillas," he advised one officer, adding that a "severe policy must be adopted in regard to them."[12]

Such a shift in policy was bound to be popular with the soldiers. "There is an old man near here who signals with the Rebs, and it is known that he does so, and doubtless gives them much information regarding our movements in this vicinity," a Connecticut Yankee complained bitterly, "yet the government, so far from having him arrested or put where he can do no harm, keeps a guard around his house to *protect his property*." The soldier welcomed the new leeway that allowed the men "to *burn* every home we come across and not waste our time in *guarding* secesh property." He later boasted, "Every house about here has been laid in ashes with the exception of those we use for hospitals."[13]

Even with such strictures in place, Anna Riddick considered returning from North Carolina to Nansemond County at least, if not to Suffolk itself. She had relatives with whom she could stay until it became clearer how things would be for her in her hometown. The ever-active Samuel Spear seems to have been the most she would have to worry about. "The town is thoroughly patrolled and every avenue well guarded," he informed General Getty from Suffolk on August 25.[14] Five days later he complained that he could not "coax" the enemy cavalry into crossing the Blackwater.[15]

In October, Anna's mother, Missouri, dashed off a note from Petersburg asking her to purchase items that were scarce or excessively expensive, as virtually everything was getting caught in the runaway inflation that accompanied a weak currency. She was also to do what she could to secure the family's possessions "if you go to Suffolk." Then, perhaps by way of encouragement, Missouri Riddick added, "The Yanks do not interfere with ladies going in and out."[16]

On this point, however, Missouri Riddick was only partially correct. Anna would have to be careful, although she could certainly count on the assistance of friends and relatives. There were inherent dangers that ranged from travel over uncertain routes to lawless elements. Getty had replaced Naglee as commander in the region in September; but given his nature, he was unlikely to relax the vigilance.[17] Under such tight security measures, no one would go undisturbed if they ran across a Union patrol or picket post. Still, for the anxious mother, forced to remain a refugee, the possibility that her daughter might be able to ascertain the condition of affairs in Suffolk must have offered a considerable source of hope.

If the year 1863 brought the temptation for some to return to the area, it raised additional issues for whites in the region, as well as their distant refugeeing friends and families, to face. One of the most significant of these was the implementation of Abraham Lincoln's Emancipation Proclamation. Issued primarily as a war measure, the proclamation also represented the Union president's great moral force. It had gone into effect on January 1, 1863, when the Confederate States remained in a state of rebellion against the United States. Because it was to apply to those rebellious regions, at that point beyond Lincoln's reach, it did not have much impact upon the people of the South, white or black, until it could be implemented. Even so, for many white Virginians the Emancipation Proclamation meant a direct challenge to their social order and to the existence of their "peculiar institution."[18]

The flourish of letters in the Riddick family between mother and daughter did not mention the proclamation or its effects until December 1863. On Christmas Eve, Missouri reported, "The poor Norfolk people all have been compelled to take the oath." Then she added with disgust, "And not only the oath to support the U.S. gov. and laws but also the Emancipation proclamation." Missouri saw in this the first evidence of the decay of her social system. "A negro kissed a white lady on the street in Norfolk last week," information she hastily threw in the letter as if the very mention of the scene, one which she could not have possibly witnessed herself, would somehow contaminate her. Like so many other white Southerners, Missouri Riddick was having difficulty coming to grips with the changes being wrought by war and emancipation.[19]

Union soldiers in the field in southeastern Virginia had their own response to Lincoln's actions. One soldier recalled watching large groups of runaway slaves appear periodically while he was on picket duty. "They were not always received in the spirit of the emancipation proclamation," he admitted. Yet when told to return to their masters, the fugitives would drift off in pretended compliance only to reappear as soon as the new pickets came to relieve the others. The soldier quoted one refugee's expression of a willingness to "keep a-tryin' cause some sojer or udder would let us in some time or udder."[20]

Writing from Suffolk in June to a friend, another Federal explained, "In regard to black soldiers, you know my sentiments. . . . I am in favor of using the black slaves, and think they can be made very useful (as they have been in many instances) in building fortifications, roads, etc."[21] Another lauded the Union president's sense of timing in the matter. Coming sooner, he postulated, the emancipation and arming of the slaves would have been disastrous.[22] Large numbers of blacks from the region would soon be in uniform, vying with whites for the right to serve their country and fight for freedom, whether others were ready for them do to so or not.

One Rhode Islander was particularly pleased with the effect of the Emancipation Proclamation on some of the people of southeastern Virginia. In a series of letters written while on the return to Suffolk from an expedition to the Blackwater River, Henry Simmons related the lot of one group of slaves to his wife, Anna. "We are encamped on a secesh farm whose owner was a Baptist minister. He has 18 or 19 slaves but I think they will all go with us tonight when we go on our way. One woman has 7 children 4 of them by her masters son so they are the old rascals grand children almost white & smart as steel. Her black husband ran away a year ago & is in Suffolk now."[23]

Later that day, he found a few more minutes to continue the story:

> We expected to have got away from here before this but we have so much on hand to do in enforcing "Uncle Abe's" Proclamation of freedom that we can't go tonight. The old scamp of whom I wrote you lost "eight chattels" & the U.S. have gained or will gain eight freemen. Thank God I belong to the 11th R.I. a regt. that believes in freeing the slaves. We sent the mother & seven children of whom I wrote you away this PM and they are now at a house some 5 miles from here protected by our pickets and a Lieut. is responsible for them. . . . We *intend* to take the other 11 with us tomorrow and if we can the old scamp himself to put him in jail & if we get a chance burn down his buildings. I don't know as we will get a good chance to burn him out but you may be assured we will do it if we can. One of his slaves has been hired by Capt. Taft of Co. F & he gave information of a lot of stuff he [the owner] had hid in the woods and our teams have gone to get it & one has come back with a load of corn. He has refused to take "the oath" and I understand last winter his house was a rendevous for guerillas & we hope Genl. Corcoran will order him burnt out.

Simmons noted that members of the 8th Connecticut "undertook to make fun of us for rescuing the negroes," but reminders of that regiment's poor performance in an earlier engagement "shuts them up mighty quick."[24]

The Rhode Islander ended the saga with a note he wrote from Suffolk when his unit finally returned from its expedition. "We remained at Isle of Wight on Miles Barrett's plantation until near 4 PM yesterday and had the pleasure of starting of[f] 16 or 17 of his slaves in fact all but one old man . . . and this morning they are all safe in Suffolk & *free* & that is more than all."[25]

As for the refugees from the region, the months of war and psychological distance from their vacated homes seemed to drag on forever. The inevitable signs of homesickness among those displaced from southeastern Virginia began to appear clearly and unmistakably. One of the first in the Riddick family to express such sentiments on paper was the youngest boy, Nathaniel Henley Riddick. In a short letter to his big sister Anna, he groaned in late 1863, "I want to see old Suffolk once more."[26] Before long, other members of the family were saying the same thing, even more forcefully than this young lad.

The soldiers continued their patrols and scouts. In September a detachment of the 11th Pennsylvania Cavalry consisting of seven companies under Lieutenant Colonel George Stetzel rode out of the Union lines near Bower's Hill. His goal was to proceed eastward through Suffolk and on to the Blackwater River line, conducting a thorough reconnaissance of the region. In order to cover the most ground, Stetzel divided his command, leading the largest of the contingents himself in the direction of Franklin, where he expected the most significant body of enemy troops to be situated. It was a familiar operation for the soldiers and the people of the region alike.

Little transpired during the expedition beyond gathering information from the local population, but some of these people seem to have been quite willing to render assistance. Perhaps most helpful was a man who lived at Carrsville. Stetzel observed of him, "I have every reason to believe [that he] is a loyal Union man, although he has a son in the rebel army (by conscription)." Through him the Union colonel learned that "there were not more than between 500 and 600 men along the entire line of the Blackwater."[27] Subsequent events, including reports from other units, corroborated this statement. For the Confederates it would appear that the Blackwater line was a backwater, and a brackish one at that.

Another member of the same unit noted both the dangers that prompted these raids and their effectiveness in a letter to his mother in mid-October from "Camp Getty, Near Portsmouth." He explained that "our company had one man killed by a Bushwhacker, we caught the chap and hung him to a tree." He noted proudly that the raid had gone beyond this act of retribution against a single Southern guerrilla. The 11th Pennsylvania had also targeted furloughed soldiers, mail carriers, local means of transportation, and economic assets. "We caught several Rebel officers and some Blockade runners, we destroyed several boats and some salt works."[28] This was all part of a continuous Union policy of disruption of Confederate activities in the region.

Likewise, the Confederates tried their hands at reconnaissance and raiding. In November, Lieutenant Colonel Arthur Herbert decided to conduct a raid with his infantry regiment, the 17th Virginia, three pieces of artillery, and a cavalry regiment under Colonel Valentine H. Taliaferro. The plan was to move rapidly against advanced pickets of the enemy and whatever outposts they may have established in the Suffolk area. Again the benefits of local intelligence came into play. An area citizen warned the Confederate colonel that the Federals anticipated his raid. Through the recent capture of a Confederate junior officer, the Federals had caught wind of the scheme and were on the alert. Any attempt to carry out the operation would not only prove futile in gathering prisoners but might lead the Confederates into a trap.

Herbert decided to use a ploy of his own to lure any Union forces that might be in the area out into the open where he could strike them. He dispatched a company of Taliaferro's cavalry to Suffolk, while he kept the bulk of his mixed command in Windsor. These horsemen were to dash into the town, capture what they could, and lead any pursuers back into the trap being set for them. The unwitting Union forces would be well beyond support from other units and "give us a chance at them that way." But this "chance" was not to be. Having captured a handful of prisoners, Taliaferro's cavalry could not entice the Federals to venture as far as Windsor.[29]

Such cat-and-mouse games marked military activities in southeastern Virginia for the remainder of the war. In neighboring North Carolina the combat was more brutal, the rules more easily discarded. When an expedition left Norfolk for South Mills, North Carolina, the commander of the force, Brigadier General Edward A. Wild, reported considerable guerrilla activity and illicit crossline trading. "The guerrillas pestered us. They crept upon our pickets at night, waylaid our expeditions and our cavalry scouts, firing upon us whenever they could." Wild's attempts to combat this nuisance often met with frustration. He laid ambushes and organized pursuit, but found these efforts generally "useless." He managed to capture quantities of equipment and one guerrilla, Daniel Bright, "whom I afterward hanged, duly placarding [him] thus: 'This guerrilla hanged by order of Brig-Genl. Wild.'"

Wild had more success in liberating slaves and transporting them to

Union lines. He estimated that he brought out some 2,500 people but admitted that "few results were gained, as the able-bodied negroes have had ample opportunities for escape [to Union lines] heretofore, or have been run over into Dixie, perhaps 70 or 100 in all." In fact, many of the previous escapees had found their way to Suffolk while it was held by the Federals. Some would soon be in Union uniforms.

Two points seem to have made an impression upon the general during the expedition. The first was the exceptional conduct of his black troops. The second was the vociferous nature of the guerrilla activity he encountered. Of the former, Wild wrote, "The men marched wonderfully, never grumbled, were watchful on picket, and always ready for a fight. They are most reliable soldiers."

Perhaps it was the use of such troops that intensified the guerrilla activity, which prompted the Union general to suggest a revision in his nation's war strategy. In physical terms this new strategy called for an expansion of Federal control beyond its current limits. "Much more might be said in favor of a frontier line to include the Chowan, Blackwater, Suffolk, etc." By this means, he argued, "a very extensive territory would be gained to us and lost to the rebels—a region notoriously productive, from which the rebels have been and are at this moment drawing vast supplies for their army." In addition, Wild thought such a change would have significant ramifications: "A great channel of contraband trade through our own lines would be cut off."

Wild was advocating nothing less than an alteration in Union policy from a protective and passive attitude toward the Southern civilians over whom they had authority, for the purpose of winning them over, to a more adversarial and aggressive approach that recognized the majority as enemies and treated them as such. The Union commander was prepared to place the "hard hand of war" upon the people, first upon those in northeastern North Carolina but then inevitably across the entire region, including southeastern Virginia. "Finding ordinary measures of little avail," he explained in describing his expedition, "I adopted a more rigorous style of warfare; burned their houses and barns, ate up their live stock, and took hostages from their families." This last measure was a precaution against ill-treatment of any of his men who happened to fall into the hands of the enemy. Wild was convinced that given a free hand in regard to the guerrillas, "I could rectify [the situation in the region] in two weeks of stern warfare"[30]

Wild was describing exactly the conditions historian Stephen Ash has characterized as a "no-man's-land," traditionally the designation for an area between enemy forces and popularized during the trench warfare of the First World War. Ash included both the positive and the negative aspects of the term. "The Northern occupiers claimed this territory as their own, and so it was, in a strictly military sense: Union forces regularly patrolled it, could project their power at will anywhere within it, and were able to exclude Confederate power and authority from it (aside from the occasional Rebel cavalry raid). By that reckoning, the citizens there were—and they considered themselves to be—in enemy hands."[31] This description could certainly be applied to the people living in Chuckatuck, Windsor, or Suffolk or along the roads leading to and from the Blackwater to Bower's Hill.

For Wild and many other Union commanders, there was a negative side to be considered. As Ash noted, "At the same time it was unpacified territory, seething with hostility and guerrilla violence: Federal authority prevailed only when and where Union troops were actually present, and it extended no farther than the range of their muskets and carbines." The extension of this reach was precisely what Wild had envisioned. Under the present conditions neither Union nor Confederate troops could establish themselves permanently in this area, leaving the residents "in a kind of vacuum of authority, a twilight zone neither Union nor Confederate."

There was also the strong possibility that Wild's tactics would backfire and produce more sympathy for the Southern cause rather than less. He tacitly admitted as much at the same time he was touting the effectiveness of his "stern warfare" policy. "We learned that they were disgusted with such unexpected treatment; it bred disaffection, some wishing to quit the business, others going over the lines to join the Confederate Army." Still, the Union general professed to find "the majority of people along our track to be reasonably neutral," whatever their real sentiments might be. He was also pleased to note "the rapid development of loyal sentiment as we progressed with our raid." For some this loyalty was certainly genuine; for others, any such demonstration need last only as long as the blue-coated soldiers remained in their vicinity.[32]

Confederate general George Pickett, assigned to the Department of Virginia and North Carolina since returning from the disastrous Gettysburg campaign, was aware of this vacuum. When Union major general John G. Foster implemented a policy removing "paupers and old persons," as well as those people "inimical to the Government," from Union-held territory,[33] Pickett considered the policy diabolical. "An extra published in Norfolk says a flag of truce with 350, mostly women and children, will be in Suffolk today, he informed Adjutant General Samuel Cooper on October 15. "What these poor creatures are to do for food or transportation I do not know. The proximity of the enemy forbids any assistance being sent them."[34] Pickett received authorization to send wagons to pick up the expelled refugees. They were to be given "all proper assistance" to "come into our lines." Transportation was to be made available to them for "a reasonable distance."[35] Pickett was finding it more and more difficult to tolerate what he saw as Yankee excesses. By the end of the year, he would have enough, inaugurating his own policy of hard war on foes who had placed themselves "against the laws of Christian warfare."[36]

The plight of the civilians, whether refugees or those remaining at home, remained burdensome. As letters found their way in and out of the region, more than one began with a notation thanking some individual for his or her kindness in delivering the mail. Traveling was difficult. One person attempting to get home wrote of finding her way across a river blocked by a gunboat. Because these gunboats were usually patrolling, rather than remaining at anchor in one place, she was soon able to cross. Some of the soldiers were taking advantage of the Union evacuation of Suffolk to return home for brief visits. "There is no news to write," one person explained in a letter from Nansemond County on August 19, "except some of the confederate soldiers have come home to see their friends and are now about to leave."[37]

There was time to think of the future. Jennie Riddick spent part of the summer thinking her "beau" had been killed. When she learned that he had been wounded and captured, not killed, she was as angry at the rumors as she was grateful for the news. She resumed planning for their wedding. "Mrs. Gwynn will prefer that we be married in Petersburg since the Yankees have frequented Suffolk so often. However, we will be married as soon as he can get a leave of absence after he is exchanged."[38]

Residents continued to follow their daily patterns, while coping with the demands warfare placed upon them. Sometimes this led to extraordinary situations. One such event occurred on Christmas Day, 1863, when several citizens of Nansemond County forwarded a petition for the release of a neighbor being held in Libby Prison in Richmond. Although it was not unusual for individuals to ask that cases be reviewed and prisoners released, this request was out of the ordinary in that the prisoner, Jesse Langston, was a "free man of Colour," and the authors of the petition were white men.

The petitioners expressed astonishment at their neighbor's arrest and detention since "Genl. Longstreet & Army were here in May." The men vouched for Langston's character, noting that he had not been charged. As far as they could determine, he had done nothing to warrant arrest. "We furthermore assert," they explained to the prison commandant, "that we know of no family of free Negroes that has been more respected, that has been of more service to the neighborhood, and that has conducted itself with more propriety, than this one." Should the charges not be of such a nature as to demand his imprisonment, they hoped to obtain his release. "He has a young family dependent on him," they argued, "and being a shoemaker by trade, would be of great service to the neighborhood, and to the Army also." Indeed, many soldiers were having shoes repaired in Nansemond County and "sent to them in the Army." "Could he come home?" they wanted to know.[39]

As the Thanksgiving and Christmas seasons approached, military activity seems to have increased. Certainly, heated rhetoric glowed white. A Confederate army officer wrote Secretary of War Seddon on November 26 to protest, "Butler is enrolling everything in [the] shape of men, black and white." What was worse, the Union general was threatening to hang the officer's scouts, even when "caught within his lines, uniformed as soldiers of the Confederacy."[40] Colonel Joel Griffin, commanding cavalry in the area, bombarded George Pickett with the outrages of the enemy. They were "committing all kinds of excesses," he wrote impassionedly. Pickett informed the secretary of war: "It is impossible with my force to prevent these raids. The section of country that the enemy is now operating in is too far from our line to do more than watch their operations."[41]

Finally, Pickett exploded. "I will not stand upon terms with these fellows any longer," he exclaimed. "Butler's plan, evidently, is to let loose his swarm of blacks upon our ladies and defenseless families, plunder and devastate the country." Solutions did not readily present themselves. He could not stop the "outrages" without more troops and did not wish to advise people to flee their homes. "Against such a warfare there is but one resource," he finally concluded: "to hang at once every one captured belonging to the expedition [of General Wild], and afterward any one caught who belongs to Butler's department." "Let us come to a definite understanding with these heathens at once," Pickett urged. "His course must be stopped."[42]

Pickett was not bluffing. He issued orders to Colonel Griffin on December 15 that were crystal clear. "Any one caught in the act (negroes or white men) of burning houses or maltreating women, must be hung on the spot, by my order."[43] Chivalric and paternalistic, Pickett may have been motivated in part by his own recent marriage to LaSalle Corbell, the young lady from Chuckatuck. Whatever the justification, his anger was slow to subside.

On the twentieth, Pickett cataloged Union wrongs to Adjutant General Cooper and stated plainly, "My orders were to spare no one."[44] He submitted a number of enclosures that illustrated the situation, including a letter out of North Carolina from Colonel Griffin. In it the colonel detailed the effect of Union raiding, adding, "They hung Private Daniel Bright, of Company L, of my Sixty-second Georgia Regiment; hung him to a beam in a house; body remained suspended forty hours." With women being arrested and jailed and a child allegedly killed, the Federals in Wild's expedition were guilty of "committing all . . . kinds of excesses."[45]

Furthermore, the Federals were threatening to extend their activities. Two ladies from Suffolk had come to a Confederate officer in Weldon, North Carolina, with troubling news. They told him, "General Butler has notified the citizens of Suffolk that they must take the oath of allegiance to the Federal Government or leave immediately." Such demands presented them with a dilemma. "They are loyal to the South," the officer explained to his superior, Brigadier General Matthew Ransom, "and wish your advice on the subject." If they took the oath, they would be disloyal; if they refused or fled their homes, they would "lose their all."[46]

Pickett had received the dispatch from Ransom. "Can we do anything for the people of Suffolk?" he had inquired.[47] Now, Pickett was passing the note on to Cooper. "You will see likewise that they are going to play the same game in Suffolk that they did in Norfolk," he observed; "make all take the oath of allegiance to the Federal Government or confiscate their property." The desperate plea of a deputation of ladies had worked its way through the chain of command to him. "I really do not know what advice to give in answer to the question they ask me," Pickett confessed. "With my force it is impossible to protect such distant points. Still it makes my blood boil to think of these enormities being practiced, and we have no way of arresting them." Desirous of taking some action, he observed, "I will give orders to the cavalry now at or near Franklin to make an expedition to Suffolk and the vicinity. We of course cannot hold the place, but might possibly do the enemy some damage."[48]

Before sending the letter and its attachments along to President Davis, who made a habit of reading correspondence personally, Adjutant General Cooper endorsed it, noting: "It is impossible for the Department to answer the question propounded by General Pickett in respect to the deputation of ladies from Suffolk further than to state that taking the compulsory oath exacted of them by an infuriated [foe], for their safety, etc, should not, under the pressing necessities of the case represented by them, be considered as an indication of their want of fidelity to the Southern cause. General Pickett, in all other respects, appears to have taken the necessary measures, to the extent of his means, to check the outrages complained of."[49]

The year ended with the Confederates contemplating a raid on Union lines.[50] Pickett had his men scattered from Franklin to Ivor, one stop northwest of Zuni, guarding the Blackwater line just as Roger Atkinson Pryor had done a year earlier.[51] Although much had transpired, little had changed in the region, except that the war was taking a greater toll on soldiers and civilians alike.

"This county is in a most deplorable condition."
State Senator William Day to Governor William Smith on Isle of Wright County

"Do hurry friends or they will get away."
Suffolk residents urging Southern troops along

⊰ 12 ⊱ *"Do Hurry Friends"*

A S THE CONFEDERATE STATES OF AMERICA ENTERED 1864, THE prospects for victory appeared bleak. Robert E. Lee had failed in his second invasion of the North at Gettysburg in July 1863. On the fourth day of that month the beleaguered garrison under John Pemberton surrendered at Vicksburg, and the subsequent loss of Port Hudson closed the Mississippi River to the Confederates. A brief glimmer attended the victory at Chickamauga, Georgia. Yet when Braxton Bragg failed to follow it up with more than a lackluster "siege" of Chattanooga, which the Federals swept away in November, the darkness returned over Confederate fortunes in the West. On the last day of the year 1863, a Richmond *Examiner* editorial summarized, "To-day closes the gloomiest year of our struggle."[1]

Still, there was hope, not yet born entirely of desperation. The war might turn, as it had in the past, to the advantage of the men in gray and butternut. Certainly if valor and sacrifice had anything to do with it, there was reason to believe that they might win out in the end, particularly if the Lincoln administration fell in the elections to come. But the opponent was just as certain that numbers and right were finally proving out. What was more, President Lincoln seemed to have found a general capable of performing to his satisfaction. He would shortly invest Ulysses S. Grant with the authority to bring the war to the Southerners on a scale they could not imagine.

For the people of southeastern Virginia, there would be no saucy predictions of victory and liberation, such as had come from the likes of Roger Pryor. He was now a private, and the region a military backwater. But life had to continue under whatever conditions prevailed, and the people of Nansemond, Southampton, Isle of Wight, and Suffolk understood that fact all too well. For them the war remained much as it had been since Longstreet's departure from the region the previous spring: a daily struggle for survival.

One of the issues with which some people in the region had to contend was the collection of back taxes. A flurry of correspondence passed between various members of the local political establishment and the governor's office in Richmond. The common theme was the desire for relief from the tax burden, at least until times could return to some semblance of normalcy. James L. Wilson, longtime member of the General Assembly, took the lead in making the request known to the governor. In a letter dated March 12 from Smithfield in Isle of Wight County, Wilson expressed his "surprise" at returning from a session of the legislature to find that "the sheriff of the County proposed and in some cases had actually proceeded to collect the taxes due from the County to the State of Va. for the year 1862." Wilson stressed that the taxes for that year had not been collected "at the usual time" for the very sufficient reason that "the exposed situation of our County after the evacuation of Norfolk by our forces and the frequent and destructive raids of the enemy" rendered proper assessments impossible. Although similar conditions prevailed in 1863, the commissioner of the revenue had managed to complete his books for 1862, enabling the sheriff to commence his collections.

There were significant problems to be overcome, the delegate explained. The assessment took as its base property values that existed before the fall of Norfolk, while Confederate forces protected and maintained order for the region. "Since that time," Wilson observed, "more than three fourths of our entire Slave labor has been taken from us by the enemy and we have had to dispose of much of our other property . . . at reduced prices to prevent its falling into the hands of the enemy." Thus the taxpayers faced a double blow. "We are required to pay taxes upon this property which has been taken from us by the enemy when our means of payment has been greatly diminished by the loss of that property."

Wilson explained to the governor that had he and other members of the legislature expected such action, they would have asked for exemptions for "our people from this burden." Still, if no remedy could be found, he was certain that the people of the county would comply, as they "are a patriotic people" who "have always paid their taxes cheerfully." Mustering his full rhetorical capabilities, the legislator pleaded, "They are a law-abiding people and are at all times willing to 'render unto Caesar the things that are Caesars,'" but "this tax for 1862 will fall heavily upon them at this time, especially upon that large class of our citizens who have lost by capture at the hands of the enemy the very property upon which they are required to pay taxes, and in this class are included many of our soldiers who are in the service of the Confederate States Army."

Then there was the additional burden of Confederate taxation. "The Confederate assessor whenever the *situation* will permit it is proceeding to assess our property and our people are willing and expect to pay the heavy taxes which the Confederate Government has imposed upon the property we are permitted to hold, although we are beyond the lines of our army and the Government, through inability we know, is unable to protect us." This latter point sheds light upon the conditions prevailing along the Confederate frontier. Although nominally under the protection of the Confederate government, the area remained vulnerable to Union incursion, which was precisely the point Wilson was trying to make to the governor.

The demands were greater than Wilson thought his constituents ought to bear. "It seems very hard to us to have to pay these heavy taxes [to the Confederate government] and at the same time to pay back taxes—taxes that could not be collected because of the actual presences or proximity of the enemy, and taxes too upon property which has yielded us nothing [with which to pay them]."[2] It was an eloquent argument on behalf of the people of property in the county, one of whom was Wilson himself. Certainly Governor Smith understood that the upper crust in Isle of Wight County and throughout southeastern Virginia was operating under extreme duress to maintain its prewar positions. Wilson spoke passionately as a representative of people adversely affected by the war and as a man who had a vested interest in obtaining relief for them and himself.

To add force to his request, Wilson had state senator William H. Day and Confederate congressman Robert H. Whitfield draft short supporting letters to the governor. Day stated: "I have read a letter addressed to you by Mr. James Wilson of this county, and concur in the views presented by him. This county is in a most deplorable condition as regards provisions. The heavy loss of slave labor has caused much distress, and I feel confident that no county in the state similarly situated will pay taxes."[3] Congressman Whitfield observed, "It requires no argument to show the hardships of numbers of our Citizens under such action as the sheriff is undertaking," although he quickly added, "I attach no blame to him, he is an excellent officer." In any case, "to pay taxes for the year 1862, on property, negroes, lost to the owners, under the existing circumstances, will I fear, indeed I know, press exceedingly heavy on them." Then, perhaps realizing the class-oriented nature of his call for relief, the congressman added a more general flavor to his closing. "Your assistance in this matter," he assured the governor, "will be kindly remembered by our unfortunate people."[4]

Even the sheriff corresponded with the governor on the issue, but his letter had a decidedly different tone than the others. Tellingly, he did not send his letter until five days after the others had been written, and he wrote his as much in response to theirs as anything else. "Sir I have been informed that there has been a Letter addressed to you from a few persons of my county requesting the suspension of the collection of taxes which was assessed for the year 1862." For his part Sheriff Thomas J. Clements had continued to fulfill the obligation of his office. "I have proceeded to collect the said tax," he explained matter-of-factly, "and have in hand, at the present over $1,200 collected in the old currency, and it is the wishes of the taxpayers of my county to pay said tax."

Absent from his correspondence was the note of desperation and the demand for relief so apparent in the others. Had the sheriff encountered any widespread opposition to his actions, he would surely have mentioned it. Indeed, the sheriff's letter reveals no significant disaffection, beyond the usual grumbling that would accompany any tax collection. The first and only challenge Clements deemed worthy of mention was the letter he learned had been sent to the governor. The sheriff's straightforward language in his March 17 communication with the governor suggests that he considered the business no more than a part of his normal routine. Even Clement's final appeal held no particular sense of urgency or concern: "Hope to hear from you on the subject if it be necessary."[5]

Despite the wishes of the prominent individuals, Governor Smith felt that his hands were tied. On the back of two of the letters, he wrote notations indicating that he had no authority to bring the relief they sought. As for the sheriff, Smith instructed his secretary, "Inform him that I have no power to suspend collection of taxes," an answer that the secretary made on his behalf on March 21, 1864.[6]

At about the same time that the representatives of the people of the Isle of Wight were writing the governor to obtain relief from the collection of back taxes, the people of Suffolk were enjoying a brief respite from Union raiding parties. The occasion was a Confederate expedition through the area that benefited from the complacent attitude of the Federals in the immediate vicinity. It began with the early arousal of the Southerners from their camps and the formation of columns, although the men remained unclear as to their destination or purpose. Some of them had already spent the better part of the previous two weeks marching and skirmishing in northeastern North Carolina, often hampered by rain and cold winds, in addition to the fatigue that accompanied the long treks along the winding country roads. The morning's activities offered the dim prospect of more of the same.

Soon it was apparent, however, that this would be no ordinary patrol. The soldiers from neighboring North Carolina formed into a line of battle some three miles outside Suffolk on the old Somerton Road in the vicinity of Bethlehem Church. Joining other units, they crossed over the tracks of the Norfolk and Petersburg Railroad near where they converged with the Seaboard and Roanoke Railroad west of the town. Henry Chambers, a captain in the 49th North Carolina, recorded what transpired on this Wednesday, March 9, in his diary. As the men advanced, they "for the first time could see the spires and housetops of Suffolk." The pace quickened with the energy of an imminent clash with the enemy. "We now began to double quick," Chambers explained, "and the nearer town the faster we were required to go."[7] One of Ransom's marathoners subsequently wrote, "We ran three miles through deep sand." The pace was exhausting. "I never was so tired in my life," he explained in a letter written on March 13 and published in a Petersburg newspaper over a week later.[8]

For the jaded marchers there may have seemed to be no justification for such haste, until the sudden appearance of a rider sent to urge them along. Chambers noted that the man wore the uniform of a "Franco-Louisiana Zouave," but his words created as much sensation as his unique military dress. "'Colonel for God's sake hurry your men on,' he called out, 'or you will be too late.'" To the nearest men in the ranks, his message was even more direct. "Run boys, run, and we will catch the G—d d——d niggers yet!" It was a message they instantly grasped. The news spurred them on with the incentive of catching, fighting, and defeating men who had been their slaves or social inferiors not so very long ago and who now had the gall, in their eyes, to oppose them wearing uniforms and shoul-dering weapons.

If the rider chose his words for maximum effect, they could not have been more successful. Chambers observed, "We were nearly exhausted with our long double quick but when told 'that the hated negroes had been encountered,' we received as it were renewed vigor and on we pushed." The sound of artillery supporting their advance must have added to their elation, as well as their sense of urgency. The same shelling that gave them covering fire would also prod the Union cavalrymen to increase the pace of their retreat back toward their lines and safety. Yet if the quarry was in danger of getting away, the men on foot simply could not keep up the frenzied pace. "Again we began to flag," Chambers admitted, but "again were we revived by the sight that met our eyes as we passed through the town."[9] One participant recalled that he would probably "have sunk with fatigue" had he and his comrades not received encouragement from the "excitement and kindly cheer" demonstrated "by the patriotic ladies of Suffolk."[10]

Some of the civilians offered containers of water to refresh the Southerners as they rushed along in pursuit of the retreating Federals. But practicality mingled with compassion. Even as they ladled dippers of water into parched throats, they warned the soldiers not to drink too much. The men resumed the marathon with the words "Take a swallow and hurry on" ring-ing in their ears. Others cheered the men as if the whole business were a sporting contest. Some assumed the posture of prayer for their delivery from the Northern troops. "Oh, I do hope they will catch them!" one observed. Another cried out, "Do hurry friends or they will get away." Others, aware of the fatigue gripping the men as they raced along, admonished them sup-portingly, "Do, do hold out a little longer!"

As the Southerners raced forward, a detached party of Union troop-ers broke through the rapidly encircling forces and dashed for safety. The Confederate artillery played havoc with the retreating bluecoats. Unlimbering and firing a few shots before limbering up once again to race forward to new positions, the crews frequently left the infantrymen to keep up as best they could. "Every now and then the artillery would stop and fire a few shots at the retreating minions of Yankeedom, when it would whirl away again to the front with us after it." Surprisingly, even at this pace the artillery marksmanship was remarkable. Regarding the firing as "excel-lent," Chambers added, "We could see the negroe cavalry scatter when the shells would fall in their midst."

The race could not continue indefinitely. Men could only stand so much. "We thus followed them for nearly a mile when they got into the swamp and the exciting chase ended." Despite their efforts, the bulk of the enemy force had gotten away. To be sure, they had rid the community of a menace, at least temporarily, but they had failed to ensnare their opponents or defeat them decisively. The Confederates felt they had done the best they could, but Henry Chambers lamented in his diary, "Had we only been accompanied by cavalry, good cavalry, the results of this day would have been more important."[11] Another Southerner concurred. Calling the experience "a romantic charge—infantry in pursuit of cavalry," he pointed to the same source for his disappointment. "Unfortunately, for us," he observed, "we had no horsemen, and most of them escaped us."[12] The Union commander of the department, Brigadier General Charles Heckman, seems to have sensed the Confederate frustration. He observed in his report on the action, "I think the object of the enemy was to capture Cole's cavalry, a result in which they failed most decidedly."[13]

Still, for the Confederates and the civilians who had urged them on, the day was important enough. For a brief moment the latter knew that Union raiders were on the run. For the former there was the always-welcome opportunity to plunder the enemy's abandoned camps. "We captured a camp," one excited Southerner gloated, "and many of our boys got a supply of clothing, blankets, etc. etc." The soldier did not neglect to treat himself to the spoils. "I was lucky enough to get two blankets" and a hat, although, he added disappointedly, "(probably a negroes, but I don't know)."[14] Returning from a reconnaissance, Chambers joined the brigade as it "marched down to the Yankee camps and the men were permitted to plunder to their heart's content." His description undoubtedly beggars the commotion that followed: "It was a scene of indescribable confusion—'confusion worse confounded'—and clothing and implements, papers, books, baker's bread, etc. etc. were handled in regular rampant rebel fashion."[15]

For their part, the Union reports naturally tried to minimize the damage. "The enemy, however, advanced no farther than Bernard's Mills, where they either destroyed or carried off the camp and garrison equipage of the three companies of the One hundred and eighteenth New York Volunteers," wrote General Heckman.[16] From Bower's Hill, David F. Dobie of the 118th New York explained that two companies of his regiment "were detached from the regiment and were at Bernard's Mills"; then "while I was North the rebels came down & drove the three companies in (back to this place)." The Southerners seem to have enjoyed a fine sense of timing with their advance, catching these troops unprepared for defense. Unlike the generals in their official reports, Dobie did not try to gloss over what he had heard in camp about the affair. "It was just about noon," he related; "the men's dinner was just ready, but the rebs. came down on them so unexpectedly that they had hardly time to put on their cartridge boxes & get their guns, & of course had to march off & leave all their clothing, excepting what little was on their backs." The subsequent retreat to Bower's Hill gave the men no chance to return for their gear and left the Confederates with a bonanza of spoils to salve any disappointment they may have felt over the enemy cavalry's escape.[17]

Whatever the outcome of the action at Suffolk, Union general Benjamin Butler, writing to Secretary of War Stanton on March 12, was positively giddy. The 2d U.S. Cavalry had "Handsomely repulsed" the Confederate cavalry force it encountered, "with large loss." In the close-hand combat that marked a portion of the fight, the black troops had taken on their white counterparts, "and the enthusiastic testimony of their officers is that they behaved with utmost courage, coolness, and daring." Butler, the man who first used the term *contraband* to describe the slaves who sought refuge within Union lines, concluded, "I am perfectly satisfied with my negro cavalry."[18]

Brigadier General Heckman had a similar reaction to the actions of the black troops under his command. In his report to Butler, he exuded: "Never did soldiers display more bravery, nor officers more coolness and courage than that displayed by Colonel Cole's command. Almost entirely surrounded by ten times their number they fought their way out, losing no prisoners or horse except those that were killed."[19] There may have been more truth to the Union general's remarks than he realized. In a March 11 letter from his post at Franklin, Confederate lieutenant Angus McDonald wrote his mother, "General Ransom is falling back he has had one or two fights with the yankeys this week." Ransom "had a fight day before yesterday at Suffolk & killed a bout thirty negrows but took no prisners." Then the Confederate artilleryman added, "But that Is something that our souldiers are apt not to do to take any negro souldiers [as prisoners]."[20] Another Southerner repeated this ominous message in a letter two days later. "We did not take *any* prisoners. Officers and men were perfectly enthusiastic in *killing* the 'd——d rascals' as I heard many call them." Then the same soldier added firmly, "Ransom's brigade never takes any negro prisoners."[21]

Henry Chambers noted, "Although we are known as 'Ransom's foot cavalry,' we can hardly overtake fresh and well fed horses, ridden by frightened negroes, especially after the hard marching we have so recently undergone."

This contemptuous tone continued as the officer recounted stories related to the Confederates by local residents:

> The citizens say negroe troops have been at Suffolk before but none were so impudent as these last. They boasted that "the white Yankees could not take Richmond, but that they were the boys that could do it"; that they "wished the d——d rebels would dare to put their feet in Suffolk." This desire had not been long expressed before the valiant Africans were flying in good, swift style before these "d——d rebels" they had so desired to see. It is said that there were three regiments of cavalry and a few white infantry in the force we had caused "to change its base" to a point nearer [their] Department Headquarters at Fortress Monroe.

One of the sidelights to this running fight through and beyond Suffolk reveals as much as any single incident could the unforgiving nature of the Civil War in 1864. While racing in pursuit of the Union cavalry, Chambers noticed "a crowd of excited men" gathering around a residence located at "the eastern edge of the town." Although prompted to continue the chase, the Confederate officer stopped long enough to learn the reason for the commotion. "We were told that there were negroes in it." he wrote. "This house was set on fire and burned before the negroes could be gotten out and killed." Chambers attested to their unwillingness to go down without a fight. "In the 'melee' around it," Chambers observed, "a man named Green of Co. 'B' of our regiment was shot through the breast by a negroe and killed."[22]

Another participant offered corroborating and gruesome detail. He believed that the men had occupied the home "for the purpose of picking off our officers." Indeed, in the initial charge the Confederates suffered two men killed and several wounded. The black soldiers "fought with desperation," he wrote with grudging respect mingled with contempt, "seeing the hopelessness of their situation." Torches were applied to the building, and as the flames quickly rose, it began to disgorge its occupants.

> Soon the fire and smoke had its effect—suffocation commenced— one of the infernals leaped from the window to escape the horrible death of burning; a minute more and a dozen bayonets pierced his body; another and another followed, and shared the same fate. Three stayed and met their doom with manly resolution. They were burnt to cinders. After the flames had enveloped the house and immense clouds of smoke were issuing from the burning building, where noth-

ing could be seen within, the crack of a rifle was heard above, and one
of the artillery men fell severely wounded in the knee. This was the
last fire from the house. See with what determination they continued
their work. Twas worthy of a better cause. But death was their doom,
and the flames were their choice.[23]

This incident makes it clear that Southern whites in southeastern
Virginia were as capable as any of expressing their outrage at challenges
to the racial and social order in the most violent ways. The Confederates
apparently could not even bring themselves to dispose of the victims. "Our
soldiers would not even bury the negroes—they were buried by negroes,"
one participant of the fight explained. Yet this Southerner understood quite
well the implications for him, should fortunes ever be reversed. "If some
of us should be captured by them," he observed coldly, "our fate would
be hard."[24]

These observations, found in the diary and letters of Confederates in
the region, are reminiscent of the actions other white Southerners took
against soldiers of African descent at places like Fort Pillow, Saltville, and
the Crater. Far from being an aberration, the war in southeastern Virginia
was proving to be as brutal as that fought anywhere else.[25]

It is ironic that many of the men wearing blue that day hailed from the
region themselves, most having been members of the 2d U.S. Cavalry for
only a few months. Numerous participants in the fighting on March 9 had
listed Suffolk or Nansemond, Southampton, or Isle of Wight County as their
place of birth. Many of these until recently had been laborers or farmers;
some had been servants or craftsmen of various sorts. Now they shared a
bond greater than birthplace, as black men in blue uniforms fighting to make
themselves and their brethren free.[26]

Despite the mixed results of this fight, and the overblown rhetoric of
official Union reports, it made eminently good sense to send these local
men on such missions. Many of them knew the confusing road network
well, and on March 9 that knowledge probably saved some of their lives.
An after-action report noted, "A majority of the missing will doubtless come
in, as most of them are men whose horses were shot, and the men ran into
the swamp and will find their way [back] in [to Union lines]," which is precisely what happened.[27]

In a follow-up report made two days later, the colonel of the 2d Cavalry
observed, "I have the honor to report the return of all men who took the
swamps when their horses were shot, except 2, as well as 1 (George Ames,
Company K) [earlier] reported killed." Ames's case presented an extraor-

dinary instance of cunning and valor. When Confederate artillery fire killed his horse, it appeared to his comrades that Ames was dead, too, pinned beneath the animal's carcass. His lack of motion, probably from the concussion of the bursting shell, if not from his precipitate fall, led to the erroneous report of his death. Instead, he regained consciousness and, according to the report, "crawled out and took [to] the swamp, hiding his arms." His quick thinking saved him from probable death; his unexpected return must have surprised and cheered his comrades.[28]

Others were not so fortunate, although casualties for the affair on both sides were relatively light. A Confederate recalled shortly afterward, "Our entire loss was two killed and five wounded."[29] Union reports placed their losses at between five and six men killed and one, a lieutenant named Van Lew, who had been wounded in the action and since that time had died. In addition, the report counted two men as still missing.[30] Because of the circumstances of some of the fighting, an exact figure of Union dead may never be known.

One of the black soldiers who participated in the running fight in Suffolk was a laborer from Southampton County named William Moff. Joining Company K of the 2d U.S. Cavalry at Fort Monroe on January 1, 1864, Moff was a young man of seventeen. By the end of the fighting on March 9, he was dead. Another Union trooper, William Lawrence, also a laborer and a Suffolk native, returned to his hometown as a member of Company C. The wounded Lawrence managed to reach the safety of Union lines at Bower's Hill with the rest of his comrades but died the following day.[31] The struggle for freedom had cost these men their lives.

As for Confederate casualties, there is no accurate account. The earlier of two Union reports stated simply, "The loss of the enemy was much greater than ours." In addition it noted, "The commanding officer of the enemy's cavalry was killed by Colonel Cole." Two days later Cole himself explained: "From the report of fugitives I am sure I underestimated the rebel loss very much. I am certain that it will exceed 50."[32] Given the nature of the fighting, it is unlikely that the number of Confederates lost in the engagement was as large as the Federals boasted it was.

Regardless, the correspondent from the *Philadelphia Inquirer* made a valid point when he observed, "Our front is well protected, and all these petty demonstrations of the Rebels is only a waste of powder on their part." What was worse, he was also correct in asserting that "the real sufferers by their presence are the farmers who live between the lines of the two forces. They are being robbed ruthlessly of their scanty stores." Even so, "few of them ought to complain," he noted, "as nearly all of them are secessionists, ever ready to render such aid to the enemy as will tend to interfere with or cripple the movements of our army."[33]

The Confederates who engaged in the Suffolk firefight did not remain in the area for long. The same civilians who had cheered their coming were distraught at their departure. "The patriot fair of Suffolk were exceedingly kind to us and wept to see us leave," one of the men explained. He attributed the intensity of this reaction to the recent presence of the black troops. From Suffolk, the soldier marched into North Carolina, where he met with a more muted reception, which he credited to the people's fear of Union retaliation against them. He concluded that despite the lack of "open demonstrations," the inhabitants were uniformly "loyal and liberal."[34]

Any respite won from this Confederate advance proved short lived, for other swiftly mounted raiding parties crisscrossed the no-man's-land between Bower's Hill and the Blackwater River in April. At least one of the goals of these expeditions was to sweep the area of Southerners visiting home on furlough, messengers carrying news and letters, and guerrillas who were attempting to harass the Union war effort. Admiral Samuel P. Lee, now quite familiar with the rivers and creeks in the region, wrote to Benjamin Butler suggesting that they undertake active defensive measures to rid the area of such pests. "The vicinity of Smithfield and Chuckatuck are known to be infested by guerrillas, who are reported to have boats concealed up those creeks and their tributaries," he explained on April 9. "I respectfully suggest that you send at once a sufficient force to capture these rebels and destroy their boats on the upper creeks and to co-operate with a naval force to prevent their escape by the river, which I will send as soon as you are ready."[35]

The request was music to Butler's ears. He was always ready to strike a blow. "I have your note in relation to the pirates of the creeks and inlets of the James River and the means of destroying them and am desirous of co-operating with you in that object," he responded the next day.[36] Within two days meticulous orders went out specifying the exact size and nature of the force, the roads along which its elements would fan out, and the area to be scoured. The chief of staff gave explicit instructions that part of this force should begin by "occupying all the houses to prevent information being taken to the enemy." Another part should make "a close examination of the country between the Chuckatuck [Creek] and [the] Nansemond, arresting all males found and destroying all small boats." No differentiation was offered between craft used by guerrillas and those used by legitimate fishermen and oystermen. "General [Charles K.] Graham," the leader of the operation, "will understand the object of the expedition is to capture all small parties of rebel soldiery, all guerrillas, the destruction of all boats found in the waters that are examined, and the capture of all property that may be valuable to the United States Government."[37]

Such expeditions depended upon interservice cooperation for success. Even then, other elements could deprive them of victory. An earlier joint operation, which had occurred at the end of January and early into February, taught the Federals valuable, if terribly painful, lessons about tangling with the Confederates in the creeks and streams of southeastern Virginia. The commander of the Union gunboat *Smith Briggs,* Captain Frederick A. Rowe, later recalled that when he set a small force of infantry and a portion of his crewmen on land near Smithfield, disaster was not long in coming. The combined force of approximately 200 men from the 99th New York, under Captain John C. Lee, ran into a Confederate force twice its size. Rowe ordered a naval lieutenant assigned to him to retrieve the crewmen with the ship's launch. With a full complement of crew, he planned to turn the vessel and lay a covering fire for the infantry force as it fell back.

Astonishingly, the naval lieutenant refused to accept his orders, forcing Rowe to use the vessel itself to extricate his crewmen. As the *Smith Briggs* pulled up to the dock, the infantrymen saw their opportunity for escape and broke off their defense to flee for safety. The Confederates dashed after them, blasting them as they ran, "picking off the men and wounding others, besides disabling the vessel." Still, Rowe managed to get the vessel away from the dock, where it promptly ran aground, still within range of the Southern guns. Captain Lee jumped overboard, while the naval lieutenant took the remaining launch and headed for safety. This left Rowe in command of a vessel in danger of being overwhelmed. He put up a valiant defense before being struck "in the throat, causing great loss of blood and almost choking me." His wound and the failure of any help to materialize convinced him that surrender was his only reasonable choice.[38]

In the meantime, the other elements of the operation lay stranded in and near the Nansemond. A dense fog rolled in on the thirty-first, grounding the vessels that might otherwise have come to the aid of the *Smith Briggs.* In his after-action report, Union general Graham noted that when one of these ships reached "the mouth of the Nansemond, the pilot stated that he could not go up, as it would be impossible to keep the channel." These vessels had the task of supporting another land force near Chuckatuck. Despite the risk of running aground, Graham ordered the lightest-draft boat to proceed and succeeded in reaching and reclaiming the Chuckatuck land force.

Word arrived later in the day that the Smithfield expedition had encountered trouble. Graham immediately instructed the vessels under his command to go to the relief of that force, but they were not able to make it in time. "On reaching the mouth of Pagan Creek [near Smithfield], about 4 P.M.," Graham wrote afterward, "the information was communicated to me . . . that the Smith Briggs with a detachment of Captain Lee had been captured, and a few moments afterward a terrific explosion occurred." He concluded that the Confederates had "blown up the Smith Briggs to prevent her recapture."[39] In point of fact, Rowe and his men set the fires that destroyed the vessel when they reached her powder magazine, detonating the vessel with such force that it shattered "every pane of glass in Smithfield."[40] Captain Lee and three others who swam to safety signaled one of the Union vessels and were rescued.[41]

It took the Federals a couple of months to recover from this setback before the annoyance of Confederate activity in the region prompted Admiral Lee to propose a cleansing operation to General Butler on April 9. Perhaps as a vote of confidence, Butler chose General Graham as the coordinator of this campaign, one which must have struck the Union commander as uncomfortably similar in style to the botched expedition in January–February. Although the operation that occurred April 13–15 avoided the disasters of the previous one, it achieved only modest results. Graham reported the capture of "one signal officer, 5 privates, C.S. Army; also 1 piece of artillery (brass), and a quantity of ammunition." His men also took ten horses, harness, saddles, boots, and sundry other items at a cost to them of five men wounded, one mortally, and "1 man accidentally drowned."[42] The artillery piece was believed to have been aboard the *Smith Briggs* when the Confederates captured her near Smithfield.[43]

The ship's log of one of the participating vessels indicates that once again the Confederates peppered the ships and launches with musketry, but they failed to repeat their success of two months earlier. Not wishing to lose his ship, the master of the *Stepping Stones* kept up his fire from a safe distance. The log report suggests the nature of the fighting: "From Merid. To 4 [April 14, 1864] at 1:30 the launches went up the Creek & were fired on from the Woods at 2:40 [the *Stepping Stones*] fired 4 Shells 1 Shrapnel in the Woods at guerrillas which were firing on the Launches at 3:15 launches returned and brought on board A. Master Wilder killed and H. H. Miller Seaman wounded with ball in the back."[44]

At the same time the Federals and Confederates traded fire near Smithfield, elements of the 118th New York joined with other units to cross the Nansemond River. The 118th moved through the village of Chuckatuck, "where we confiscated nine or ten horses, six mules, etc., arrested one rebel soldier connected with the signal service, & also some citizens." Returning to the river, these men united with the other forces in time to take on "about one hundred rebs. who thought that we only had about one hundred and fifty men; but they very unexpectedly run against the 9th N.J. about 900 strong & had to beat a precipitate retreat."

In the aftermath of this little tussle, the Union force moved on to Benn's Church and then to Smithfield, which one Federal described as "a very pretty little town." While there, two companies of the 118th received orders to locate and destroy "that torpedo boat which attempted to blow up the Minnesota a short time since." The raiding party confronted some opposition in carrying out their "hunt." "We skirmished up a little creek where the boat was thot. to be," the soldier explained in a letter home, but they failed to find the vessel or do much damage besides destroying "four small boats."[45]

Private William Lind in the 27th Massachusetts Infantry participated in the operation as well. On April 18 he wrote his brother Thomas a straightforward explanation of what had been accomplished. "Well, Tom, we have just got back from a 3 days march up 12 miles beyond Suffolk, Va. but the Rebels found out that we was coming and they left us. we captured one guerrellie thats all." He found more than the march distasteful: "We was 24 hours without anything to eat. Only what we could pick up on the road." Such fruitless expeditions had him counting the days until his term of service was up, but with orders to "go somewhere," he was certain that more lay in store. "It looks as [if] we was going to see a littel more fighting yet before we get out of it."[46]

Regardless of this soldier's expectations, it was clear from the two combined operations in the first half of 1864 that such expeditions failed to garner enough results to justify the losses sustained in carrying them out. They did little more than irritate the Confederates by snagging the occasional prisoner and confiscating or destroying some military property. The flow of information and supplies soon resumed as the Southerners created new means of relaying them to and from the region.

But larger-scale military operations were not the only ones conducted in the region. Often small lightning raids into the no-man's-land of Nansemond and Isle of Wight Counties proved more successful at less cost. Such efforts seem to have been carried out by smaller groups of soldiers led by volunteers from among the officer corps. An indication of this kind of operation appears in two letters written in April by a member of the 118th New York, stationed at Bower's Hill.

On April 2 Captain David Dobie wrote his friend Hattie that the lieutenant colonel had called upon him at his tent "and asked if I was well acquainted [with] Suffolk." When Dobie wondered about the reason for the inquiry, the colonel answered that he "proposed making a night raid into that place to capture some rebel officers who were home on leave." The captain noted that "I with three others, officers in the Regt. in command of a large squad, or detachment of men, were to do the business." The weather forced a temporary postponement in the operation but did not dampen their spirits for it.

In his next letter, on April 11, Dobie picked up the story. "You will perhaps remember I spoke about being detailed to go on a raid into Suffolk," he reminded Hattie. The next day he had accompanied the band of raiders to a midway point between Bower's Hill and Suffolk, where they waited until early in the morning for the dash into the town. By the time the men were ready to set out, Dobie had become quite ill. Other officers volunteered to take his place, but he would have none of it. "I was determined, having been selected, to go if I shook to pieces on the way."

The sick soldier managed to stay in his saddle, and the squad reached Suffolk at about 3:30 A.M. "We took the men we went after," he recalled, "and left about 8 o'clock." The hit-and-run raid had proved successful, but it left Dobie with a strange sense of déjà vu. "We saw our old camping ground of last summer," he explained, "the church we used as a Chapel, the everything familiar except the stir around the stores & market so common last spring when the place was occupied by a large number of Union troops." Whether this lack of activity could be attributed to the withdrawal of those troops or the early hour of his visit, the quiet of the town left an impression upon the Union soldier.[47]

A great deal more was about to occur to the north in an area of central Virginia known as the Wilderness. On May 5 Lieutenant General Ulysses S. Grant launched his "Overland Campaign" when the lead elements of the Army of the Potomac plunged into that thickly forested region. Ultimately, Grant committed 115,000 men to the enterprise, but Robert E. Lee had chosen his ground for defense well. The mass of undergrowth and the bisecting roads offered him advantages that would offset the superior numbers the Federals brought to bear against him and his 60,000 men.

Two days of hard and bloody combat followed. Men fell in astounding numbers. Then fires spread among the dry undergrowth, adding terror and death of a different kind. A participant observed in his journal: "The woods have caught fire, darkening the sun and filling the air with stench. The smell of burning bodies is horrible." What made matters worse was the combatant's inability to help the wounded soldiers threatened by the blazes. "We heard the cries and saw the sickening blue flames of their bodies, but there was nothing we could do to help them."[48] Even the severe wounding of Lee's "War Horse" James Longstreet by friendly fire did not prevent another Confederate victory and a costly Union defeat. Altogether, Grant lost some 18,000 men. He then did something that no other Union commander had done to Lee. He moved forward, instead of retreating to lick his wounds. Grant had the weight of numbers on his side, and everyone, including Lee, knew it.[49]

Grant's next destination was a hamlet known as Spotsylvania Courthouse. The action there spread over the next several weeks, adding the name "Bloody Angle" to the lexicon of the war. Men of Major General Winfield S. Hancock's 2d Corps smashed through the Confederate defenses at a point the soldiers called the "Mule Shoe" because of its shape. Bitter counterattacks contained the break, and the Confederates toiled steadily to reestablish their broken lines farther to the rear. Again the death toll was horrendous. The Federals lost another 18,000 men, while the Confederates lost between 9,000 and 10,000. Yet once more Grant sent his men south.[50]

So far in this campaign the combatants had been like boxers. Each slugged at the other for awhile, inflicting as much damage as possible. Then there would come maneuvering, as they looked for weaknesses to exploit. Finally, there was more slugging. The Southerners, smaller in number, had to wait for their larger opponent to leave himself open to the blow that would finish him off, or for him simply to tire of the match. The Northerners continued their pounding, realizing that weight of numbers was on their side and that repeated blows would inevitably have to tell.

The next point of contention in the Overland Campaign was along the North Anna River. Lee made the first mistake here when he miscalculated Union intentions. This allowed some of the Federals to seize the important Telegraph Road bridge, while others crossed the river on the Confederate left. Rather than panic, the Southern commander turned the misfortune to his own good. By establishing his army in a strong defensive position between these forces, Lee kept the enemy divided. He planned to use quick concentration to hit one portion when the opportunity allowed. Both sides had lost another 2,500 to 2,600 men before Grant realized the gravity of the situation and pulled back into his own earthworks.[51]

The Union commander moved once more around the Confederate right flank. This kept him close to his water communications and supplies and forced Lee to abandon his formidable line of defenses along the North Anna or leave the road to Richmond open. Grant's men managed to take the crossroads at Cold Harbor, but when Lee refused to withdraw behind the Chickahominy River as he might have done, the Federal commander decided to blast him out of his entrenchments. Grant launched a powerful frontal attack against the Confederate lines. Three Union corps faced a withering fire that decimated their ranks, producing some 7,000 casualties in the space of thirty minutes. It was Malvern Hill in reverse.[52]

Yet, Grant's last feat in this campaign was his finest. He decided once more to maneuver his men around the Confederates. Crossing the James River on massive pontoon bridges, he carried his army to the south side of the river. From there he could threaten to take the vital city of Petersburg. He not only threatened but almost captured it. On June 9 a scratch force of soldiers, "old men and boys," kept the city in Confederate hands as Lee, now painfully aware of his critical position, rushed his army to defend it. Over four days, June 15–18, Petersburg lay within the Union grasp. But assaults by William F. "Baldy" Smith's 18th Corps on the fifteenth, Hancock's 2d Corps on the sixteenth, Ambrose Burnside's 9th Corps on the seventeenth and the 2d, 9th, and 5th Corps on the eighteenth failed to do more than dent the powerful Confederate Dimmock Line. In the meantime, Lee and his army had arrived in time to reinforce the beleaguered defenders. Grant's hope of a swift capture of Petersburg was gone.[53]

Throughout the course of the month and a half of sharp fighting that characterized this campaign, soldiers from Nansemond, Southampton, Isle of Wight, and Suffolk saw their share of combat. Their casualties attest to the human cost of a war of attrition, in which the Union forces sought to wear down their Confederate opponents with repeated blows. The South simply could not replace its losses in manpower, while the North could.

The 41st Virginia took most of its casualties in the Wilderness. Seven of its members received wounds, one mortal. Elden Casey of Company G had to have an arm removed. Lieutenant Walter C. Jones and Private Thomas J. Holland both died in the fighting on the sixth. Lieutenant Colonel Richard Owen Whitehead of the 16th Virginia took a round in the chest on that same day.[54] At Spotsylvania it was the 16th that suffered the most. Lieutenant Thomas Washington Smith and three sergeants fell wounded. One of them, John Walter Roberts, lost an arm to amputation. Colonel Thomas E. Upshaw of the 13th Virginia Cavalry was captured on the fourteenth. Then at North Anna, Captain Robert B. Brinkley and Sergeant Oliver H. P. Holland, both of the 41st, were killed in action. On June 3 Private James T. Conley of the 3d Virginia fell at Cold Harbor, and on the next day Private William Lester of the 16th Virginia died on Turkey Ridge. On June 8 two Harrells, Wilson and James, both of the 41st, were wounded. Two days later John Harrell fell into Union hands as a prisoner of war.[55]

While soldiers from the lower tidewater fell on battlefields in other parts of the state, many civilians sought to make sense of the changes being wrought in their lives. Their comments about the events affecting their lives show that many of them had different and conflicting interests to protect or advance. A letter to Anna Mary Riddick from a cousin in May 1864 suggests the naïveté of at least some white Southerners about the motives and desires of their African-American servants. The writer observed that her family anticipated the arrival of "the Yankees every moment." As a precaution "we had negro men posted at the kitchen gate with orders to tell us as soon as they saw Yankees approaching and then to take to the woods immediately so as not to be forced to leave." She failed to realize the possibility that they might actually want to leave. Unwittingly she continued, "But some of them were so curious that as soon as they saw any one coming [they] would run to take the horse and I verily believe if the Yankees had come, some of them would have been at the gate to hold their horses."[56]

Soldiers from both sides continued to cross through the no-man's-land between the Blackwater River and Bower's Hill, usually via the town of Suffolk. A newspaper in North Carolina described such a raid in June. "Raiding parties, says the Christian Sun, are going out in every direction from Suffolk, robbing the farmers of horses, provisions, etc." Laying the blame for such depredations on "Beast" Butler, the paper noted that he had ordered his patrols "to have all the horses taken in Nansemond, Isle of Wight, and Gates County, N.C., so as to prevent the making of a crop." This was a deliberate policy of starvation as far as the writer was concerned. "A party came into Suffolk last Friday with 114 horses and mules taken from their owners." The newspaper reported that "another party was at Chuckatuck and captured Dr. William T. Jordan of the Signal Corps, and a citizen, carrying them off. Great distress and consternation pervade the whole section of the country now given up to the ravages of the cruel enemy."[57]

Patrols and expeditions had occurred so often that some of the troops became quite familiar not only with road systems and crossings but with the inhabitants of the houses and farms along the routes they commonly used. In some cases these occupants proved helpful in providing news and information or in meeting the more tangible needs of the soldiers for sustenance. According to a Union trooper who belonged to the well-traveled 1st New York Mounted Rifles, one such family, the Ely family, lived just beyond Providence Church, outside the 1863 Union lines. The Elys were decidedly Confederate in sympathy but wisely sought to accommodate the men in blue. The tightwire act appears to have worked. "I always found the head of the family very candid in his statements," the soldier later explained, "but it was his express desire to remain neutral and to give no information to either side." Ely apparently had a son in Confederate service but was wise enough to realize that his proximity to Union forces required that he remain as neutral as possible, at least publicly. The family remained openly receptive to its Union visitors, with Mrs. Ely playing the role of hostess to perfection. The writer remembered that all of the Union troopers appreciated her "refined and womanly qualities and cheerful hospitality."

Then, during one of the visits, tragedy struck. As usual, Mrs. Ely had invited the officers of the regiment in for a meal, cheerily supervising at table, when noise from the yard and the cry "Fire!" disturbed the diners. Despite all of the efforts of the Union officers and men to save the nearby barn, the flames rapidly engulfed the structure. To make matters worse, the fire threatened the Ely home as well; in a matter of minutes, the wind carried firebrands from the burning barn to the "handsome mansion." The flames spread too rapidly for the men to prevent the destruction of both structures. The swiftness of the flames prevented the Elys from salvaging more than the clothes on their backs. They lost everything to the fire. The accident hit the Union officers nearly as hard as it did the Ely family. Feeling "deeply mortified and distressed," they decided it would be best to move the regiment along. Some of them noticed that the wife stood at the roadside as they rode off, visibly stunned. In the aftermath of the fire, the Elys took up residence in a former blacksmith shop nearby.

The story did not end there. At some point "toward the close of the war," an unnamed Union infantry regiment stopped nearby. Some of the officers asked the lady of the dilapidated homestead for some milk, which she readily supplied to them. Shortly the ones who had accepted and consumed the milk became "violently ill." The men accused the woman of attempting to poison them and took her into custody. According to the writer, "she fought her guards like a wounded tigress and had to be tied with cords before she could be placed in a cart and taken to jail in Suffolk." It was not until the end of the war that Mrs. Ely, once the willing hostess, gained her freedom.[58]

The Elys became victims not of vengeful Union hard-war policies but of misfortune that might have befallen them at any time. Many others suffered more directly from the activities of men on both sides who sought their goods for requisition or confiscation. Such was the price of war for many who lived in the vast no-man's-land between the main Union lines at Bower's Hill and the Confederate outposts along the Blackwater River in 1864. The only certainty that they could expect was that the coming year would bring more of the same.

"I hope you have tried to prepare yourself for
this sad event and that God may give you grace
to bear it."

*The Reverend W. B. Wellons comforting the widow of
Thaddeus Williams upon his death near Petersburg*

"It was Christmas day and the gloomiest that
I ever spent."

Mary Riddick in a letter, December 26, 1864

⊰ 13 ⊱ *An Autumn of Despair*

THADDEUS GRASHAW WILLIAMS NEVER KNEW WHAT HIT HIM. THE captain in the 6th Virginia Infantry was leading his men in a charge on June 22, 1864, near the Wilcox farm at Petersburg when the fatal shot struck him down. The Reverend William B. Wellons forwarded the sad news to the widow the next day. Wellons had chanced to visit with the captain a few days earlier and believed that he had "never seen him look better and more cheerful." Then in that fateful charge Williams fell. "A minnie ball passed through his head above the right eye and he died immediately," the preacher explained in hopes of providing the comforting knowledge that the soldier had not lingered in pain. "We found him after 9:00 o'clock at night and brought him into town," Wellons noted, adding that "Mr. Nathl. Riddick accompan[ied] me." Then, with the body safely retrieved, "over his remains we all wept, because a brave and good man had fallen."

Williams had married Mary Josaphene Person in 1847. His death left her with four children to raise. "I prayed and laid him to rest [with] the cannons roaring in our ears the whole time," Wellons wrote. "I hope you have tried to prepare yourself for this sad event and that God may give you grace to bear it." The same attack left the preacher with much to do. "Near him sleeps the body of (poor) Francis E. Jones who was killed in the same charge. I write his dear wife today." Another soldier, William P. Wright, had to be buried "in the field."[1]

Ulysses S. Grant was not finished with his opponents in Petersburg. Demonstrating the same tenaciousness that he had displayed at Vicksburg and Chattanooga and in the Overland Campaign, Grant held the city with a bulldog grip. All the while he probed for weaknesses while extending the Confederate lines to the breaking point. Perhaps the most famous confrontation in this process occurred when men from the mining country of Pennsylvania attempted to blast their way through the Southern defensive works. Soldiers from the 48th Pennsylvania pushed a tunnel over 500 feet beneath a strongpoint known as Elliott's Salient. The Confederates became suspicious and dug countermines, but they failed to locate the Union shaft before the Federals could jam the two chambers with black powder and light the fuse. A faulty fuse line provided a few tense moments before a volunteer scrambled into the darkness to relight it.

Then, at approximately 4:45 in the morning of July 30, a tremendous explosion rocked the earthworks. Hurling men, artillery, and equipment skyward, the blast created a 170-foot gap. Hardly had the smoke, dust, and debris cleared when a Union bombardment signaled the advance that was meant to exploit the gap and open the road into Petersburg itself. But political considerations had led to a last-minute change in the elements of the attack. Fearing a debacle that would sacrifice the black troops chosen and specially prepared to lead the operation, the Federals substituted white troops who had no idea what they would be required to do. Compounding the problem with ineffective and incompetent leadership, as well as poor preparation (the men had no ladders, for instance), the troops rushed into the crater itself rather than going around it as planned. Some men stopped to take in the awful spectacle; others tried to dig out Confederates as prisoners. The attack lost all momentum and bogged down hopelessly.

In the meantime, the Confederates regained their equilibrium. Brigadier General William Mahone pulled his men out of line, marching them undetected through a series of covered ways to a point within 200 yards of the crater. The men caught their breath, fixed bayonets, and lunged into the cauldron of battle. The counterattack contained the Union advance, pressing those Federals who had managed to reach the opposite side back into the gaping hole. From that point the fighting degenerated into a vicious hand-to-hand affair. The Confederates on the ridge fired into the seething mass of blue below as their opponents desperately sought to ascend the slippery slopes, only to fall back into pools of blood gathering beneath them.[2] When the fighting finally ended, a curious Confederate took advantage of a flag of truce, walked over, and "examined the crater." For Franklin Riley of the 16th Mississippi, the "Sight was horrible. Dead and wounded lie every-where." As he looked around at the compactness of the battleground, the soldier concluded coldly, "With 1000's of men crowded into a 2–acre plot, it would have been difficult not to have hit them."[3]

Men from southeastern Virginia participated in the action. Henry Pruden, a Nansemond County farmer serving with the Isle of Wight Avengers, took a wound in the foot, while John W. Pruden was thought to have been killed in the fighting. Actually, John managed to get himself cap-tured in the chaos and confusion. He spent a brief time in Point Lookout Prison in Maryland before being transferred to notorious Elmira Prison in New York. Like so many prisoners in the war on both sides, he never returned home, dying of typhoid fever on the day after Christmas, 1864.[4]

Because of the close-hand nature of the fighting, the deaths and wounds among these men were substantial. Captain Beverly B. Hunter of the 41st must have been in the thickest of the fighting on every battlefield, for he had already been wounded once at Seven Pines and again at Second Manassas; he died at the head of his command at the Crater. Captain William Wallace Broadbent died leading the 16th Virginia into action. Stephen H. Pierce had been an eighteen-year-old farmer when he joined the Isle of Wight Rifle Greys at Windsor in 1861. He died at the Crater, along with James M. Niblett, John W. Westbrook, and William J. White, all members of the same regiment. Richard Goodman Holland of the 41st Virginia suffered a wound in the chest from a bullet that lodged against his shoul-der blade and a bayonet wound in the mouth that knocked out two of his teeth. Solomon K. Savage of the same regiment died the next day from his wounds, while Corporal John H. Ivy of the 16th lingered until August 10 before dying of his. Three sergeants in the 6th Virginia were casualties, including Milton Babb, who died in the battle.[5]

The disaster at the Crater cost both sides dearly. The Union's 3,798 casu-alties prompted the normally stoic General Grant to observe, "It was the saddest affair I have ever witnessed in the war."[6] Deprived of a quick vic-tory, the Union commander opted to challenge his opponent's supply and communications lines. This process continued through the summer, with fighting at Globe Tavern on August 18–21 as Federals under Gouverneur K. Warren sought to cut the Weldon Railroad.

On the nineteenth, Major General William Mahone, promoted since his exploits at the Crater, participated in a flank assault that netted 2,700 prisoners for the Confederacy. On the twenty-first, Mahone tried unsuccessfully to drive the Federals from their strong defensive works. All of this combat meant that more names went on the casualty rolls, including Sergeant William Jackson Lassiter of the 41st Virginia, wounded at Davis's farm and dead in just a little over a week. Others, like William H. Cross of the 41st and Graves Niblett of the 16th, were wounded and captured. Cross had been a student in 1860, joining the South Quay Guards the next year. He took a round in the head while trying to defend the Weldon Railroad, and although a surgeon succeeded in extracting it, the soldier died shortly thereafter. At one point earlier in the war, Niblett had been detailed as a guide for the Confederates on the Blackwater line. In addition to these losses, several more men became prisoners, including Sergeant William Robinson Smith of the 16th and Josiah Joyner of the 6th Virginia.[7]

Mahone's men played a lesser role in the defeat of Major General Winfield S. Hancock's 2d Corps at Ream's Station on August 25. But each Union thrust meant that Robert E. Lee had to stretch his defenses ever more thinly. By late October his forces stood poised to protect the Boydton Plank Road and the Southside Railroad. Hancock and Mahone soon would be facing each other again, and their combat on this occasion would be much more direct. The hero of Gettysburg, George Gordon Meade, who remained in nominal command of the Army of the Potomac but was taking his orders directly from General Grant, selected Hancock's 2d Corps to lead another Union push against Lee's supply lines. The orders called for Hancock to seize a foothold on the Southside Railroad, thereby cutting the vital link. But when the attack began in the early hours of October 27, poor weather and enemy resistance slowed the advance, prompting the two supporting corps to halt. Although he did not realize it yet, Hancock had already lost the extra punch he would need to accomplish his mission. What was more, as the 2d Corps pushed on toward Burgess's Mill, Hancock was putting himself into a relatively exposed position.

Had everything been equal, Hancock would have proceeded anyway. One of the Union army's finest fighting generals, he relished any scrap with the Confederates, even an unequal one. Meade recognized the precariousness of his situation and ordered him back. His primary target, the Southside Railroad, was still miles away, and with the supporting units stalled, any continued advance threatened to isolate the 2d Corps almost entirely. Even with the orders to pull back, the 2d Corps was vulnerable to attack. Now it was the Southerners who saw a chance to strike a blow. Major General Mahone believed his men held the key to the 2d Corps's destruction. He planned to seize the Darby Mill Road, thereby forcing Hancock into a box from which there would be no escape. As they attempted to carry out their commander's orders, the Confederates seemed to possess all the momentum. Mahone's men smashed into the Union lines, taking prisoners and capturing cannon. When the Confederates succeeded in reaching the Darby Mill Road, it must have looked as if Hancock's men were doomed.

But Hancock did not want a repetition of the punishment his men had received earlier at Ream's Station. He fought on this day as if his hard-won reputation rested in the balance. Executing movements that threatened to cut the Confederates off instead, the Union commander turned the tables on them. His counterthrust worked, as Mahone's men turned their attention to saving themselves rather than destroying the enemy. In fierce combat both sides suffered nearly equal casualties. The fighting reached an impasse. Hancock could not proceed toward his intended target; the Confederates could not destroy his corps or even prevent him from withdrawing intact if he chose.[8]

More southeastern Virginia boys became casualties at Burgess's Mill, although the substantial proportion of them became prisoners. Half a dozen Isle of Wight soldiers fell into Union hands and spent the remainder of the war at Point Lookout Prison in Maryland. Altogether at least thirty-three men from the 6th, the 16th, and the 41st Virginia, all hailing from the region, were captured. John E. Norfleet and Jon Oliver of the 6th Virginia sustained wounds, as did Robert Rawls of the 41st. Rawls's commander, Captain John Hobday Jr., a father and businessman from Portsmouth who had enlisted near Bower's Hill, died in the fighting. Captain John Brenan of the 16th, a twenty-seven-year-old saddler who had enlisted in the Suffolk Continentals in 1861, fell into enemy hands wounded, lost his leg to amputation, and subsequently died on November 25.[9]

These repeated Union assaults placed tremendous pressure on Lee's lines. Somehow they held. For many of the families who had sought refuge in the city of Petersburg, the agonies were every bit as real as for the soldiers. A relative of the Riddicks sent a brief note on September 24, 1864: "The children ask very often if you are living in a tent. I hope you are not; now that it is getting so cool, I should think it would be very unpleasant."[10] That is apparently what some of the Riddicks had been doing. On October 8 Missouri wrote her daughter Anna to tell her: "We are now in Petersburg living at Mr. Dunn's house on High Street. It became so uncomfortable in tents we could not stand it." She seems to have traded one sort of discomfort for another. "It is very much exposed to the roar of shells and has been struck once but a poor refugee can do no better." Still, "we are more comfortable [here]," she observed, "than we have been since we left Suffolk."

A sick relative had to remain in the hospital rather than join the family in the High Street abode, for "your father thought he would not be able to get him below [the] stairs if the shells were to come." There was consolation in knowing that he would be under Missouri's brother's care and that "the shells never go out there." As for Anna, living temporarily with kinfolk in Nansemond County, Missouri remarked, "Your father thinks it safer in Suffolk and Chuckatuck than up here and wants you to stay so long at your uncle's [as is necessary]." She suggested other places her daughter might go should the need arise. Then, with a tone only a parent could have, Missouri added, "Wherever you stay try to conform to their rules and make yourself useful." Appearances, even in these distressing times, counted for something.

Even if they were now better situated, Missouri Riddick was not happy with any of the choices she and her family faced. "It is indeed distressing and humiliating to have no home and to have to trouble other people." She would have much preferred to return to the sense of power she had once known as the mistress of a household. Missouri concluded regretfully of her decision to leave her home in Suffolk, "I would rather have remained with the Yankees."[11] Of course, had she remained in the Suffolk area, Missouri Riddick might have seen things differently. In August 1864 a circular emanated from "Head Quarters Defences Norfolk & Portsmouth," designed to provide greater security for the Union forces in the region. "Hereafter," it decreed, "all prisoners, refugees, deserters or contrabands coming inside our lines will be searched by the officer in command of the outpost where they are received, and an invoice taken of all property and papers found in their possession."[12]

Anna received a letter from her father in early November reiterating the news his wife had written earlier. "We are now you know living on High Street not entirely removed from the range of Yankee Shells," he told her. "To this arrangement I was forced to submit rather with the advancing cold weather continue to occupy the tents at Grassland." Other moves remained possible, depending on family economics, but for the time being Nathaniel urged his daughter to stay where she was. Given the uncertain military situation and his heavy expenses in trying to accommodate others in need, conditions were too volatile in Petersburg for her to attempt to rejoin her parents.

Nathaniel hoped that by winter the circumstances would be different.

He took some solace in the failure of the Federals to capture the city thus far, confidently predicting that the defense of Petersburg would continue to "stand against the mightiest efforts of the Enemy." Whatever might transpire, he had begun to take steps to secure his property, including "my negroes," for removal should an evacuation become necessary. With all this in mind, Nathaniel emphasized, "It is therefore that I am anxious that you should not return to Petersburg now."[13] Anna's mother wrote her on the same day. "Petersburg is not safe," she argued, disagreeing with Nathaniel's more upbeat assessment of the city's chances. "A big battle is daily expected." Then, referring to the fighting at the end of October over the Southside Railroad, she added, "We thought it had certainly commenced last Wednesday. There was a simultaneous attack at three points but it ended in nothing of importance." Issuing her catalog of casualties, Missouri noted, "Col. R. O. Whitehead was wounded Capt. Brenan wounded and captured Beny Hannaford and Tim Whitehead captured."[14]

On November 4 Missouri passed on the usual family news. But events in Petersburg continued to intrude. Like everyone, she tried to predict what might happen next. "The big guns have just commenced firing and Grant has massed a very heavy force on the right so I fear the fight is about to take place, but what looks more ominous, Gen. Lee has come to Petersburg from Richmond, stayed here a few days and has now gone back to Stoney Creek."[15] Grant continued to apply pressure, but it would be spring before another major Union assault threatened Lee's supply lines at Petersburg.

By mid-November, Nathaniel Riddick was back in Richmond. The Virginia House of Delegates was due to reconvene its session on December 7, but he also had personal matters to attend to in the capital. "I am now boarding at the American hotel and may continue to do so for some time," he wrote his son Mills on the tenth, "at a cost of $25 per day. This is much less than the usual price, I mean to transient customers." Among the matters he mentioned was the imprisonment of a relative, "Lt. Clem. Dissosway," in Libby Prison. Having chosen to join the Union army, the soldier was finding it difficult to obtain sympathy from his Southern kinsmen. One relative who went to see him in prison advised him "that he need not expect a visit from any of his kind—that he himself, was the only one who would do such a thing." The contrite-sounding prisoner responded that "he really did not expect it—perhaps did not deserve it." The visitor explained that the family could not do much for him anyway, because he had helped "to make them beggars, etc., etc."[16]

However, if Lieutenant Israel Clement Disosway felt some discomfort as he lay amid the straw and stench in Libby Prison, it was nothing in comparison to what he had felt on the way to his own execution. He was one of seven men, selected by lot, who were due to be executed for what the Confederate partisan John Singleton Mosby saw as the murder of his men by the Federals. Six of his Rangers had met their unmerciful fate on September 23 in Front Royal, and the seventh had been hanged about a month later. Now seven Union soldiers must die in retribution. Mosby viewed this as an act of justice, not vengeance, although he wanted the condemned men to come from the command of the Union officer he held personally responsible for the outrage, George Armstrong Custer. To that end, he had let it be known that retaliation would come with each murder, starting with these.

Thus Clem Disosway found himself bound and mounted on a horse to his final destination. Or so he thought, until he caught a glimpse of a Masonic pin on the lapel of a Confederate officer returning to camp with a detachment. Thinking quickly in his desperation, the lieutenant flashed the distress sign of a Mason. The Confederate, Richard P. Montjoy, saw it and convinced the trooper leading the prisoners to allow an exchange for one of the men Montjoy was holding for the lieutenant. All of Montjoy's prisoners also came from Custer's command, so the exchange came off. Disosway wound up in Libby Prison. Two of the condemned men managed to escape, three were hanged, but so haphazardly that two of them survived the ordeal, and two others were shot to death. For his part, Montjoy received an icy reply when he reported to Mosby what he had done. His command "was no Masonic lodge," the partisan leader snarled, but he let the exchange stand without correction.[17]

In a letter to his son Mills, Nathaniel Riddick related the story, although with the distortions that come from obtaining information secondhand. "He was captured by Mosby—and with four other officers was selected to be shot in retaliation for the shooting of 2 or 3 of Mosby's men, who had been hung and shot by the Yankees," Nathaniel explained. "Some friend, (Captain Lovejoy) who knew Clement, interposed in his behalf, and being a 'Free Mason', he was sent to Richmond instead, as a prisoner." Riddick closed with the assurance, "This is Clem's account as given to me by Julian [Clem's visitor in prison]."[18]

Subsequent family letters revealed the disdain in which Disosway was held. On November 25 Mills wrote his sister Anna: "Father received a letter from Cousin Clement Disosway a few days ago. He is a prisoner in the Libby Prison [and] wrote Father asking him to come to see him.'" Mills then threw in a rhetorical question. "Don't you think he ought to keep in Prison until the war is over[?]" It was not such a strange question for a Confederate soldier who had been wounded, even if this fellow was fam-

ily.[19] Missouri added a note of her own the next day. Of the Union prisoner's letter to her husband, she noted, "What impudence."[20] A later piece
of correspondence from another Riddick relative to Wilbur Disosway, who
was almost certainly Clem's brother, continued the scorn. "I feel truly thank-
full," Mary Taylor Riddick wrote on the day after Christmas, "that [there]
is not another of your *mother's* [children] that is willing to beggar them and
kill up there kindred."[21]

As winter approached, shortages promised to make life difficult throughout war-ravaged Virginia. On December 9 Missouri wrote Anna that everyone was doing reasonably well where they were now, but that conditions
in Petersburg had deteriorated badly. "The people of Petersburg will have
to suffer for fuel this winter, coal is used [up] altogether, both by the citizens and the army." It was the Confederate army that created the shortage, she observed. "Gen. Lee has ordered 3000 grates to be put in the
trenches, so you know coal will be very high and scarce." Missouri again
told her daughter uneasily, "I feel entirely too dependent."[22]

Affairs were just as disturbing for those who remained in southeastern
Virginia. Southampton County farmer Daniel Cobb continued to keep his
"hands" busy but increasingly noted shortages and requisitions in his diary.
On June 5 he grumbled that "the Crual war has reduced our Table to no
Shugar & Coffee no flower."[23] Despite this, historian Daniel Crofts noted
that the Cobb household endured better than most, with ample crops and
creative substitutes for the items that were absent from the table.[24]

In September, Cobb bemoaned the fact that while the Northerners talked
of going to war to restore the Union, the cause seemed now to be a quite
different one. The war "has turned out to be [about] slavery," he concluded,
adding, "They love our soles [souls or slaves] so well." With the fighting in
Petersburg bringing the war closer than ever, Cobb observed, "What a
bloody & cruel war this is."[25]

At the end of the month, he complied with the requirements of the tax-
in-kind, complaining of the low prices he obtained for his goods from the
government agents. "I sent My sheap to Mrfrees Station that was Called
for, for the N. Army of Virginia They loud me 50 Cts. per lbs per Gross for
no 1 Lambs &c."[26] Later he "sent some 95 Gallons of Brandy to the Depot
for Lees Army if [it] reaches"; that supply seems to have fallen victim to a
sudden raid by Union cavalry.[27]

There were unsettling rumors of his son Asbury's capture, but then letters and news from comrades on leave eased his mind. In late November,
Asbury even came home for a short time himself.[28] Cobb was keeping "his
foalks" busy "picking out Cotton" and "getting up Corn." He settled

accounts with the government agents, noting of his assessment for the tax-in-kind, "Better this year than last." "To day is the grate Northan Presadent Election," he noted on that November Tuesday. "The struggle of the north I wait a he[a]ring." Cobb made no note of the result, although he could not have been pleased with Lincoln's reelection to the presidency.[29]

Asbury returned for Christmas. It would be the last time that his father recorded seeing his son alive.[30] Earlier, on October 11, 1864, Daniel W. Cobb had celebrated his fifty-third birthday. "God shall I see 54 and feel as I now do feele," he wondered then. "Shall I see a nother 12 M[onths] of War Oh! how cruel." Punctuating his despairing words were the sounds of the distant rumbling of artillery pieces. "At 10 of the night I think we had the Studest [steadiest] & heavyest Cannonading [there has] been since Grant has been near P[eters]burgh for it was a continuel rower of Cannon."[31]

Nor was Daniel Cobb alone in this frame of mind. On December 26 Mary Taylor Riddick wrote, "It was Christmas day and the gloomiest that I have ever spent." Aside from the work that she was unaccustomed to doing and her advanced years, she had to maintain a house full of refugees.

> I am here in my house with Mills & family whose house was
> burned over his wife and children's heads while he was prisoner
> and I am not the only one of my family who is in this condition
> all except Rich who has more left than the others and is doing all he
> can to help us he has made some crop of grain which has not been
> distroyed. The most distressing part of my poverty is seeing my chil-
> dren so much in need and not as heretofore have it in my power to
> aid them in any way. There is little or nothing in the way of provision
> made in this or the adjoining county as it was well known that it would
> be distroy[ed] as it was in many many places after it was made which
> make provision very dear and scarce and nothing but specie or green-
> backs is current in this section. Mills has lost everything he had but
> there clothes and some furniture. Nat has his house left a perfect wreck
> his farm ruined all the houses burned and timber cut down fences dis-
> troyed R. T. Rid. had house all burned and every damage that could be
> done. W.L.R. has lost much his family are in Florida I fear in suffering
> circumstances.

Despite these devastating losses, Mary Riddick remained defiant. "Oh it is heart rending and sick[en]ing to tell of the [destruction] say nothing of the deaths and bodyly suffering of our family and the people in general but there is still the same firm spirit of resistance as ever." Even so, the strain was difficult to bear. "You can hardly conceive of our situation in this place," she explained; "not one Store of any kind either dry goods or grocery so that those who have money can get nothing but what is smuggled in not even a pair of shoes."[32]

Just after Christmas, Nathaniel Riddick wrote to his daughter Anna, still living with either extended family or friends in southeastern Virginia. The rest of her family was elsewhere, with her mother and sisters now in Louisa County in the central part of the state. Nathaniel left Richmond to join them as soon as he had finished with his official duties with the House of Delegates.

"Well, I am up here to spend a portion of my Christmas holiday," he began, "for you know that in the Confederacy *that* holiday is still observed, whatever may have been its fate in Yankeedom." But if the holiday promised gaiety and joy in the bosom of one's family, it was also a reminder of the realities of war. "It is true we don't have the big 'Christmas fixings' that used to distinguish it, but still we have a right good time 'considering' all things," he explained. Missouri and the youngest girls were enjoying "a good easy, quiet time 'with none to molest or make them afraid' and if not 'under their own vine and fig-tree,' they feel quite at home, amidst kind friends, with good fires, plenty to eat, and served as such things used to be, when the sound of war was not aloud in the land." Such reminders of a better past, tempered by the hardships of refugee life, caused him to believe that the respite for his wife and daughters was "a great and happy privilege, which they know how to appreciate, and for which they are duly thankful."

The anxious father felt some consolation "in the assurance that you are well and tenderly cared for, under the protection of one of our dearest and most valued friends; that Henley is similarly provided for [in Leasburg], and that John and Mills are at least at their posts of duty." Even so, he wished that by the following Christmas he could reunite his family "at home again."[33]

But the Riddicks remained a family torn apart by war, like so many other people in the region. With sons in the service and the other children scattered far and wide, Missouri and Nathaniel felt a deep sense of powerlessness. Having no control over one's fate or that of one's family was surely the most difficult burden for these families to endure. For the people whose kinsmen wore either gray or blue, there was the all-too-frequent letter observing as the Reverend Mr. Wellons had to the widow of Thaddeus Williams, "I hope you have tried to prepare yourself for this sad event."

"I do not approve of families being separated
at such times. . . . If we suffer let us suffer
together."

Missouri Riddick to her daughter

"I need them as guards and as a lesson to
[the] Rebels."

*Union general George H. Gordon on black troops
under his command, May 5, 1865*

⊰ 14 ⊱ *"Let Us Suffer Together"*

THE NEW YEAR BROUGHT THE RESIDENTS OF SOUTHEASTERN
Virginia little to hope for, except that the war would soon grind to
a halt and the surviving relatives in the service could make their
way home. Years of exposure to raids and enemy incursions had left many
of the people destitute. Others coped with the exigencies of war by trading across Union lines or carrying such goods as they could to distant mar-
kets. All faced an uncertain future that promised to challenge the social order
of the postwar world.

For Missouri Riddick the toll of caring for her children, some of whom
were beyond her physical reach, and worrying about her sons in the
Confederate service was mounting. Life as a refugee and concern for the
home she had left behind compounded her burden. On January 5, 1865,
she confided to her daughter Anna Mary, "I do wish I had a comfortable
little home and had my dear girls and Henley with me. . . . I am so tired of

this dependent life. I had rather live on a crust of bread than to live as we are now living."[1] To her husband Nathaniel, Missouri argued: "It seems to me it would be better at such critical times that we should all be together. I do not approve of families being separated at such times, particularly with both armies between them. If we suffer let us suffer together." Then, tellingly, she repeated, "I had rather have a crust of bread for my own than to live on any one and have all the luxuries that could be mentioned."[2]

Nathaniel Riddick held out the hope that independence could still be obtained, although he seems increasingly to have pinned his hopes upon a negotiated settlement rather than an outright military victory. "There is no doubt but we are at the crisis of this great Revolution," he wrote his daughter on January 16, "and that a few weeks or months will develop the issue."[3] For the moment there was a glimmer of hope. "I would here say that we have sent peace Commissioners to Washington at the invitation of Lincoln," Riddick noted. "Vice-President Stephens, Senator [R. M. T.] Hunter [of Virginia] and Judge [John A.] Campbell, late Asst. Sect. Of War, are the men." Riddick was unequivocal about the individuals. "Capital selections," he told Anna confidently, then added, "The prospects of peace brighten."[4]

Within a matter of days, those hopes would be effectively crushed as the two sides met on the *River Queen* in Hampton Roads near Fort Monroe. As one historian has explained, "Mr. Lincoln told a few stories, everyone was reasonably friendly, but nothing came of it or could come of it, considering the Federal demand for unconditional restoration of the Union and the Confederate demand for terms between two independent nations."[5]

On February 2 Nathaniel explained almost apologetically about his heavy workload in the House of Delegates, "I dislike to be absent from my duties here even for a day, and have not been this Session." These were momentous times, and the tone of his letter reflected the tension. "Our Sessions now are mostly secret ones and much is transpiring of which it would not do for me to write." Even so, he expressed the desire "for a speedy close of 'this cruel War' upon the basis of independence and other rights for which we contend."[6] If by the latter he meant retaining control over his slave property, then the Virginia legislator and family patriarch had failed to grasp the change in the nature of the war and its potential effect upon the Southern social order.

Even for this stalwart, signs of the defeat looming just months away must have been impossible to ignore. Still, he felt it best to be prepared if an evacuation of Petersburg and Richmond became necessary. As he explained to his son John in late February, "You have no doubt heard of preparations in Petersburg and in this city also [Richmond] looking to an Evacuation.

The cotton and the tobacco are being gotten together ready for destruction. Medical stores and some other things are being sent away." For him, those "things" had to include "negroes . . . [although] I should not know what to do with them or where to carry them."[7]

The Federals in southeastern Virginia continued to perfect their measures for controlling an increasingly pacified region. Special Orders No. 13 directed Colonel George W. Lewis of the 3d New York Cavalry to "proceed to Suffolk and occupy the defensive works in his front with the companies of his command now stationed at Camp Getty [at Bower's Hill] and Bernard's Mills," along with a section of artillery. He was to "dispose his forces in the most favorable manner for guarding the several approaches to the place, keeping a sufficient force in reserve to be used in scouting the country between Suffolk, South Quay, Franklin and Smithfield."[8] It was almost as if the clock had been turned back to 1862. Once more the area would come under the direct scope of Federal authority.

This sense of a return to earlier times generally fit the Union policy toward the people of the region as well. In March the provost marshal at Suffolk received authorization to grant "market passes and permits to carry out supplies for persons residing inside the line of outposts viz: from Suffolk," as well as "passes to persons living inside the lines to visit Norfolk and Portsmouth, good for one trip only."[9] Soon individuals such as Robert M. Darden of Suffolk made application "to purchase cotton this side of the Blackwater, and bring the same within the Federal lines." Colonel Lewis happily endorsed the application, "Mr. Darden is a loyal citizen living on the road from Suffolk to Edenton."[10] Even so, enough uncertainty remained for the demand to be made that "the applicant will state the names of the parties from where the purchases are to be made, and the place or places in which the cotton was raised," before the request received final approval.[11]

Some individuals simply sought to return to their homes. Jonas Walsavens requested permission "to visit his farm near Chuckatuck, in Nansemond Co., for the purpose of attending to his crops." Union general Charles K. Graham endorsed the request, explaining that Walsavens had been "brought within the Union lines by my command about 13 mo[n]ths ago as a refugee at the time a raid was being made near Chuckatuck, and at that time gave me much valuable information." He added, "If the indulgence asked for is granted, I believe it will not be abused."[12]

The situation was apparently settled enough for L. G. Heath to obtain permission "to take articles to Suffolk for the purpose of opening an Eating Saloon for officers."[13] Indeed, the war must have seemed a long way away from southeastern Virginia.

Then the final tide of war broke upon Richmond and Petersburg. Ulysses S. Grant launched an offensive that swept Robert E. Lee's thinned and worn forces out of their entrenchments in Petersburg. The impasse broke at a road junction called Five Forks. George Pickett, whose troops guarded this key point, had the correct initial instinct when he pulled back to the critical crossroads after making a strong probe of Major General Philip H. Sheridan's command. The arrival of heavy columns of Union infantry caused the Confederate commander to retreat to the intersection and order his men to improve their defenses as much as possible.[14]

Lee had given his fellow Virginian explicit instructions: "Hold Five Forks at all hazards." These were strong and unmistakable words for the Confederate chieftain to use. He followed with a relatively mild criticism of Pickett's decision to give up so readily the ground he had gained in attacking Sheridan on March 31.[15] This must not be done at Five Forks, whatever the cost. Yet having established his defensive line, Pickett left the field to attend a shad bake with several officers some two miles away.

Unlike at Suffolk in 1863, when the Federals unleashed their assault this time the Confederates paid dearly for Pickett's absence. Employing pressure along the entire line, the Union advance promised to test the Southern defenses severely. Even had Pickett been present from the outset, it is doubtful that he could have done much, if anything, to alter the outcome. The Union attack on the Confederate left hit the line in the flank and the rear. It quickly disintegrated. Although groups of men tried to buy time for their comrades to escape by putting up a stubborn defense, such resistance was quickly overcome. The day, and Petersburg with it, were lost.[16]

At Five Forks the mob of routed Confederates contained Virginians from the southeastern part of the state. The number of men captured who had enlisted in Suffolk and the surrounding counties rivaled those taken at Gettysburg and Burgess's Mill. Three men in the 3d Virginia, including Sergeant Everett M. Pond, died at Five Forks. Perhaps the sergeant had tried to rally the men or merely sought to give them a chance to run for safety, but at least twenty-five men from the 3d Virginia failed to do so and were captured.[17] One of the soldiers captured in the sweep of these days remarked when he arrived at the depot at City Point, "Prisoners are everywhere, more prisoners than guards (but the guards have rifles)."[18] At the same place a North Carolina soldier became aware of the futility of his cause. "I knew much about our army, its size, equipment and strength, but I was simply amazed at the evidences that met my gaze on every hand, of the size, equipment and strength of the army that opposed us, and I wondered, and we all wondered, how our little army had so long held at bay so mighty a force."[19] The Southerners probably were too dispirited to have offered much resistance anyway. The darkness was descending upon the Confederacy, as they now knew better than anyone.

Confederate president Jefferson Davis was in worship at St. Paul's Church in Richmond when he received notice of General Lee's intention to evacuate Petersburg. "I see no prospect of doing more than holding our position here till night," the general wired the war office as nonchalantly as he would any routine report. Then came a hint of the numbing reality of the desperate situation he faced, "I am not certain I can do that."[20] The final words were the heaviest. "I advise that all preparation be made for leaving Richmond tonight," Lee explained, promising to "advise you later, according to circumstances."[21]

Davis read the words dispassionately and quickly left the church service. He, as much as anyone, clung to the hope of a revival of Confederate fortunes. For his part, Lee would have to evacuate his lines or risk becoming entrapped in them. The only legitimate chance for the Army of Northern Virginia would be to make it to North Carolina and join forces with Joseph E. Johnston's forces there. Perhaps together they could carry on the fight.

With all of the thoughts that surely inundated them as they contemplated the future, President Davis and the rest of the members of official Richmond spent the remainder of the day packing. Late in the day they scrambled into the train station and boarded the special cars being held for them. The president and his cabinet left the Confederate capital in the early hours of the next morning, bound west-southwest, seeking safety from the Union forces closing in on them. Richmond was soon in utter chaos. A firestorm swept through the capital once the Confederate government abandoned it, consuming all the supplies the army and the looters had not already carried off and providing an eerie backdrop to the movement of Lee's dejected warriors as they set out on their westward march from the trenches they had defended for so long.[22]

At Amelia Courthouse the Confederates found boxcars on the tracks, but they contained ammunition, not food. Searching for something to sustain the army cost it a day's march and allowed the Union cavalry a chance to catch up. In the meantime, the 13th Virginia Cavalry sparred with the Federals. Among the casualties in this affair was Captain Charles Henry Riddick, taken as a prisoner of war. It had not been so very long ago that he had gone to Richmond to woo political support for a cavalry command. Now he was riding away in the custody of his enemies.[23]

Confederate soldiers from Nansemond, Southampton, Isle of Wight, and Suffolk struggled along with the other remnants of Lee's army as it moved away from Petersburg and Richmond. Some of them stood at Sailor's Creek, where the Southerners endured another crushing defeat on April 6. Others became prisoners at places along the way as the Federals added capture to the hemorrhage of desertion and straggling that lessened the Army of Northern Virginia's fighting potential, and thus its chances of survival, daily. As is so often the case in every war, there were the unfortunate few who, having survived on so many fields in the worst fighting, fell in the conflict's final hours. One such man was William Mason, a member of Company G in the 41st Virginia, who had received a $50 bounty to reenlist. He was killed in fighting at Cumberland Church only two days before Robert E. Lee agreed to surrender terms.[24]

From Louisa County, Nathaniel Riddick sent word of the latest developments to his daughter in Nansemond County. "The 'military situation' has become gloomier," he wrote. "Poor Richmond is now in the hands of the Yankees." He was uncertain of the fate of his family's longtime refuge, having heard "nothing definite as to the evacuation of Petersburg, but I think the probabilities are that the place is now in possession of the Enemy." Nathaniel still felt compelled to cast this "very gloomy aspect of affairs" in the best light. "If it [the Army of Northern Virginia] moves off in the direction of Lynchburg and Danville as many suppose, Isle of Wight [and] Nansemond . . . may be among the most quiet parts of the State on the presumption that we are already under their rule."[25]

In fact, the Army of Northern Virginia had tried to head for Danville, only to find the road blocked. Further westward movement ended in the area of Appomattox Court House. There, in the parlor of Wilmer McLean, who had desperately sought to get away from the war ever since it came to his home near Manassas in 1861, Lee accepted Grant's terms. The war had ended in Virginia. It would be days before the soldiers finished the paroling process and made their respective ways home. It would be weeks before the Federals brought other Confederate armies to bay, culminating in the final surrender of organized Southern resistance in June 1865.

For the people of southeastern Virginia, the long nightmare of war was finally over. Yet they faced the uncertainties of reunion, possibly even a reconstruction of some form. The Riddick family at long last could reassemble in Suffolk, although they could not yet move back into their home. Used as a military headquarters since mid-1862, Riddick's Folly remained in Union hands for that purpose following the close of the war in Virginia.

A cousin writing to Anna in June summarized the frustrating conditions of peacetime and their effects. "I feel very old now," she wrote on the first. "I hope things will get more settled soon." Then commiserating with her

Suffolk relatives' plight, she added, "I am sorry that your father can not get his house, I hope however it will be given up very soon."[26] When the Riddicks finally returned to Riddick's Folly in November, they found that its wartime occupants had stripped it of its belongings and some of the walls in the attic were marred by graffiti.[27] Nevertheless, Missouri Riddick and her family were home, with the bitterness and hardship of the war and refugeeing behind them. If they were to suffer more, they would do so together, as she had wished during the darkest days of her life.

Even with hostilities ended in Virginia, the Federal bureaucracy maintained its sense of inertia. Throughout April requests poured in to the offices in Portsmouth for permission to bring goods into Suffolk, open stores there, or purchase produce from the area. A sutler from a New York battery wanted to ship supplies to Suffolk. He gained approval, but under the stipulation that these goods were "to be sold to soldiers only[,] not in quantities to be resold by them to citizens & others." Whether this restriction was intended to protect the people from speculation or, more likely, to keep these items out of their hands, the recommendation added that the "sutler within named" is "to be held responsible that nothing goes without [outside] the lines."[28]

The most enthusiastic endorsement came when H. A. Brandt of Portsmouth asked permission "to open a store in Suffolk, Va., for sale of Clothing and Furnishing Goods, etc." The local Federal agent forwarded the request with the notation, "If any stores at all are permitted at Suffolk, I can approve the within application. The Messers. Brandt are dealers in this city, loyal men and obedient to all orders."[29] At about this time onetime newspaperman, legislator, and attorney John R. Kilby asked to have the official records of Nansemond County returned from safekeeping in Norfolk.

The Federals also began to consider rebuilding the infrastructure in southeastern Virginia. On April 29 Brigadier General George H. Gordon asked the assistant superintendent of military telegraph lines in Washington to send supplies for restoring telegraphic communications along the Seaboard and Roanoke Railroad line. "C. W. Peterson and a detail direct from Maj. Genl. Sherman have arrived at Suffolk . . . with orders to extend the telegraph line from Weldon to Norfolk," General Gordon explained, adding that he "wishes them [the supplies] sent to Suffolk at once."[30] But they would have to wait their turn, for Major Thomas T. Eckert, the assistant superintendent, replied that same day, "The material asked for by Mr. C. W. Peterson for rebuilding [the telegraph] line on [the] Seaboard and Roanoke Rail Road will not be furnished."[31]

Although General Gordon was willing to help in restoring communication lines, he did not want the civilians to assume that all was forgiven and forgotten. On May 5 he made an impassioned plea to keep "the colored troops in this Dist. for a short time longer." He explained to his superiors, "I need them as guards and as a lesson to [the] Rebels."[32]

Guards would certainly be needed, because on the same day General Gordon issued strict instructions from his headquarters in Norfolk to Colonel George W. Lewis, the commanding officer in Suffolk. "Stop all negroes who attempt to come into Suffolk from the surrounding country and turn them back from whence they came," he ordered peremptorily, "informing them that they must hire themselves to work on the plantation." Given the press of refugees, both black and white, Gordon wanted to gain a handle on the situation before it got completely out of hand. "The Government cannot care for negros here," he continued. "The order is imperative."[33]

Almost a month later, the Suffolk commander still had refugees coming into town to plead their cases. One apparently argued that he could sustain himself and his family if the Union troops would let him through to Norfolk. General Gordon, still not wishing to impose upon the Federal government any particular obligation, responded, "If the negro who wishes to bring his family into Norfolk can show that he can support them without aid from [the] Government, he can be passed on. Not otherwise." Nor was his wish to avoid such obligations limited to black refugees. "Issue no rations whatever to destitute whites within your District," he told Colonel Lewis, "and none to Blacks except at the Poor Farms upon the requistions of Provost Marshals."[34]

By May 12 the war had truly ended in southeastern Virginia. Special Orders No. 36 designated Colonel Lewis to detail Captain J. M. Starr "to proceed to Smithfield, Va., to be stationed there as a Provost Guard until further orders, for the purpose of protecting the inhabitants desiring to return to their former allegiance to the U.S. Government." Lewis was to send Captain J. A. Allis to Isle of Wight Court House on the same errand.[35] Troop assignments followed to give these officers enforcement capabilities should the need arise.[36]

The Bureau of Refugees, Freedmen, and Abandoned Lands did its best to safeguard the interests of the freed men and women. Set up as a government agency, the Freedmen's Bureau depended upon military officers and a military structure for support of its operations. Thus, as historian William McFeely has assessed it, "Congress had called for the nation's most advanced experiment in social welfare but had grafted it onto the most conservative of American institutions."[37]

Still, the army could provide enforcement if it was necessary. At the end of May, a circular went out under General Orders No. 102 noting that bureau officers in the field were to seek military assistance if they needed it in order to "discharge" their "official duties" safely.[38] A few weeks later another circular reminded the agents that the wartime ration for "adult refugees and to adult freedmen, when they are not employed by the Government," would continue in force, but such supplies should not be distributed for more than seven days.[39] Freed men and women would be expected to sustain themselves through their work and without any permanent government assistance. The Freedmen's Bureau was expected to help the former slaves make the transition from slavery to freedom as easily as possible. At the same time it had to conduct an internal census to determine exactly who had been hired to work for the agency.[40]

Oliver Otis Howard, a Union major general and the commissioner of the bureau, laid down strict guidelines for the officers in the field on July 12. There was to be no "compulsory unpaid labor," except for criminals, and no "substitute" to replace slavery. If planters found this simple dictum unbearable, then such was "to some degree the necessary consequence of events." There was much to do to ensure meaningful freedom for the former slaves, but nothing less than that "will be tolerated," Howard made clear.[41]

High-sounding rhetoric was important, but it soon faced a grueling reality. Orlando Brown, a Union colonel and the assistant commissioner, issued General Orders No. 3 on July 18. "Ass't Superintendents will see that the Freedmen within their sub-Districts are not defrauded, in their contracts for labor, by their employers," he demanded. The officers were "to examine, and record, all contracts made with the Freedmen, in their respective Sub districts and report such as are injurious and unfair, to their District Superintendent, who will, if just cause exists, annul them." In case these officers thought the orders were only cosmetic, he added, "Superintendents will hold their Assistants to a strict accountability under this order."

It was soon obvious that the Freedmen's Bureau would be inundated by more than its share of problems to be solved and issues to be resolved. Andrew Johnson had assumed the presidency after the assassination of Abraham Lincoln at Ford's Theater on April 14. Despite his credentials as a strong Tennessee Unionist, he did not favor a liberal policy toward the freedmen. After a brief period of philosophical jousting with the Freedmen's Bureau leadership and its congressional supporters, it also became clear that Johnson's main goal was to use the agency to get the former slaves back into agricultural production as quickly as possible. Civil rights would have to wait. The president wanted civil order, even if this left the white planters in the position of power over their former slaves. For this reason, he favored

the restoration of abandoned and confiscated lands to their prewar owners over the redistribution of them.[42]

A subtle indication of how such a policy would be implemented
emanated from the office of the superintendent for District No. 1, State
of Virginia. Apparently in response to complaints, it pronounced, "It
appearing that the *Freedmen* in many parts of the State, are in the habit of
engaging in *hunting with fire-arms on the Sabbath, Superintendents* will instruct
their *Assistants to seize all arms found* in the hands of *Freedmen on the Sabbath*,
and hold such arms subject to the order of the *Assistant Commissioner.*"[43]
Such an order, as well intended as it was meant to be, was an invitation by
bureau officials to disarm the freedmen. In effect, this order mirrored the
demand that white leaders like Nathaniel Riddick would make to Virginia
governor Francis H. Pierpont for the disarmament of the freedmen. The
orders had an unsettling effect on some army officers. Union major general Alfred H. Terry, commanding the Department of Virginia, worried
for the safety of freedmen deprived of the means to defend themselves.
He would agree to obey such instructions if there was any indication that
the freedmen planned violence, but with a touch of bitterness he observed
that the blacks had been "our friends when nearly every white man was
our enemy."[44]

Historian William McFeely has criticized Howard for not demanding
more of those who worked with him in the form of sympathy for the plight
of the freedmen. He also considered the general too quick to undermine
those who were, for the sake of good political relations, particularly close
to the president. He has concluded that as the president moved toward a
conservative policy, the army, upon which the bureau depended, went with
him. By September, Circular No. 13, signed by General Howard on July 28
and calling for the redistribution of abandoned and confiscated lands to the
freedmen, was dead on the books. The army would content itself with trying to prevent violence against freedmen, while acquiescing in allowing
white Southerners to reassert their dominance. As McFeely explained it,
"The United States Army was preventing the Freedmen's Bureau from doing
its job, as defined by Congress."[45] Congress may have established the
bureau, but the president was still commander in chief of the military
officers who were required to run it.

In Southampton County, Daniel Cobb, who had endured the travails of
war and had lost a son, now hoped to maintain control over a labor force
that would enable him to continue cultivating, planting, and harvesting as
he had done since the early 1840s. He knew that he had to pay a wage to
free laborers, rather than demand work from slaves, but the arrangements

Cobb made with his workers clearly favored him. As historian Daniel Crofts has noted, "Although the specific details are difficult to decipher, Cobb's workforce apparently agreed to terms that offered them one-quarter of the corn and cotton crops plus small cash wages in exchange for food and housing. Cobb plainly retained the upper hand."[46] Consequently, as Crofts concluded, "Many things on his farm did not change, at least not at first."[47] Because Cobb's 1865 diary is not known to exist, his attitudes in these critical days are unavailable. Yet by looking at the entries for 1866, one can catch a glimpse of what the old farmer must have been thinking. Time and again during 1866, he made diary entries that could have been written before the war.[48] Surprisingly, even the gang system of labor remained in place, a holdover of slavery that former slaves themselves usually made sure was one of the first things to go.

Yet the white Southampton farmer could not completely reconcile himself to even the smallest changes in his long-established patterns. Unwilling to make the slightest concession without complaint, Cobb wrote in 1866, "The hands I hired to tend a Crop on shars looses at least 25 or 30 minutes every morning after sun rise." Instead of working strictly as he would have insisted they do as slaves, these freedmen slept longer and worked less. And while such lack of effort might cost him only a little bit "per day or per week or say month," the loss could become quite hefty. "Per year will count," he moaned. The troubles and difficulties just seemed to get worse for the farmer, who himself faced an uncertain future in which it looked as if the bottom rail of the social order really had gotten on top. "White men At home ploughing and Nigars frolickin," he decried, expressing a worldview that many other white Southerners echoed.[49]

Of course, when it came time to settle accounts, Daniel Cobb exhibited a sense of power over his labor force that suggested little had changed since the days of slavery. Deductions and charges ensured that when "paying out," as the process was known, he would get the lion's share of profits from the sale of the crops. Workers who poured their energy into producing that crop were undoubtedly dismayed to find their dreams of self-sufficiency so easily thwarted. However, even if Cobb experienced "some trouble with some of the hands" when settling accounts for the year, he held the upper hand in the arrangement and knew it.[50]

Just as Daniel Cobb clung stubbornly to the past, other whites in the region tried to resist the changes thrust so rapidly upon them. They rejected efforts to bring education to the former slaves and targeted schools, educators, and supporters of black education. In Nansemond County angry white vigilantes burned a schoolhouse and a Quaker meetinghouse in

Somerton. Not wanting the former slaves to have any opportunity for advancement, these individuals hoped to thwart that advancement by attacking its symbols.[51] In a mind-set that would be repeated a hundred years later, the "ringleader" of the attack "did not deny his guilt but seemed to be proud of being accused of such a crime," according to the local Freedman's Bureau agent, Major J. R. Stone. This was the point at which white leaders from the region made their disarmament request of Governor Pierpont.[52]

Thus, in less than a year following the close of a war that supposedly brought their world crashing about them, many Southern whites were demonstrating a remarkable resiliency. Early signs, such as the burning of the schoolhouse, pointed to the likelihood of another struggle in the immediate future as black Southerners sought first to learn and then to expand the limits of their hard-won freedom and white Southerners worked to restore prewar conditions as closely as possible.[53]

Yet as January 1, 1866, dawned, such a struggle must have seemed somewhat distant. It had been three years since the Emancipation Proclamation had gone into effect. Many slave and freed men and women, before and since that proclamation, had taken upon themselves the responsibility for obtaining and securing their liberty. For much of the conflict, Suffolk had been one of their destinations. So much had transpired in the intervening time. The Confederate surrenders at Appomattox, Durham, and elsewhere sealed the Union victory. It was a victory that thousands of African Americans helped to achieve, by the sweat of their brows as much as by the blood they had shed when finally allowed to wear their nation's uniform and carry its arms. Then the House of Representatives dealt a deathblow to the formal institution of slavery in the United States of America with the passage of the Thirteenth Amendment to the Constitution. The matter went to the states for ratification, but slavery's demise was already a fait accompli, at least officially.

On January 1, 1866, Ben and Henry King must have watched with real anticipation and hope as the Freedmen's Bureau agent scratched words on a piece of paper that would serve as their labor contract for the coming year. With an X the two men signed these papers, drawn up in Suffolk, that promised them the princely sum of $6.25 per month, a total of $75.00 for the twelve months they were to work as laborers for George W. Briggs. This local doctor also hired two women for $2.00 a month as servants.

Others signed contracts of varying types on this New Year's Day. L. D. Parker, a farmer near Somerton, agreed to pay his "farm hand" $38, while Solomon Eley offered Bob Eley, an "old man," the position of "servant" for

$48. Eley also employed two women as servants, giving both "clothes for herself & children" as compensation. Charles H. Darden signed contracts by which he would employ Cherry Darden and Senior Darden as "Laborers on farm." The former was supposed to receive "Board and clothes [for] herself and her seven children," while the latter, a "Col'd [man] aged 72 years," was to be given similar consideration.[54]

In Isle of Wight County, Hardy Chapman had a busy day on January 1 making contracts with hands for the coming year. He signed Hannah Chapman and one child as servants for twelve months at $27 and Robin Chapman and Jeffrey Williams at $72 to work as servants. He also agreed to provide Catherine Chapman, a "Col'd afflicted woman," her "usual clothing" as compensation. Robert R. Pope demonstrated a similar disposition by hiring an "old woman," Suckey Pope, to act as "cooker, washer, etc.," for $36 and a young "boy," Frank Pope, to be his "servant" for $48. William N. Gray offered Lewis Gray $66 to function as a "Laborer on farm." William W. Joyner hired Mary Joyner as a "House servant" and Lavinia Joyner and her two children as "servants." Mary could draw $1 a month, or $12 for the coming year, while Lavinia would receive $3 a month, for a total of $36. Others placed their X on documents that would put them in similar positions throughout the region.[55]

Over the next year government agents remained busy trying to keep an eye on the contracts being signed. Although these documents carried penalties for violating them "without legal cause," it appears to have been very rare for agents to take such action, at least in Isle of Wight and Nansemond Counties. One occasion arose concerning the agreement between John Tate and William G. Northworthy. Assistant Superintendent J. R. Stone witnessed a contract in "Suffolk, Nansemond Co.," on January 26, 1866, in which John Tate agreed that his son Joseph would act as "Farm hand or house servant" for Northworthy for "Six and a half" dollars per month, or $78 for the year. The contract also contained a penalty clause in which either party who violated the agreement "without legal cause" would forfeit damages "to the other" party, up to "twenty (20)" dollars. The situation seems to have deteriorated from the start, for the government agent noted on the outside of the original document, "Contract annulled and wages of Boy paid except $2.00," further adding, "Paid Tate Senior $8.60." Since Joseph was to have received all of the $78.00 owed to him with the exception of $2.00, the latter sum must have constituted a penalty meted out to William Northworthy and paid to the young man's father.[56]

For their part, the workers accepted contracts that placed stipulations upon their newly won freedoms. These early contracts merely required that they "faithfully and diligently perform the duties" required of them, but later ones became more explicit in exactly what would and would not be tolerated. One set of contracts used at this time in Mississippi even carried an elaborate list of "Rules and Regulations" for the freed men and women to follow, including deductions for time lost and charges for lost or broken tools. The contracts gave the planter or manager sole discretion to determine the kind of behavior they found acceptable among the former slaves, with penalties that ranged from deduction to outright forfeiture of wages.[57] Such terms made the position of power clear. But even when such strictures did not appear on paper, planters carried the same kind of expectations that they had always held for their slaves when it came to production and deference, as Cobb's journal amply illustrates.

These months realigned the focus of individuals from the war just finished to the peace now at hand. President Johnson sought to give some indication that conditions were returning to a sense of normalcy. On August 29 he announced that material once banned as contraband of war could now be traded with the South.[58] By the next August, Johnson proclaimed "that the said insurrection is at an end and that peace, order, tranquility, and civil authority now exist in and throughout the whole of the United States of America."[59]

The declaration had a distinctly hollow ring to it. As historian Stephen Ash has written, "Indeed, of the five great conflicts that had convulsed the occupied South, it was clear that two had been wholly resolved: the Federal government had stamped out all resistance to its authority, and the forces of order had put to rout the forces of disorder in no-man's-land. But as the summer wore on, it became obvious that the other conflicts—those of politics, race, and class—were not at all resolved but were merely entering a new phase."[60]

What Washington L. Riddick wrote to a relative in November 1867 seems to confirm such an assessment. The relative, Ella Taylor Disosway, had requested information on the Riddick family coat of arms. He replied that the original sketch he had of it was a victim of the war. "That drawing or sketch is lost," he noted. "I rather think it was among my baggage on the retreat from Petersburg in 1865, and was captured on the 6th of Apl. and probably now adorns the album of some trophy [collector] in a more Boreal region." Riddick was fearful that circumstances would require the family to return to the "predatory inclinations" of its forebears in the Highlands of Scotland, reflected in their motto, which translated to "Compelled by Necessity." He halfheartedly jested, "Whatever place or distinction we may have reached in [recent] times past, I much fear that we are fast approaching a period when we may have to go back to our first principles, and bring into practice the deeds suggested by our crest and motto."

For now, times were hard. At the moment the family was mostly interested in obtaining sufficient clothing to endure the winter, demonstrating a preference for "overcoats" to "coats of arms." Nor were circumstances likely to improve in the immediate future. Riddick thought he knew why: "What the end of it will be I am sure I am unable to conjecture. Black is the favorite color with the nation just now, and as long as the taste and fashion tends in that direction, we of the opposite tint find ourselves not in request."[61]

Difficult days lay before the people of southeastern Virginia. With the same determination that had characterized their wartime sacrifices, they would find ways to cope with the future come what may. For most it was a simple matter of meeting the needs as they arose day to day. For others there was the hope and dream of a better world just over the horizon. But for each one, in his or her own way, there was a legacy to be remembered of the time when war had hit home for them. Certainly none of them would ever be the same again.

"Nervously they stood watch at the borders,
and nervously they stood watch at home."
Historian Stephen Ash on life in the occupied South

⊰ CONCLUSION ⊱ *Nervously Standing Watch*

THE EXPERIENCES OF MEN, WOMEN, AND CHILDREN LIVING IN southeastern Virginia during the American Civil War suggest a number of themes. The first is that the communities in this region dealt with the war in successive waves, responding to each in a different fashion to meet the requirements of that unique set of circumstances. These waves were the third of the war during which Confederates defended the region, the third when Union forces occupied it, and the third in which the chaos of being a no-man's-land held sway.

The second theme that unfolds is the change in Union policy toward civilians in the region and the impact such policies had upon the lives of those people. The third is the remarkable resiliency and fortitude with which Southerners of all races and genders adapted to the changing situations. A fourth theme is an affirmation of Stephen Ash's contention that there were differences between the experiences of those living in towns garrisoned by

Union troops, those caught in the no-man's-land between the opposing forces, and those who lived on the Confederate periphery, or "frontier."

Finally, strong evidence suggests that a sense of Confederate nationalism existed and that for some, at least, it remained in force until the end of the war. This evidence flies in the face of those who contend that such nationalism never truly emerged or faded quickly with adverse military results. A latter-day Thomas Paine would have found reason to chastise the Confederacy's "sunshine patriots," but he would not have stood alone in devotion to the cause had he lived in southeastern Virginia in the 1860s.

Indeed, there was no single or overriding response to all the sets of conditions that the war imposed upon the people of southeastern Virginia. It would be convenient to claim that all remained ardent Confederate nationalists or loyal Unionists, or that people in the counties surrounding Suffolk reacted in markedly different ways from the manner in which the townsfolk did. When Confederate forces filled the area, entrepreneurs sought to meet the needs of those troops and enrich themselves in the process. Local residents seem to have gone about their daily tasks without much interruption, beyond the novelty of having to share space and resources with so many new people. Confederate officers like William Dorsey Pender could attest that local people took a great interest in the martial activities and ceremonies that he and his men performed, often acting as hosts at gatherings in their honor.

When the Confederates evacuated Suffolk in April 1862, white Southerners reacted with trepidation based upon rumors and stereotypical views of their enemies. Those enemies proved themselves relatively restrained and courteous at first, exhibiting mostly a sense of curiosity and humor of their own. Yet as Southern resistance on the homefront continued, and in some cases intensified, Union policy changed. Restrictions and requirements increased, particularly once Union general John Peck arrived in October 1862.

Confederate generals Roger A. Pryor and James Longstreet added further to Federal concerns when they brought their commands east of the Blackwater River, the line beyond which the Confederates had withdrawn in 1862. At the battle of Kelly's Store, or Deserted House, Pryor clashed with Federals under General Michael Corcoran in a bloody but indecisive affair at the end of January 1863. Three months later Longstreet arrived before Suffolk with his battle-tested legions. The "Siege of Suffolk" or Suffolk campaign brought the war home to many in the area in ways they had never dreamed. Civilians suffered particularly harshly in the loss through destruction of significant amounts of personal property.

By the time the campaign ended, General Lee was busily engaged with

Joseph Hooker at Chancellorsville. In that battle, as in most of those that took place in the eastern theater of the war, units from southeastern Virginia participated, often at a fearful toll. Throughout, the soldiers attempted as well as circumstances would permit to maintain ties to the communities they had left behind through letters, newspapers, furloughs, and visits from friends and relatives. Many would never return to their homes, dying more often of disease than of wounds.

For slaves and "free people of color" in the region, 1863 also proved to be a pivotal year. Although records indicate that many slaves sought freedom on their own before President Lincoln's actions could take effect, the Emancipation Proclamation offered others incentive to do likewise. For many this flight for freedom turned into a fight for freedom when they took up arms and joined the Union forces. Confrontations in 1864 involving white Confederates and black Federals injected race into the combat that occurred on the battlefields of the region.

Whatever might be happening around them, most civilians sought to survive as best they could. Some sold to both the Confederates and the Federals, seeing the two sides as targets of economic opportunity. Others tried to obtain goods that could be smuggled to people beyond Confederate lines. Such activities led to increased Union crackdowns as the Federals attempted to demonstrate their control over the usually uncooperative residents. Despite the arrests, boat seizures, and surprise lightning raids the Union forces made, the network that whites referred to as their own Underground Railroad continued, connecting through correspondence and trade with people inside Confederate-held territory.

For all of their hardening rhetoric and actions, the Union troops often interacted in less threatening ways with local civilians. Provost guards ensured an order that citizens no doubt missed once the Union forces withdrew from Suffolk to Bower's Hill in July 1863. What is more, far from burning the town, as many civilians feared and assumed they would, the Federals obeyed General Dix's instructions to hold private property inviolate. This, too, came in the face of Dix's admission that the region's people remained stubbornly adherent to their cause.

The last year of the war brought additional shortages and privation. Loyal Southerners continued to submit to the tax-in-kind and other levies, however much they might grumble in the process. Others found the means to express their patriotism in different ways. Even so, only the most die-hard among them failed to see, or chose not to see, that the end was closing upon them. Ulysses S. Grant kept his death grip on Petersburg until the pressure proved too much for the Confederate defenders. Then he overwhelmed

Lee's retreating army. The surrender of the Army of Northern Virginia at Appomattox ended the hopes for Confederate independence and left the survivors to find their own way home. They had much to do to renew their lives. Yet the former Confederates proved remarkably adept at reestablishing their strength. Slavery was officially dead, but former slaves found few options open to them beyond returning to the farms and plantations they had worked on before the war.

There is no doubt that the demands of war proved more than some could take. Many Confederates probably shared the sentiments expressed by one angry farmer, who proclaimed, "The sooner this damned Government [falls] to pieces the better it will be for us."[1] Still, complaining out of sheer frustration was one thing, rejecting any notion of nationalism another. It is true that this farmer and others with similar feelings wished the agent of their frustrations, the Confederate government, would simply go away. We do not know if he was driven to take up arms against it, or accept exile in order to escape it, or actively resist its dictates. That some did is proof that they failed to have a sufficient sense of nationalism inculcated within them, not that all, or even most, individuals did so.

Much of the evidence used to dismiss or diminish Southern nationalism is anecdotal, as is that used to establish its existence and durability. Numbers to prove either view are virtually impossible to obtain. The Riddick family of Suffolk and the people with whom they corresponded remained steadfast in support of the Confederacy. No one complained more than Daniel Cobb of Southampton, yet he too was loyal to the end. The fact that Union recruiters failed miserably in securing enlistees from southeastern Virginia for service in the Union forces, even with the inducement of a sizable bounty, speaks for Southern nationalism. To be sure, self-interest motivated people in the region as it did people anywhere else, but many remained loyal to the Confederacy even after it was clearly in their self-interest not to do so.

The major exception to all this was the black Southerner. Slaves quickly demonstrated their feelings for the Confederacy, and for their masters, by seeking refuge behind Union lines in occupied Suffolk. Others sought to fight for freedom as soon as the opportunity became available, enlisting in a wide variety of Union regiments. Some died in battle in the very region in which they had lived as slaves. Indeed, they made the sacrifice that the disgruntled farmer most likely did not make in expressing through their deeds their attitudes toward the Confederate States of America.

Of course, the women and men in Suffolk, Virginia, and the surrounding area were not the only ones deeply affected by the war. The same issues of combat and camp, conscription and emancipation, patriotism and self-preservation, faced Southerners of both races throughout the Confederacy. Likewise, people in the region who had to adapt to critical shortages in almost anything of value mirrored the ordeal of others finding conditions unimproved once the firing stopped. Reconstruction promised only to offer new, and perhaps more formidable, challenges.

The experience of war in Suffolk and Nansemond, Isle of Wight, and Southampton Counties, Virginia, represents that war in microcosm. People bore the contest because they had no choice, or because they believed in the cause for which they fought. It is their struggle that continues to draw us these many decades later. For them the American Civil War had truly hit home. It is a tribute to so many, of both races and genders, at the front and at home, on both sides of the conflict, that their legacy endures.

⤙ APPENDIX A ⤚ THE DAYS AFTER

DANIEL WILLIAM COBB

The Southampton farmer emerged from the war years a wrecked man in many ways. He suffered physically from ailments and mentally from the loss of his son Asbury and the changes he saw taking place in the society he had known. Cobb complained incessantly about labor conditions, becoming just as disenchanted with white tenant farmers as he was with free black laborers. He also continued to struggle with his farm. In the late summer of 1872, while attempting to demonstrate how to pull corn fodder properly, he experienced a chill. A month later Daniel Cobb was dead, buried beneath the soil he had tried to make productive for decades.

MICHAEL CORCORAN (USA)

The fiery Irishman suffered no official sanction for killing Colonel Kimball at Suffolk. A court-martial convened on May 7, 1863, only to exonerate him. Subsequently he transferred to the Department of Washington. Then, on

December 22, 1863, while riding with fellow Irish general Thomas Meagher, Corcoran fell as his horse stumbled. The animal could not regain its footing and dropped on the general, killing him.

WILLIAM BARKER CUSHING (USN)

Cushing's sense of adventure remained unabated after his service in Suffolk. He undertook various daring and dangerous exploits, the most famous of which was the sinking of the Confederate ironclad CSS *Albemarle*. The expedition earned him a promotion to lieutenant commander at the age of twenty-one. Cushing led a company of sailors and marines in the assault on Fort Fisher on January 15, 1865. He continued to serve in the U.S. Navy after the Civil War, both in the Pacific and Atlantic Squadrons. Promoted to commander in 1872, Cushing soon suffered from ill health and died in Washington on December 17, 1874.

SAMUEL GIBBS FRENCH (CSA)

After the Suffolk campaign French transferred to Mississippi, where he served under Joseph E. Johnston. He fought with the Army of Tennessee during the Atlanta and Nashville campaigns before being relieved from duty when a serious eye infection rendered him almost blind. After recovering, French served in Mobile until the end of the war. He returned to planting and devoted much time to his autobiography. French died in Florala, Alabama, on April 20, 1910, still bitter about his experiences in the Suffolk campaign.

GEORGE WASHINGTON GETTY (USA)

Getty served in Virginia until early in 1864, when he became acting inspector general of the Army of the Potomac. He was severely wounded during the battle of the Wilderness but recovered to serve at Petersburg and in Philip Sheridan's Shenandoah Valley campaign. During that campaign he performed exceptionally, particularly in the action at Cedar Creek where his stout defense bought critical time for the Federals to rally and win the day. Getty became a major general in March 1865, before participating in the Appomattox campaign. After the war he remained in the regular army and commanded the artillery school at Fort Monroe. He died on his farm at Forest Glen, Maryland, on October 1, 1901.

JOHN BELL HOOD (CSA)

Hood followed Longstreet to Gettysburg, where he suffered a debilitating wound in the arm while trying valiantly to turn the Union left flank. He later went to the western theater with Longstreet and lost his right leg at Chickamauga. Then, promoted to the temporary rank of full general (July 18, 1864), Hood replaced Joseph E. Johnston as commander of the Army of Tennessee but waged a losing struggle to save Atlanta, Georgia from capture.

Later in 1864 he marched into Tennessee, where he smashed his army at Franklin and Nashville. In May 1865 Hood surrendered at Natchez, Mississippi. He resided in New Orleans after the war until his death on August 30, 1879, from the same yellow fever epidemic that killed his wife and one of their children. Hood's romance with Buck Preston failed to survive the war, fluttering only briefly before finally dying out in 1864.

Roswell Hawkes Lamson (USN)

After his service on the Nansemond River in April 1863, Lamson continued to perform admirably in the U.S. Navy. One of the vessels he commanded was the USS *Nansemond,* which, he wrote, had been named "as a compliment to me." Lamson suffered a severe wound in the assault on Fort Fisher and resigned from the navy in 1866. He married his beloved Kate in 1867 and returned to Oregon in 1870. In his remaining years he farmed, served as county clerk, and taught math at Pacific University in Forest Groves, Oregon. Appointed clerk of the U.S. court in Portland, Lamson held the post for seventeen years before resigning due to ill health. He died on August 14, 1903. Always proud of his Suffolk service, he was laid to rest in a casket covered with the flag that had flown from the *Mount Washington* those many years ago. At one point of very slow activity during the war, he had written despairingly, "One week of Nansemond service would be worth five years of this sort of life."

Samuel Phillips Lee (USN)

Lee remained in command of the North Atlantic Blockading Squadron, rendering effective service against Southern blockade runners. In 1864 he transferred to the Mississippi Squadron and assisted George Thomas against Hood in Tennessee. At war's end Lee served at the head of the Signal Service before commanding the North Atlantic Squadron in 1870–72. After retiring from the military, he died of a stroke at Silver Springs, Maryland, on June 5, 1897.

James Longstreet (CSA)

The "War Horse" was too late to rejoin Lee at the battle of Chancellorsville, but he fought with him at the battle of Gettysburg, commanding Lee's right wing. In September 1863 Lee sent Longstreet to reinforce Braxton Bragg. "Old Peter" helped to secure the Confederate victory at Chickamauga but was terribly unsuccessful in a second independent command at Knoxville. He suffered a severe wound from an accidental shooting by his men during the battle of the Wilderness but recovered to surrender at Appomattox in April 1865. After the war he lived in New Orleans before moving to Gainesville, Georgia, where he died on January 2, 1904. Longstreet incurred the wrath of his former colleagues by working with the victorious Republicans and criticizing the now dead and venerated General Lee. Longstreet would serve as U.S. minister to Turkey in the 1880s and commissioner of Pacific railroads under Presidents William McKinley and Theodore Roosevelt.

JOHN JAMES PECK (USA)

After a brief leave of absence to recover from his horse-riding accident at Suffolk, Peck assumed command in North Carolina from August 14, 1863, to April 25, 1864. During this period he wrote to a fellow officer: "On the 9th [of October] I mounted my horse for the first time since April, when my horse was thrown upon me with great violence while forming line of battle. The experiment was not as satisfactory as I wish, but I hope to recover from the blow near the spinal column." That did not happen. Peck returned home to regain his health, eventually assuming command on the Canadian frontier until the end of the war. He resumed civilian life at Syracuse, New York, organizing the New York State Life Insurance Company in 1867 and serving as the company's president until his death on April 21, 1878. To the end of his days he seemed to regret that he did not receive his due for the defense of Suffolk.

GEORGE EDWARD PICKETT (CSA)

The disastrous results of his charge against the Union center at Gettysburg left Pickett with bitter feelings concerning the decimation of his division. Nevertheless he continued to court LaSalle Corbell, marrying her on September 5, 1863. Pickett commanded the Department of Virginia and North Carolina, served at Petersburg in 1864–65, and suffered a crushing defeat at Five Forks on April 1, 1865. General Lee subsequently relieved him of command. Following his surrender at Appomattox, Pickett became an insurance salesman. He died in Norfolk, Virginia, in July 1875.

ROGER ATKINSON PRYOR (CSA)

Pryor remained incensed that he had lost his command on the Blackwater. He resigned from the army in August 1863, only to join it again as a private. Pryor fell into Union hands in November 1864 and remained in a prison camp until near the end of the war. Following the conflict he went to New York, studied and then practiced law, and became a judge. On March 14, 1919, the former secessionist and Southern "fire-eater" who had once gathered shrapnel from the shelling of Fort Sumter to give to President Jefferson Davis died in New York City and was buried in Princeton, New Jersey.

THE RIDDICK FAMILY

The Riddicks struggled to restore their lives and home, Riddick's Folly. The house, now the headquarters for the Suffolk-Nansemond Historical Society, still bears some of the scars of this period in the form of graffiti left by Union soldiers when the upper rooms housed wounded men. One wrote a paraphrase of the famous motto: "E Pluribus Union." Anna Riddick, who had lost her sweetheart Jonny Smith in the war, never married. Despite the hardships, the Riddick family was able to endure the conflict intact. To be sure, Anna lost Jonny and Mills suffered a wound, but the immediate family faced the uncertainties of the future together in their own home, as Missouri and Nathaniel had once hoped.

⊰ APPENDIX B ⊱ CONFEDERATE ORDER OF BATTLE, SUFFOLK CAMPAIGN, APRIL–MAY 1863

ARMY OF NORTHERN VIRGINIA: GEN. ROBERT E. LEE

Department of Virginia and North Carolina: Lt. Gen. James Longstreet

Pickett's Division: Maj. Gen. George E. Pickett

Kemper's Brigade: Brig. Gen. James L. Kemper

1st Virginia	11th Virginia
3d Virginia	24th Virginia
7th Virginia	

Garnett's Brigade: Brig. Gen. Richard B. Garnett

8th Virginia	28th Virginia
18th Virginia	56th Virginia
19th Virginia	

Armistead's Brigade: Brig. Gen. Lewis A. Armistead

9th Virginia	53d Virginia
14th Virginia	57th Virginia
38th Virginia	

Corse's Brigade: Brig. Gen. Montgomery D. Corse

15th Virginia	30th Virginia
17th Virginia	32d Virginia
29th Virginia	

Light Artillery Battalion: Maj. James Dearing

Dearing's Virginia Battery
Stribling's Virginia Battery (Fauquier Artillery)
Macon's Virginia Battery (Richmond Fayette Artillery)
Caskie's Virginia Battery
Bradford's Mississippi Battery (Confederate Guards Artillery)
Hood's Division: Maj. Gen. John Bell Hood
Law's Brigade: Brig. Gen. Evander McI. Law

4th Alabama	47th Alabama
15th Alabama	48th Alabama
44th Alabama	

Robertson's Brigade: Brig. Gen. Jerome B. Robertson

3d Arkansas	4th Texas
1st Texas	5th Texas

Anderson's Brigade: Brig. Gen. George T. Anderson

7th Georgia	10th Georgia Battalion
8th Georgia	11th Georgia
9th Georgia	59th Georgia

Toomb's Brigade: Brig. Gen. Henry L. Benning

2d Georgia	17th Georgia
15th Georgia	20th Georgia

Light Artillery Battalion

Maj. Henry Lane's North Carolina Battery
Reilly's North Carolina Battery (Rowan Artillery)
Backman's South Carolina Battery (German Artillery)
Garden's South Carolina Battery (Palmetto Light Artillery)

Department of Southern Virginia: Maj. Gen. Samuel G. French

French's Division: Maj. Gen. Samuel G. French
Jenkins's Brigade: Brig. Gen. Micah R. Jenkins
1st South Carolina (Hagood's)
2d South Carolina Rifles

  5th South Carolina
  6th South Carolina
  Palmetto (South Carolina) Sharpshooters
  Hampton (South Carolina) Legion
Davis's Brigade: Brig. Gen. Joseph R. Davis
  2d Mississippi 42d Mississippi
  11th Mississippi 55th Mississippi
  26th Mississippi
Artillery: Maj. L. M. Shumaker
  Moseley's Battery
  Sturdivant's Battery
Cavalry: Col. John A. Baker
  41st North Carolina Cavalry

Source: Cormier, *Siege of Suffolk*, 316–18.

⊰ APPENDIX C ⊱ CASUALTIES OF SELECTED COMPANIES FROM SOUTHEASTERN VIRGINIA COMPILED BY ENGAGEMENT

Note: This list contains casualties only from companies of selected regiments with men from Suffolk, Nansemond, and the parts of Southampton, Isle of Wight, and Bower's Hill areas encompassed by this study. It is not meant to be comprehensive but is intended to offer the reader a glimpse at the price these men paid in this conflict. Two large classifications of soldiers are not included: prisoners, except those who were also wounded or died in captivity, and those who died from disease. The number of those who perished from illnesses was many times the number of those included in this list.

Some names appear more than once because they were casualties in more than one battle. The rank given is current to that battle. Those with no rank were privates at the time of the engagement in which they became casualties.

The age given was the individual's age at the time of enlistment in the service, where known. Finally, there is often more than one spelling for names featured below. This list uses the primary, or first, spelling given. The source is the H. E. Howard Regimental series volume for the particular regiment, and each is listed in the bibliography.

ABBREVIATIONS

WIA	Wounded in action
MWI	Mortally wounded (will die of wounds)
KIA	Killed in action
POW	Prisoner of war or captured
MIA	Missing in action

Deaths in italics

UNITS

3d Virginia Infantry (Co. D, Southampton Greys; Co. F, Nansemond Rangers; Co. G, Rough and Ready Guards)

6th Virginia Infantry (Co. E, Nansemond Guards)

9th Virginia Infantry (Co. E, Isle of Wight Blues; Co. F, Chuckatuck Light Artillery; Co. I, Craney Island Light Artillery)

16th Virginia Infantry (Co. A, Marion Rangers; Co. B, Suffolk Continentals; Co. D, Isle of Wight Rifle Greys)

41st Virginia Infantry (Co. G, Bilisoly Blues—Bower's Hill area; Co. I, Nansemond—Cypress Chapel area; Co. K, South Quay Guards)

61st Virginia Infantry (Co. F, Isle of Wight Avengers)

ENGAGEMENTS

Seven Pines or Fair Oaks, Va., May 31–June 1, 1862
Jesse T. Parker, age 18, WIA (leg), Co. D, 3d
Sgt. Francis Bailey, age 19, WIA, Co. G, 9th
John B. Brooks, age 24, WIA, Co. F, 9th
Lucien J. B. Godwin, age 27, WIA (cheek & side), Co. F, 9th
Henry Gwynn, age 24, WIA, Co. F, 9th
Thomas D. Moody, WIA (arm), Co. F, 9th
Lt. Caleb L. Upshur, age 21, WIA, Co. F, 9th
Jethro H. Franklin, farmer, WIA, Co. I, 41st
Capt. Beverly B. Hunter, medical student, WIA, Co. K, 41st
Thomas Pierce, MWIA & POW, Co. K, 41st [Died 6/15/62]
William Stephens Wright, WIA (arm), Co. F, 61st

Listed Generally as Seven Days, Va., June–July 1862
Alfred B. Cross, farmer, age 22, WIA, Co. F, 3d

John R. Dixon, sailor-oysterman, age 24, WIA, Co. F, 3d
George H. Gasley, KIA, Co. D, 3d
James R. Jones, farmer, age 41, WIA, Co. F, 3d
William J. Lassiter, farmer, age 26, WIA (hand), Co. F, 3d
William A. Phelps, farmer, age 20, WIA, Co. F, 3d
Robert Edward Riddick, WIA, Co. F, 3d
Sgt. George Washington Turner, farmer, age 30, WIA, Co. G, 3d
Joseph Turner, laborer, age 18, WIA, Co. G, 3d

Gaines's Mill, Va., June 27, 1862
William F. Edwards, age 18, MWIA, Co. D, 3d
William H. Felts, age 22, KIA, Co. D, 3d
Benjamin F. Harrison, WIA, Co. G, 3d
Richard Hill, overseer, age 30, MWIA, Co. G, 3d
Benjamin B. Ivey, farmer, age 28, WIA, Co. G, 3d
Joseph W. James, farmer, KIA, Co. G, 3d
Matthew Joyner, age 24, WIA, Co. D, 3d
James C. Laine, age 24, WIA, Co. D, 3d
William H. Pittman, age 18, WIA, Co. D, 3d
Benjamin B. Pulley, WIA, Co. G, 3d
William H. Webb, age 20, KIA, Co. D, 3d
Henry Kinchen Williams, WIA, Co. D, 3d

Glendale, Va., June 30, 1862
Cpl. Benjamin C. Britt, farmer, age 21, KIA, Co. G, 3d
Sgt. Melza Allen Jenkins, MWIA, Co. D, 3d
William H. Leigh, farmer, age 21, WIA, Co. G, 3d
Nathaniel T. Livesay, overseer, age 33, KIA, Co. G, 3d
James H. Marks, MWIA, Co. G, 3d
Thomas E. Peete, overseer, age 18, WIA, Co. G, 3d
George T. Rawls, age 22, WIA (shoulder), Co. D, 3d
William V. Turner, age 24, WIA (face and breast), Co. D, 3d
Lt. William T. Eley, physician, MWIA, Co. E, 6th
Lt. William J. Haslett, KIA, Co. K, 41st

Malvern Hill, Va., July 1, 1862
Lt. Joseph Boykin Whitehead, WIA, Co. E, 6th
Sgt. William J. Barradall, age 23, WIA, Co. F, 9th
Lt. Cornelius M. Dozier, KIA, Co. I, 9th
Sgt. John Hack, age 22, WIA, Co. F, 9th
Bray B. Walters, age 19, WIA, Co. F, 9th
George W. Bailey, MWIA, Co. E, 16th

Euclid Borland Jr., WIA, Co. E, 16th
Julius C. Darden, student, WIA, Co. D, 16th
Buxton W. Gale, painter, age 29, KIA, Co. D, 16th
Lt. Napoleon B. Hawes, merchant, WIA, Co. A, 16th
Lafayette W. Hodges, student, WIA, Co. A, 16th
Maj. Francis David Holladay, hotelkeeper, WIA, Co. B, 16th
Fabius C. Johnson, farmer, WIA, Co. D, 16th
Adolphus H. Outland, farmer, WIA, Co. D, 16th
William H. Powell, farmer-overseer, WIA, Co. D, 16th
Albert J. Rawls, farmer, WIA, Co. A, 16th
Julius J. Rawls, farmer, MWIA, Co. A, 16th
Sgt. John Walter Roberts, farmer, WIA, Co. D, 16th
Charles William Rowland, age 20, MWIA, Co. E, 16th
Cpl. John Henry Sledge, age 19, WIA, Co. E, 16th
Lt. Thomas Washington Smith, businessman-clerk, WIA, Co. A, 16th
Richard P. Spiers, teamster, WIA (head), Co. E, 16th
Lt. Hugh G. Brinkley, WIA (hand), Co. I, 41st
Jackson Richard Brinkley, farmer, WIA (head), Co. I, 41st
Lt. James H. Goodman, WIA ("minie ball entered left eye, exited behind left
    ear"), Co. I, 41st
John G. Holland, farmer, WIA, Co. K, 41st
Joseph J. Hunter, KIA, Co. I, 41st
Archibald Redd, farm laborer, WIA (hand), Co. I, 41st
Commodore Saunders, WIA, Co. I, 41st

Second Manassas/Bull Run, Va., August 30, 1862
Sgt. James M. Emmerson, clerk, age 20, WIA, Co. F, 3d
Cpl. Alexander Higginbotham, farmer, age 41, WIA, Co. F, 3d
Sgt. William J. Sullivan, sailor, age 22, WIA (hand), Co. F, 3d
Cpl. William H. Babb, KIA, Co. E, 6th
Sgt. Milton Babb, WIA, Co. E, 6th
John T. Holland, KIA, Co. E, 6th
John T. Luke, MWIA, Co. E, 6th
Charles Nelms, MWIA, Co. E, 6th
Augustus B. Norfleet, MWIA & POW, Co. E, 6th
Sgt. Kinsey J. Norfleet, WIA, Co. E, 6th
Francis W. Hotchkiss, age 27, KIA, Co. F, 9th
Benjamin F. Ashburn, WIA, Co. A, 16th
John Henry Avent, KIA, Co. E, 16th
Sgt. Thomas Hardy Cross, WIA (twice), Co. A, 16th
Sgt. John Darden, clerk, KIA, Co. A, 16th

John P.C. Eley, farmer, age 32, KIA, Co. D, 16th
Robert Gale, painter, age 34, WIA (leg), Co. D, 16th
Francis W. Hotchkiss, KIA, Co. F, 16th

Crampton's Gap, Md., September 14, 1862
William H. Pierce, WIA, Co. E, 6th
Cpl. Solomon V. Butler, clerk, age 22, WIA, Co. D, 16th
Jethro Raymond, farmer, age 18, WIA & POW, Co. D, 16th
Lemuel J. Stephens, farmer, age 20, KIA, Co. D, 16th

Gettysburg, Pa., July 1–3, 1863
Cpl. Benjamin F. Armes, age 28, MWIA, Co. F, 3d
Lt. John Calvin Arthur, farmer, age 23, MWIA, Co. F, 3d
George H. Bailey, age 26, KIA, Co. D, 3d
John H. Barrett, age 19, WIA, Co. D, 3d
John H. Branch, age 24, KIA, Co. D, 3d
Robert J. Dunford, farmer, age 18, POW (possibly *KIA*), Co. F, 3d
Cpl. Joseph R. Edwards, MIA (later learned KIA), Co. D, 3d
Sgt. Richard B. L. Everett, age 24, KIA, Co. D, 3d
Richard A. Felts, farmer, age 20, KIA, Co. G, 3d
Charles S. Gardner, age 18, POW, Co. D, 3d *[Died in prison]*
William J. Gardner, KIA, Co. D, 3d
Matthew Holland, farmer, age 18, POW, Co. F, 3d *[Died in prison]*
Richard T. Holland, farmer, age 21, WIA & POW, Co. F, 3d
Cornelius E. James, farmer, age 18, WIA & POW, Co. F, 3d
James K. Jelks, age 25, KIA, Co. D, 3d
John C. Jordan, student, age 19, WIA (thigh) & POW, Co. F, 3d *[Died July 12]*
William Thomas Lancaster, farmer, age 22, WIA & POW, Co. F, 3d
Elisha Murray, farmer, age 28, MWIA, Co. F, 3d [Died July 21]
John S. Norsworthy, farmer, age 16, WIA (leg) & POW, Co. G, 3d
Lt. C. Crawley Phillips, professor, age 26, KIA, Co. F, 3d
Cpl. Joseph W. Pope, farmer, age 23, WIA & POW, Co. G, 3d [Died July 11]
Peter Simmons, laborer, age 18, POW, Co. G, 3d *[Died in prison]*
Sgt. James D. Taylor, farmer, age 24, WIA, Co. F, 3d
Henry G. West, laborer, age 24, WIA & POW, Co. G, 3d [Died July 16]
Sgt. William J. Barradall, age 23, POW, Co. F, 9th *[Died in prison]*
Cpl. John T. Beach, age 23, WIA (arm & leg) & POW, Co. F, 9th
William H. Brittingham, WIA, Co. F, 9th
Lt. Walter Butts, age 20, POW, Co. F, 9th [Died July 11]
Lt. John Hack, age 22, WIA & POW, Co. E, 9th
Wilfred J. Hobsden, age 18, WIA (foot) & POW, Co. D, 9th
Daniel Miltier, WIA & POW, Co. D, 9th

William Morgan, POW, Co. D, 9th *[Died in prison]*

Amos Riddick, WIA & POW, Co. I, 9th

Lt. Richard Franklin Chapman, farmer, age 32, WIA (leg) & POW, Co. E, 16th [Leg amputated and died]

John R. Clemments, farmer, age 33, WIA, Co. A, 16th

Beverly Proctor Baker, WIA, Co. I, 41st

Elias W. Cherry, POW, Co. G, 41st *[Died in prison]*

Solomon J. Holland, WIA, Co. I, 41st

Julius Ward, KIA, Co. G, 41st

John H. Duck, age 19, POW, Co. F, 61st *[Died in prison]*

Mills A. Gay, age 18, MWIA, Co. F, 61st [Died July 4]

Wilderness, Va., May 4–5, 1864

Cpl. Addison Ashburn, MWIA, Co. E, 6th [Died May 22]

Francis Columbus Roberts, farmer, WIA (arm), Co. D, 16th

Lt. Col. Richard Owen Whitehead, WIA (chest), 16th

John R. Ballard, farmer, WIA, Co. I, 41st

Elden K. Casey, WIA (arm amputated), Co. G, 41st [Later in Co. F, 61st]

William E. Gardner, MWIA, Co. K, 41st

Thomas J. Holland, KIA, Co. K, 41st

Lt. Walter C. Jones, KIA, Co. D, 41st

James H. Pearce, farmer, WIA, Co. I, 41st

Thomas J. Rawles, WIA, Co. K, 41st

Luther Rawls, WIA (shoulder), Co. K, 41st

Joseph B. Skinner, WIA, Co. I, 41st

Spotsylvania Courthouse, Va., May 12, 1864

Sgt. Richard A. Channell, clerk, age 21, WIA, Co. A, 16th

Cpl. Julius C. Darden, student, WIA, Co. D, 16th

David R. Daughtrey, farmer, age 20, WIA, Co. D, 16th

Henry R. Ellis, farmer, age 18, WIA, Co. B, 16th

Robert L. Harris, shoemaker, WIA, Co. A, 16th

Robert E. Norfleet, student, WIA (head), Co. A, 16th

Sgt. John T. Pierce, clerk, age 26, WIA, Co. B, 16th

Benjamin Claudius Roberts, farmer, WIA, Co. D, 16th

Sgt. John Walter Roberts, farmer, WIA (arm amputated), Co. D, 16th

Lt. Thomas Washington Smith, businessman-clerk, WIA, Co. A, 16th

James T. Wilson, painter, age 23, WIA (head), Co. B, 16th

Robert Beale, KIA, Co. K, 41st

Mills Rogers Jr., WIA (leg), Co. I, 41st

Joshua Skinner, farmer, WIA (arm), Co. I, 41st

William Bracy, age 30, WIA (thigh), Co. F, 61st

William Corbit, KIA, Co. F, 61st
Benjamin C. Eley, age 35, KIA, Co. F, 61st

Drewry's Bluff and North Anna, Va., May 16 and May 25, 1864
Lt. John E. Cowling, KIA, Co. F, 9th
Capt. Robert B. Brinkley, merchant, KIA, Co. I, 41st
Sgt. Oliver H.P. Holland, student, KIA, Co. K, 41st

Cold Harbor and Turkey Ridge, Va., June 1–8, 1864
James T. Conley, overseer, age 23, KIA, Co. G, 3d
George T. Folk, MWIA, Co. E, 6th
William Lester, age 29, KIA, Co. E, 16th
James Harrell, WIA (shoulder), Co. K, 41st
Wilson Harrell, WIA (thigh), Co. K, 41st
William T. Daughtrey, age 28, POW, Co. F, 61st *[Died in prison]*

Wilcox's Farm, Va., June 22, 1864
Capt. Thaddeus G. Williams, farmer, KIA, Co. E, 6th
James Brown, clerk, age 21, WIA (side), Co. D, 16th
Sgt. Francis E. Jones, engineer, age 28, KIA, Co. A, 16th
John Frederick Lotzia, WIA, Co. A, 16th
Sgt. Mills W. Roberts, farmer, WIA, Co. A, 16th
Josiah C. Bradshaw, age 23, KIA, Co. F, 61st
James P. Butler, age 18, WIA (leg), Co. F, 61st [Died July 2]
Isaiah Turner, age 30, KIA, Co. F, 61st
Jacob Turner, WIA, Co. F, 61st
James H. Turner, WIA (face), Co. F, 61st

The Crater, Petersburg, July 30, 1864
Sgt. Milton Babb, KIA, Co. E, 6th
Sgt. William H. Pierce, WIA, Co. E, 6th
Lt. James M. Bailey, clerk, age 22, MWIA, Co. B, 16th
Richard J. Bendall, age 21, WIA, Co. E, 61st
Capt. William Wallace Broadbent, age 27, KIA, Co. E, 16th
Jesse Augustus Hamilton, farmer, WIA, Co. E, 16th
Cpl. Julian C. Hines, medical student and schoolteacher, age 18, WIA, Co. B, 16th
Cpl. John H. Ivy, age 27, WIA, Co. E, 16th [Died August 10]
James N. Niblett, age 22, KIA, Co. E, 16th
Benjamin F. Northcross, farmer, age 18, WIA, Co. E, 16th
Stephen H. Pierce, farmer, age 18, KIA, Co. D, 16th
Robert A. Purvis, lawyer and farmer, age 19, WIA, Co. A, 16th [Died July 31]
John W. Westbrook, age 19, KIA, Co. E, 16th

William J. White, clerk, KIA, Co. I, 41st

Jackson Richardson Brinkley, farmer, WIA (leg), Co. I, 41st

John G. Brinkley, farmer, WIA, Co. I, 41st

James E. Ellis, farmer, KIA, Co. I, 41st

Richard Goodman Holland, WIA ("minie ball, left breast, bullet lodged against shoulder blade, bayonet wound in the mouth knocking out 2 teeth"), Co. K, 41st

Capt. Beverly B. Hunter, medical student, KIA, Co. K, 41st

Leroy Parker, MWIA (right side, head), Co. I, 41st

Solomon K. Savage, MWIA, Co. I, 41st [Died July 31]

Smith Toppin, KIA, Co. G, 41st [Transferred to 61st]

Parker Duke, WIA, Co. F, 61st

Henry H. Pruden, WIA (foot), Co. F, 61st

John W. Pruden, age 20, POW, Co. F, 61st *[Died in prison]*

Weldon Railroad and Davis's Farm, Va., August 19, 1864

Benjamin F. Cutchin Jr., clerk, age 21, WIA (leg), Co. A, 16th

Henry R. Ellis, farmer, age 18, WIA (eye), Co. B, 16th

Sgt. William Jackson Lassiter, carpenter, age 33, WIA, Co. B, 16th [Died August 28]

James J. Morriss, farmer, age 28, WIA, Co. D, 16th

Graves Niblett, WIA & POW, Co. D, 16th

Alexander W. Oliver, farmer, WIA, Co. A, 16th

James T. Saunders, farmer, age 20, WIA, Co. D, 16th

William H. Cross, student, MWIA (head), & POW, Co. I, 41st [Died August 23]

William H. Holland, farmer, Co. K, 41st

Cpl. William Augustus Butler, age 19, WIA (arm amputated), Co. F, 61st

Lt. Robert R. Owens, WIA (thigh), Co. F, 61st

Thomas Peel, POW, Co. F, 61st *[Died in prison]*

Burgess's Mill, Va., October 27, 1864

Capt. John Brenan, saddler, age 27, WIA & POW, Co. B, 16th [Died November 24]

Frederick Brinkley, student, WIA (hip) & POW, Co. I, 41st

Capt. John Hobday Jr., KIA, Co. G, 41st

Robert Rawls, WIA (hand), Co. I, 41st

Hatcher's Run, Va., February 7, 1865

Lt. Thomas Washington Smith, businessman-clerk, WIA, Co. A, 16th

James Harrell, WIA (hip), Co. K, 41st

Five Forks, Va., April 1, 1865

Seth N. Barnett, age 18, Co. D, 3d

Retreat to Appomattox Courthouse, Va., April 1865

William Mason, KIA, Cumberland Church, Co. G, 41st

⊰ APPENDIX D ⊱ UNION ORDER OF BATTLE, SUFFOLK CAMPAIGN, APRIL–MAY 1863

DEPARTMENT OF VIRGINIA AND 7TH CORPS: MAJ. GEN. JOHN A. DIX

Suffolk Garrison: Maj. Gen. John J. Peck

 1st Division, 7th Corps: Brig. Gen. Michael Corcoran
  1st Brigade: Brig. Gen. Henry D. Terry [15 KIA, 68 WIA]

26th Michigan	152d New York
1st Battalion New York	167th Pennsylvania
Sharpshooters	11th Rhode Island
130th New York	

  2d Brigade: Col. Robert S. Foster [2 KIA, 27 WIA, 1 MIA]

13th Indiana	169th New York
6th Massachusetts	165th Pennsylvania
112th New York	166th Pennsylvania

3d Brigade (Corcoran's Irish Legion): Col. Michael Murphy
[1 KIA, 14 WIA]

10th New Jersey	170th New York
155th New York	182d New York
164th New York	

3d Division, 9th Corps: Brig. Gen. George W. Getty
1st Brigade: Col. Rush Hawkins [6 KIA, 27 WIA]
10th New Hampshire
9th New York (Hawkins' Zouaves) [Lt. Col. Edgar A. Kimball
killed by Gen. Corcoran]
89th New York
103d New York [Col. Benjamin Ringold, MWIA]
117th New York
2d Brigade: Brig. Gen. Edward Harland [10 KIA, 44 WIA]

8th Connecticut	15th Connecticut
11th Connecticut	16th Connecticut

3d Brigade: Col. Arthur S. Dutton [7 KIA, 36 WIA]

21st Connecticut	25th New Jersey
13th New Hampshire	4th Rhode Island

Light Artillery Battalion [3 WIA]
Battery A, 1st Pennsylvania Light Artillery
Battery A, 5th U.S. Artillery

Reserve Division: Col. William Gurney
2d Brigade: Col. Burr Porter [No loss reported]
22d Connecticut
40th Massachusetts
141st New York
3d Brigade: Col. Robert S. Hughston [No loss reported]

127th New York	143d New York
142d New York	144th New York

Reserve Brigade: Col. Robert W. Wardrop [No loss reported]
99th New York [Casualties listed in App. F]
118th New York
9th Vermont
19th Wisconsin
Cavalry [4 WIA, 1 MIA]
1st New York Mounted Rifles
11th Pennsylvania
1st Dragoons—19th New York

Unattached Artillery (Heavy) [No loss reported]
    2d Battalion (Cos. A, B, F, and G)
    3d Pennsylvania Battery
Unattached Artillery (Light) [No loss reported]

1st Delaware Battery	Battery D, 4th U.S.
7th Massachusetts Battery	Battery L, 4th U.S.
16th New York Battery	2d Wisconsin Battery
19th New York Battery	4th Wisconsin Battery

Unassigned [No loss reported]
    3d New York

Sources: Cormier, *Siege of Suffolk,* 312–14; Return of Casualties in the Union forces, n.d., OR 18:286–88.

⊰ APPENDIX E ⊱ UNION NAVAL VESSELS

NORTH ATLANTIC BLOCKADING SQUADRON:
ACTING REAR ADM. SAMUEL P. LEE [9 KIA, 16 WIA, 4 MIA]

Lower Nansemond Flotilla: Lt. William B. Cushing

	TYPE	TONS	CREW	GUNS
USS *Commodore Barney*	sw. f.	513	96	7
USS *Yankee*	sw. st.	328	48	3
USS *Primrose*	sc. st.	94	25	2
USS *Cohasset*	sc. st.	100	12	2

Upper Nansemond Flotilla: Lt. Roswell H. Lamson

USS *Stepping Stones*	sw. st.	266	21	5
USS *Mount Washington*	sw. st.	500	40	1
USS *Alert*	sc. st.	65	15	2

	TYPE	TONS	CREW	GUNS
USS *Zouave*	sc. st.	127	25	2
USS *Coeur de Lion*	sw. st.	110	29	3
USS *Teaser*	sc. st.	96	25	2

Army Quartermaster Boats:
  West End
  Smith Briggs

Abbreviations: sw.—sidewheel; sc.—screw propeller; f.—ferryboat; st.—steamer.

Sources: Cormier, *Siege of Suffolk,* 315; Merrifield, "The Seaboard War," 274, 275, 277, 278, 279, 280.

⊰ NOTES ⊱

Abbreviations

AMR	Anna Mary Riddick
BRFAL	Bureau of Refugees, Freedmen and Abandoned Lands, NA
CPC	Confederate Papers Relating to Citizens or Business Firms, NA
DU	Perkins Library, Duke University, Durham, N.C.
EU	Woodruff Library, Emory University, Atlanta, Ga.
LVA	Library of Virginia, Richmond
MAJKR	Missouri Ann Jones Kilby Riddick
MHI-CB	U.S. Army Military History Institute, Carlisle Barracks, Pa.
MOC	Eleanor S. Brockenbrough Library, Museum of the Confederacy, Richmond, Va.
NA	National Archives, Washington, D.C.
NR	Nathaniel Riddick
NCDHA	North Carolina Department of History and Archives, Raleigh

OR   *The Official Records of the Union and Confederate Armies in the War of*
            Rebellion
ORN   *Official Records of the Union and Confederate Navies*
RFP   Riddick Family Papers
SHC-UNC   Southern Historical Collection, University of North Carolina,
            Chapel Hill
UGA   University of Georgia, Athens
UM   William L. Clements Library, University of Michigan, Ann Arbor
USMA-WP   United States Military Academy Library, West Point, N.Y.
UVA   University of Virginia Library, Charlottesville
VHS   Virginia Historical Society, Richmond
VPI&SU   Virginia Polytechnic Institute and State University, Blacksburg

Introduction: "War on Their Doorsteps"

1. *Harper's Weekly,* May 2, 1863, 276.
2. Ibid.
3. Henry E. Simmons to My Darling Anna, Camp 11th R.I.V., May 7, 1863, Henry E. Simmons Papers, SHC-UNC.
4. Henry Grimes Marshall to Dear Folks at Home, Suffolk, Va., May 11, 1863, Henry Grimes Marshall Papers, UM.
5. For these ideological components, see Foner, *Free Soil,* and Wyatt-Brown, *Southern Honor,* as a starting point.
6. Massey, *Refugee Life,* 282.
7. Quoted in Wills, *Battle,* 136.
8. The debate over Confederate nationalism continues to rage. Some historians argue either that the South failed to develop any meaningful sense of nationalism or that it faded quickly under the pressures of war and defeat. Others argue that the Confederate States of America succeeded in developing as a nation, even amid the demands of war, and that a sense of nationalism proved remarkably endurable. For examples of these views, see Faust, *Creation of Confederate Nationalism,* and Thomas, *Revolutionary* and *Confederate Nation.* A good discussion of these issues can be found in Owens and Cooke, *Crucible of War.* For a more recent examination of this issue, see Gallagher, *Confederate War.*

1. "Blood Thursty for Lincoln"

1. Daniel William Cobb 1859 Diary, "Thursday 27 [Oct.]" entry, Daniel William Cobb Papers, VHS. See also Crofts, *Southampton,* which uses the Cobb diaries extensively, and Crofts, *Cobb's Ordeal.*
2. See McPherson, *Battle Cry,* 213–33, for an assessment of the election of 1860.
3. Elliott L. Story 1860 Diary, [Nov.,] "Tues. 6," "Mon. 12," "Mon. 19," and "Thurs. 22" entries, Elliott L. Story Diaries, VHS; see also Crofts, *Southampton,* which uses the Story diaries in addition to those of Daniel Cobb.
4. Quoted in Thomas, *Lee,* 186.

5. Annual Board Meeting, July 1860, Norfolk and Petersburg Railroad, Norfolk and Petersburg Railroad Papers, VPI&SU.

6. Long, *Day by Day*, 5.

7. Charleston *Mercury*, special edition, Dec. 20, 1860.

8. See Thomas, *Confederate Nation*, 37–72.

9. Quoted in Long, *Day by Day*, 32.

10. Ibid., 41–42.

11. Cobb Diary, "1861 Sunday 13 [Jan.]"

12. Story Diary, "Sat. 12 [Jan. 1861]"

13. Cobb Diary, "1861 Saturday 19 [Jan.]"

14. Ibid., "1861 Munday 4 [Feb.] "; Crofts, *Southampton*, 176–77.

15. Crofts, *Southampton*, 177.

16. Story Diary, "Tues. 5 [Feb. 1861]."

17. Cobb Diary, "1861 Munday 11 [Feb.]"

18. Ibid., "1861 Thursday 14 [Feb.]"

19. Ibid., "1861 Teusday 12 [March]," "1861 Saturday 16 [March]."

20. L. P. Walker to P. G. T. Beauregard, April 10, 1861, OR 1:297. See also Swanberg, *First Blood*.

21. P. G. T. Beauregard to Maj. Robert Anderson, April 11, 1861, OR 1:13.

22. L. P. Walker to Beauregard, April 11, 1861, ibid., 301.

23. Swanberg, *First Blood*, 296–331.

24. Cobb Diary, "1861 Sunday 14 [April]."

25. Quoted in Roland, *American Iliad*, 35.

26. Davis, *Making of the Confederacy*, 321.

27. Ibid.

28. Ibid., 324.

29. Cobb Diary, numerous entries in March and April 1861.

30. Ibid., "1861 Thursday 18 [April]."

31. Hobbs, *Storm over Suffolk*, 2; Hobbs and Paquette, *Suffolk: A Pictorial History*, 57.

32. Cobb Diary, "1861 Saturday 20th [April]."

33. Ibid., "1861 Sunday 21 [April]."

34. Story Diary, "May 1861."

35. Ibid., "June 1861."

36. Cobb Diary, "1861 Saturday 20th [April]."

37. Flanders, "The Night They Burned the Yard"; Long, "The Gosport Affair, 1861."

38. Cobb Diary, "1861 Monday 22nd [April]."

39. Ibid.

40. Composite of Suffolk taken from numerous letters, diaries, etc. See also Hobbs, *Storm over Suffolk*, 2, and Pollack, *Sketchbook*.

41. Johnston, *Virginia Railroads*, 4, 11; Black, *Railroads*, 39.

42. Hobbs, *Storm over Suffolk*, 2; Pollack, *Sketchbook*, 82.

43. R. S. Garnett to Walter Gwynn, April 30, 1861, OR 2:791.

44. Benjamin Butler to Winfield Scott, May 29, 1861, ibid., 54.

45. Lee to Huger, May 27, 1861, ibid., 882.
46. Cobb Diary, "1861 Monday 29 [April]."
47. Ibid., "1861 Sunday 12 [May]."
48. Ibid., "1861 Teusday 14 [May]."
49. Crofts, *Southampton,* 59, 194. See also Balfour, *13th Virginia Cavalry,* for the history and roster of this regiment.
50. Cobb Diary, "1861 Teusday 23 [April]," "1861 Sunday 28 [April]."
51. Balfour, *13th Virginia Cavalry,* 3.
52. Cobb Diary, "1861 Saturday 25 [May]," "1861 Friday 31st [May]."
53. See Wallace, *Guide,* for a complete listing of units from this region and throughout the state of Virginia. See also Crofts, *Southampton,* 194–95; Hobbs, *Storm over Suffolk,* 24; and various volumes from the Virginia Regimental Series (Lynchburg, Va.).
54. Wallace, *Guide,* 53, 69, 109, 114, 126, 164, 286.
55. Trask, *61st Virginia Infantry,* 1, 3.
56. Cavanaugh, *6th Virginia,* 124; Petersburg *Daily Express,* July 8, 1862.
57. Jonathan Smith to AMR, Craney Island, May 14, 1861, RFP.
58. Cobb Diary, "1861 Thursday 23 [May]."
59. See Thomas, *Revolutionary.*
60. Cobb Diary, "1861 Monday 27 [May]," "1861 Thursday 3 [May]."

2. *A "Lion" Is in the Streets*

1. Pender, *General to His Lady,* 3–6.
2. Ibid., 25.   5. Ibid., 27–28.   8. Ibid., 39.
3. Ibid., 38.   6. Ibid., 27.   9. Ibid., 40.
4. Ibid., 26.   7. Ibid., 30–31.   10. Ibid., 42–44.
11. Ibid. Various post-Suffolk letters attest to the personal growth Dorsey Pender underwent in the course of the war, including in regard to his relationship with his wife and family.
12. Ibid., 35.
13. Ibid., 37–38.
14. Coz to AMR, near Weldon, N.C., Jan. 16, 1862, RFP.
15. See, for example, Wallace, *3rd Virginia,* 9, 13–14; Trask, *9th Virginia,* 1–7.
16. Jonny Smith to AMR, Craney Island, May 14, 1861, RFP.
17. To My Dear Friend, Camp Huger, Suffolk, Va., Nov. 28, 1861, William Dunlap Simpson Papers, DU.
18. Pender, *General to His Lady,* 32.
19. Ibid., 27.   20. Ibid., 27, 33, 35.   21. Ibid., 34.
22. J. T. Hambrick to Dear Wife, Camp Suffolk, Va., June 24, 1861, Hambrick and Paylor Papers, NCDHA.
23. R. J. Stallings to Cousin Emma, Suffolk, Va., June 20, 1861, Lucinda Sugg Moore Papers, SHC-UNC.
24. To My Dear Friend, Camp Huger, Suffolk, Nov. 28, 1861, William Dunlap Simpson Papers, DU.

25. Crews and Parrish, *14th Virginia*, 83–156 passim. See also rosters of various units in the Virginia Regimental Series.

26. L. Robert Moore to Dear Mother, Suffolk, Nansemond Cty, Va., June 15, 1861, L. Robert Moore Papers, VHS.

27. Hambrick to Dear Wife, Suffolk, Va., June 6, 1861, Hambrick and Paylor Papers, NCDHA.

28. Trask, *16th Virginia*, 79, 81, 105, 112.

29. Crews and Parrish, *14th Virginia*, 106, 135, 150.

30. Wallace, *3rd Virginia*, 101, 109.

31. Henry Clay Carter to Dear Brother, Suffolk, March 14, 1862, Carter Family Papers, VHS.

32. Quoted in Wert, *Brotherhood of Valor*, 81. Disease ravaged the common soldiers of both sides, particularly early in the war, thinning their ranks and reducing the combat effectiveness of even the finest military units, as Wert ably demonstrates.

33. Jonny Smith to AMR, Craney Island, April 10, 1862, RFP.

34. Petersburg *Daily Express*, Saturday, Sept. 28, 1861.

35. Tom Parramore, "The Roanoke-Chowan Story," 110, F. Roy Johnson Papers, NCDHA. See also Trotter, *Ironclads and Columbiads*, 214–15.

36. To My Dear Friend, Camp Huger, Nov. 28, 1861, William Dunlap Simpson Papers, DU.

37. Alvin Coe Voris to My Dear Wife, Suffolk, Va., Sept. 28, 1862, Alvin Coe Voris Papers, VHS.

38. To My Dear Friend, Camp Huger, Nov. 28, 1861, William Dunlap Simpson Papers, DU.

39. R. Channing Price to Dear Mother, Suffolk, Va., March 9, 1862, R. Channing Price Papers, SHC-UNC.

40. Price to Dear Mother, Howitzer Camp at Suffolk, Mar. 28 [1862], and Camp Randolph near Suffolk, April 4, 1862, ibid.

41. Receipts for various individuals, CPC, microcopy no. 346, roll no. 1088.

42. T. M. R. Talcott to the Quartermaster at Suffolk, Day's Neck Battery, July 4, 1861, Samuel J. Hunt to T. M. R. Talcott, Suffolk, July 4, 1861, Hunt to Talcott, July 6, 1861, Talcott Family Papers, VHS.

43. See additional correspondence between Hunt and Talcott, July 15, 16, 17, 18, 1861, ibid., concerning the movement of supplies and the requirement for proper documentation of requisitions.

44. Willis Riddick Receipts, CPC.

45. Archibald Riddick Receipts, ibid.

46. Jordan, *Black Confederates*, 214.

47. Willis Riddick Receipts, CPC.

48. Cobb Diary, "1861 Wednesday 21 [Nov.]," "1861 Saturday 24 [Nov.]"

49. Thomas, *Confederate Nation*, 196.

50. R. J. Stallings to Cousin Emma, Suffolk, Va., June 20, 1861, Lucinda Sugg Moore Papers, SHC-UNC.

51. Pender, *General to His Lady*, 37.
52. John E. Wool to George B. McClellan, William J. Whipple enclosure, Nov. 11, 1861, *OR* 4:629–31.
53. Ibid.
54. Cobb Diary, "1861 Sunday 9 [June].
55. Ibid., "1861 Thursday 13 [June]
56. Pender, *General to His Lady*, 34. Big Bethel was a small engagement, particularly by later standards, with 2,500 Federals confronting 1,200 Confederates, producing 76 and 8 casualties respectively.
57. Long, *Day by Day*, 84. Exultant Southerners displayed captured trophies in Richmond storefront windows following Big Bethel and boasted of a rapid end to the conflict following First Manassas.
58. Thomas E. Upshaw to Charlie Riddick, Suffolk, Friday night [Jan. 3, 1862], RFP.
59. C. H. Riddick to NR, Portsmouth, Va., Jan. 6, 1862, ibid.
60. See Balfour, *13th Virginia Cavalry*, for regimental history and roster.
61. Thomas, *Travels*, 13.
62. Samuel McGuire to My dear [brother], near Pocotaligo, S.C., Saturday, Feb. 22, 1862, Webb-Prentiss Papers, UVA.
63. See Wiley, *Road to Appomattox*.
64. Petersburg *Daily Express*, Thursday, Feb. 20, 1862.
65. McGuire to [brother], near Pocotaligo, S.C., Saturday, Feb. 22, 1862, Webb-Prentiss Papers, UVA.
66. Price to Dear Mother, Suffolk, Va., March 9, 1862, R. Channing Price Papers, SHC-UNC.
67. Newspaper clipping in file, Executive Papers, Governor John Letcher, March 1862, LVA.
68. See correspondence relating to military and civil authority in Norfolk, Va.: R. E. Lee to Maj. Gen. B. Huger, Richmond, March 22, 1862, to George M. Munford, Richmond, March 22, 1862, and notation by Governor Letcher, ibid.
69. Wallace, *Surry Light Artillery*, 6.
70. Price to Dear Mother, Camp Randolph near Suffolk, March 1862, R. Channing Price Papers, SHC-UNC.
71. Quoted in Thomas, *Confederate Nation*, 152.
72. Price to Dear Mother, Camp Randolph near Suffolk, April 1862, R. Channing Price Papers, SHC-UNC.
73. Quoted in Thomas, *Confederate Nation*, 154.
74. See Davis, *Duel*.
75. Arnie Herbert to AMR, Level Green, March 17, 1862, RFP.
76. Jonny to AMR, Craney Island, April 10, 1862, ibid.

3. *Paradise Lost*

1. Henry Clay Carter to Dear Bro., Suffolk, May 5, 1862, Carter Family Papers, VHS.
2. Jackson, Bryant, and Wills, *Three Rebels*, 61.
3. George W. Randolph to Maj. Gen. Huger, May 1, 1862, *OR*, vol. 11, pt. 3, p. 485.

4. Randolph to Huger, May 3, 1862, ibid., 490.

5. Lee to Gen. Joseph E. Johnston, May 7, 1862, ibid.,497.

6. Fannie to AMR, Bonnie Doon, May 8, 1862, RFP.

7. Randolph to Huger, May 11, 1862, *OR*, vol. 11, pt. 3, p. 507.

8. Lee to Huger, May 16, 1862, ibid., 519–20.

9. For a strong assessment of Huger's failings as a field commander, see Freeman, *Lieutenants* 1:611–13.

10. Benjamin Lyons Farinholt Diary, May 9, 1862, Benjamin Lyons Farinholt Papers, VHS.

11. Robert Mabry to My Dear Wife, Camp Dunn near Petersburg, Va., May 12, 1862, Robert C. Mabry Papers, NCDHA.

12. Price to Dear Mother, Camp at Zuni Depot, N&P RR, Isle of Wight Co., May 12, 1862, R. Channing Price Papers, SHC-UNC.

13. Farinholt Diary, May 10, 1862, VHS.

14. See unit roster, Cavanaugh, *6th Virginia*, 79–139 passim.

15. Mattie J. Prentiss to Joseph Webb, June, 1862, RFP.

16. A native of New Jersey, Dodge was born on Sept. 16, 1841. He mustered into Federal service as a captain of the Mounted Rifles shortly after his twentieth birthday and rose to the rank of brigadier general by the end of 1862. Despite his youth Dodge enjoyed wide admiration from his command, although he seems to have fallen out of favor with General Dix while in southeastern Virginia (Warner, *Blue*, 126–27).

17. Wool to Stanton, May 12, 1862, *OR*, vol. 11, pt. 3, p. 169; Ferguson, *Occupation*, 2.

18. Ash, "White Virginians," 170, 172. For a broader examination by the same author, see Ash's excellent study, *Yankees*.

19. General Orders No. 46, May 16, 1862, *OR*, vol. 11, pt. 3, p. 176.

20. Wool to E. M. Stanton, May 19, 1862, ibid., 181–82.

21. Ferguson, *Occupation*, 2.

22. Ash, "White Virginians," 172.

23. *Eleventh Pennsylvania Cavalry*, 36.

24. Nickerson, *War Experiences*, 40–41.

25. Lt. William Ryan to Maj. Richard Nixon, May 30, 1862, RG 393, U.S. Army Continental Commands, 1821–1899, Dept. of Va. and N.C. Provost Marshal (1861) Reports, 1862, 1864, NA.

26. Ash, "White Virginians," 172.

27. Wills, "In Charge," 142; "Riddick's Folly," Frank M. Roberts, Suffolk *Sun*, Jan. 11, 1981, p. 1; U.S. Census, Population and Slave Schedules, Nansemond County, Va., 1850, 1860, NA.

28. Jonny to AMR, Craney Island, April 25, 1862, RFP.

29. Jonny to AMR, June 14th, 1862, ibid..

30. Lee to Huger, May 16, 1862, *OR*, vol. 11, pt. 3, pp. 519–20.

31. Price to Dear Mother, Camp at Ivor Depot, Southampton Co, N&P RR, May 19, 1862, R. Channing Price Papers, SHC-UNC.

32. Farinholt Diary, May 13, 1862, VHS.

33. Hobbs, *Storm over Suffolk*, 5.

34. Trask, *9th Virginia*, 10–12.
35. Ibid., 12–13.
36. MAJKR to AMR, June 10, 1862, RFP.
37. Jonny to AMR, Chaffin's Farm, June 13, 1862, ibid.
38. MAJKR to AMR, June 10, 1862, RFP.
39. Mills Riddick to AMR, Camp Starvation, June 16, 1862, ibid.
40. MAJKR to AMR, June 10, 1862, ibid.
41. Ibid., June 24, 1862.
42. Ibid., June 10, 1862.
43. Ibid. See Grimsley, *Hard Hand of War,* for a recent assessment of this policy and the change it underwent during the course of the war.
44. MAJKR to AMR, June 24, 1862, RFP.
45. Ibid.
46. Ash, "White Virginians," 175.
47. See Appendix C for a listing of casualties for each major engagement for many of the units with men from the part of southeastern Virginias encompassed by this study.
48. Wallace, *3rd Virginia*, 86, 87, 90.
49. Petersburg *Daily Express.*
50. Wallace, *3rd Virginia*, 79; Henderson, *41st Virginia*, 111.
51. Jonny to AMR, Charles City Road, June 28, 1862, RFP.
52. Hill, "McClellan's Change," 394. Also quoted in Sears, *Gates,* 335, which also provides an excellent overview of the Peninsula campaign. See also Dowdy, *Seven Days.*
53. Cavanaugh, *6th Virginia*, 125.
54. MAJKR to AMR, July 2, 1862, RFP.
55. "Cousin" to AMR, Petersburg, Thursday afternoon, Aug. 15, 1862, ibid..
56. Interview with Anna W. Rollings, Suffolk, Va., Jan. 2, 1981.
57. MAJKR to AMR, July 2, 1862, RFP.
58. Trask, *9th Virginia,* 60, 96.
59. MAJKR to AMR, July 2, 1862, RFP.
60. MAJKR to AMR, Friday, July 11, 1862, ibid.
61. Robert R. Prentis to NR, University of Va., July 5, 1862, ibid.
62. MAJKR to AMR, July 2, 1862, ibid.
63. Mattie J. Prentiss to Joseph Webb, June 1862, ibid. See also Hobbs, *Storm over Suffolk,* 4–5.
64. Prentis to Webb, June 1862, RFP.
65. W. H. Casey to John Letcher, Aug. 1862, Executive Papers, Governor John Letcher, Aug. 1862, LVA.
66. Nathaniel J. Riddick, Gates, N.C., Sept. 29, 1862, CPC.
67. Dix to Stanton, July 31, 1862, *OR,* vol. 11, pt. 3, p. 345.
68. Warner, *Blue,* 309–10. For correspondence relating to the ill-fated transfer, see Mansfield to Halleck, Sept. 5, 1862, *OR* 18:385–86; Special Orders, no. 229, War Dept. A.G.O., Sept. 8, 1862, ibid., 387.
69. See Hennessy, *Return,* for an excellent account of this engagement.

70. Cavanaugh, *6th Virginia*, 80, 109, 115. See also Appendix C.
71. MAJKR to AMR, Friday evening, RFP.
72. See, for example, the MacClenny Papers, UVA.
73. MAJKR to AMR, Aug. 1, 1862, RFP.
74. MAJKR to AMR, Friday morning, ibid.
75. MAJKR to My Dear Zou, Beach Hill, Sept. 20, 1862, ibid.
76. William Henry Snow to My very dear wife, Camp Suffolk, Va., Sept. 17, 1862, William Henry Snow Papers, SHC-UNC.
77. Alvin Coe Voris to My Dear wife, Suffolk, Va., Nov. 3, 1862, Voris Papers, VHS.
78. Theodore Skinner to Dear parents, Suffolk, Sept. 20, 1862, Theodore W. Skinner Papers, Civil War Miscellaneous Collection, MHI-CB.
79. Woodward, *Memoir*, 63–64.
80. Pollack, *Sketchbook*, 85.
81. Dix to Halleck, Sept. 10, 1862, *OR* 18:388.
82. Halleck to Dix, ibid., 388–89.
83. Dix to Halleck, Sept. 13, 1862, ibid., 392.
84. MAJKR to AMR, Aug. 1, 1862, RFP.

4. A Deserted House

1. Warner, *Blue*, 364–65.
2. Hill, "Reunion," 264.
3. Peck report, May 5, 1863, and Peck to Dix, Sept. 23, 1862, *OR* 18:274–75, 401. Dix considered Peck "a very good officer" and fought to "retain" him before placing him in command at Suffolk (Dix to Halleck, Sept. 5, 1862—4 P.M., ibid., 385).
4. Dix to Halleck, Sept. 20, 1862, ibid., 397; Cullum, *Biographical Register* 2:158–60; *DAB*, s.v. "Peck, John James."
5. Peck to Dix, Sept. 23, 1862, *OR* 18:401. Samuel Perkins Spear was born in Boston in 1815 and served against the Seminole Indians before participating in the Mexican War. Spear rose to the rank of colonel at the end of August 1862.
6. Cronin, *Memoirs*, 172.
7. Peck report, May 5, 1863, *OR* 18:275.
8. Lenfest, *Diary*, 7.
9. Ingalls, *Diary*, 25.
10. Steven Cormier explains the unusual qualities of the road system in the region in his study of the 1863 Suffolk campaign. "On certain wartime maps of Suffolk and in many wartime U.S. accounts, there is confusion between the White Marsh and Edenton Roads, which in turn may confuse the casual student of the campaign. The road closest to the [Dismal] Swamp is correctly called the White Marsh Road, and is so designated by the locals and the Confederates. The Yankees, however, almost invariable called the White Marsh Road, the Edenton Road, probably because that is where the road eventually led, to Edenton, N.C. See the Curtis Map [map 4] for an example of this confusion" (Cormier, *Siege*, 328).
11. See maps 2 and 4.
12. Gordon, *War Diary*, 39–40.

13. Alvin Coe Voris to My Dear Wife, Coles Island, S.C., April 12, 1863, Voris Papers, VHS.
14. Dix to Halleck, May 23, 1863, *OR* 18:269.
15. Dix to S. P. Lee, Sept. 24, 1862, *ORN* 8:104–5.
16. Lee to C. W. Flusser, Sept. 24, 1862, ibid., 105.
17. Flusser to S. P. Lee, Sept. 26, 1862, ibid., 106.
18. Dix to S. P. Lee, Oct. 5, 1862, ibid.
19. Flusser report, Oct. 6, 1862, ibid., 108–9; Geo. W. Gale enclosure, Oct. 3, 1862, ibid., 109; *Confederate Veteran* 27 (Aug. 8, 1919): 305.
20. Flusser report, Oct. 6, 1862, *ORN* 8:108–9.
21. Roske and Van Doren, *Lincoln's Commando,* 128.
22. Edmund R. Colhoun report, Oct. 6, 1862, *ORN* 8:110–11.
23. Charles A. French report, Oct. 4, 1862, ibid., 111.
24. *Confederate Veteran* 27 (Aug. 8, 1919): 305.
25. Flusser report, Oct. 13, 1862, *ORN* 8:113.
26. Dix to Lee, Oct. 5, 1862, ibid., 106–7.
27. See, for example, Dix to Halleck, Oct. 3, 1862, to Halleck, Oct. 5, 1862, various reports, Peck to Dix, Oct. 4, 1862, Peck to Van Buren, Oct. 9, 1862, Marshall to French, Oct. 4, 1862, Dix to Halleck, Oct. 27, 1862, Peck to Dix, Nov. 2, 1862, *OR* 18:15–20; Lenfest, *Diary,* 7–8; *Eleventh Pennsylvania Cavalry,* 53; Bowen, *First New York Dragoons,* 48–50.
28. Jennie Boykin to Annie, n.d., RFP.
29. Voris to My Dear Wife, Camp Suffolk, Va., Dec. 14, 1862, Voris Papers, VHS.
30. *Eleventh Pennsylvania Cavalry,* 187.
31. *Quiet Regiment,* 11.
32. *Eleventh Pennsylvania Cavalry,* 187.
33. Quoted in Mitchell, *Civil War Soldiers,* 131.
34. William Henry Snow to My very dear wife, Camp Suffolk, Va., Nov. 2, 1862, Snow Papers, SHC-UNC.
35. Pardon Papers, Jan.–June 1863, Executive Papers, Governor John Letcher, LVA.
36. Dennis E. Frye, "South Mountain, Maryland (MD002) Washington and Frederick Counties, September 14, 1862," in Kennedy, *Guide,* 115–17.
37. Trask, *16th Virginia,* 96, 117. See Appendix C for a listing of casualties.
38. Wallace, *3rd Virginia,* 31, 108. See also Sears, *Landscape,* for a recent study of this engagement.
39. Crofts, *Southampton,* 176–77, 189; Cobb Diary, "Munday 4 [Feb.]"
40. Tommie to AMR, Camp near Winchester, Oct. 2, 1862, RFP.
41. Euclid Borland to AMR, in the woods six miles north of Winchester, Oct. 15, 1862, ibid.
42. Mills Riddick to AMR, Camp near Winchester, Oct. 19, 1862, ibid.
43. A. C. Myers to My Dearest Wife, on picket 7 miles above Franklin, Va., on the banks of the Blackwater, Nov. 3, 1862, A. C. Myers Correspondence, 1862–1864, Private Collection, NCDHA.

44. Myers to My Dear wife, Black Creek Bridge, Va., Nov. 25, 1862, ibid.

45. S. H. Pulliam to My dear Aunt, Jan. 19, 1863, Samuel Harper Pulliam Papers, VHS.

46. Pryor to Longstreet, Feb. 27, 1863, James Longstreet Papers, DU.

47. Various receipts for Archibald Riddick and Wiley Riddick, Jan.–Feb. 1863, CPC.

48. Pryor to Longstreet, Feb. 27, 1863, Longstreet Papers, DU.

49. Ibid.

50. Hyde, *One Hundred Twelfth N.Y.*, 17. See also Brown, Crane, and Hubbell, *Twenty-first Connecticut*, 107.

51. Boots, "Letters," 207.

52. Bowen, *First New York Dragoons*, 22; *Eleventh Pennsylvania Cavalry*, 71.

53. Thompson, *Thirteenth New Hampshire*, 130.

54. Voris to My Dear Wife, Camp Suffolk, Va., Dec. 24, 1862, Voris Papers, VHS.

55. Hyde, *One Hundred Twelfth N.Y.*, 17.

56. Ingalls, *Diary*, 6. For this soldier's frequent references to fatigue duty, see ibid., 6–49.

57. Ibid., 35.

58. Wallace, *3rd Virginia*, 108.

59. Dix report, Oct. 3, 1862—9:30 P.M., *OR* 18:15.

60. Peck reports, Oct. 4, 9, 1862, ibid., 16–18.

61. "Ruff" [Nate Lampheur] to D[ea]r Sister and Brother, 130th N.Y. Vols., Suffolk, Va., Oct. 3, 1862, additional note of Oct. 4, 8 P.M., Nate Lampheur Papers, DU.

62. Lenfest, *Diary*, 7.

63. Hanson, *Sixth Massachusetts*, 171.

64. Ibid., 173.

65. Dobie to My dear Friend Hattie, April 18, 1864, David F. Dobie Letters, UVA.

66. Hanson, *Sixth Massachusetts*, 173.

67. Voris to My Dear Lydia, Suffolk, Va., Oct. 12, 1862, Voris Papers, VHS.

68. *Eleventh Pennsylvania Cavalry*, 50–51; Dix reports, Oct. 3, 1862—9:30 P.M., Oct. 5, 1862—12:46 p.m., Oct. 7, 1862, *OR* 18:15–16.

69. "Ruff" to D[ea]r Sister and Brother, Oct. 4, 1862, 8 P.M. note, Nate Lampheur Papers, DU.

70. Log of USS *Stepping Stones*, Ship Logbooks, NA.

71. Ingalls, *Diary*, 12, 23.

72. "Ruff" to Dear Friends, Suffolk, Va., Nov. 2, 1862, Nate Lampheur Papers, DU.

73. Zephaniah Gooding to Dear Brother, Suffolk, Va., Oct. 29, 1862, Zephaniah Gooding Papers, DU.

74. Jennie Boykin to AMR, n.d., RFP.

75. "Ruff" to Dear Friends, Suffolk, Va., Nov. 2, 1862, Nate Lampheur Papers, DU.

76. "Ruff" to Dear Sister and Brother, Hd. Qrs. 130th N.Y. Vols., Suffolk, Va., Nov. 9, 1862, ibid.

77. Voris to My Dear Wife, Suffolk, Va., Nov. 17, 1862, Voris Papers, VHS.

78. Ibid., Suffolk, Va., Nov. 20, 1862.

79. Lenfest, *Diary*, 10–11.

80. Dix reports, Dec. 2, 4, 1862, *OR* 18:35–36; *Eleventh Pennsylvania Cavalry*, 53–55;

Ingalls, *Diary,* 23. See also Isaac S. Varnum to ——, Camp Suffolk, [Dec.] 7, 1862, Varnum Family Papers, Civil War Miscellaneous Collection, MHI-CB; Wallace, *Surry Light Artillery,* 74–75.

81. Lenfest, *Diary,* 11.
82. O. S. Ferry report, Dec. 23, 1862, *OR* 18:123; *Daily Richmond Examiner,* Dec. 25, 1862.
83. Quoted in *Daily Richmond Examiner,* Dec. 31, 1862.
84. Lenfest, *Diary,* 13; Ingalls, *Diary,* 28.
85. Voris to Wife, "Christmas in Camp," Dec. 24, 1862, Voris Papers, VHS.
86. Ibid., New Bern, N.C., Jan. 7, 1863.
87. Peck makes reference to Pryor's boast in Peck to Dix, Jan. 10, 1863, *OR* 18:511.
88. Ingalls, *Diary,* 31.   89. Ibid.   90. Ibid., 31, 34.
91. Dix to Peck, Jan. 18, 1863, *OR* 18:521.
92. Log of USS *Stepping Stones,* Ship Logbooks, NA.
93. Pryor to Smith, Jan. 6, 1863, *OR* 18:846.
94. Pryor report, Feb. 4, 1863, ibid., 142.
95. Peck report, Feb. 4, 1863, ibid., 132.
96. Cavanaugh, *Meagher,* 352–53; Warner, *Blue,* 93.
97. Jones, *Irish Brigade,* 16.
98. Ibid., 17–18.
99. Ibid., 18, 75–76, 87, 134–35; Warner, *Blue,* 93–94; Cavanaugh, *Meagher,* 402–5; Lonn, *Foreigners,* 200–201.
100. Peck report, Feb. 4, 1863, Corcoran report, Feb. 1, 1863, *OR* 18:132, 136, 139; Bowen, *First New York Dragoons,* 59; Hanson, *Sixth Massachusetts,* 199–200.
101. Pryor report, Feb. 4, 1863, *OR* 18:143.
102. Quoted in Weaver, *63rd Virginia,* 27–28.
103. Ibid., 28; see also Sherwood and Weaver, *54th Virginia,* 64.
104. Moore, *Rebellion Record,* 405–7.
105. See, for example, McPherson, *Battle Cry,* 520, which discusses the effects of the phenomenon "acoustic shadow" during the battle of Perryville in 1862.
106. Pryor report, Feb. 4, 1863, *OR* 18:142.
107. Peck report, Feb. 4, 1863, Corcoran report, Feb. 1, 1863, ibid., 132–33, 136.
108. Bowen, *First New York Dragoons,* 59–60; Lenfest, *Diary,* 18.
109. Bowen, *First New York Dragoons,* 60–61.
110. Lenfest, *Diary,* 18–19.
111. Chapla, *50th Virginia,* 64, 129, 179, 181.
112. Quoted in Sherwood and Weaver, *54th Virginia,* 63–65.
113. Quoted in Chapla, *50th Virginia,* 64.
114. Corcoran report, Feb. 1, 1863, *OR* 18:136–37.
115. Ibid.
116. Ibid., 137.
117. Bowen, *First New York Dragoons,* 60–61.
118. Pryor report, Feb. 4, 1863, *OR* 18:143.
119. Quoted in Chapla, *50th Virginia,* 64.
120. Peck report, Feb. 4, 1863, Dix to Halleck, Jan. 30, 1863, French endorsement, Feb.

10, 1863, in Pryor report, Feb. 4, 1863, *OR* 18:134–35, 531, 145; Moore, *Rebellion Record*, 405–7.

121. Peck report, Feb. 4, 1863, Corcoran report, Feb. 1, 1863, French endorsement, Feb. 10, 1863, in Pryor report, Feb. 4, 1863, *OR* 18:134–35, 139, 145.

122. Lincoln, *Collected Works* 6:84.

123. Quoted in Sherwood and Weaver, *54th Virginia*, 63.

5. *A Winter of Discontent*

1. Peck to Dix, Feb. 3, 1863, and Peck report, Feb. 4, 1863, *OR* 18:534, 134–35.

2. Peck report, May 5, 1863, ibid., 275.

3. "The Battle of Deserted House or Kelly's Store," MacClenny Papers, UVA.

4. Cobb Diary, "1863 Sunday 1st [Feb.]"

5. Jordan, *Black Confederates*, 256.

6. See Hofstadter, *Great Issues*, 411–13.

7. Jordan, *Black Confederates*, 262; Schwarz, *Slave Laws in Virginia*, 147.

8. Rufus M. Riddick, William H. Riddick, Gates, N.C., Jan. 18–Feb. 21, 1863, CPC.

9. Current, *Lincoln's Loyalists*, 24–26.

10. Johnston, *Virginia Railroads*, 119.

11. Viele to Wardrop, Jan. 16, 1863, Thomas Shepard Seabury Papers, UVA.

12. Woodward, *Memoir*, 70.

13. Ibid., 85; Robert Hatchman to Dear Friend Charles, Camp Dodge, Suffolk, Va., Mar. 20, 1863, author's collection.

14. Log of USS *Stepping Stones*, Feb. 26, 1863, Ship Logbooks, NA.

15. Butts, *Reminiscences*, 9, 10–11.

16. Dix to Halleck, Sept. 20, 1862, *OR* 18:396; Johnston, *Virginia Railroads*, 142.

17. Pulliam to My dear Aunt, Jan. 19, 1863, Samuel Harper Pulliam Papers, VHS.

18. Denny, *Prisons*, 90.

19. Pulliam to My dear Aunt, Jan. 19, 1863, Samuel Harper Pulliam Papers, VHS.

20. Peck report, May 5, 1863, Peck to Dix, Feb. 11, 12, 1863, *OR* 18:536–38. For Confederate reaction, see Lee to Seddon, Feb. 14, 1863, Seddon to Lee, Feb. 15, 16, 17, 1863, ibid., 876–77, 879, 882–83.

21. Lee to Seddon, Feb. 14, 1863, ibid., 876–77.

22. Seddon to Lee, Feb. 15, 1863, ibid., 877.

23. Ibid., 877–78.

24. Lee to Seddon, Feb. 15, 1863, ibid., vol. 25, pt. 2, p. 624.

25. Lee to Seddon, Feb. 16, 1863, ibid., 18:880.

26. Seddon to Lee, Feb. 17, 1863, ibid., 882.

27. Lee to Longstreet, Feb. 18, 1863, ibid., 883–84, and ibid., vol. 25, pt. 2, p. 632.

28. Eliot, *West Point in the Confederacy*, 4–5.

29. Longstreet, *Lee and Longstreet*, 98–100.

30. Ibid., 214.

31. Eckenrode and Conrad, *Longstreet*, 10.

32. Sorrel, *Recollections*, 23–24, 37–38.

33. Freeman, *Lieutenants* 1:xliv.

34. Pollard, *Lee,* 419.
35. Sorrel, *Recollections,* 26.
36. Fremantle, *Diary,* 218.
37. Longstreet, *Lee and Longstreet,* 215; Warner, *Gray,* 192–93.
38. Sorrel, *Recollections,* 54. For an excellent recent biography of Pickett, see Gordon, *Pickett.*
39. Patterson, "Pickett," 19.
40. Sorrel, *Recollections,* 54.
41. Eliot, *West Point in the Confederacy,* 5, Patterson, "Pickett," 19; Sadlow, "Pickett," 3–8.
42. Longstreet, *Lee and Longstreet,* 158–59; Gordon, *Pickett,* 26–28.
43. Freeman, *Lieutenants* 2:491; Gordon, *Pickett,* 34–35.
44. Warner, *Gray,* 239; Gordon, *Pickett,* 42–95.
45. Pickett, *What Happened to Me,* 110–12.
46. "Widow of General Pickett."
47. Pickett, *Soldier,* 33; Pickett, *Heart,* 70.
48. Pollard, *Lee,* 673; Steiner, *Medical-Military Portraits,* 217; Davis, *Chaplain Davis,* 149.
49. O'Conner, *Hood,* 89–90.
50. McMurry, *Hood,* 9.
51. McMurry, "Rise," 47.
52. O'Conner, *Hood,* 41–42; Dyer, *Gallant Hood,* 163–66.
53. McMurry, *Hood,* 68–69.
54. Chestnut, *Chestnut's Civil War,* 442–43.
55. Cooper to Longstreet, Feb. 25, 1863, and General Orders, No. 34, A.I.G.O., April 1, 1863, *OR* 18:895, 953; Freeman, *Lee* 2:499. Longstreet assumed command of the department after Maj. Gen. Gustavus W. Smith resigned in mid-February 1863.
56. General Orders, No. 34, A.I.G.O., April 1, 1863, *OR* 18:953; Freeman, *Lieutenants* 2:469. See also Bridges, *Maverick General,* 166–79.
57. See, for example, Jones, *Diary,* 152, 159–60; Kean, *Diary,* 41–43.
58. Thomas, *Confederate Nation,* 202–6; Thomas, *Richmond,* 119–21; Thomas, "Bread Riot." See also Furgurson, *Ashes,* 193–96.
59. Pender, *General to His Lady,* 219.
60. Lee to Seddon, Jan. 1863, *OR,* vol. 25, pt. 2, p. 597.
61. Goff, *Supply,* 67.
62. Simpson, *Hood's Texas Brigade,* 189–90.
63. See, for example, Lee to Imboden, *OR,* vol. 25, pt. 2, p. 712.
64. Goff, *Supply,* 72–74.
65. Lee to Seddon, Feb. 2, 1863, *OR,* vol. 25, pt. 2, p. 604.
66. Sanger and Hay, *Longstreet,* 121–22.
67. Seddon to Lee, Feb. 22, 1863, *OR* 18:890.
68. Lee, *Recollections,* 92.
69. Lee to Davis, April 16, 1863, *OR,* vol. 25, pt. 2, p. 725.

6. *The "War Horse" Jockeys for Provisions*

1. Lee to Longstreet, March 16, 1863, *OR* 18:921–22.
2. Longstreet to Lee, March 17, 1863, ibid., 923–24.
3. Longstreet to Lee, March 19, 1863, ibid., 926–27.
4. Withers to Longstreet, March 19, 1863, Lee to Longstreet, March 18, 1863, ibid., 927; Simpson, *Hood's Texas Brigade*, 220–22; Chestnut, *Chestnut's Civil War*, 441–43; Simpson, *Gaines' Mill*, 121; Polley, *Hood's Texas Brigade*, 141–43; Collier, *Third Arkansas*, 114; Vaughan, "Diary," 575–76; McClendon, *Recollections*, 171; Polk, *Review*, 23.
5. A variety of historians and biographers have asked such questions. For example, see Eckenrode and Conrad, *Longstreet*, 151–67; Freeman, *Lee* 2:325.
6. Longstreet, *Memoirs*, 158–59.
7. For recent assessments of the relationship between Lee and Longstreet, see Thomas, *Lee*, 247, 279–80; Wert, *Longstreet*, 206–7.
8. Pollard, *Lee*, 420.
9. Fremantle, *Diary*, 198.
10. Sorrel, *Recollections*, 76.
11. See Sutherland, *Fredericksburg and Chancellorsville*.
12. Eckenrode and Conrad, *Longstreet*, 151–67.
13. Freeman, *Lee* 3:5–6.   15. Thomas, *Lee*, 277.
14. Ibid., 2:502–3.   16. Ibid., 278.
17. Longstreet to Lee, March 19, 1863, *OR* 18:926.
18. Longstreet to Lee, March 19, 21, 1863, Lee to Longstreet, March 21, 1863, ibid., 927, 933–34.
19. Longstreet to Lee, March 21, 1863, ibid., 933.
20. Lee to Longstreet, March 21, 1863, ibid., 933–34.
21. Lenfest, *Diary*, 23.
22. Ibid., 24.
23. Ferguson, *Occupation*, 6.
24. Peck to Dix, March 6, 1863, *OR* 18:552.
25. Dix to Peck, Feb. 13, 1863, ibid., 538.
26. Peck to Dix, March 17, 1863, ibid., 562.
27. Dix to Peck, March 17, 1863, ibid., 561.
28. Spear report, March 18, 1863, ibid., 200.
29. Boulware Diary, "Tuesday 17th [1863]," LVA.
30. J. R. Boulware to Brother Bill, Camp on Blackwater River, Va., March 11, 1863, James Richmond Boulware Papers, LVA.
31. John M. White to Dear Sister Martha, Camp on Blackwater, Va., March 22, 1863, MOC.
32. *Eleventh Pennsylvania Cavalry*, 62.
33. White to Dear Sister Martha, March 22, 1863, MOC.
34. Spear report, March 18, 1863, *OR* 18:200–201.

35. Dix to Halleck, March 18, 1863—8:30 P.M., ibid., 563.

36. Spear report, March 18, 1863, ibid., 201.

37. John Habberton Diary, March 1863, John Habberton Papers, Civil War Miscellaneous Collection, MHI-CB.

38. Thompson, *Thirteenth New Hampshire,* 118–19.

39. Ferguson, *Occupation,* 6.

40. Eva to My dear Sister, Chuckatuck, March 9, 1863, MacClenny Papers, UVA.

41. Peck to Dix, March 12, 1863, *OR* 18:558.

42. Thompson, *Thirteenth New Hampshire,* 120.

43. Jenkins to Longstreet, March 24, 1863, *OR* 18:941.

44. Peck to Dix, March 31, 1863, ibid., 573.

45. Ferguson, *Occupation,* 7.

46. Ibid.

47. Cronin, *Memoirs,* 168–71.

48. Peck to Dix, March 30, 1863, *OR* 18:571.

49. Cronin, *Memoirs,* 168–71.

50. Longstreet to Lee, March 24, 1863, *OR* 18:942.

51. Wert, *Longstreet,* 206–7; Thomas, *Lee,* 279–80.

52. Lee to Longstreet, March 27, 1863, *OR* 18:943–944.

53. Longstreet to Lee, March 27, 1863, ibid., 944.

54. John Bratton to Dear Wife, March 2, 1863, John Bratton Papers, EU; Boulware Diary, March 9–10, 1863, LVA; George Newton Wise Diary, March 23–25, 1863, DU; Warfield, *Memoirs,* 143; Wise, *Seventeenth Virginia,* 137; Krick, *30th Virginia,* 35–36; Griggs, "Thirty-eight Virginia," 252; Coker, *Company G, Ninth S.C., and Company E, Sixth S.C.,* 119.

55. Thompson, *Thirteenth New Hampshire,* 119, 122–23; Jones, *Diary,* 177–78.

56. Louis (Lewis) Henry Webb Diary, March 22, 25, 1863, Louis (Lewis) Henry Webb Papers, SHC-UNC.

57. John M. White to Dear Sister Martha, Weldon, N.C., June 16, 1863, MOC.

58. Holzman, *Adapt or Perish,* 71–72.

59. Jenkins to Longstreet, March 24, 1863, *OR* 18:940.

60. Jenkins to Longstreet, March 28, 1863, ibid., 946.

61. See, for example, Lee to Longstreet, March 28, 1863, Longstreet to Lee, March 29, 1863, French to Longstreet, March 29, 1863, Lee to Longstreet, March 30, 1863, Longstreet to Lee, March 30, 1863, Longstreet to Hill, March 30, 1863, Longstreet to Whiting, March 30, 1863, Lee to Longstreet, March 30, 1863, Elzey to Longstreet, April 1, 1863, *OR* 18:946, 948, 906–7, 948–50, 953; Lee to Davis, April 2, 1863, ibid., vol. 25, pt. 2, p. 700; Lee to Longstreet, April 2, 1863, Longstreet to Lee, April 3, 1863, ibid., 18:954, 958; Lee to Davis, April 4, 1863, ibid., vol. 25, pt. 2, pp. 702–703; Lee to Longstreet, April 6, 1863, ibid., 18:966.

62. Lee to Longstreet, April 2, 1863, ibid., 18:954.

63. Longstreet to Lee, April 3, 1863, ibid., 959. For correspondence concerning the C.S. Navy, see Longstreet to Lee, March 27, 1863, 30, April 3, 1863, Longstreet to

Seddon, April 6, 1863, Seddon to Longstreet, April 7, 1863, Lee to Seddon, April 9, 1863, Longstreet to Seddon, April 17, 1863, Seddon to Longstreet, April 18, 1863, Longstreet to Seddon, April 1863, Gilmer to Seddon, April 20, 1863, ibid., 944, 950, 959, 960, 967–68, 974, 996–97, 999, 1002, 1008–9.

64. Lee to Longstreet, March 27, 1863, ibid., 944. One member of the Confederate War Department had particular insight into the problems with naval cooperation that confronted Longstreet. On April 12 R. G. H. Kean noted in his diary: "The engineers oppose making an opening in the obstructions to allow the *Richmond* to pass. The matter is referred to the President but progresses very slowly. Nothing is likely to come of it, I think" (Kean, *Diary,* 50).

65. Longstreet to Lee, April 4, 1863, *OR* 18:959–60.

66. Lee to Longstreet, April 6, 1863, ibid., 967.

67. Longstreet to Lee, April 3, 1863, ibid., 958–59.

68. Ibid., 959.

69. Jenkins to Longstreet, April 6, 1863, ibid., 963.

70. Longstreet to Jenkins, April 6, 1863, ibid.

71. Pickett to Longstreet, April 6, 1863, ibid., 967.

72. Seddon to Longstreet, April 7, 1863, ibid., 967–68. R. G. H. Kean believed that Longstreet was fortunate not to receive naval cooperation. On April 19 he wrote, "The *Richmond* is such a stupid failure, drawing fourteen feet of water [so] that she cannot get up or down the river even if the obstructions were opened to let her pass; and as she can only steam about three knots being worthless as a ram and her machinery [so] very defective, it is deemed unsafe for her to go down" (Kean, *Diary,* 52).

73. Longstreet to Lee, April 7, 1863, *OR* 18:969–70.

74. Lee to Seddon, April 9, 1863, ibid., 974.

75. Peck to Dix, Feb. 20, 1863, ibid., 542.

76. Dix to Halleck, March 2, 1863, ibid., 549.

77. Peck to Dix, March 4, 1863, ibid., 551.

78. Dix to Halleck, March 4, 1863, ibid., 551.

79. Peck to Dix, March 5, 1863, ibid., 551–552.

80. Peck to Dix, March 11, 12, 1863, ibid., 556, 557.

81. Dix to Halleck, March 13, 1863—11 A.M., to Kelton, March 27, 1863, ibid., 558, 570. For examples of Peck's state of alertness, see Peck to Dix, March 17, 1863, Dix to Halleck, March 18, 1863, Peck to Dix, March 21, 28, 1863, Peck to Hooker, April 4, 7, 1863, ibid., 562, 563, 566, 571, 582–83, 586.

82. Thomas L. Bailey to Dear Nellie, Banks of the Nansemond River, Friday, April 3, 1863, Thomas L. Bailey Papers, Northwest Corner Civil War Round Table Collection, MHI-CB.

83. Cullum, *Biographical Register,* 41–42; Warner, *Blue,* 170–71; *DAB,* s.v. "Getty, George Washington"; Stackpole, *Drama,* 202, 216.

84. Peck report, May 5, 1863, *OR* 18:275.

85. Brown, Crane, and Hubbell, *Twenty-first Connecticut,* 109. Peck was in the process of shipping reinforcements to North Carolina when he received information con-

cerning Longstreet's advance that caused him to reverse this action. He immediately recalled the troops from the train upon which they had embarked.

86. For information on these campaigns in relationship to Longstreet's in Virginia, see Cormier, *Siege*.

87. Longstreet to Jenkins, April 6, 1863, *OR* 18:963.

88. Longstreet to Whiting, April 8, 1863, Sorrel to Hill, April 9, 1863, ibid., 974, 975.

89. Warner, *Blue*, 93–94; Freeman, *Lieutenants* 2:472.

90. Freeman, *Lieutenants* 2:472; French, *Autobiography*, 160. To French, Robert E. Lee represented the consummate professional soldier. He praised Lee as "ever a gentleman, and considerate of everyone" (ibid., 150).

91. Thompson, *Thirteenth New Hampshire*, 125.

92. See, for example, Peck to Dix, Feb. 20, 1863, *OR* 18:542.

93. Longstreet to Seddon, April 10, 1863, ibid., 977.

94. Wallace, *Glencoe Diary*, 25.

95. Vaughan, "Diary," 578.

96. Boulware Diary, April 10–11, 1863, LVA; Wise Diary, April 10–11, 1863, DU; Osman Latrobe Diary, April 11–12, 1863, VHS; E. P. Reeve to My precious Wife, April 16, 1863, Edward Payson Reeve Papers, SHC-UNC; Armistead Burwell to My dear Sister, Near Suffolk, Va., April 20, 1863, Burwell Family Papers, VHS.

97. Trask, *9th Virginia*, 88.

7. *The War Hits Home*

1. Davis report, May 8, 1863, *OR* 18:273.

2. Cronin, *Memoirs*, 177; Thompson, *Thirteenth New Hampshire*, 127; Butts, *Reminiscences*, 15.

3. Corell, *99th New York*, 11.

4. Getty report, May 12, 1863, *OR* 18:301; Stevens, "Siege," 205.

5. Getty report, May 12, 1863, *OR* 18:301.

6. Stevens, "Siege," 205.

7. Cormier, *Siege*, 89.

8. McPherson and McPherson, *Lamson*, 94.

9. Dyer, *Compendium*, vol. 2, pt. 3, p. 1444.

10. Stevens, "Siege," 200; Butts, *Reminiscences*, 8; Osbon, *Handbook*, 11, 249; Merrifield, "Seaboard War," 274, 279.

11. See, for example, Van Buren to S. P. Lee, April 11, 13, 1863, *OR* 18:597, 603.

12. S. P. Lee to Keyes, April 11, 1863, *ORN* 8:712.

13. McPherson and McPherson, *Lamson*, 94.

14. Peck to John G. Foster, Oct. 12, 1863–7 P.M., *OR* 18:301. Although it is uncertain exactly what happened to John Peck at Suffolk in 1863, it is clear that a riding mishap incapacitated him for several months and haunted him for the remainder of his life. In 1871 B. B. Foster sent Peck a note which made reference to the general's continued poor health: "I was unprepared to learn, as I did from your letter, that you have suffered so severely in health and are still at a distance from recovery" (Foster to Peck, Norfolk, Va., March 24, 1871, John James Peck Papers, USMA-WP).

15. H. J. H. Thompson to Wife, April 11, 1863, Henry J. H. Thompson Papers, DU.

16. Hyde, *One Hundred Twelfth N.Y.*, 29.

17. Ferguson, *Occupation*, 8–10.

18. Ibid., 10.

19. The Richmond *Sentinel*, June 11, 1863, listed the houses burned in the area during the Suffolk campaign. See also *Quiet Regiment*, 13, which quotes the Petersburg *Express*, May 1863; Ferguson, *Occupation*, 8, 13; Butts, *Reminiscences*, 16; Thompson, *Thirteenth New Hampshire*, 128.

20. Peck report, May 5, 1863, *OR* 18:275; Wise Diary, April 11, 1863, DU; Reeve to My Precious Wife, April 16, 1863, Edward Payson Reeve Papers, SHC-UNC.

21. Butts, *Reminiscences*, 15–16.

22. Thompson, *Thirteenth New Hampshire*, 132; Thorpe, *Fifteenth Connecticut*, 45; Blakeslee, *Sixteenth Connecticut*, 34.

23. Bowen, *First New York Dragoons*, 71.

24. Lee to Welles, April 12, 1863, *ORN* 8:714–15.

25. Osbon, *Handbook*, 30, 145; Merrifield, "Seaboard War," 275, 277.

26. *DAB*, s.v. "Lee, Samuel Phillips"; Merrifield, "Seaboard War," 142–45.

27. Parker, *Chautauqua Boy*, 66.

28. Ibid., 68–69; *DAB*, s.v. "Cushing, William Barker"; McCartney, *Lincoln's Admirals*, 200.

29. *DAB*, s.v. "Cushing, William Barker"; see also Roske and Van Doren, *Lincoln's Commando*; Edwards, *Cushing*.

30. Roske and Van Doren, *Lincoln's Commando*, 151.

31. "Naval Hero Dies," *Portland Morning Oregonian*, Aug. 15, 1903.

32. Roske and Van Doren, *Lincoln's Commando*, 154; Edwards, *Cushing*, 134.

33. Porter, *Naval History*, 419.

34. S. P. Lee to Cushing and Lamson, April 13, 1863, *ORN* 8:717.

35. S. P. Lee to Cushing and Lamson, April 12, 1863, ibid., 713–14.

36. Lamson to S. P. Lee, April 12, 13, 1863, ibid., 716, 718; Butts, *Reminiscences*, 26–27. The pilot was crucial to the successful navigation of the twisting channel of the Nansemond. Consequently, the pilothouse became a favorite target of Confederate marksmen and artillerists.

37. Thompson, *Thirteenth New Hampshire*, 127. Thompson kept a good record of the daily weather conditions in the Suffolk vicinity.

38. Wise Diary, April 12, 1863, DU; Boulware Diary, April 12, 1863, LVA; Wise, *Seventeenth Virginia*, 140–41; Peck report, May 5, 1863, *OR* 18:275.

39. Graham, *Ninth New York*, 410–11; Whitney, *Hawkins Zouaves*, 174; Johnson, *Long Roll*, 227–28.

40. Graham, *Ninth New York*, 411–15; Whitney, *Hawkins Zouaves*, 175–77; Johnson, *Long Roll*, 228; *New York Times*, April 16, 1863.

41. Wightman, *Letters*, 125.

42. "An Incident at Suffolk," comp. Charles L. English, George W. Griggs Manuscript, Norwich Civil War Round Table Collection, MHI-CB.

43. Graham, *Ninth New York*, 419.

44. Johnson, *Long Roll,* 229.

45. Lamson to S. P. Lee, April 22, 1863, *ORN* 8:722–25; Butts, *Reminiscences,* 20–27.

46. French, *Autobiography,* 160–61.

47. Ibid., 161; Special Orders, *OR* 18:988; Freeman, *Lieutenants,* 482–83.

48. Latrobe Diary, April 13, 1863, VHS; Lamson to S. P. Lee, April 22, 1863, *ORN* 8:723; Butts, *Reminiscences,* 21; Stevens, "Siege," 206–7.

49. Hobbs, *Storm over Suffolk,* 19–20; see also Cormier, *Siege,* 218–21, which offers several explanations for the tragedy.

50. Thompson to Wife, Apr. 14, 63, Henry J. H. Thompson Papers, DU.

51. *Eleventh Pennsylvania Cavalry,* 66.

52. Ibid.

53. *Quiet Regiment,* 5, 38; Ferguson, *Occupation,* 10; Cormier, *Siege,* 373.

54. *Quiet Regiment,* 8.

55. *Eleventh Pennsylvania Cavalry,* 69.

56. Butts, *Reminiscences,* 22.

57. Roske and Van Doren, *Lincoln's Commando,* 153–54; Edwards, *Cushing,* 132–33.

58. Lamson to S. P. Lee, April 22, 1863, *ORN* 8:722–25; Butts, *Reminiscences,* 20–27.

59. Quoted in McPherson and McPherson, *Lamson,* 96.

60 "General Longstreet's Hd. Qrs. Are at the level plateau beyond the Petersburg R.R. where the Portsmouth R.R. crosses. None of the Confed. Genls. stay in houses, all occupy tents" (Onderdonk to B. B. Foster, April 28, 1863, John James Peck Papers, USMA-WP). Cormier suggests that the officers' use of tents indicates the influence of General Lee and his habits upon Longstreet and his subordinates (Cormier, *Siege,* 354).

61. See, for example, Sorrel to Benning, April 13, 1863, Henry Lewis Benning Papers, SHC-UNC; Sorrel to Benning, April 19–May 2, 1863, *OR,* vol. 51, pt. 2, pp. 691, 693–94, 695, 696, 697, 699, 700–701.

8. A "Knight" in Suffolk

1. Trask, *9th Virginia,* 22–23, 88.

2. N. B. Haines to Mrs. N. Riddick (MAJKR), n.d., RFP.

3. Trask, *9th Virginia,* 95.

4. Petersburg *Daily Express,* April 16, 1863.

5. Corcoran report, May 1863, Patton report, April 18, 1863, Itinerary of the Third Brigade, April 9, May 3, Dodge report, May 7, 1863, *OR* 18:289, 291–92, 296, 299–300; Wise, *Seventeenth Virginia,* 141–42; Warfield, *Memoirs,* 145.

6. Corcoran report, May 1863, R. S. Foster report, April 18, 1863, *OR* 18:289, 293; Spear to B. B. Foster, April 17, 1863, John James Peck Papers, USMA-WP.

7. Pickett, *Heart,* 74.

8. Pickett, *What Happened to Me,* 121. For a recent assessment of this impassioned relationship, see Gordon, *Pickett.*

9. Young and Young, *56th Virginia,* 74.

10. Sorrel, *Recollections,* 155–56.

11. Ibid.

12. Hunton, *Autobiography*, 84–85.

13. Gordon, *Pickett*, 99.

14. Getty report, May 12, 1863, *OR* 18:302–3.

15. See, for example, Peck to Halleck, April 16, 1863, Peck to Dix, April 16, 1863, ibid., 619, 620.

16. Getty report, May 12, 1863, ibid., 303, 307; Thompson, *Thirteenth New Hampshire*, 128; Henry E. Simmons to Anna, April 19, 1863, Papers, SHC-UNC; Foster, *New Jersey*, 531–32.

17. Davis report, May 9, 1863, *OR* 18:274.

18. S. P. Lee to Welles, April 16, 1863, *ORN* 8:729–30.

19. Lamson to S. P. Lee, April 17, 1863, ibid., 732–33.

20. French report, April 22, 1863, *OR* 18:324; French, *Autobiography*, 161.

21. Cushing to Lee, April 17, 1863, *ORN* 8:734; French to Myers, April 19, 1863, *OR*, vol. 51, pt. 2, p. 691; S. P. Lee to Welles, April 22, 1863, *ORN* 8:765; Washington, D.C., *Evening Star*, April 20, 1863.

22. Longstreet to French, April 17, 1863, *ORN* 8:795.

23. Coker, *Company G, Ninth S.C., and Company E, Sixth S.C.*, 120–22. See also Mixson, *Reminiscences*, 40–41.

24. Bratton to Dear Wife, April 20, 1863, John Bratton Papers, EU.

25. Stribling report, May 6, 1863, *OR* 18:336.

26. Vaughan, "Diary," 580.

27. Bratton to Bettie, April 19, 1863, John Bratton Papers, EU.

28. Longstreet to French, April 19, 1863, *OR* 18:1001.

29. French to Shumaker, April 19, 1863, ibid., 328.

30. French report, April 22, 1863, French to Shumaker, April 19, 1863, ibid., 325, 328.

31. Longstreet to French, April 19, 1863, ibid., 1001.

32. French to Shumaker, April 19, 1863, ibid., 328.

33. French report, April 22, 1863, Special Orders, No. 3, April 17, 1863, Sorrel to French, April 17, 1863, Connally report, April 22, 1863, Cunningham endorsement, April 22, 1863, Shumaker report, April 21, 1863, ibid., 325, 327, 998, 338, 340, 332.

34. Connally report, April 22, 1863, ibid., 338.

35. Lamson to S. P. Lee, April 18, 1863, *ORN* 8:739. The first two efforts by Lamson to help in the execution of a coordinated attack upon the Hill's Point Battery came on the nights of April 16–17 and 18–19. Both attempts failed when coordination between the army and navy broke down, causing the attacks to be aborted. See Lamson to S. P. Lee, April 17, 1863, Cushing to S. P. Lee, April 17, 1863, Lamson to S. P. Lee, April 19, 1863, ibid., 732–33, 734–35, 740–41; Stevens, "Siege," 212; Butts, *Reminiscences*, 37–38.

36. Lamson to S. P. Lee, April 17, 1863, *ORN* 8:739.

37. Lamson to S. P. Lee, April 20, 1863, ibid., 740; Getty report, May 12, 1863, *OR* 18:304; Stevens, "Siege," 213–14; Butts, *Reminiscences*, 38–39.

38. Getty to Peck, April 19, 1863, John James Peck Papers, USMA-WP.

39. Getty report, May 12, 1863, *OR* 18:304.

40. Stevens, "Siege," 214–15. Stevens won the Medal of Honor for his part in the Hill's Point assault.
41. French report, April 22, 1863, Gary Carroll report, April 20, 1863, *OR* 18:332, 329.
42. Robert M. Stribling report, May 6, 1863, John A. Jones report, April 19, 1863, ibid., 337.
43. Lamson to S. P. Lee, April 20, 1863, *ORN* 8:747; Getty report, May 12, 1863, *OR* 18:304; Stevens, "Siege," 215–16; Butts, *Reminiscences*, 42.
44. Getty report, May 12, 1863, Stribling report, May 6, 1863, *OR* 18:304, 336; French, *Autobiography*, 162; Stevens, "Siege," 216.
45. Connally report, May 12, 1863, *OR* 18:338–39; Belo, *Memoirs*, 24–25.
46. "A Visit to the Hill's Point, Nansemond County, earthworks, Sept. 7th, 1936," MacClenny Papers, UVA; Laine and Penny, *Law's Alabama Brigade*, 60; Richmond *Enquirer*, April 24, 1863.
47. Sorrel to Lt. Campbell, April 24, 1863, Eli Duvall Collection, MOC.
48. *Brooke, Fauquier, Loudoun, and Alexandria Artillery*, 14–15, 74–77, 106–19.
49. Longstreet to French, April 19, 1863, *OR* 18:1002; French, *Autobiography*, 162.

9. *"Waiting for the Wagons"*

1. French, *Autobiography*, 159–77.
2. Richmond *Daily Examiner*, May 2, 1863.
3. Jones, *Diary*, 192.
4. Edmonston, *Journal*, 386.
5. Oates, *War*, 176–78; Laine and Penny, *Law's Alabama Brigade*, 60.
6. Oates, *War*, 178; Laine and Penny, *Law's Alabama Brigade*, 60; Belo, *Memoirs*, 25–26.
7. Oates, *War*, 178.
8. Laine and Penny, *Law's Alabama Brigade*, 61.
9. *Rome (Ga.) Tri-Weekly Courier*, May 7, 12, 1863.
10. McMurry, *Hood*, 70.
11. Chestnut, *Chestnut's Civil War*, 443.
12. McMurry, "Rise," 42.
13. Hood, *Advance and Retreat*, 52.
14. Hood to Lee, April 29, 1863, *OR*, vol. 51, pt. 2, p. 697; ibid., copy in Charles Scott Venable Papers, SHC-UNC.
15. John Bell Hood to James Longstreet, June 28, 1875, in *Southern Historical Society Papers* 4 (Oct. 1877): 147.
16. U.S. Dept. of the Army, *Medal of Honor*, 123.
17. Stevens, "Siege," 215.
18. S. P. Lee to Cushing, April 19, 1863, *ORN* 8:743.
19. S. P. Lee to Cushing and Lamson, April 20, 1863, Cushing to S. P. Lee, April 20, 1863, ibid., 748–49.
20. Getty report, May 12, 1863, *OR* 18:305.
21. Lamson to S. P. Lee, April 20, 1863, *ORN* 8:749.
22. Lamson to S. P. Lee, April 21, 1863, *OR*, vol. 51, pt. 2, p. 693.

23. T. W. Clements Diary, ca. April 26, 1863, UGA.
24. Sorrel to French, April 21, 1863, *OR* 18:1009–10.
25. French to Sorrel, April 21, 1863, ibid., 1010.
26. Sorrel to French, April 21, 1863—11:15 P.M., ibid.
27. Longstreet to Seddon, April 22, 1863, ibid., 1014.
28. Sorrel to French, April 22, 1863, ibid., 1016.
29. Sorrel to Hood, April 22, 1863, ibid., vol. 51, pt. 2, p. 693.
30. Sorrel to French, April 27, 1863, ibid., 18:1026.
31. Sorrel to Pickett, April 22, 1863, ibid., vol. 51, pt. 2, p. 693.
32. John T. Riddick to AMR, Virginia Military Institute, April 19, 1863, RFP.
33. Ibid., April 28, 1863.
34. Thaddeus G. Williams to Col. J. R. Copeland, Hd Qrs., Mahone's Brigade, Army Northern Va., Spotsylvania County, April 22, 1863, letter in possession of Thad Williams, Suffolk, Va.
35. Lamson to S. P. Lee, April 24, 1863, *ORN* 8:773.
36. Longstreet to Seddon, April 17, 1863, *OR* 18:97.
37. Seddon to Longstreet, April 18, 1863, ibid., 999, addresses the problems of adequate transportation. In addition to having to obtain sufficient transportation, Longstreet's agents also found themselves in the field competing with agents representing the Confederate commissary general, which had the effect of driving up prices for foodstuffs and forage (Longstreet to Seddon, April 19, 1863, ibid., 1002).
38. John Riddick Receipts, CPC.
39. Jethro Riddick Receipts, ibid.
40. Edward C. Riddick Receipts, ibid.
41. Lamson to Peck, April 13, 1863, John James Peck Papers, USMA-WP.
42. Sorrel to Benning, April 13, 63, Henry Lewis Benning Papers, SHC-UNC.
43. Cormier, *Siege,* 176.
44. Holt, *Letters,* 129–30.
45. Quoted in Cormier, *Siege,* 176–77.
46. Ibid., 177.
47. Longstreet to Lee, April 3, 1863, *OR* 18:958–59; Sorrel to Benning, April 19–May 2, 1863, ibid., vol. 51, pt. 2, pp. 691–701; Sorrel to Benning, April 13, 1863, Henry Lewis Benning Papers, SHC-UNC.
48. Trotter, *Ironclads and Columbiads,* 211–19.
49. Longstreet to Lee, April 3, 1863, *OR* 18:958–59;
50. Wightman, *Letters,* 129; see also Cunningham, *Diaries,* 60; *New York Tribune,* April 22, 1863; Ripley, *Vermont General,* 102.
51. Corell, *99th New York,* 13.
52. Quoted in Ibid., p. 14.
53. Ibid.; Thompson, *Thirteenth New Hampshire,* pp. 129–31. The sharpshooting led the men to compose a short verse, "Show your head—and soon you are dead."
54. Longstreet, *Memoirs,* 325–26.
55. Henry Simmons to Anna, Suffolk, Va., April 20, 1863, Simmons Papers, SHC-UNC.

56. Wightman, *Letters,* 129.

57. Corell, *99th New York,* 13–14.

58. Thompson, *Thirteenth New Hampshire,* 158.

59. Peck to Halleck, April 16, 1863, Dix to Halleck, April 16, 1863, Peck to Dix and Viele, April 16, 1863, *OR* 18:619, 620; Onderdonk to B. B. Foster, April 16, 1863, John James Peck Papers, USMA-WP; Longstreet, *Memoirs,* 324. One of the men Longstreet sent behind Union lines may have been James Harrison. Longstreet mentions the "scout" reporting to him while before Suffolk. The mysterious Harrison later acted as the eyes of Lee's army in the absence of Jeb Stuart during the Gettysburg campaign. See Blakeless, "James Harrison"; Stuart, "Of Spies," 313–15.

60. Martin Buffum to Capt. L. Siebert, April 25, 1863, John James Peck Papers, USMA-WP; Thompson, *Thirteenth New Hampshire,* 154. See also Allen, *Fourth R.I.,* 196–97.

61. *Rome (Ga.) Tri-Weekly Courier,* April 28, 1863.

62. William Dalzell to Dear Lizzy, April 28, 1863, William Dalzell Papers, EU.

63. Cushing to S. P. Lee, April 23, 1863, Harris to Cushing, April 22, 1863, *ORN* 8:771–72, 762; S. P. Lee to Gideon Welles, April 23, 1863—8 a.m., *OR* 18:650–51; S. P. Lee to Dix, April 29, 1863, Stone endorsement, May 22, 1863, *ORN* 8:762–63; Butts, *Reminiscences,* 56–62; Stevens, "Siege," 219–20.

64. Peck to Dix, quoted in Dix to Halleck, April 24, 1863—9:30 p.m., Peck report, May 5, 1863, Corcoran report, May 1863, John McConile report, May 8, 1863, Itinerary of the Third Brigade, April 9–May 3, 1863, Dodge report, May 7, 1863, Stedman report, May 5, 1863, Peck to Dix, April 24, 1863, 653, 277, 289, 295, 297, 300, 315, 653; H. G. Marshall to family, April 26, 1863, Marshall Papers, UM; Smith Brown to Friend, Suffolk, Va., April 26, 1863, Johnson Family Papers, MHI-CB; Blakeslee, *Sixteenth Connecticut,* 35–36; Thorpe, *Fifteenth Connecticut,* 46–47; McGrath, *127th New York,* 40; Pickett report, April 26, 1863, *OR* 18:340–41; Wise Diary, April 24, 1863, DU; Chamberlayne, *Richmond Fayette Artillery,* 4.

65. Lee to Longstreet, April 27, 1863, *OR* 18:1025.

66. Cooper to Longstreet, April 29, 1863, ibid., 1029.

67. Cooper to Longstreet, April 30, 1863, ibid., 1032.

68. French, *Autobiography,* 166.

69. Cooper to Longstreet, May 1, 1863, *OR* 18:1034.

70. Sorrel to Mitchell, May 1, 1863, ibid., vol. 51, pt. 2, p. 700.

71. Sorrel to Benning, May 2, 1863 (two communications), ibid., 700–701.

72. Longstreet to Cooper, May 2, 1863, ibid., 701.

73. Sorrel to Baker, May 2, 1863, ibid..

74. John Bell Hood to James Longstreet, June 28, 1875, in *Southern Historical Society Papers* 4 (Oct. 1877): 146–47.

75. Hood, *Advance and Retreat,* 52.

10. No-Man's-Land

1. Corell, *99th New York,* 2.

2. Wightman, *Letters,* 132.

3. Corell, *99th New York,* 2 and roster.

4. Belo, *Memoirs*, 27–28.

5. Itinerary of the Reserve Brigade, April 24–May 1, *OR* 18:299. See also William Dalzell to Dear Lizzy, Camp 142d Regt., N.Y.S.V., Suffolk, Va., "Sunday, May 2 [i.e., May 3]," 1863, Dalzell Papers, EU. Dalzell noted of the fighting on May 1: "Friday afternoon we had quite a little skirmish our [loss] was between forty and fifty killed and wounded."

6. Corell, *99th New York*, 3.

7. Thompson, *Thirteenth New Hampshire*, 139.

8. Stevens, "Siege," 220–21. See also Foster, *New Jersey*, 533.

9. Thompson, *Thirteenth New Hampshire*, 141–43.

10. Ibid., 144, 147, 151.

11. Peck report, May 5, 1863, Getty report, May 12, 1863, *OR* 18:278, 306; Kimball, *103rd New York*, 30–31, 104–5; Stevens, *Siege*, 221. In his desire for absolution, George W. Griggs, the sutler at Suffolk who attributed Col. Kimball's death to whiskey he had sold him, also accepted responsibility for Ringold's death. He confessed that "liquor bought the night previous [to] the crossing was indirectly the cause, as the Lieut.-Colonel afterward told me, of his foolishness and death." Whether or not Ringold's consumption of alcohol on the night before the attack contributed to his death by his "getting in advance of his men and rashly exposing himself [to enemy fire]," Griggs felt guilty enough to write in this manner in 1895 ("An Incident at Suffolk," George W. Griggs Manuscript, Norwich Civil War Round Table Collection, MHI-CB).

12. Getty report, May 12, 1863, *OR* 18:306.

13. Foster, *New Jersey*, 534.

14. Thompson, *Thirteenth New Hampshire*, 151.

15. Arthur Dutton report, May 1863, *OR* 18:319–20.

16. Hiram B. Crosby report, May 5, 1863, ibid., 321–22. See also Brown, Crane, and Hubbell, *Twenty-first Connecticut*, 116; Cormier, *Siege*, 269.

17. Crosby report, May 5, 1863, *OR* 18:322.

18. McPherson and McPherson, *Lamson*, 105.

19. Special Orders, May 2, 1863, Sorrel to French, May 3, 1863, *OR* 18:1038, 1041.

20. Dodge report, May 7, 1863, ibid., 300–301.

21. Morgan, *Reminiscences*, 163. See also Loehr, *First Virginia*, 34.

22. Trask, *9th Virginia*, 50, 62, 65, 70, 76, 77, 89, 91.

23. Peck report, May 5, 1863, Corcoran report, May 1863, Dodge report, May 7, 1863, *OR* 18:278, 289–90, 300–301; Lenfest, *Diary*, 30; *Eleventh Pennsylvania Cavalry*, 70–71; Clarke, *Back Home*, 77.

24. Two recent studies of this campaign and battle are Furgurson, *Chancellorsville*, and Sears, *Chancellorsville*.

25. Thomas, *Jeb Stuart*, 210–13.

26. Trask, *16th Virginia*, 76; Henderson, *41st Virginia*, 94, 115, 134, 135.

27. Peck report, May 5, 1863, *OR* 18:279. A revision of the list of casualties showed 266 men killed, wounded, captured, or missing. Nevertheless, the list remains incomplete ("Return of Casualties," ibid.,286–88).

28. Stevens, "Siege," 222.

29. Peck report, May 5, 1863, *OR* 18:279.

30. Gorgas, *Diary*, 33.

31. Hood to Lee, April 29, 1863, *OR*, vol. 51, pt. 2, p. 697; ibid., copy in Charles Scott Venable Papers, SHC-UNC.

32. Hood, *Advance and Retreat*, 52; Simpson, *Hood's Texas Brigade*, 229–30.

33. Hood to Lee, April 29, 1863, *OR*, vol. 51, pt. 2, p. 697; ibid., copy in Charles Scott Venable Papers, SHC-UNC.

34. Ellis to Dear Charles, Camp near Suffolk, Va., April 25, 1863, Munford-Ellis Family Papers, DU.

35. Cormier, *Siege*, 214.

36. Hyde, *One Hundred Twelfth*, 33.

37. Clarke, *Back Home*, 77.

38. Lenfest, *Diary*, 30.

39. Charles Clark to Parents, Suffolk, Va., May 5, 1863, Charles N. Clark Papers, Civil War Miscellaneous Collection, MHI-CB.

40. Habberton Diary, May 12, 1863, John Habberton Papers, ibid.

41. Dix to Halleck, May 10, 1863, *OR* 18:711–12.

42. Halleck to Dix, May 14, 1863, ibid., 718.

43. S. P. Lee to Dix, May 11, 1863, Dix to S. P. Lee, May 14, 1863, ibid., 713, 717.

44. Halleck to Dix, May 14, 1863, ibid., 718.

45. Lenfest, *Diary*, 31.

46. Ibid.

47. Hyde, *One Hundred Twelfth*, 34–35. See also Hanson, *Sixth Massachusetts*, 237–40.

48. Lenfest, *Diary*, 31–32.

49. Hyde, *One Hundred Twelfth*, 35,

50. Lenfest, *Diary*, 31–32.

51. U.S. Dept. of the Army, *Medal of Honor*, 128.

52. Hanson, *Sixth Massachusetts*, 242–43.

53. Hyde, *One Hundred Twelfth*, 36.

54. John M. White to Dear Sister Martha, Camp near Franklin, Va., May 22, 1863, John M. White Letters, MOC.

55. Habberton Diary, May 20, 1863, John Habberton Papers, Civil War Miscellaneous Collection, MHI-CB.

56. Lenfest, *Diary*, 32–33.

57. Franklin A. Stratton report, June 11, 1863, *OR*, vol. 27, pt. 2, p. 788.

58. William McEvily report, June 24, 1863, ibid., 789.

59. Lewis Henry Webb to ——, June 12, 1863, Webb Papers, SHC-UNC.

60. Corcoran to Dix, June 18, 1863, *OR*, vol. 27, pt. 3, p. 207.

61. Joseph C. Brooks to My Dear Friend, Camp of Reserve Brigade, Suffolk, Va., June 10, 1863, Thomas Walker and J. C. Brooks Letters, UVA.

62. John Newton Smith to Dear Sister, Essex Co., Va., Feb. 20, 1863, John Newton Smith Papers, VPI&SU.

63. Smith to Dear Pa, Essex Co., Va., Feb. 25, 1863, ibid.

64. Charles Crofts to Dear Uncle, Hanover "Ecedemy" Hosp., June 2, 1863, ibid.

65. Crofts to Dear Uncle, Hanover "Ecedemy hospitle," June 8, 1863, ibid.

66. Crofts to Dear Uncle, Hanover "Ecedemy Hospitile," June 9, 1863, ibid.

67. S. Meredith to A. Savage, Hanover Academy Hospital, Sept. 29, 1863, ibid.

68. Alexander Savage to B. R. Smith, Hamilton's Crossing near Fredericksburg, Va., March 18, 1864, ibid.

69. White to Dear Sister Martha, Weldon, N.C., June 16, 1863, John M. White Letters, MOC.

70. D. H. Hill to Seddon, June 21, 1863, *OR*, vol. 27, pt. 3, p. 911.

71. C. H. Causey to Maj. Norris, June 26, 1863, ibid., 939.

72. Aaron Blake to Sister, Camp near Portsmouth, Va., June 11, 1863, to Mother, Camp Bowers near Portsmouth, Va., June 15, 1863, Aaron K. Blake Papers, Civil War Miscellaneous Collection, MHI-CB.

73. Brooks to My Dear Friend, June 10, 1863, Thomas Walker and J. C. Brooks Letters, UVA.

74. Henry C. Smith to Dear Katie, Suffolk, Va., May 30, 1863, Henry C. Smith Papers, VHS.

75. Dix to Corcoran, June 20, 1863, *OR*, vol. 27, pt. 3, p. 241.

76. Dix to Corcoran, June 28, 1863, ibid., 395.

77. Confederate major general D. H. Hill correctly speculated that the Union forces in Suffolk would pull back to positions closer to Portsmouth and Norfolk in a message to Secretary of War Seddon on June 21: "Still, I have no idea that they will fall back farther than Bowers' Hill, 8 miles from Portsmouth, if, indeed, they go back that far" (ibid., 911).

78. John A. Baker to D. H. Hill, enclosed in D. H. Hill to Seddon, June 25, 1863—1 P.M., ibid., 933–34.

79. Harkey to H. A. Wise, June 24, 1863, ibid., 928.

80. Corcoran to Capt. Barstow, July 4, 1863, ibid., 529.

81. Smith to Dear friend, Bowers Hill, July 4, 1863, Henry C. Smith Letters, VHS.

82. E. B. Montague to Seddon, July 7, 1863, *OR*, vol. 27, pt. 3, pp. 978–79.

83. Henry Lyle to Mother, Camp Bower's Hill, July 24, 1863, Henry Lyle Papers, Norman Daniels Collection, Harrisburg Civil War Round Table Collection, MHI-CB.

11. *"Nothing but Glory"*

1. MacClenny Papers, UVA.

2. See Reardon, *Pickett's Charge*. See also William Faulkner, *Intruder in the Dust* (New York, 1948), 194–95. There remains no more powerful and eloquent statement of the mythic qualities of "Pickett's Charge" than this.

3. Trask, *9th Virginia*, 26.

4. See Appendix C; Wallace, *3rd Virginia*, 37–39 and roster.

5. Trask, *9th Virginia*, 80; Henderson, *41st Virginia*, 144.

6. Quoted in Foote, *Civil War* 2:564.

7. Mollie to AMR, Nansemond County, Aug. 19, 1863, RFP.

8. Special Orders, Aug. 1, 1863, *OR,* vol. 29, pt. 2, pp. 58–60.

9. George H. Johnston to Capt. John C. Lee, Aug. 14, 1863, ibid., 48.

10. Henry M. Naglee to Capt. F. A. Rowe, Aug. 20, 1863, ibid., 80.

11. General Orders, No. 8, Aug. 21, 1863, ibid., 88.

12. Naglee to Lt. Col. William Lewis, Sept. 12, 1863, ibid., 174.

13. Mitchell, *Civil War Soldiers,* 139.

14. Spear to Getty, Aug. 25, 1863, *OR,* vol. 29, pt. 2, pp. 99–100.

15. Spear to Getty, Aug. 30, 1863, ibid., 114.

16. MAJKR to AMR, Oct. [1863], RFP.

17. Special Orders, No. 65, Sept. 23, 1863, *OR,* vol. 29, pt. 2, pp. 226–27.

18. See McPherson, *Battle Cry,* for a discussion of the Emancipation Proclamation, its content and impact.

19. MAJKR to AMR, Oct. [1863], RFP.

20. Habberton, "When Boys Were Men," 33, John Habberton Papers, Civil War Miscellaneous Collection, MHI-CB.

21. Joseph C. Brooks to My Dear Friend, Camp of Reserve Brigade, Suffolk, Va., June 10, 1863, Thomas Walker and J. C. Brooks Letters, UVA.

22. Cronin, *Memoirs,* 171.

23. Henry Simmons to My Sweet One, Monday [May 24, 1863] A.M. 9 o clock, Simmons Papers, SHC-UNC.

24. Simmons to wife, May 24, 7½ P.M., ibid.

25. Simmons to My Darling Wife, Camp 11th R.I.V., Suffolk, May 27, 1863, ibid.

26. Nathaniel Henley Riddick to AMR, Petersburg, Oct. 23, 1863, RFP.

27. George Stetzel report, Sept. 17, 1863, *OR,* vol. 29, pt. 1, pp. 135–36.

28. Henry Lyle to Mother, Camp Getty near Portsmouth, Oct. 18, 1863, Lyle Papers, Norman Daniels Collection, Harrisburg Civil War Round Table Collection, MHI-CB.

29. Arthur Herbert report, Nov. 11, 1863, ibid., 638.

30. Edward A. Wild reports, Dec. 21, 28, 1863, ibid., 910–18. These reports contain extraordinary statements pertaining to the desire Union generals Wild and Butler shared to "exterminate" guerrilla activity through whatever means necessary and of their willingness to employ black troops as a psychological weapon against white Southerners. For more information on this change of Union policy, see Grimsley, *Hard Hand of War.*

31. Ash, *Yankees,* 99.

32. Ibid.

33. J. G. Foster to Lt. Col. J. A. Hardie, Oct. 14—9:10 A.M., *OR,* vol. 29, pt. 2, p. 320.

34. Pickett to Cooper, Oct. 15, 1863, ibid., 789.

35. J. A. Campbell to Adjutant General, Oct. 22, 1863, ibid., 799.

36. This quotation from Confederate signal officer J. F. Milligan doubtless reflects Pickett's indignation as well (J. F. Milligan, Nov. 26, 1863, ibid., 850).

37. Mollie to AMR, Nansemond County, Aug. 19, 1863, RFP.

38. Jennie Riddick to AMR, Home, Aug. 30, 1863, RFP.

39. Daniel Brinkley et al. to Major Turner, Dec. 25, 1863, CSA Army Department of Henrico, sec. 8, VHS.
40. J. F. Milligan to Seddon, Nov. 26, 1863, *OR,* vol. 29, pt. 2, pp. 849–50.
41. Joel Griffin to Pickett, Dec. 15, 1863, Pickett to Cooper, Dec. 15, 1863, ibid., 872–73.
42. Pickett to Cooper, Dec. 15, 1863, ibid., 873.
43. Pickett to J. R. Griffin, Dec. 15, 1863, ibid., 874.
44. Pickett to Cooper, Dec. 20, 1863, ibid., 881–82.
45. Ibid.; enclosure no. 2, Griffin to Pickett, [Dec.] 19, [1863], ibid., 883.
46. Enclosure no. 4, DeBordenave to M. W. Ransom, [Dec.] 20, [1863], ibid., 884.
47. Enclosure no. 3, M. W. Ransom to Pickett, Dec. 20, 1863, ibid., 884.
48. Pickett to Cooper, Dec. 20, 1863, ibid., 881–82.
49. Cooper endorsement, ibid., 882.
50. Pickett to Cooper, Dec. 31, 1863, ibid., 897.
51. Abstract from Return of the Department of North Carolina, Dec. 31, 1863, ibid., 906.

12. *"Do Hurry Friends"*

1. Quoted in Long, *Day by Day,* 450.
2. James L. Wilson to Gov. William Smith, Smithfield, Isle of Wight Co., Va., March 12, 1864, Executive Papers, Governor William Smith, LVA.
3. William H. Day to Gov. Smith, Smithfield, March 12, 1864, ibid.
4. Robert H. Whitfield to Gov. Smith, Smithfield, Isle of Wight, Va., 1864, March 12, ibid.
5. Thomas J. Clements to Gov. Smith, Isle of Wight Co., Va., March 17, 1864, ibid.
6. Gov. Smith to Clements, notation on letter of March 17, 1864, ibid.
7. Henry A. Chambers Diary, "Wednesday March the 9th [1864] Affair at Suffolk, Va.," Henry A. Chambers Papers, NCDHA. For a published version, see Chambers, *Diary,* 182–84.
8. Suderow, "Suffolk Slaughter," 38.
9. Chambers Diary, "Wednesday, March the 9th: Affair at Suffolk, Va.," Henry A. Chambers Papers, NCDHA.
10. Suderow, "Suffolk Slaughter," 38.
11. Chambers Diary, "Wednesday, March the 9th: Affair at Suffolk, Va.," Henry A. Chambers Papers, NCDHA.
12. Suderow, "Suffolk Slaughter," 38.
13. Charles A. Heckman report, March 12, 1864, *OR* 33:238.
14. Suderow, "Suffolk Slaughter," 38.
15. Chambers Diary, "Wednesday, March the 9th: Affair at Suffolk, Va.," Henry A. Chambers Papers, NCDHA.
16. Heckman report, March 12, 1864, *OR* 33:238.
17. David F. Dobie to Hattie, March 1864, David F. Dobie Letters, UVA.
18. Benjamin F. Butler report, March 12, 1864, *OR* 33:237–38.
19. Heckman report, March 12, 1864, ibid., 238.

20. Angus McDonald to Mother, Franklin Depot, Southampton County, Va., March 11, 1864, MOC.
21. Suderow, "Suffolk Slaughter," 38, 39.
22. Chambers Diary, "Wednesday, March the 9th: Affair at Suffolk, Va.," Henry A. Chambers Papers, NCDHA.
23. Suderow, "Suffolk Slaughter," 38–39.
24. Ibid.
25. See, for example, Wills, *Battle,* 169–99, for a discussion of Fort Pillow. See also comments and quotations from Wiley, *Johnny Reb,* 314; Mitchell, *Civil War Soldiers,* 174–75; and Robertson, *Soldiers Blue and Gray,* 32–35, on the subject of race and the Civil War.
26. Paquette, *U.S. Colored Troops,* 10–16, 23.
27. Heckman report, March 12, 1864, *OR* 33:238.
28. George W. Cole report, March 14, 1864, ibid., 239.
29. Suderow, "Suffolk Slaughter," 39.
30. Cole report, March 14, 1864, ibid., 239.
31. Paquette, *U.S. Colored Troops,* 13, 23.
32. Heckman report, March 12, 1864, *OR* 33:238; Cole report, ibid., 239.
33. "Interesting from Norfolk," *Philadelphia Inquirer,* Monday, March 14, 1864, p. 2.
34. Suderow, "Suffolk Slaughter," 39.
35. S. P. Lee to Butler, April 9, 1864, *OR* 33:834.
36. Butler to S. P. Lee, April 10, 1864, ibid., 837.
37. J. W. Shaffer, Instructions to C. K. Graham, [April 12, 1864], ibid., 850–51.
38. Corell, "Captain F. A. Rowe's Reminiscences," in Corell, *99th New York.*
39. Charles K. Graham report, Feb. 2, 1864, *OR* 33:105.
40. Corell, "Rowe's Reminiscences," in Corell, *99th New York.*
41. Graham report, Feb. 2, 1864, *OR* 33:105.
42. Graham report, April 16, 1864, ibid., 273.
43. Andrew Ewell report, ibid., 274.
44. Log of USS *Stepping Stones,* Naval Log Books, NA.
45. David F. Dobie to My dear friend Hattie, Picket Line near Bower's Hill, Va., April 18, 1864, Dobie Letters, UVA.
46. William Lind to Thomas, April 18, 1864, in Lind, *Long Road,* 166.
47. David F. Dobie to Hattie, April 2, 11, 1864, Dobie Letters, UVA.
48. Dobbins, *Grandfather's Journal,* 191–92.
49. See Rhea, *Wilderness.*
50. See Matter, *Spotsylvania;* Rhea, *Spotsylvania Court House.*
51. See Trudeau, *Bloody Roads.*
52. Ibid.
53. See Trudeau, *Last Citadel.*
54. Henderson, *41st Virginia,* 95, 114, 118; Trask, *16th Virginia,* 123.
55. Trask, *16th Virginia,* 79, 102, 111, 113, 117; Balfour, *13th Virginia Cavalry,* 100; Henderson, *41st Virginia,* 91, 111, 114; Wallace, *3rd Virginia,* 81.
56. Coz to AMR, Woodlawn, May 29, 1864, RFP.

57. Quoted in *Quiet Regiment*, 29.

58. Cronin, *Memoirs*, 179–80.

13. An Autumn of Despair

1. William B. Wellons to Mary Williams, June 25, 1864, Thaddeus G. Williams Papers, Thad Williams, Suffolk, Va. See Cavanaugh, *6th Virginia*, 49, 136

2. See Power, *Lee's Miserables*, 135–40.

3. Dobbins, *Grandfather's Journal*, 207.

4. "The Crater, Virginia (VA070), Petersburg, July 30, 1864," Kennedy, *Guide*, 355–56.

5. Henderson, *41st Virginia*, 114, 116, 135; Trask, *16th Virginia*, 76, 98, 107, 123; see also Appendix C.

6. Quoted widely. For example, see "The Crater," Kennedy, *Guide*, 335–56.

7. Henderson, *41st Virginia*, 98; Trask, *16th Virginia*, 107, 117; Cavanaugh, *6th Virginia*, 106.

8. Christopher M. Calkins, "Reams Station II, Virginia (VA073), Dinwiddie County, August 25, 1864," in Kennedy, *Guide*, 360–62.

9. Cavanaugh, *6th Virginia*, 116; Trask, *16th Virginia*, 76; Henderson, *41st Virginia*, 113, 132.

10. Coz to AMR, Woodlawn, Sept. 24, 1864, RFP.

11. MAJKR to AMR, Oct. 8, 1864, ibid.

12. Circular, Head Quarters Defences Norfolk & Portsmouth, Portsmouth, Va., Aug. 6, 1864, RG 393, pt. 2, NA.

13. NR to AMR, Petersburg, Va., Nov. 1, 1864, RFP.

14. MAJKR to AMR, Nov. 1, 1864, ibid.

15. Ibid., Nov. 4, 1864.

16. NR to Mills Riddick, Dec. 10, 1864, ibid.

17. Wert, *Mosby's Rangers*, 244–50.

18. NR to Mills Riddick, Ho. of Delegates, Nov. 10, 1864, RFP.

19. Mills to AMR, Nov. 25, 1864, ibid.

20. MAJKR to AMR, Nov. 26, 1864, ibid.

21. Mary Taylor Riddick to Wilbur Disosway, Dec. 26, 1864, ibid.

22. MAJKR to AMR, Dec. 9, 1865, ibid.

23. Cobb Diary, "1864 Friday 2 [Sept.]"

24. Crofts, *Cobb's Ordeal*, 238.

25. Cobb Diary, "1864 Friday 2 [Sept.]"

26. Ibid., "1864 Friday 23 [Sept.]"

27. Ibid., "1864 Saturday 15 [Oct.]"

28. Ibid., "1864 Sunday 27 [Nov.]"

29. Ibid., "1864 Friday 28–Wednesday 9 [Oct.–Nov.]," "1864 Tuesday 8 [Nov.]"

30. Ibid., "1864, 24 [Dec.]"

31. Ibid., "1864, 11 [Oct.]"

32. Mary Taylor Riddick to Wilbur Disosway, Dec. 26, 1864, RFP.

33. NR to AMR, Harris's P.O., Louisa County, Va., Thursday, Dec. 29, 1864, ibid.

14. "Let Us Suffer Together"

1. MAJKR to AMR, Jan. 5, 1865, RFP.
2. MAJKR to NR, Sunday, Jan. 16, 1865, ibid.
3. NR to AMR, Richmond, 16 Jan., 1865, ibid.
4. Ibid., Feb. 1, 1865.
5. Long, *Day by Day*, 633.
6. NR to AMR, Feb. 2, 1965, RFP.
7. NR to John Thompson Riddick, Richmond, Feb. 25, 1865, ibid.
8. Special Orders No. 13, Hd. Qrs. Defence Norfolk & Portsmouth, Portsmouth, Va., Feb. 4, 1865, RG 393, NA.
9. Circular, Hd. Qrs. Norfolk, Portsmouth & Defences, Portsmouth, Va., March 6, 1865, RG 393, pt. 2, ibid.
10. Darden, Robert M., Suffolk, March 1, 1865, ibid.
11. Darden, Robt. M., Suffolk, March 1865, ibid.
12. Walsavens, Jonas, Norfolk, April 4, 1865, ibid.
13. Heath, L. G., Suffolk, March 8, 1865, ibid.
14. Christopher M. Calkins, "Five Forks, Virginia (VA088), Dinwiddie County, April 1, 1865," in Kennedy, *Guide*, 417–19.
15. See Bearss and Calkins, *Five Forks*.
16. Ibid.
17. See Appendix C; Wallace, *3rd Virginia*.
18. Dobbins, *Grandfather's Journal*, 242.
19. Quoted in Trudeau, *Out of the Storm*, 58.
20. Thomas, *Richmond*, 193–96.
21. Trudeau, *Last Citadel*, 376.
22. Davis, *Davis*, 604–6; Furgurson, *Ashes of Glory*, 319–25. The fate of the city itself is discussed in Thomas, *Richmond*, 196, and Furgurson, *Ashes of Glory*, 332–36.
23. Balfour, *13th Virginia Cavalry*, 95.
24. Henderson, *41st Virginia*, 123.
25. NR to AMR, Louisa County, April 5, 1865, RFP.
26. "Cousin" to AMR, Woodlawn, June 1, 1865, ibid.
27. Hobbs, *Storm over Suffolk*, 23; Cormier, *Siege*, 327–28; Frank M. Roberts, "Yankee Occupiers Left Mark on Home," Suffolk *Sun*, Nov. 1, 1979, p. 5.
28. Ladd, J. S., 8th Ind. NY Batty., April 8, 1865, RG 393, pt. 2, NA.
29. Bran[d]t, H. A., Portsmouth, April 25, 1865, ibid.
30. George H. Gordon to T. T. Eckert, April 29, 1865, ibid.
31. Thomas T. Eckert to G. W. Lewis, April 30, 1865, ibid.
32. G. H. Gordon to Edward W. Smith, May 5, 1865, ibid.
33. G. H. Gordon to G. W. Lewis, May 5, 1865, ibid.
34. Ibid., May 25, 1865.
35. Special Orders, No. 36, May 12, 1865, ibid.
36. G. H. Gordon to G. W. Lewis, June 3, 1865, ibid.

37. McFeely, *Yankee Stepfather*, 65. See also Foner, *Reconstruction*, for an excellent study of the Reconstruction era.

38. General Orders, No. 102, May 31, 1865, BRFAL, NA.

39. Circular, No. 8, June 20, 1865, ibid.

40. Circular, No. 10, July 11, 1865, ibid.

41. Circular, No. 11, July 12, 1865, General Order, No. 3, July 18, 1865, ibid.

42. President Johnson's plan to restore lands to white Southerners and thereby subvert the goals of the Freedmen's Bureau is a subtext of McFeely's study.

43. Circular, Dec. 11, 1865, BRFAL, NA.

44. Crofts, *Southampton*, 224.

45. McFeely, *Yankee Stepfather*, 129.

46. Crofts, *Cobb's Ordeal*, 281.

47. Crofts, *Southampton*, 222.

48. For a summary, see Crofts, *Cobb's Ordeal*, 287–92.

49. Cobb Diary, "1866 Thursday 1 [March]."

50. Cobb Diary, "1866, Friday 7 [Dec.]"; Crofts, *Cobb's Ordeal*, 281–82.

51. Crofts, *Southampton*, 224.

52. Ibid.

53. In addition to Foner, *Reconstruction*, see Foner, *Nothing but Freedom*.

54. Various labor contracts, Nansemond County, Va., BRFAL, NA.

55. Various labor contracts, Isle of Wight County, Va., ibid.

56. John Tate and William G. Northworthy, Labor Contract, Suffolk, Va., ibid.

57. Various labor contracts, Mississippi, ibid.

58. Long, *Day by Day*, 695.   59. Ibid., 696–97.   60. Ash, *Yankees*, 231.

61. Washington L. Riddick to Ella Taylor Disosway, Nov. 1867, RFP.

Conclusion: Nervously Standing Watch

1. Quoted in Paul D. Escott, "The Failure of Confederate Nationalism: The Old South's Class System in the Crucible of War," in Owens and Cooke, *Crucible of War*, 20.

⊰ BIBLIOGRAPHY ⊱

PRIMARY SOURCES

Manuscripts

William R. Perkins Library, Duke University, Durham, N.C.

Oscar Brown Ireland Papers   William Dunlap Simpson Papers

Nate Lampheur Papers   Henry J. H. Thompson Papers

James Longstreet Papers   George Newton Wise Diary

Munford-Ellis Family Papers

Robert W. Woodruff Library, Emory University, Atlanta

John Bratton Papers   John A. Everett Papers

William Dalzell Papers   Theodore Turner Fogle Papers

Robert F. Davis Diary

Library of Virginia, Richmond

James Richmond Boulware Papers

David F. Dobie Letters

Executive Papers, Governor John Letcher

Executive Papers, Governor William Smith
Henry T. Owens Papers
Eleanor S. Brockenbrough Library, Museum of the Confederacy, Richmond
Eli Duvall Collection
Angus McDonald Letter
John M. White Letters
National Archives, Washington, D.C.
Bureau of Refugees, Freedmen, and Abandoned Lands. General Orders and
Circulars.
———. Labor Contracts, Isle of Wight County, Va.
———. Labor Contracts, Nansemond County, Va.
Confederate Papers Relating to Citizens or Business Firms. Microcopy no. 346,
roll no. 1088.
Letters. Record Group 393, pt. 2
U.S. Bureau of the Census. Seventh Census of the United States, 1850.
———. Eighth Census of the United States, 1860.
USS *Stepping Stones* Log Book, Naval Log Books
North Carolina Department of History and Archives, Raleigh
Henry A. Chambers Papers
Hambrick and Paylor Papers
F. Roy Johnson Papers
Private collection
A. C. Myers Correspondence, 1862–64
Personal Collections
Robert Hatchman Letter. Author's personal collection.
Riddick Family Papers. Personal collection of Mrs. Anna W. Rollings, Suffolk,
Va. Typescript copies given to the author.
Thaddeus G. Williams Papers. Letter in possession of Thad Williams, Suffolk,
Va. Copy made available to the author.
U.S. Army Military History Institute, Carlisle Barracks, Pa.
Civil War Miscellaneous Collection
Aaron K. Blake Papers   Newell B. Richardson Papers
Charles N. Clark Papers   Theodore F. Skinner Papers
John Habberton Papers   Varnum Family Papers
Andrew J. Lorish Papers
Harrisburg Civil War Round Table Collection
Norman Daniels Collection
Henry Lyle Papers
Johnson Family Papers
Smith Brown Letter
Lewis Leigh Collection
John M. Hughes Papers
C. D. W. Nelson Collection
Charles Sayles Papers

Northwest Corner Civil War Round Table Collection
    Thomas L. Bailey Papers
Norwich Civil War Round Table Collection
    George W. Griggs Manuscript
U.S. Military Academy Library, West Point, N.Y.
    John James Peck Papers
University of Georgia, Athens
    T. W. Clements Diary
    Samuel L. Roe Papers.
William L. Clements Library, University of Michigan, Ann Arbor
    Henry Grimes Marshall Papers
Southern Historical Collection, University of North Carolina, Chapel Hill
    Henry Lewis Benning Papers   William Henry Snow Papers
    Lucinda Sugg Moore Papers   Charles Scott Venable Papers
    R. Channing Price Papers   Louis (Lewis) Henry Webb Papers
    Edward Payson Reeve Papers   Lewis Neal Whittle Papers
    Henry E. Simmons Papers
University of Virginia Library, Charlottesville
    David F. Dobie Letters   Thomas Walker and J. C. Brooks Letters
    MacClenny Papers   Webb-Prentiss Papers
Virginia Historical Society, Richmond
    Burwell Family Papers
    Carter Family Papers
    C.S.A. Army Dept. of Henrico, Section 8, Letter, Daniel Brinkley et al., Dec. 25,
        1863
    Daniel William Cobb Diaries   Henry C. Smith Papers
    Benjamin Lyons Farinholt Diary   Elliott L. Story Diaries
    Osman Latrobe Diary   Talcott Family Papers
    L. Robert Moore Papers   Alvin Coe Voris Papers
    Samuel Harper Pulliam Papers
Virginia Polytechnic and State University, Blacksburg
    Norfolk and Petersburg Railroad Papers
    John Newton Smith Papers

Published Records of the U.S. Government

U.S. Department of the Army. *The Medal of Honor of the United States Army.* Washington,
    D.C., 1948.
U.S. Department of War. *Atlas to Accompany the Official Records of the Union and
    Confederate Armies.* 2 vols. Washington, D.C., 1891–95.
——. *The War of the Rebellion: A Compilation of the Official Records of the Union and
    Confederate Armies.* 70 vols. in 127 serials and index. Washington, D.C., 1880–95.
U.S. Naval War Records Office. *Official Records of the Union and Confederate Navies in the
    War of the Rebellion.* 30 vols. Washington, D.C., 1894–1922.

Newspapers

Charleston *Mercury*	Richmond *Daily Enquirer*
Harper's Weekly	Richmond *Daily Examiner*
New York Times	Richmond *Sentinel*
New York Tribune	Richmond *Whig*
Philadelphia Inquirer	*Rome (Ga.) Tri-Weekly Courier*
Portland Morning Oregonian	*Suffolk News Herald*
North Carolina Standard (Raleigh)	Suffolk *Sun*
Petersburg *Daily Express*	*Washington (D.C.) Evening Star*
Richmond *Daily Dispatch*	

Published Memoirs and Personal Papers

Belo, Alfred H. *Memoirs of Alfred Horatio Belo Dictated by Him to and with a Short Introduction by Charles Peabody, May 1902.* Boston, 1904.

Butts, Frank B. *Reminiscences of Gunboat Service of the Nansemond: Personal Narratives of Events in the War of the Rebellion.* Papers Read before the Rhode Island Soldiers and Sailors Historical Society, 3d ser., no. 8. Providence, 1884.

Cavanaugh, Michael. *Memoirs of Gen. Thomas Francis Meagher, Comprising the Leading Events of His Career Chronologically Arranged, with Selections from His Speeches, Lectures, and Miscellaneous Writings, Including Personal Reminiscences.* Worcester, Mass., 1892.

Chambers, Henry A. *Diary of Captain Henry A. Chambers.* Ed. T. H. Pearce. Wendell, N.C., 1983.

Chestnut, Mary Boykin. *Mary Chestnut's Civil War.* Ed. C. Vann Woodward. New Haven, 1981.

Clarke, Hermon. *Back Home in Oneida: Hermon Clarke and His Letters.* Ed. Larry F. Jackson and Thomas F. O'Donnell. New York, 1965.

Cronin, David E. (Seth Eyland). *The Evolution of a Life, Described in the Memoirs of Major Seth Eyland, Late on the Mounted Rifles.* New York, 1884.

Davis, Nicholas A. *Chaplain Davis and Hood's Texas Brigade.* Ed. Donald E. Everett. San Antonio, 1962.

Dawson, Francis W. *Reminiscences of Confederate Service, 1861–1865.* Charleston, S.C., 1882.

Dix, John Adams. *Memoirs of John Adams Dix.* Comp. Morgan Dix. 2 vols. New York, 1883.

Dobbins, Austin C., ed. *Grandfather's Journal: Company B, Sixteenth Mississippi Infantry Volunteers, Harris' Brigade, Mahone's Division, A. P. Hill's Corps, A.N.V., May 27, 1861–July 15, 1865.* Dayton, Ohio, 1988.

Dooley, John E. *John Dooley, Confederate Soldier: His War Journal.* Ed. Joseph T. Durkin, S.J. Foreword by Douglas S. Freeman. Washington, D.C., 1945; Ithaca, N.Y., 1945.

Edmonston, Catherine Ann Devereux. *"Journal of a Secesh Lady": The Diary of Catherine Ann Devereux Edmonston, 1869–1866.* Ed. Beth G. Crabtree and James W. Patton. Raleigh, N.C., 1979.

Edwards, E. M. H. *Commander William Barker Cushing of the United States Navy: Genealogy, Reminiscences of Childhood, Boyhood, and Manhood, Incidents of His Naval Career,*

Especially the Sinking of the Albemarle, *Original Letters, with Numerous Illustrations, Portraits of Himself and Others.* New York, 1898.

Ferguson, Emma L. McGuire. *The Occupation of Suffolk by the Yankees during the War between the States: A Paper Read by Mrs. Emma L. McGuire Ferguson before the Chapter of the U.D.C., of Suffolk, Va.* N.p., n.d.

Fletcher, William Andrew. *Rebel Private Front and Rear.* Ed. Bell I. Wiley. Austin, Tex., 1954.

Fremantle, James Arthur Lyon. *The Fremantle Diary: Being the Journal of Lieutenant Colonel James Arthur Lyon Fremantle, Coldstream Guards, on His Three Months in the Southern States.* Ed. Walter Lord. Boston, 1954.

French, Samuel G. *Two Wars: An Autobiography of Gen. Samuel G. French, An Officer in the Armies of the United States and the Confederate States: A Graduate from the U.S. Military Academy, West Point, 1843: His Experience: Incidents, Reminiscences, etc.* Nashville, 1901.

Giles, Valerius C. *Rags and Hope: The Recollections of Val C. Giles, Four Years with Hood's Brigade, Fourth Texas Infantry, 1861–1865.* Comp. and ed. Mary Lasswell. New York, 1961.

Gordon, George H. *A War Diary of Events in the War of the Great Rebellion, 1863–1865.* Boston, 1882.

Goree, Thomas J. *Longstreet's Aide: The Civil War Letters of Major Thomas J. Goree.* Ed. Thomas W. Cutrer. Charlottesville, Va., 1995.

Gorgas, Josiah. *The Civil War Diary of General Josiah Gorgas.* Ed. Frank E. Vandiver. Tuscaloosa, 1947.

Holt, John Lee. *"I Wrote You Word": The Poignant Letters of Private Holt, John Lee Holt, 1829–1863.* Lynchburg, Va., 1993.

Hood, John Bell. *Advance and Retreat: Personal Experiences in the United States and Confederate States Armies.* Philadelphia, 1880.

Houghton, Mitchell B. and William R. *Two Boys in the Civil War and After.* Montgomery, Ala.,, 1912.

Hunter, Alexander. *Johnny Reb and Billy Yank.* New York, 1905.

Hunton, Eppa. *Autobiography of Eppa Hunton.* Richmond, 1933.

Ingalls, Henry H. *The Diary of Henry H. Ingalls, Sixth Regiment of Massachusetts Volunteer Militia, Company K, Suffolk, Va., August 31, 1862, to May 26, 1863.* Ed. Giles L. Newsome. Suffolk, Va., 1986.

Jackson, Edgar Allan, James Fenton Bryant, and Irvin Cross Wills. *Three Rebels Write Home: Including the Letters of Edgar Allan Jackson (September 7, 1860–April 15, 1863), James Fenton Bryant (June 20, 1861–December 30, 1866), Irvin Cross Wills (April 9, 1862–July 29, 1863), and Miscellaneous Items.* Franklin, Va., 1955.Johnson, Charles F. *The Long Roll: Being a Journal of the Civil War, as Set Down during the Years 1861–1863 by Charles F. Johnson, Sometime of Hawkins Zouaves.* East Aurora, N.Y., 1911.

Johnston, David E. *Four Years a Soldier.* Princeton, W.Va., 1887.

——. *The Story of a Confederate Boy in the Civil War.* Introd. C. E. Cline. Portland, Ore., 1914.

Jones, John Beauchamp. *A Rebel War Clerk's Diary at the Confederate States Capital.* Ed. Earl Schenck Miers. New York, 1961.

Jordan, William C. *Some Events and Incidents during the Civil War.* Montgomery, Ala., 1909.

Kean, Robert Garlick Hill. *Inside the Confederate Government: The Diary of Robert Garlick Hill Kean.* Ed. Edward Younger. New York, 1957.

Lee, Robert E. *Recollections and Letters of General Robert E. Lee.* Garden City, N.Y., 1926.

Lenfest, Solomon Augustus. *The Diary of Solomon Augustus Lenfest, Co. G, Sixth Massachusetts Infantry, While Stationed at Suffolk, Virginia, August 28, 1862, to May 29, 1863.* Suffolk, Va., 1975.

Lincoln, Abraham. *The Collected Works of Abraham Lincoln.* Ed. Roy P. Basler. New Brunswick, N.J., 1953.

Lind, Henry C., ed. *The Long Road for Home: The Civil War Experiences of Four Farm Soldiers of the Twenty-seventh Massachusetts Regiment of Volunteer Infantry as Told by Their Personal Correspondence, 1861–1864.* Rutherford, N.J., 1992.

Longstreet, James. *From Manassas to Appomattox: Memoirs of the Civil War in America.* Philadelphia, 1896.

McClendon, W. A. *Recollections of War Times, by an Old Veteran While under Stonewall Jackson and Lieutenant General James Longstreet: How I Got In, and How I Got Out.* Montgomery, Ala., 1909.

McPherson, James M., and Patricia R. McPherson, eds. *Lamson of the* Gettysburg: *The Civil War Letters of Lieutenant Roswell H. Lamson, U.S. Navy.* New York, 1997.

Mixson, Frank M. *Reminiscences of a Private.* Columbia, S.C., 1910.

Moore, Frank, ed. *The Rebellion Record: A Diary of American Events, with Documents, Narratives, Illustrative Incidents, Poetry, etc.* New York, 1863.

Morgan, William H. *Personal Reminiscences of the War of 1861–5, in Camp—en Bivouac—on the March—on Pickett—on the Skirmish Line—on the Battlefield—and in Prison.* Lynchburg, 1911.

Nickerson, Ansel D. *A Raw Recruit's War Experiences.* Providence, 1888.

Parker, David B. *A Chautauqua Boy in '61 and Afterward.* Ed. Torrance Parker. Boston, 1912.

Pender, William Dorsey. *A General to His Lady.* Ed. Warren W. Hassler. Chapel Hill, N.C., 1962. Rept. as *One of Lee's Best Men: The Letters of William Dorsey Pender.* Chapel Hill, N.C., 1999.

Pickett, George E. *The Heart of a Soldier: As Revealed in the Intimate Letters of Genl. George E. Pickett, CSA.* New York, 1913.

——. *Soldier of the South: General Pickett's War Letters to His Wife.* Ed. Arthur Crew Inman. Boston, 1928.

Pickett, LaSalle Corbell. *What Happened to Me.* New York, 1917.

Polk, J. M. *The North and South American Review.* Austin, Tex., 1914.

Prince, Henry W. *Civil War Letters and Diary of Henry W. Prince, 1862–1865, the "Monitor," 127th New York State Volunteers.* Comp. Helen Wright Prince. N.p., 1979.

Pryor, Sara A. R. *Reminiscences of Peace and War.* New York, 1904.

Ripley, Edward H. *Vermont General: The Unusual War Experiences of Edward Hastings Ripley, 1862–1865.* Ed. Otto Eisenschiml. New York, 1940.

Sorrel, G. Moxley. *Recollections of a Confederate Staff Officer.* New York, 1905.

Stevens, John W. *Reminiscences of the Civil War by John W. Stevens, a Soldier in Hood's Texas Brigade, Army of Northern Virginia.* Hillsboro, Tex., 1902.

Taylor, Walter H. *Four Years with General Lee.* Ed. and Introd. James I. Robertson Jr. New York, 1962.

Thomas, Joseph P. *Memoirs of Joseph P. Thomas.* Richmond, 1919.

Wallace, Elizabeth Curtis. *Glencoe Diary: The War-Time Journal of Elizabeth Curtis Wallace.* Ed. Eleanor P. and Charles B. Cross Jr. Chesapeake, Va., 1968.

Warfield, Edgar. *A Confederate Soldier's Memoirs.* Richmond, 1936.

Wightman, Edward King. *From Antietam to Fort Fisher: The Civil War Letters of Edward King Wightman, 1862–1865.* Ed. Edward G. Longacre. Rutherford, N.J., 1985.

Woodward, John B. *John B. Woodward: A Biographical Memoir.* Ed. Elijah R. Kennedy. New York, 1897.

Unit Histories

Allen, George H. *Forty-six Months with the Fourth R.I. Volunteers, in the War of 1861–1865, Comprising a History of Its Marches, Battles, and Camp Life, Compiled from Journals Kept While on Duty in the Field and Camp, by Corp. Geo. H. Allen, of Company B.* Providence, 1887.

Blakeslee, Bernard F. *History of the Sixteenth Connecticut Volunteers.* Hartford, 1875.

Botsford, T. F. *A Sketch of the 47th Alabama Regiment, Volunteers, C.S.A.* N.p., 1909.

Bowen, James R. *Regimental History of the First New York Dragoons (Originally the 130th N.Y. Vol. Infantry).* N.p., 1900.

Brown, Delos D., Alvin M. Crane, and William S. Hubbell. *The Story of the Twenty-first Regiment, Connecticut Volunteer Infantry, during the Civil War, 1861–1865, by Members of the Regiment.* Middleton, Conn., 1900.

Chamberlayne, Edwin H., Jr. *War History and Roll of the Richmond Fayette Artillery, 38th Virginia Battalion Artillery, Confederate States Army, 1861–1865.* Richmond, 1883.

Clarke, Walter, ed. *Histories of Several Regiments and Battalions from North Carolina in the Great War, 1861–1865, Written by Members of the Respective Commands.* 5 vols. Raleigh and Goldsboro, N.C., 1901.

Coker, James L. *History of Company G, Ninth S.C. Regiment, Infantry, S.C. Army, and of Company E, Sixth S.C. Regiment, Infantry, S.C. Army.* Greenwood, S.C., 1979.

Corell, Phillip, ed. *History of the Naval Brigade: 99th New York Volunteers, Union Coast Guard, 1861–1865.* New York, 1905.

Cunningham, John L. *Three Years with the Adirondack Regiment, 118th New York Volunteer Infantry, from the Diaries and Other Memoranda of John L. Cunningham, Major, 118th New York Volunteer Infantry, Brevet Lieutenant Colonel United States Volunteers.* Norwood, Mass., 1920.

Graham, Matthew J. *The Ninth Regiment New York Volunteers (Hawkins' Zouaves): Being a History of the Regiment and Veteran Association from 1860–1900.* New York, 1900.

Hamilton, D. H. *History of Company M., First Texas Volunteer Infantry, Hood's Brigade, Longstreet's Corps, Army of the Confederate States of America.* Waco, Tex., 1962.

Hanson, John W. *Historical Sketch of the Old Sixth Regiment of Massachusetts Volunteers during Its Three Campaigns in 1861–1862, 1863, and 1864. Containing the History of the*

Several Companies Previous to 1861, and the Name and Military Record of Each Man Connected with the Regiment during the War. Boston, 1866.

Herbert, Arthur. *Seventeenth Virginia Regiment; Papers Read before R. E. Lee Camp, Confederate Veterans, by Col. Arthur Herbert, at Their Request, Briefly Sketching Incidents and Movements of the 17th Virginia Infantry during the Four Years War between the States.* N.p., n.d.

History of the Eleventh Pennsylvania Volunteer Cavalry, Together with a Complete Roster of the Regiment and Regimental Officers. Philadelphia, 1902.

Hyde, William L. *History of the One Hundred Twelfth Regiment N.Y. Volunteers.* Fredonia, N.Y., 1866.

Irby, Richard. *Historical Sketch of the Nottoway Grays, Afterwards Company G, Eighteenth Virginia Regiment, Army of Northern Virginia: Prepared at the Request of the Surviving Members of the Company at Their First Re-union at Bellefont Church, July 21, 1877.* Richmond, 1878; rept. Gaithersburg, Md., 1983.

Kimball, Orville S., comp. *History and Personal Sketches of Company I, 103 N.Y.S.V., 1862–1864.* Elmira, N.Y., 1884.

Loehr, Charles T. *War History of the Old First Virginia Infantry Regiment, Army of Northern Virginia.* Richmond, 1884.

McGrath, Frank, comp. *The History of the 127th New York Volunteers, "Monitors," in the War for the Preservation of the Union—September 8, 1862, June 30, 1865.* N.p., n.d.

McKee, James H. *Back "In the War Times": History of the 144th Regiment, New York Volunteer Infantry, with Itinerary, Showing Contemporaneous Date of the Important Battles of the Civil War.* N.p., 1903.

Mowris, James A. *A History of the One Hundred and Seventeenth Regiment, N.Y. Volunteers (Fourth Oneida,) from the Date of Its Organization, August 1862, till That of Its Muster Out, June 1865.* Hartford, Conn., 1866.

Mowry, William A. *Camp Life in the Civil War, Eleventh R.I. Infantry.* Boston, 1914.

Oates, William C. *The War between the Union and the Confederacy and Its Lost Opportunities, with a History of the 15th Alabama Regiment and Forty-eight Battles in Which It Was Engaged.* New York, 1905.

Polley, J. B. *Hood's Texas Brigade: Its Marches, Its Battles, Its Achievements.* Dayton, Ohio, 1976.

The Quiet Regiment. Suffolk, Va., 1990.

Roback, Harry, ed. and comp. *The Veterans Volunteers of Herkimer and Ostego Counties in the War of the Rebellion; Being History of the 152nd N.Y.V. with Scene, Incidents, etc., Which Occurred in the Ranks of the 34th N.Y., 97th N.Y., 121st N.Y., 2nd N.Y. Heavy Artillery, and 2nd N.Y. Mounted Rifles.* Utica, N.Y., 1888.

Robertson, Jerome B. *Touched with Valor: Civil War Papers and Casualty Reports of Hood's Texas Brigade, Written and Collected by General Jerome B. Robertson, Commander of Hood's Texas Brigade, 1862–1864.* Ed. and with Biography of General Robertson by Harold B. Simpson. Hillsboro, Tex., 1964.

Thompson, John C. *History of the Eleventh Regiment, Rhode Island Volunteers, in the War of the Rebellion.* Providence, 1881.

Thompson, S. Millett. *Thirteenth Regiment of New Hampshire Volunteer Infantry in the War of the Rebellion, 1861–1865: A Diary Covering Three Years and a Day.* Cambridge, Mass., 1888.

Thorpe, Sheldon B. *The History of the Fifteenth Connecticut Volunteers in the War for the Defense of the Union, 1861–1865.* New Haven, 1893.

Whitney, J. H. E. *The Hawkins Zouaves (Ninth N. Y. V.): Their Battles and Marches.* New York, 1866.

Wise, George. *History of the Seventeenth Virginia Infantry, C.S.A.* Baltimore, 1870.

Articles

Boots, Edward N. "Civil War Letters of E. N. Boots, Virginia, 1862." Ed. Wilfred W. Black. *Virginia Magazine of History and Biography* 69 (April 1961): 194–209.

Chaplain, C. T., and J. M. Keeling. "Operations on the Blackwater River." *Confederate Veteran* 27:8 (Aug. 1919): 304–5.

Cody, Barnett H. "Letters of Barnett Hardeman Cody and Others, 1861–1864." Ed. Edmund Cody Burnett. *Georgia Historical Quarterly* 23 (1939): 265–99.

Goodson, Joab. "The Letters of Captain Joab Goodson, 1862–1864." Ed. W. Stanley Hoole. *Alabama Review* 10 (1957): 126–53, 215–31.

Gordon, John W. "Pleasant Days in War Time." *Confederate Veteran* 37:3 (March 1929): 93–95.

Griggs, George K. "Memoranda of Thirty-eight Virginia Infantry; from the Diary of Colonel George K. Griggs." *Southern Historical Society Papers* 14 (1886): 25–257.

Hightower, Harvey J. "Letters from H. J. Hightower, a Confederate Soldier, 1862–1864." Ed. Dewey W. Grantham Jr. *Georgia Historical Quarterly* 40 (1956): 174–89.

Hill, Daniel H. "McClellan's Change of Base and Malvern Hill." *Battles and Leaders of the Civil War, Being for the Most Part Contributions by Union and Confederate Officers: Based upon "The Century" War Series,* vol. 2. New York, 1887–88.

———. "Reunion of the Virginia Division Army of Northern Virginia Association." *Southern Historical Society Papers* 3 (1885): 259–84.

Hood, John Bell, to James Longstreet, June 28, 1875. *Southern Historical Society Papers* 4 (1877): 146–47.

Stevens, Hazard. "The Siege of Suffolk, April 11–May 3, 1863." In *Operations on the Atlantic Coast, 1861–1865, Virginia, 1862, 1864 Vicksburg.* Papers of the Military Historical Society of Massachusetts, 9. Boston, 1912.

Suderow, Bruce. "The Suffolk Slaughter: 'We Did Not Take Any Prisoners.'" *Civil War Times Illustrated* 23:3 (May 1984): 37–39.

Vaughan, Turner. "Diary of Turner Vaughan, Co. 'C,' 4th Alabama Regiment, C.S.A., Commenced March 4th 1863 and Ending February 12th 1864." *Alabama Historical Quarterly* 18 (1956): 573–604.

"Widow of General Pickett." *Confederate Veteran* 39 (1931): 151.

SECONDARY SOURCES

Alderman, John Perry. *29th Virginia Infantry.* Lynchburg, Va., 1989.

Ash, Stephen V. *When the Yankees Came: Conflict and Chaos in the Occupied South, 1861–1865.* Chapel Hill, N.C., 1995.

Balfour, Daniel T. *13th Virginia Cavalry.* Lynchburg, Va., 1985.

Bearss, Ed, and Chris Calkins. *The Battle of Five Forks.* Lynchburg, Va., 1985.

Black, Robert C., III. *The Railroads of the Confederacy.* Chapel Hill, N.C., 1952.

Blair, William. *Virginia's Private War: Feeding Body and Soul in the Confederacy, 1861–1865.* New York, 1998.

Boney, F. N. *John Letcher of Virginia: The Story of Virginia's Civil War Governor.* Tuscaloosa, Ala., 1966.

Brewer, James H. *The Confederate Negro: Virginia's Craftsmen and Military Laborers, 1861–1865.* Durham, N.C., 1969.

Bridges, Hal. *Lee's Maverick General: Daniel Harvey Hill.* New York, 1961.

The Brooke, Fauquier, Loudoun, and Alexandria Artillery. Lynchburg, Va., 1990.

Burton, Ann H. *History of Suffolk and Nansemond County, Virginia.* Suffolk, Va., 1970.

Cavanaugh, Michael A. *6th Virginia Infantry.* Lynchburg, Va., 1988.

Chapla, John D. *50th Virginia Infantry.* Lynchburg, Va., 1997.

Collier, Calvin L. *"They'll Do to Tie To!": The Story of the Third Regiment, Arkansas Infantry, C.S.A.* Little Rock, Ark., 1959.

Connelly, Thomas L. *The Marble Man: Robert E. Lee and His Image in American Society.* Baton Rouge, La., 1977.

Connelly, Thomas L., and Archer Jones. *The Politics of Command: Factions and Ideas in Confederate Strategy.* Baton Rouge, La., 1973.

Cormier, Steven A. *The Siege of Suffolk: The Forgotten Campaign, April 11–May 4, 1863.* Lynchburg, Va., 1989.

Crews, Edward R., and Timothy A. Parrish. *14th Virginia Infantry.* Lynchburg, Va., 1995.

Crofts, Daniel W. *Cobb's Ordeal: The Diaries of a Virginia Farmer, 1842–1872.* Athens, Ga., 1997.

———. *Old Southampton: Politics and Society in a Virginia County, 1834–1869.* Charlottesville, Va., 1992.

Cullum, George W. *Biographical Register of the Officers And Graduates of the U.S. Military Academy at West Point, N.Y., from Its Establishment, in 1802 and 1890, with the Early History of the United States Military Academy.* 2 vols. Boston, 1891.

Current, Richard Nelson. *Lincoln's Loyalists: Union Soldiers from the Confederacy.* Boston, 1992.

Davis, William C. *Duel between the First Ironclads.* Garden City, N.Y., 1975.

———. *"A Government of Our Own": The Making of the Confederacy.* New York, 1994.

———. *Jefferson Davis, the Man and His Hour: A Biography.* New York, 1991.

Denny, Robert E. *Civil War Prisons and Escapes: A Day-by-Day Chronicle.* New York, 1993.

Dowdy, Clifford. *Lee.* Boston, 1965.

———. *The Seven Days: The Emergence of Lee.,* 1964.

Dunn, Joseph B. *The History of Nansemond County Virginia.* N.p., n.d.

Durrill, Wayne K. *War of Another Kind: A Southern Community in the Great Rebellion.* New York, 1990.

Dyer, Frederick H. *A Compendium of the War of the Rebellion.* Dayton, Ohio, 1979.

Dyer, John P. *The Gallant Hood.* Indianapolis, 1950.

Eckenrode, H. J., and Bryan Conrad. *James Longstreet: Lee's War Horse.* Chapel Hill, N.C., 1936.

Eliot, Ellsworth, Jr. *West Point in the Confederacy.* New York, 1941.

Faust, Drew Gilpin. *The Creation of Confederate Nationalism: Ideology and Identity in the Civil War South.* Baton Rouge, La., 1988.

Foner, Eric. *Free Soil, Free Labor, Free Men: The Ideology of the Republican Party before the Civil War.* New York, 1970.

———. *Nothing but Freedom: Emancipation and Its Legacy.* Baton Rouge, La., 1983.

———. *Reconstruction: America's Unfinished Revolution, 1863–1877.* New York, 1988.

Foote, Shelby. *The Civil War: A Narrative.* New York, 1963.

Foster, John Y. *New Jersey and the Rebellion: A History of the Services of the Troops and People of New Jersey in Aid of the Union Cause.* Newark, N.J., 1868.

Freeman, Douglas Southall. *Lee's Lieutenants: A Study in Command.* New York, 1943.

———. *R. E. Lee: A Biography.* New York, 1935.

Furgurson, Ernest B. *Ashes of Glory: Richmond at War.* New York, 1996.

———. *Chancellorsville 1863: The Souls of the Brave.* New York, 1992.

Gallagher, Gary W. *The Confederate War.* Cambridge, Mass., 1997.

Goff, Richard D. *Confederate Supply.* Durham, N.C., 1969.

Gordon, Lesley J. *General George E. Pickett in Life and Legend.* Chapel Hill, N.C., 1998.

Gregory, G. Howard. *38th Virginia Infantry.* Lynchburg, Va., 1988.

Grimsley, Mark. *The Hard Hand of War: Union Military Policy toward Southern Civilians, 1861–1865.* Cambridge, 1995.

Henderson, William D. *41st Virginia Infantry.* Lynchburg, Va., 1986.

Hennessy, John J. *Return to Bull Run: The Campaign and Battle of Second Manassas.* New York, 1993.

Hobbs, O. Kermit, Jr. *Storm over Suffolk: The Years 1861–1865.* Suffolk, Va., 1979.

Hobbs, O. Kermit, Jr., and William Paquette. *Suffolk: A Pictorial History.* Norfolk, Va., 1987.

Hofstadter, Richard, ed. *Great Issues in American History: From the Revolution to the Civil War, 1765–1865.* New York, 1958.

Holzman, Robert S. *Adapt or Perish: The Life of General Roger A. Pryor, C.S.A.* Hamden, Conn., 1976.

Johnston, Angus James, II. *Virginia Railroads in the Civil War.* Chapel Hill, N.C., 1961.

Jones, Paul. *The Irish Brigade.* Washington, D.C., 1969.

Jordan, Ervin L., Jr. *Black Confederates and Afro-Yankees in Civil War Virginia.* Charlottesville, Va., 1995.

Kennedy, Frances H., ed. *The Civil War Battlefield Guide.* 2d ed., Boston, 1998.

Krick, Robert K. *30th Virginia Infantry.* Lynchburg, Va., 1983.

Laine, J. Gary, and Morris M. Penny. *Law's Alabama Brigade in the War between the Union and the Confederacy.* Shippensburg, Pa., 1996.

Long, E. B. *The Civil War Day by Day: An Almanac, 1861–1865.* Garden City, N.Y., 1971.

Longacre, Edward G. *Pickett, Leader of the Charge: A Biography of George E. Pickett, C.S.A.* Shippensburg, Pa., 1995.

Longstreet, Helen D. *Lee and Longstreet at High Tide: Gettysburg in the Light of the Official Records.* Gainesville, Ga., 1904.

Lonn, Ella. *Foreigners in the Union Army and Navy.* Baton Rouge, La., 1951.

Massey, Mary Elizabeth. *Refugee Life in the Confederacy.* Baton Rouge, La., 1964.

Matter, William D. *If It Takes All Summer: The Battle of Spotsylvania.* Chapel Hill, N.C., 1988.

McCartney, Clarence Edward. *Mr. Lincoln's Admirals.* New York, 1956.

McFeely, William S. *Yankee Stepfather: General O. O. Howard and the Freedmen.* New Haven, 1968.

McMurry, Richard M. *John Bell Hood and the War for Southern Independence.* Lexington, Ky., 1982.

McPherson, James M. *Battle Cry of Freedom: The Civil War Era.* New York, 1988.

———. *For Cause and Comrades: Why Men Fought in the Civil War.* New York, 1997.

Mitchell, Reid. *Civil War Soldiers: Their Expectations and Their Experiences.* New York, 1988.

O'Conner, Richard. *Hood: Cavalier General.* New York, 1949.

Osbon, Bradley S. *Handbook of the United States Navy: Being a Compilation of All the Principal Events in the History of Every Vessel of the United States Navy, from April 1861 to May 1864.* New York, 1974.

Owens, Harry P., and James J. Cooke, eds. *The Old South in the Crucible of War.* Jackson, Miss., 1983.

Paquette, William. *U.S. Colored Troops from Lower Tidewater in the Civil War.* Portsmouth, Va., 1982.

Parramore, Thomas C. *Southampton County, Virginia.* Charlottesville, Va., 1978.

Piston, William Garrett. *Lee's Tarnished Lieutenant: James Longstreet and His Place in Southern History.* Athens, Ga., 1987.

Pollack, Edward. *Sketchbook of Suffolk, Va.* Portsmouth, Va., 1886.

Pollard, Edward A. *Lee and His Lieutenants. . . .* New York, 1867.

Porter, David D. *The Naval History of the Civil War.* New York, 1886.

Power, J. Tracy. *Lee's Miserables: Life in the Army of Northern Virginia from the Wilderness to Appomattox.* Chapel Hill, N.C., 1998.

Reardon, Carol. *Pickett's Charge in History and Memory.* Chapel Hill, N.C., 1997.

Rhea, Gordon C. *The Battle of the Wilderness, May 5–6, 1864.* Baton Rouge, La., 1994.

———. *The Battles for Spotsylvania Court House and the Road to Yellow Tavern, May 7–12, 1864.* Baton Rouge, La., 1997.

Robertson, James I., Jr., *Soldiers Blue and Gray.* Columbia, S.C., 1988.

Roland, Charles P. *An American Iliad: The Story of the Civil War.* New York, 1991.

Roske, Ralph J., and Charles Van Doren. *Lincoln's Commando: The Biography of Commander W. B. Cushing, U.S.N.* New York, 1957.

Sanger, Donald R., and Thomas R. Hay. *James Longstreet: I. Soldier. II. Politician, Officeholder, and Writer.* Baton Rouge, La., 1951.

Schwarz, Philip J. *Slave Laws in Virginia.* Athens, Ga., 1996.

Sears, Stephen W. *Chancellorsville.* Boston, 1996.

———. *Landscape Turned Red: The Battle of Antietam.* New York, 1983.

———. *To the Gates of Richmond: The Peninsula Campaign.* New York, 1992.

Sherwood, George L., and Jeffrey C. Weaver. *54th Virginia Infantry.* Lynchburg, Va., 1993.

Simpson, Harold B. *Gaines' Mill to Appomattox: Waco and McLennan County in Hood's Texas Brigade.* Waco, Tex., 1963.

———. *Hood's Texas Brigade: Lee's Grenadier Guard.* Waco, Tex., 1970.

Sommers, Richard J. *Richmond Redeemed: The Siege of Petersburg.* Garden City, N.Y., 1981.

Stackpole, Edward J. *Drama on the Rappahannock: The Fredericksburg Campaign.* Harrisburg, Pa., 1957.

Steiner, Paul E. *Medical-Military Portraits of Union and Confederate Generals.* Philadelphia, 1968.

Sublett, Charles W. *57th Virginia Infantry.* Lynchburg, Va., 1985.

Sutherland, Daniel E. *Fredericksburg and Chancellorsville: The Dare Mark Campaign.* Lincoln, Nebr., 1998.

Swanberg, W. A. *First Blood: The Story of Fort Sumter.* New York, 1957.

Thomas, Emory M. *Bold Dragoon: The Life of Jeb Stuart.* New York, 1986.

———. *The Confederacy as a Revolutionary Experience.* Englewood Cliffs, N.J., 1971.

———. *The Confederate Nation, 1861–1865.* New York, 1979.

———. *The Confederate State of Richmond: A Biography of the Capital.* Austin, Tex., 1971.

———. *Robert E. Lee: A Biography.* New York, 1995.

———. *Travels to Hallowed Ground: A Historian's Journey to the American Civil War.* Columbia, S.C., 1987.

Thomas, Wilbur. *General James "Pete" Longstreet: Lee's War Horse, Scapegoat for Gettysburg.* Parsons, W.Va., 1979.

Trask, Benjamin H. *9th Virginia Infantry.* Lynchburg, 1984.

———. *16th Virginia Infantry.* Lynchburg, 1986.

———. *61st Virginia Infantry.* Lynchburg, 1988.

Trotter, William R. *Ironclads and Columbiads: The Civil War in North Carolina, The Coast.* Winston-Salem, N.C., 1989.

Trudeau, Noah Andre. *Bloody Roads South: The Wilderness to Cold Harbor, May–June 1864.* Boston, 1989.

———. *The Last Citadel: Petersburg, Virginia, June 1864–April 1865.* Boston, 1991.

Wallace, Lee A., Jr. *A Guide to Virginia Military Organizations, 1861–1865.* Richmond, 1964.

———. *17th Virginia Infantry.* Lynchburg, 19.

———. *Surry Light Artillery and Martin's, Wright's, Coffin's Batteries of Virginia Artillery.* Lynchburg, Va., 1995.

———. *3rd Virginia Infantry.* Lynchburg, Va., 1986.

Warner, Ezra J. *Generals in Blue: Lives of Union Commanders.* Baton Rouge, La., 1964.

———. *Generals in Gray: Lives of Confederate Commanders.* Baton Rouge, La., 1959.

Waugh, John C. *The Class of 1846, from West Point to Appomattox: Stonewall Jackson, George McClellan, and Their Brothers.* New York, 1994.

Weaver, Jeffrey C. *63rd Virginia Infantry.* Lynchburg, Va., 1991.

Wert, Jeffry D. *A Brotherhood of Valor: The Common Soldiers of the Stonewall Brigade, C.S.A., and the Iron Brigade, U.S.A.* New York, 1993.

———. *General James Longstreet, the Confederacy's Most Controversial Soldier: A Biography.* New York, 1993.

———. *Mosby's Rangers*. New York, 1990.

Wiley, Bell I. *Johnny Reb: The Common Soldier of the Confederacy*. Baton Rouge, La., 1978.

———. *The Road to Appomattox*. Memphis, 1956; rept. New York, 1977.

———. *Southern Negroes, 1861–1865*. Baton Rouge, La., 1965.

Williams, Kenneth P. *Lincoln Finds a General: A Military Study of the Civil War*. 5 vols. New York, 1949–59.

Wills, Brian Steel. *A Battle from the Start: The Life of Nathan Bedford Forrest*. New York, 1992. Rept. as *The Confederacy's Greatest Cavalryman: Nathan Bedford Forrest*. Lawrence, Kans., 1998.

Woodworth, Steven. *Davis and Lee at War*. Lawrence, Kans., 1995.

Wyatt-Brown, Bertram. *Southern Honor: Ethics and Behavior in the Old South*. New York, 1982.

Young, William A., Jr., and Patricia C. *56th Virginia Infantry*. Lynchburg, Va., 1990.

Articles

Ash, Stephen. "White Virginians under Federal Occupation, 1861–1865." *Virginia Magazine of History and Biography* 98:2 (April 1990): 169–92.

Blakeless, John. "James Harrison: Rebel Enigma." *Civil War Times Illustrated* 9 (April 1970): 12–15, 18–20.

Crofts, Daniel W. "A Journey Back: Old Southampton in the Mid-Nineteenth Century." *Virginia Cavalcade* 42 (winter 1993): 130–43.

Flanders, Alan B. "The Night They Burned the Yard." *Civil War Times Illustrated* 8 (Feb. 1980): 30–39.

Graham, Martin. "An Affair of Regimental Honor." *Civil War Times Illustrated* 26 (Jan. 1988): 22–24, 42–43.

Johnson, Ludwell H., III. "Blockade or Trade Monopoly?: John A. Dix and the Union Occupation of Norfolk." *Virginia Magazine of History and Biography* 93 (Jan. 1985): 54–78.

Long, John S. "The Gosport Affair, 1861." *Journal of Southern History* 23 (1957): 155–72.

McMurry, Richard M. "Rise to Glory: A Speculative Essay on the Early Career of John Bell Hood." In *Rank and File: Civil War Essays in Honor of Bell Irvin Wiley*, ed. James I. Robertson Jr. and Richard M. McMurry, pp. 39–54. San Rafael, Calif., 1976. Patterson, Gerald A. "George E. Pickett." *Civil War Times Illustrated* 5 (May 1966): 18–24.

Robertson, W. Glenn. "The Siege of Suffolk, 1863: Another Name for Futility?" *Virginia Cavalcade* 27 (spring 1978): 164–73.

Spraggins, Tinsley Lee. "Mobilization of Negro Labor for the Department of Virginia and North Carolina, 1861–1865." *North Carolina Historical Review* 24 (April 1947): 160–97.

Stuart, Meriwether. "Of Spies and Borrowed Names: The Identity of Union Operatives in Richmond Known as 'The Phillipses' Discovered." *Virginia Magazine of History and Biography* 89:3 (July 1981): 308–27.

Thomas, Emory M. "The Richmond Bread Riot of 1863." *Virginia Cavalcade* 18 (summer 1968): 41–44.

Weinert, Richard P. "The Suffolk Campaign." *Civil War Times Illustrated* 7 (Jan. 1969): 31–39.

Unpublished Papers

Cormier, Steven A. "Forgotten Campaign: The Siege of Suffolk, April 11–May 4, 1863." M.A. thesis, Old Dominion University, 1982.

Holland, Reginald. "A Brief Summary of Events during the Federal Occupation of Suffolk and Nansemond County, 1862–1863." Typescript in possession of the author.

Merrifield, Edward F. "The Seaboard War: A History of the North Atlantic Blockading Squadron, 1861–1865." Ph.D. diss., Case Western Reserve University, 1975.

Sadlow, Jeane Louise. "Life and Campaigns of General George Edward Pickett." M.A. thesis, St. John's University, 1959.

Wills, Brian Steel. "In Charge: Command Relationships in the Suffolk Campaign, 1863." M.A. thesis, University of Georgia, 1985.

A NATION DIVIDED:
NEW STUDIES IN CIVIL WAR HISTORY

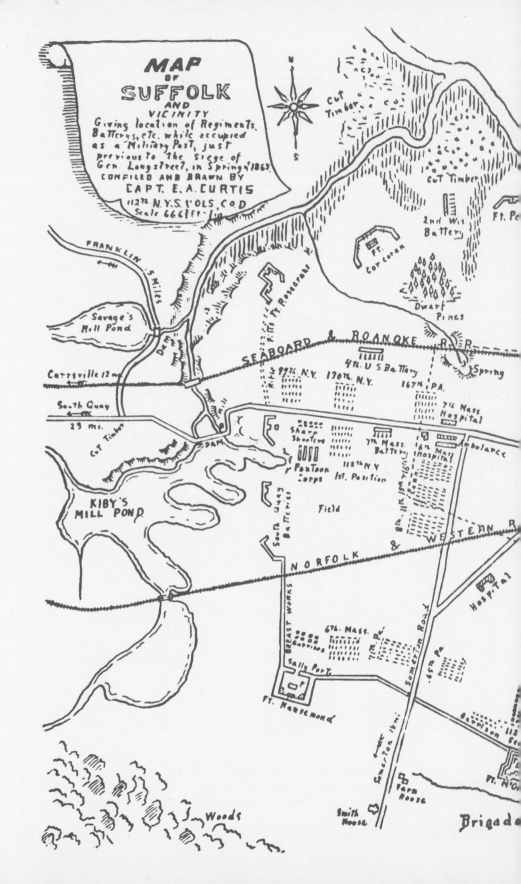